DOCUMENTS ON BRITISH FOREIGN POLICY

1919–1939, 3rd. Ser.

EDITED BY

ROHAN BUTLER, M.A.

Fellow of All Souls College, Oxford

AND

J. P. T. BURY, M.A.

Fellow of Corpus Christi College, Cambridge

ASSISTED BY

I. BAINS, M.A.

Third Series   Volume X
INDEX

LONDON
HER MAJESTY'S STATIONERY OFFICE
1961

First published 1961

© *Crown Copyright 1961*

Published by

HER MAJESTY'S STATIONERY OFFICE

To be purchased from
49 High Holborn, London W.C.1
13A Castle Street, Edinburgh EH2 3AR
109 St. Mary Street, Cardiff CF1 1JW
Brazennose Street, Manchester M60 8AS
50 Fairfax Street, Bristol BS1 3DE
258 Broad Street, Birmingham 1
7 Linenhall Street, Belfast BT2 8AY
or through any bookseller

SBN 11 591535 4

PRINTED IN ENGLAND
UNDER THE AUTHORITY OF HER MAJESTY'S STATIONERY OFFICE
BY GALLIARD LTD., GREAT YARMOUTH

PREFATORY NOTE

THIS index-volume to the nine volumes of the completed Third Series, covering the period from March 1938 to September 1939, is published in accordance with the announcement in the Preface to the Collection: see Volumes I of the First and Second Series, also Volume IX of the Third Series. The Assistant Editor of the present volume, Miss I. Bains, M.A., has compiled all the tables and indexes in it, and the Editors are most grateful for her long and careful labour. They would also like to thank the Deputy Librarian of the Foreign Office, Mr. C. H. Fone, I.S.O., M.B.E., for his valuable advice.

The volume is designed to provide a general index for convenient reference, and is divided into four parts, as indicated in the table of contents on p. vii and as explained below.

Part I. *Summary Contents of Volumes*

Part I lists the tables of contents in each of the volumes. It thus provides a general guide to the Third Series, and a quick view of the main subjects treated in each volume and of the periods covered.

Part II. *Reference Tables of Sovereigns and Holders of Office*

The chief purpose of this Part is to list the leading personalities in the countries with which the Series is concerned and, in addition, other personalities mentioned in the text, even if only by office. The tables list, for every country: (*a*) the names of the Head of State, and, where applicable, of the Prime Ministers or Presidents of the Council and of the Ministers for Foreign Affairs; (*b*) the holders of the numerous offices mentioned in the documents. The tables are divided into two sections: (i) the British Commonwealth and Empire, beginning with the United Kingdom; (ii) Foreign States in alphabetical sequence: under this heading the League of Nations is also included.

In these tables personal names, titles and ranks are in general given as for the period in question. In the list for the United Kingdom the dates of tenure of office which follow the names include the month as well as the year. For holders of office in H.M. Government these dates are those of appointment and of resignation, as publicly announced. For members of the Foreign Office and diplomatic and consular representatives the dates are generally based upon information in the annual Foreign Office Lists. Where, however, in the case of a senior representative serving abroad, it has been possible from other Foreign Office records to determine the months in which he assumed or relinquished charge of a post these dates have been substituted for those in the Foreign Office Lists. For example, according to these lists Sir

Sydney Waterlow was transferred to Athens on 30 November 1933, and retired on 29 June 1939. Foreign Office records, however, show that he took charge of the British Legation at Athens on 4 December 1933, and left Athens on 31 May 1939. Therefore the dates here given are December 1933–May 1939.

For countries other than the United Kingdom, months are normally given in the dating of appointments only when a change of office occurred during the period covered by the Third Series. And, in general, dates of tenure are recorded only for the more senior offices. The information for foreign countries has been derived from many sources including the various national Year Books and the Almanach de Gotha as well as other published records and Foreign Office files. In a few instances it has proved impossible to trace the names of foreign holders of lesser offices mentioned in documents, and they have accordingly been omitted from the tables.

Part III. Index of Persons

The Index of Persons includes the names of all persons living in the period 1919–39 who are mentioned in the Third Series either by name or by office (except as noticed above). Brief notes of positions held at the time have been added in parentheses. After the page references to mentions of each person, standard subheadings have been added, as appropriate, referring in particular to speeches or statements by him, to his visits and conversations with other persons, and his outward correspondence; in the case of official despatches and telegrams from the person indexed, only the subheading *To* is prefixed to the name of his correspondent.

Part IV. Subject Index

In the Subject Index much of the material has been indexed under the names of countries and the relations of one country with another. Territorial subheadings have also been used under other main headings, e.g. under Guarantees, Jews, Rearmament.

Where a territorial designation has been used as a main heading and elsewhere as a subheading, the main heading has been printed in bold type for ease of reference; thus Germany is in bold type on pages 118–22 but elsewhere in ordinary type.

In most instances alphabetical order has been retained for entries concerning the relations between any two countries. For example, relations between Italy and France are indexed under the heading France, with subheading Italy; those between the U.S.S.R. and Roumania under the heading Roumania, with subheading U.S.S.R. Where this order has occasionally been reversed, cross-references are given to the main entries, e.g. under 'Austria, Germany. *See* Germany (Austria).' As in this example, in cross-references subheadings are printed in parentheses.

Standard subheadings have been used, so far as appropriate, under the main entry for each country, e.g. Armed Forces, Internal Situation, Military

Measures, Minorities, Political Parties, Press, Public Opinion. Under the subheading 'Press', individual papers are listed after the entries of subjects dealt with by the press.

Main headings, besides those for particular countries, also include general headings such as Air Warfare, Balkan Entente, Commissions, Committees, Communism, Conferences, Four-Power Declaration, Guarantees, Jews, Little Entente, Missions, Munich, Plebiscites, Rearmament, Refugees, Self-determination, South-East Europe, Sudeten German Question, Treaties.

In both the Index of Persons and the Subject Index the following practices have been adopted.

Volume numbers are printed in small roman numerals in bold type.

References to footnotes are indicated by *n* placed after the number of the page, e.g. 50*n*. Where a name or subject occurs in the main text and in a footnote on the same page, the page-reference only is printed.

Subheadings are usually arranged in alphabetical order according to the first word. In some entries, however, the chronological order has been followed when precise dates are given. For instance, in the Index of Persons, under the main heading Chamberlain, the chronological order has been adopted in listing his Communications with Herr Hitler and Communications with Signor Mussolini; and under the main heading Sudeten German Question in the Subject Index it has been followed under the subheading Attitude of France and Great Britain.

It may sometimes be found helpful to use the indexes in conjunction with the Chapter Summaries printed at the beginning of each volume of the Third Series. For instance, the occasional references in the indexes to passages *passim* may be conveniently supplemented by the Chapter Summaries, which provide a chronological page-register to the contents of each volume.

R. D'O. B.
J. P. T. B.

15 August 1960

CONTENTS

Part I

Summary Contents of Volumes

Volume I

Pages

Chapter I. Attitude of His Majesty's Government towards the German annexation of Austria: German assurances to the Czechoslovak Government. (March 9–16, 1938) 1–60

Chapter II. Attitude of His Majesty's Government with regard to possible German action against Czechoslovakia: approach to French and Czechoslovak Governments. (March 16–April 26, 1938) 61–196

Chapter III. Anglo-French conversations, April 28–29: instructions for proposed *démarches* at Prague and Berlin, May 4. (April 27–May 18, 1938) . . 197–316

Chapter IV. The crisis of May 19–22: consideration by His Majesty's Government of the possibility of an International Commission in the event of a breakdown in the negotiations between the Czechoslovak Government and Herr Henlein: Mr. Strang's visit to Prague and Berlin. (May 19–30, 1938) 317–416

Chapter V. Further negotiations with a view to facilitating a settlement of the Sudeten question. (May 31–July 14, 1938) 417–565

Chapter VI. Proposal by His Majesty's Government to send Viscount Runciman on a special mission to Prague: acceptance of proposal by the Czechoslovak Government. (July 15–23, 1938) 566–620

Appendixes

I. Additional exchange of letters between Lord Halifax and Sir N. Henderson. March 20–July 18, 1938 621–629

II. Record of Herr Henlein's statements to Mr. Churchill, Sir A. Sinclair, and Sir R. Vansittart while on a visit to London in May, 1938 . . 630–635

III. Memoranda explaining the negotiations between the Czechoslovak Government and the Sudeten Germans in June, 1938 636–646

IV. Foreign Office memorandum setting out considerations for and against proposals for the neutralization of Czechoslovakia 647–652

V. Record of a conversation between Herr Forster, Gauleiter of Danzig, Professor Noe, and Sir A. Cadogan 653–655

Volume II

Chapter VII. German military measures: Lord Runciman's negotiations in Prague: Sir J. Simon's speech at Lanark on August 27. (July 24–August 27, 1938) 1–175

Chapter VIII. German military measures: breakdown of negotiations between the Czechoslovak Government and the Sudeten Germans: Mr. Chamberlain's decision to visit Herr Hitler. (August 28–September 13, 1938) . 176–314

Pages

Chapter IX. Mr. Chamberlain's meeting with Herr Hitler at Berchtesgaden: Anglo-French conversations of September 18: Anglo-French approach to Czechoslovak Government: acceptance by Czechoslovak Government of Anglo-French proposals. (September 13–21, 1938). 315–445

Chapter X. Mr. Chamberlain's meetings with Herr Hitler at Godesberg: Anglo-French conversations of September 25 and 26: Mr. Chamberlain's letter of September 26 to Herr Hitler. (September 21–26, 1938) 446–542

Chapter XI. Sir H. Wilson's conversations of September 26 and 27 with Herr Hitler: negotiations preceding the Munich Conference: the Munich Conference: Mr. Chamberlain's conversation of September 30 with Herr Hitler. (September 26–30, 1938) 543–645

Appendixes

I. Additional letters from Sir N. Henderson, August–September, 1938 . 646–655

II. Additional correspondence on Lord Runciman's Mission . . . 656–679

III. Text of the Prime Minister's statement to the Press on September 11, 1938 680–682

IV. Unofficial German approaches, August–September, 1938 . . . 683–692

Maps

I. Sketch map based on the Memorandum handed to the Prime Minister by Herr Hitler on September 23, 1938 . . . . . . *At end*

II. Sketch map based on the map annexed to the Agreement signed at Munich on September 29/30, 1938 . . . . ,, ,,

Volume III

Chapter I. Correspondence with regard to Polish and Hungarian claims to Czechoslovak territory. (September 14–30, 1938) 1–55

Chapter II. The execution of the Munich Agreement: i. (September 30–October 7, 1938.) Meetings of the International Commission: Polish and Hungarian claims to Czechoslovak territory 56–137

Chapter III. The execution of the Munich Agreement: ii. (October 8–14, 1938.) Meetings of the International Commission: Polish and Hungarian claims to Czechoslovak territory 138–183

Chapter IV. The execution of the Munich Agreement: iii. (October 15–November 25, 1938.) The Settlement of Polish and Hungarian claims to Czechoslovak territory 184–243

Chapter V. German press attacks on Great Britain: correspondence regarding anti-Semitic measures in Germany: Anglo-French conversations of November 24. (October 20–November 24, 1938) 244–311

Chapter VI. Correspondence regarding the entry into force of the Anglo-Italian Agreement of April 16, 1938. (October 1–November 16, 1938) . 312–362

Chapter VII. The Franco-German Declaration of December 6: German-Czech relations: the British guarantee to Czechoslovakia: German decision with regard to the building of submarines. (November 25–December 31, 1938) . 363–457

Chapter VIII. Anglo-Italian relations from the entry into force of the Anglo-Italian Agreement to the visit of Mr. Chamberlain and Lord Halifax to Rome: correspondence with regard to Franco-Italian relations. (November 16, 1938–January 19, 1939) 458–540

Pages

Chapter IX. German designs in Europe: the question of Danzig. (December 28, 1938–January 20, 1939) 541–614

Appendixes

    I. Two letters from Sir N. Henderson, October 1938 615–617
    II. Extracts from additional letters by Sir E. Phipps to Viscount Halifax . 618–621
    III. Memorandum on Military Measures taken by Germany in connexion with the Sudeten question. 622–628
    IV. Additional correspondence on Financial Assistance to Czechoslovakia . 629–638
    V. Additional correspondence on the International Commission . . 639–656
    VI. Letter from M. Burckhardt on the question of Danzig . . . 657–661
    VII. Additional documents relating to the Anglo-German Naval Agreement . 662–674
    VIII. Note of interview with Dr. Schacht on December 15, 1938 . . . 675–682

Map

Sketch map showing the Frontier between Germany and Czechoslovakia based on the map attached to the Protocol of November 20, 1938 . . . *At end*

Volume IV

Chapter I. The European situation: estimates of German intentions: the Danzig question: Herr Hitler's speech of January 30: the international guarantee of Czecho-Slovakia. (January 23–February 9, 1939) 1–99

Chapter II. Further correspondence on the European situation and estimates of German intentions: German–Polish relations: the international guarantee of Czecho-Slovakia. (February 10–March 9, 1939) 100–209

Chapter III. The German violation of the Munich Agreement and the destruction of Czech independence. (March 9–17, 1939) 210–291

Chapter IV. Attitude of His Majesty's Government towards Italian claims against France. (January 20–April 2, 1939) 292–359

Chapter V. British proposals for the organization of mutual support against further German aggression: Memel: Anglo-French conversations of March 21–22. (March 17–23, 1939) 360–491

Chapter VI. The announcement of the British guarantee to Poland. (March 24–April 3, 1939) 492–588

Appendixes

    I. Additional letters on the German situation, February–March, 1939 . 589–596
    II. Report by Mr. Ashton-Gwatkin on his visit to Germany and interviews with German statesmen, February 19–26, 1939 597–610
    III. Letter from H.M. Embassy at Moscow on Soviet policy in connexion with the possibilities of negotiating a war trade agreement in the event of war between Germany and the Western Powers 611–614
    IV. Foreign Office memorandum on the situation after the absorption of Czecho-Slovakia, and on the policy of His Majesty's Government . 615–622
    V. Memorandum on the German military situation 623–627

Pages

VI. Negotiations concerning a voluntary limitation of capital ships and the exchange of information on naval matters 628–637

VII. Additional correspondence on the situation in Memel. (December 7–20, 1938) 638–647

Volume V

Chapter I. M. Beck's visit to London, April 4–6: events leading to the announcement of the British guarantee to Roumania. (April 4–13, 1939) . . 1–115

Chapter II. The Italian attack on Albania: the announcement of the British guarantee to Greece. (April 3–14, 1939) 116–197

Chapter III. The European situation: Italy, Turkey and the Balkans: correspondence with the French and Soviet Governments with regard to proposals for checking further German aggression. (April 14–21, 1939) . . 198–274

Chapter IV. The European situation: visit of the Roumanian Foreign Minister to London, April 23–26: Herr Hitler's speech of April 28: further correspondence with the French and Soviet Governments: Anglo-Turkish negotiations. (April 22–30, 1939) 275–381

Chapter V. The European situation: Polish–German relations: further British proposals and Soviet counter-proposals: correspondence with the Vatican. (May 1–6, 1939) 382–457

Chapter VI. The European situation: Polish–German relations: further correspondence with the Soviet Government: Anglo-Turkish Declaration of May 12. (May 7–12, 1939) 458–546

Chapter VII. The European situation: further correspondence with the Soviet Government: Anglo-Turkish negotiations: the Danzig question. (May 13–20, 1939). 547–621

Chapter VIII. The European situation: Anglo-Russian negotiations: the Danzig question. (May 21–26, 1939) 622–699

Chapter IX. The European situation: Anglo-Italian relations: the position in Danzig: decision to send Mr. Strang to Moscow: Anglo-French proposals to Soviet Government. (May 27–June 7, 1939) 700–794

Appendixes

I. Additional letters on the European situation, April–May, 1939 . . 795–808

II. Foreign Office memorandum on the Danzig question with additional comments by Sir N. Henderson 809–818

Volume VI

Chapter I. Further proposals to the Soviet Government and instructions to Sir W. Seeds: the situation in Danzig: records of M. Burckhardt's conversations in Danzig, Warsaw, and Berlin. (June 8–13, 1939). . . . 1–64

Chapter II. Russian rejection of Anglo-French proposals: further instructions to Sir W. Seeds: Anglo-Turkish negotiations: the situation in Danzig. (June 14–20, 1939) 65–125

Pages

Chapter III. Russian rejection of revised Anglo-French proposals: British memorandum to the German Government on the latter's denunciation of the Anglo-German Naval Agreement: Anglo-Turkish negotiations: the situation in Danzig. (June 21–28, 1939) 126–186

Chapter IV. Further Russian objections to Anglo-French proposals: M. Zhdanov's article of June 29: the situation in Danzig: message from the Prime Minister to Signor Mussolini: Anglo-Turkish negotiations. (June 29–July 5, 1939) 187–271

Chapter V. Further Anglo-French discussions with the Soviet Government: Anglo-Turkish negotiations: the Danzig question and German–Polish relations. (July 6–12, 1939) 272–343

Chapter VI. Further Anglo-French discussions with the Soviet Government: Mr. Strang's summary of the position on July 20: General Sir E. Ironside's visit to Poland: Anglo-Polish financial negotiations: the situation in Danzig. (July 13–20, 1939) 344–426

Chapter VII. Further Anglo-French discussions with the Soviet Government: Danzig and the German–Polish situation: Anglo-Polish financial negotiations: Anglo-Turkish negotiations. (July 21–27, 1939) 427–520

Chapter VIII. Further Anglo-French discussions with the Soviet Government: Anglo-French Military Missions to Moscow: Danzig and the German–Polish situation: Anglo-Turkish negotiations. (July 28–August 4, 1939) . 521–608

Chapter IX. German–Polish relations and the situation in Danzig: the Anglo-French Military Missions in Moscow: Herr Hitler's statements to M. Burckhardt. (August 5–14, 1939) 609–701

Appendixes

I. Additional correspondence on the German situation, June–August, 1939 . 702–720

II. Additional correspondence with M. Burckhardt, June–July, 1939 . . 721–735

III. Record of a conversation and correspondence with M. Wenner-Gren, June–July, 1939 736–742

IV. Records of conversations with M. Dahlerus, July–August, 1939 . . 743–761

V. Instructions to the British Military Mission to Moscow, August, 1939 . 762–789

Volume VII

Chapter I. Anglo-Franco–Soviet military conversations: attempts to secure Polish consent to the Russian demands with regard to the possible passage of Russian troops through Poland: suggestions for an approach by His Majesty's Government to Herr Hitler: Anglo-Italian exchanges. (August 15–20, 1939) 1–95

Chapter II. German military measures: announcement of the Soviet–German Non-Aggression Pact: message of August 22 from His Majesty's Government to Herr Hitler: Herr Hitler's reply of August 23: the attitude of Italy. (August 21–23, 1939) 96–179

Chapter III. Attempt to secure direct Polish–German negotiations: estimate of German intentions: Herr Hitler's communication of August 25 to Sir N. Henderson: signature of the Anglo-Polish Treaty. (August 24–25, 1939) . 180–260

Pages

Chapter IV. Exchanges with the Turkish Government: further exchanges with the Italian Government: proposals for relieving German–Polish tension. (August 26–27, 1939). 261–317

Chapter V. Reply of His Majesty's Government to Herr Hitler's communication of August 25: Sir N. Henderson's interviews of August 28 and 29 with Herr Hitler: Herr Hitler's communication of August 29. (August 28–29, 1939). 318–390

Chapter VI. Reply of His Majesty's Government to Herr Hitler's communication of August 29: Anglo-Turkish negotiations: Sir N. Henderson's interview of August 30 with Herr von Ribbentrop: negotiations of August 31: Italian decision to remain neutral: German communication of August 31. (August 30–31, 1939) 391–467

Chapter VII. The German attack on Poland: Note of September 1 from His Majesty's Government to the German Government: Italian proposal for a conference: Anglo-Turkish negotiations: the British ultimatum to Germany, September 3. (September 1–4, 1939) 468–546

Appendixes

I. Additional correspondence on the German situation, August 1939 . . 547–557

II. Further material on the Anglo-Franco–Soviet military conversations in Moscow, August 1939 558–614

III. Speech by M. Molotov on the ratification of the Soviet–German Non-Aggression Pact, August 31, 1939 615–622

IV. Material relating to previous volumes in this Series 623–633

Volume VIII

Chapter I. British attitude towards the Sino-Japanese conflict: attempts to reach an understanding with Japan on the treatment of British interests in China: Japanese statement of September 14 on relations with Germany and Italy. (August 4–September 30, 1938) 1–113

Chapter II. Further attempts to improve Anglo-Japanese relations in China: Sir R. Craigie's interview of October 11 with the Japanese Prime Minister: British, French and United States Notes to Japan on the navigation of the Yangtze: Sir A. Clark Kerr's interview of November 6 with Generalissimo Chiang Kai-shek. (October 1–November 11, 1938) 114–223

Chapter III. Further correspondence with regard to Japanese attacks upon British interests in China: the situation in Tientsin: financial aid to China: Japanese statement of December 22, 1938. (November 12–December 31, 1938) 224–358

Chapter IV. Further correspondence with regard to Japanese attacks upon British interests in China: the situation in Tientsin and Shanghai: Chinese appeals for increased British assistance: reports of the conclusion of an alliance between Germany, Italy and Japan. (January 1–February 21, 1939) 359–462

Chapter V. Further correspondence with regard to Japanese attacks upon British interests in China: the situation in Tientsin and Shanghai. (February 22–April 8, 1939) 463–541

Appendixes

I. Additional correspondence on the naval situation in the Far East . . 542–550
II. Additional correspondence dealing with the arrest and internment of Ssu Ching-wu. (October 4–November 1, 1938) 551–560

Volume IX

Chapter I. Correspondence with regard to Japanese attacks on British and French interests in China: the situation in Tientsin and Shanghai: Japanese relations with the Axis Powers. (April 10–May 14, 1939). . . . 1–68

Chapter II. The Tientsin dispute: refusal of His Majesty's Government to accede to Japanese demands: Japanese announcement of measures against the British Concession at Tientsin: Japanese attacks on Chinese currency. (May 15–June 7, 1939) 69–147

Chapter III. The Tientsin dispute: the Japanese blockade of the British Concession. (June 8–29, 1939) 148–238

Chapter IV. Negotiations at Tokyo over the Tientsin dispute: Anglo-Japanese statement of July 22: the Chinese currency question. (June 30–July 23, 1939) 239–318

Chapter V. Negotiations at Tokyo over the Tientsin dispute: attitude of the United States to the Japanese demands. (July 24–August 3, 1939) . . 319–396

Chapter VI. Negotiations at Tokyo over the Tientsin dispute: failure to reach agreement with the Japanese over the question of silver stocks in North China. (August 4–16, 1939) 397–462

Chapter VII. Refusal of His Majesty's Government to accede to the Japanese demands: Japanese reaction to the Soviet–German pact. (August 17–September 5, 1939) 463–527

Appendixes

I. Memorandum on British Policy in the Far East 528–532
II. Foreign Office memorandum on the legal aspects of the dispute regarding the disposal of alleged anti-Japanese terrorists arrested in the British Concession at Tientsin. 533–535
III. Foreign Office memorandum respecting silver stocks in North China . . 536–538
IV. Document relating to Volume VII in this Series 539

Part II

Reference Tables
of Sovereigns and Holders of Office

(i) British Commonwealth and Empire

KING AND EMPEROR .   . HIS MAJESTY KING GEORGE VI (Dec. 1936–Feb. 1952)

UNITED KINGDOM

Prime Minister and 1st Lord of the Treasury .	Mr. A. Neville Chamberlain (May 1937–May 1940)
Secretary of State for Foreign Affairs .	Mr. Anthony Eden (Dec. 1935–Feb. 1938)
	Viscount Halifax (Feb. 1938–Dec. 1940)
Chancellor of the Exchequer	Sir John Simon (May 1937–May 1940)
Lord Chancellor	Lord Maugham (Mar. 1938–Sept. 1939)
Lord Privy Seal	Earl de la Warr (May 1937–Oct. 1938)
Secretary of State for the Home Department .	Sir Samuel Hoare, Bt. (May 1937–Sept. 1939)
Secretary of State for the Dominions . .	Mr. Malcolm MacDonald (June 1935–May 1938, Nov. 1938–Jan. 1939)
Minister for Co-ordination of Defence . .	Sir Thomas W. H. Inskip (Mar. 1936–Jan. 1939)
	Admiral of the Fleet Lord Chatfield (Jan. 1939–April 1940)
Chancellor of the Duchy of Lancaster . .	Earl Winterton (May 1937–Jan. 1939)
	Mr. W. S. Morrison (Jan. 1939–April 1940)
1st Lord of the Admiralty	Mr. A. Duff Cooper (May 1937–Oct. 1938)
	Earl Stanhope (Oct. 1938–Sept. 1939)
Secretary of State for War	Mr. Leslie Hore-Belisha (May 1937–Jan. 1940)
Secretary of State for Air	Viscount Swinton (June 1935–May 1938)
	Sir Kingsley Wood (May 1938–April 1940)
President of the Board of Trade . . .	Mr. Oliver F. G. Stanley (May 1937–Jan. 1940)
Minister of Supply	Dr. E. Leslie Burgin (July 1939–May 1940)
Minister of Agriculture and Fisheries . .	Mr. W. S. Morrison (Oct. 1936–Dec. 1938)
Chief Diplomatic Adviser to Secretary of State for Foreign Affairs	Sir Robert Vansittart (June 1938–June 1941)
Permanent Under-Secretary of State for Foreign Affairs	Sir Alexander Cadogan (Jan. 1938–Feb. 1946)
Parliamentary Under-Secretaries of State for Foreign Affairs	Earl of Plymouth (July 1936–May 1939)
	Mr. R. A. Butler (Feb. 1938–July 1941)
Parliamentary Under-Secretary of State for War	Earl of Munster (Jan.–Sept. 1939)
Parliamentary Secretary, Department of Overseas Trade	Mr. R. S. Hudson (May 1937–April 1940)
Parliamentary Secretary, Mines Department .	Mr. G. W. Lloyd (April 1939–May 1940)

Diplomatic Representatives

Ambassador at Angora . . .	Sir Percy L. Loraine, Bt. (Jan. 1934–Feb. 1939)
	Sir Hughe M. Knatchbull-Hugessen (Feb. 1939–Sept. 1944)
Ambassador at Berlin	Sir Nevile Henderson (April 1937–Sept. 1939)
Ambassador at Brussels . . .	Sir Robert H. Clive (July 1937–Nov. 1939)
Ambassador at Cairo	Sir Miles W. Lampson (1943 Baron Killearn) (Dec. 1936–Mar. 1946)
Ambassador in China	Sir Archibald Clark Kerr (Feb. 1938–Feb. 1942)

UNITED KINGDOM (*cont.*)

Ambassador at Moscow . . .	Viscount Chilston (Oct. 1933–Nov. 1938)
	Sir William Seeds (Jan. 1939–Jan. 1940)
Ambassador at Paris . . .	Sir Eric C. E. Phipps (April 1937–Oct. 1939)
Ambassador at Rome . . .	Earl of Perth (Sir Eric Drummond) (Oct. 1933–April 1939)
	Sir Percy L. Loraine, Bt., (May 1939–June 1940)
Ambassador at Tokyo . . .	Sir Robert L. Craigie (Sept. 1937–Dec. 1941)
Ambassador at Warsaw . .	Sir Howard W. Kennard (Jan. 1935–Sept. 1939)¹
Ambassador at Washington . .	Sir Ronald C. Lindsay (Mar. 1930–Aug. 1939)
	Marquess of Lothian (Aug. 1939–Dec. 1940)
Minister at Athens . . .	Sir Sydney P. Waterlow (Dec. 1933–May 1939)
	Sir Michael Palairet (June 1939–April 1941)²
Minister at Bangkok . . .	Sir Josiah Crosby (Aug. 1934–Feb. 1942)
Minister at Belgrade . . .	Sir Ronald H. Campbell (Aug. 1935–Oct. 1939)
Minister at Berne . . .	Sir George Warner (Jan. 1935–Dec. 1939)
Minister at Bucharest . .	Sir Reginald H. Hoare (Feb. 1935–Feb. 1941)
Minister at Budapest . . .	Sir Geoffrey George Knox (Oct. 1935–May 1939)
	Mr. Owen St. Clair O'Malley (May 1939–April 1941)
Minister at Copenhagen . .	Sir Patrick W. M. Ramsay (Oct. 1935–Sept. 1939)
Minister at Durazzo . . .	Sir Andrew Ryan (Sept. 1936–June 1939)
Minister at The Hague . .	Sir Nevile Bland (Sept. 1938–May 1940)³
Minister at Helsingfors . .	Mr. Thomas Maitland Snow (Mar. 1937–Feb. 1940)
Minister at Oslo . . .	Mr. C. (1937 Sir Cecil) F. J. Dormer (June 1934–April 1940)⁴
Minister at Paris . . .	Mr. R. I. Campbell (May 1938–Dec. 1939)
Minister at Prague . . .	Mr. B. (1939 Sir Basil) C. Newton (Mar. 1937–April 1939)
Minister at Riga, Tallinn and Kovno .	Mr. C. W. Orde (April 1938–July 1940)
Minister at Sofia . . .	Mr. G. W. Rendel (June 1938–Mar. 1941)
Minister at Stockholm . .	Sir Edmund St. J. D. J. Monson, Bt. (Jan. 1938–Jan. 1940)
Minister at The Vatican . .	Mr. F. D'A. G. (1943 Sir Francis d'Arcy Godolphin) Osborne (Feb. 1936–June 1947)
Minister at Vienna . . .	Mr. C. M. (June 1938, Sir Michael) Palairet (Dec. 1937–Mar. 1938)
Agent at Burgos	Sir Robert Hodgson (Dec. 1937–Feb. 1939; Chargé d'Affaires, Feb.–April 1939)
Chargé d'Affaires at Belgrade .	Mr. T. A. Shone (Secretary)
Chargé d'Affaires at Berlin . .	Sir George A. D. Ogilvie-Forbes (Counsellor)
Chargé d'Affaires at Bucharest .	Mr. J. H. Le Rougetel (Secretary)
Chargé d'Affaires at Budapest .	Mr. A. D. F. Gascoigne (Secretary)
Chargé d'Affaires at Kovno . .	Mr. T. H. Preston (June 1930–Sept. 1940)
Chargé d'Affaires at Moscow .	Mr. G. G. M. Vereker (Counsellor)
Chargé d'Affaires at Paris . .	Mr. R. I. Campbell (Minister)

¹ Sir H. Kennard continued to hold the position of H.M. Ambassador to Polish Government until May 1941, but the British Diplomatic Mission was transferred to Angers in Nov. 1939 and to London in June 1940: Sir H. Kennard left Warsaw in September 1939.

² Sir M. Palairet continued to hold the position of H.M. Minister to Greek Government until May 1942, but the British Diplomatic Mission was transferred to London in Sept. 1941: Sir M. Palairet left Athens in April 1941. From 1942 to 1943 Sir M. Palairet was H.M. Ambassador to Greek Government.

³ Sir N. Bland continued to hold the position of H.M. Minister to the Netherlands Government until May 1942, but the British Diplomatic Mission was transferred to London in May 1940. From 1942 to 1948 Sir N. Bland was H.M. Ambassador to the Netherlands Government.

⁴ Sir C. Dormer continued to hold the position of H.M. Minister to Norwegian Government until May 1941, but the British Diplomatic Mission was transferred to London in June 1940: Sir C. Dormer left Oslo in April 1940.

Chargé d'Affaires at Prague . .	Mr. J. M. Troutbeck (Secretary)
Chargé d'Affaires at Rome . . .	Sir Noel H. H. Charles, Bart. (Counsellor)
Chargé d'Affaires at Vienna. . .	Mr. W. H. B. Mack (Secretary)
Chargé d'Affaires at Warsaw . .	Mr. C. J. Norton (Counsellor)
Counsellor at Angora	Mr. J. Morgan (Oct. 1930–Sept. 1940)
Counsellor at Berlin . . .	Sir George A. D. Ogilvie-Forbes (Mar. 1937–Sept. 1939)
Counsellor in China	Mr. P. M. Broadmead (Dec. 1938–April 1941)
Counsellor at Moscow . . .	Mr. G. G. M. Vereker (Nov. 1937–Feb. 1940)
Counsellor at Rome	Sir Noel H. H. Charles, Bart. (Oct. 1937–Oct. 1939)
Counsellor at Tokyo . . .	Mr. J. L. Dodds (Mar. 1936–Sept. 1940)
Counsellor at Warsaw . . .	Mr. C. J. Norton (Dec. 1937–Oct. 1939)
Counsellor at Washington . .	Mr. V. A. L. Mallet (Jan. 1936–Dec. 1939)
Secretary at Angora	Mr. E. A. Walker (May 1939–May 1941)
Secretary at Athens . . .	Mr. H. L. d'A. Hopkinson (Feb. 1938–June 1939)
Secretary at Belgrade	Mr. T. A. Shone (Nov. 1936–Nov. 1939)
Secretary at Berlin . . .	Mr. I. A. Kirkpatrick (Aug. 1933–Dec. 1938)
	Mr. A. Holman (Dec. 1938–Sept. 1939)
	Mr. C. E. Steel (July 1936–June 1939)
Secretary at Bucharest. .	Mr. H. L. Farquhar (Dec. 1935–Jan. 1939)
	Mr. J. H. Le Rougetel (Jan.–Nov. 1939)
Secretary at Budapest . . .	Mr. A. D. F. Gascoigne (April 1936–Aug. 1939)
Secretary in China . . .	Mr. J. D. Greenway (Nov. 1937–April 1940)
	Mr. G. P. Young (Oct. 1935–Oct. 1938)
	Mr. W. D. Allen (Jan. 1938–Oct. 1941)
Chinese Secretary in China . .	Sir Arthur D. Blackburn (Sept. 1935–Nov. 1942)
Chinese Secretary (Acting) in China	Mr. H. I. Prideaux-Brune (Oct. 1938–Nov. 1939)
Secretary at Moscow	Mr. F. H. R. Maclean (Feb. 1937–April 1939)
	Mr. A. R. Dew (Sept. 1938–Feb. 1940)
Secretary at Paris	Mr. W. H. B. Mack (Aug. 1938–June 1940)
	Mr. V. G. Lawford (Mar. 1937–Sept. 1939)
Secretary at Prague	Mr. J. M. Troutbeck (Oct. 1937–May 1939)
Secretary at Rome	Mr. A. F. Yencken (Jan. 1937–April 1939)
	Mr. P. J. Dixon (Feb. 1938–Jan. 1940)
	Mr. W. H. B. Mack (April–Aug. 1938)
	Mr. P. F. Grey (Oct. 1938–Sept. 1939)
Secretary at Vienna	Mr. W. H. B. Mack (Dec. 1934–April 1938)
Secretary at Warsaw	Mr. R. M. A. Hankey (Nov. 1936–Sept. 1939)
Naval Attaché at Berlin . .	Captain T. H. Troubridge (Aug. 1936–April 1939)
Naval Attaché at Moscow . .	Captain H. Clanchy (Oct. 1936–Jan. 1942)
Naval Attaché at Paris . . .	Captain C. S. Holland (Jan. 1938–June 1940)
Naval Attaché at Rome . . .	Captain R. H. Bevan (July 1936–Jan. 1939)
	Captain Sir Philip W. Bowyer-Smyth, Bart. (Jan. 1939–Jan. 1940)
Naval Attaché at Tokyo . .	Captain H. B. Rawlings (Jan. 1936–Jan. 1939)
Assistant Naval Attaché for Europe	Commander Glyn Hearson (Sept. 1937–Sept. 1939)
Military Attaché at Angora .	Lt.-Col. A. Ross (Feb. 1936–Aug. 1939)
Military Attaché at Belgrade .	Lt.-Col. H. C. T. Stronge (Nov. 1936–Mar. 1939)
Military Attaché at Berlin . .	Colonel F. N. Mason-Macfarlane (Dec. 1937–May 1939)
	Colonel T. D. Daly (May–Sept. 1939)
Military Attaché at Brussels . .	Lt.-Col. D. K. Paris (Feb. 1935–Feb. 1939)
	Lt.-Col. F. A. A. Blake (Feb. 1939–May 1940)
Military Attaché in China . .	Lt.-Col. C. R. Spear (Oct. 1938–Dec. 1939)

UNITED KINGDOM (*cont.*)

Military Attaché at Moscow . .	Colonel R. C. W. G. Firebrace (April 1937–Dec. 1939)
Military Attaché at Paris . . .	Colonel William Fraser (Aug. 1938–Nov. 1939)
Military Attaché at Prague . . .	Lt.-Col. H. C. T. Stronge (Nov. 1936–Oct. 1938)
	Major G. A. C. Macnab (Oct. 1938–May 1939)
Military Attaché at Rome . . .	Colonel M. B. Burrows (May 1938–May 1940)
Military Attaché at Tokyo . . .	Major-General F. S. G. Piggott (May 1936–Sept. 1939)
Military Attaché at Vienna . . .	Major K. V. B. Benfield (Jan. 1935–May 1938)
Military Attaché at Warsaw. .	Lt.-Col. J. T. Godfrey (Oct. 1935–June 1938)
	Lt.-Col. E. R. Sword (June 1938–Sept. 1939)
Assistant Military Attaché at Berlin .	Major K. W. D. Strong (Jan. 1938–Aug. 1939)
Assistant Military Attaché at Paris .	Major C. A. de Linde (Aug. 1936–June 1940)
Assistant Military Attaché at Rome .	Major W. P. Barclay (Nov. 1937–Mar. 1939)
	Major A. R. Barter (Mar. 1939–June 1940)
Air Attaché at Berlin (and Warsaw) .	Group Captain J. L. Vachell (Oct. 1937–Sept. 1939)
Air Attaché at Brussels . . .	Wing Commander E. P. M. Davis (July 1937–May 1940)
Air Attaché in China	Wing Commander H. S. Kerby (Sept. 1936–Nov. 1938)
Air Attaché at Moscow . . .	Wing Commander C. Hallawell (Mar. 1937–Nov. 1941)
Air Attaché at Paris	Wing Commander D. Colyer (June 1936–June 1940)
Air Attaché at Prague . . .	Wing Commander A. H. H. MacDonald (Feb. 1938–May 1939)
Air Attaché at Rome	Group Captain C. E. H. Medhurst (Aug. 1937–June 1940)
Air Attaché at Tokyo . . .	Group Captain W. E. G. Bryant (Dec. 1937–Dec. 1941)
Air Attaché at Vienna. . . .	Wing Commander A. H. H. MacDonald (Feb.–Mar. 1938)
Air Attaché at Warsaw . . .	(as at Berlin)
Assistant Air Attaché at Berlin and Warsaw	Squadron Leader A. A. Adams (Sept. 1938–Sept. 1939)
Press Attaché at Berlin. . . .	Mr. R. F. O'N. Bashford (Oct. 1938–Sept. 1939)
Press Attaché at Budapest . . .	Mr. F. G. Redward (July 1935–April 1941)
Press Attaché at Paris	Sir Charles Mendl (June 1926–May 1940)
Financial Adviser at Berlin . . .	Mr. G. H. S. Pinsent (Nov. 1932–April 1939)
	Mr. E. N. R. Trentham (April–Sept. 1939)
Financial Adviser at Paris . . .	Mr. E. Rowe-Dutton (Oct. 1934–April 1939)
Financial Adviser at Shanghai and Tokyo	Mr. E. L. Hall-Patch (June 1936–Sept. 1939)
Financial Adviser at Washington . .	Mr. T. K. Bewley (Feb. 1933–May 1937; Mar. 1938–May 1939)
Commercial Counsellor at Berlin . .	Mr. J. H. Magowan (Nov. 1937–Sept. 1939)
Commercial Counsellor at Paris . .	Mr. J. R. (1932 Sir Robert) Cahill (Feb. 1921–July 1939)
Commercial Counsellor at Rome . .	Mr. R. L. Nosworthy (Oct. 1934–June 1940)
Commercial Counsellor at Shanghai .	(*See below* Commercial Secretary in China)
Commercial Counsellor at Tokyo . .	Mr. G. (1935 Sir George) B. Sansom (Mar. 1925–Sept. 1940)
Commercial Counsellor at Warsaw .	Mr. A. J. Pack (Aug. 1937–May 1939)
Commercial Secretary at Angora . .	Mr. S. R. Jordan (Aug. 1938–July 1943)
Commercial Secretary at Berlin . .	Mr. A. F. Merry (Jan. 1938–Sept. 1939)

Commercial Secretary in China . .	Mr. A. H. George (Oct. 1935–July 1940) Mr. J. C. Hutchison (H.M. Trade Commissioner at Hong Kong, Nov. 1938–Jan. 1940)
Commercial Secretary at The Hague	Mr. R. V. Laming (April 1920–May 1940)
Commercial Secretary at Moscow .	Mr. F. H. Todd (Aug. 1938–May 1940)
Commercial Secretary at Prague .	Mr. W. Hough (July 1937–May 1939)
Commercial Secretary at Tokyo .	Mr. H. A. Macrae (Nov. 1929–Sept. 1940)
Consul-General at Amoy . . .	Mr. N. Fitzmaurice (April 1938–June 1943)
Consul-General at Canton . . .	Mr. A. P. Blunt (Feb. 1937–July 1943)
Consul-General at Danzig . . .	Mr. E. H. G. Shepherd (Nov. 1937–July 1939) Mr. F. M. Shepherd (in charge: July–Sept. 1939)
Consul-General at Genoa . . .	Mr. A. G. Major (Jan. 1935–Aug. 1939)
Consul-General (Acting) at Hankow .	Mr. C. E. Whitamore (May 1938–Sept. 1939)
Consul-General at Milan . . .	Mr. W. S. Edmonds (Oct. 1938–Aug. 1939)
Consul-General at Moscow . . .	Mr. J. P. Trant (June 1939–Mar. 1943)
Consul-General at Munich . . .	Mr. D. St. Clair Gainer (Oct. 1932–Mar. 1938) Mr. J. E. M. Carvell (April 1938–Aug. 1939)
Consul-General at Naples . . .	Mr. D. F. S. Filliter (Nov. 1937–June 1940)
Consul-General at Shanghai. . .	Mr. H. (1938 Sir Herbert) Phillips (Sept. 1937–July 1940)
Consul-General at Tientsin . . .	Mr. J. B. Affleck (Feb. 1935–Aug. 1938) Mr. E. G. Jamieson (Aug. 1938–Oct. 1939)
Consul-General at Tunis . . .	Mr. W. L. C. Knight (April 1937–July 1940)
Consul-General at Vienna . . .	Mr. D. St. Clair Gainer (Mar. 1938–Sept. 1939)
Consul at Bratislava	Mr. P. Pares (Dec. 1938–Sept. 1939)
Consul at Dresden	Mr. H. B. Livingston (July 1936–April 1938) Mr. F. M. Shepherd (June 1938–July 1939)
Consul at Florence	Mr. C. O. Wakefield-Harrey (Sept. 1936–Mar. 1939)
Consul (Acting) at Hankow . . .	Mr. L. H. Whittall (Mar. 1939–Feb. 1940)
Consul at Katowice	Mr. J. A. Thwaites (April–Oct. 1939)
Consul (Acting) at Palermo . .	Mr. H. H. Clark (1936–8)
Consul at Peking	Mr. H. A. F. B. Archer (July 1937–Aug. 1939)
Consul at Shanghai	Mr. G. V. Kitson (Jan. 1939–April 1941)
Consul at Tallinn	Mr. W. H. Gallienne (Sept. 1935–June 1941)
Consul at Tientsin	Major G. A. Herbert (Oct. 1938–Nov. 1939)
Consul at Tripoli	Mr. A. E. Watkinson (Oct. 1938–July 1940)
Consul at Turin	Captain R. H. Tottenham Smith (Nov. 1937–June 1940)
Consul at Venice	Mr. A. Napier (Nov. 1924–June 1940)
Vice-Consul at Breslau . . .	Mr. R. F. O'N. Bashford (May 1936–Oct. 1938)
Vice-Consul (Acting) at Brno . .	Mr. O. Neumark (1938–9)
Vice-Consul at Danzig . . .	Mr. G. H. Baker (July–Sept. 1939)
Vice-Consul at Dresden . . .	Mr. C. J. Girling (July 1936–Dec. 1938; Mar.–Sept. 1939)
Vice-Consul at Durazzo . . .	Mr. F. H. Gamble (June 1938–June 1939)
Vice-Consul at Gdynia . . .	Mr. C. H. Jeffrey (Mar. 1931–Sept. 1939)
Vice-Consul at Katowice . . .	Mr. J. A. Thwaites (Aug. 1938–April 1939, then Consul)
Vice-Consul at Liberec . . .	Mr. S. P. Elliott (1923–39; in charge of post, 1936–9)
Vice-Consul at Lodz . . .	Mr. E. Gilbert (Feb. 1924–Sept. 1939)
Vice-Consul at Spezia . . .	Mr. R. A. Guattari-Stafford (June 1924–Nov. 1939)
Pro-Consul at Shanghai . . .	Mr. W. H. Williams (May 1938–Sept. 1942)
Judge of H.B.M. Supreme Court for China	Mr. A. (1937 Sir Allan) G. Mossop (1933–43)
Assistant Judge of H.B.M. Supreme Court for China	Mr. P. Grant Jones (1931–45)
The Crown Advocate, Shanghai . .	Mr. V. Priestwood (1934–9)

UNITED KINGDOM (*cont.*)

The Royal Navy

1st Sea Lord and Chief of Naval Staff .	Admiral of the Fleet Sir Dudley Pound (1939–43)
Deputy Chief of Naval Staff. . .	Vice-Admiral Sir A. B. Cunningham (1938–9)
	Rear-Admiral T. S. V. Phillips (1939–41)
Director of Naval Intelligence . .	Rear-Admiral J. A. G. Troup (1935–9)
	Rear-Admiral J. H. Godfrey (1939–42)
Commander-in-Chief, Mediterranean .	Admiral Sir Dudley Pound (1936–9)
China Command:	
Commander-in-Chief . . .	Vice-Admiral (1939 Admiral) Sir Percy L. H. Noble (1938–40)
Senior Naval Officer Yangtze . .	Rear-Admiral R. V. Holt (1937–9)

The Army

Chief of Imperial General Staff (C.I.G.S.)	General the Viscount Gort (1937–9)
Director of Military Operations and Intelligence	Major-General H. (1940 Sir Henry) R. Pownall (1938–40)
Inspector-General of Overseas Forces .	General Sir Edmund Ironside (July–Sept. 1939)
British Troops in China: General Officer Commanding	Major-General A. E. Grasett (1938–41)
British Troops in China: Commander, Shanghai Area	Major-General F. K. Simmons (1939–40)
British Troops in China: Commander, Tientsin Area	Brigadier A. H. Hopwood (1935–9)
	Brigadier Sir John E. Laurie (1939–40)

The Royal Air Force

Chief of Air Staff	Air Chief Marshal Sir Cyril L. N. Newall (1937–40)

AUSTRALIA

Governor-General	Brigadier-General Lord Gowrie (1936–41)
Prime Minister	Mr. J. A. Lyons (1937–9)
Minister for External Affairs . .	Mr. W. M. Hughes (1937–9)
High Commissioner in London .	Mr. S. M. Bruce (1933–45)

EIRE

President	Dr. Douglas Hyde (1938–45)
Prime Minister and Minister for Foreign Affairs	Mr. Eamon de Valera (1937–48)
Minister at Rome	Mr. Michael MacWhite (1938–50)

NEW ZEALAND

Governor-General	Viscount Galway (1935–41)
Prime Minister and Minister for External Affairs	Mr. M. J. Savage (1935–40)
High Commissioner in London .	Mr. W. J. Jordan (1936–51)

SOUTH AFRICA, UNION OF

Governor-General	Sir Patrick Duncan (1937–43)
Prime Minister	General J. B. M. Hertzog (1924–39)
Minister for Foreign Affairs . .	General J. B. M. Hertzog (1929–39)
Minister of Defence . . .	Dr. Oswald Pirow (1933–9)
High Commissioner in London .	Mr. C. T. te Water (1929–39)
Minister at Berlin . . .	Dr. S. F. N. Gie (1934–9)
Minister at Rome . . .	Dr. Albert Heymans (1934–40)

(ii) Foreign States

ALBANIA

King	Zog I (Sept. 1928–April 1939)
Prime Minister	M. Constantine Kotta (Nov. 1936–April 1939)
Minister for Foreign Affairs . . .	M. Ekrem Libohova (Nov. 1936–April 1939)
Minister of the Interior . .	M. Malik Bushati

Diplomatic Representatives

Minister at London	M. Lec Kurti (May 1936–April 1939)
Minister at Rome . . .	General Zef Sereggi (Mar.-April 1939)
Chargé d'Affaires at Bucharest .	M. Pandeli Nasse (1937–9)

ARGENTINA

President	Dr. Roberto M. Ortiz (Feb. 1938–June 1942)
Vice-President	Dr. Ramon S. Castillo (Feb. 1938–June 1942)
Minister for Foreign Affairs . .	Señor J. M. Cantilo (1938–40)

Diplomatic Representatives

Ambassador at Berlin	Dr. Eduardo Labougle (1936–9)
Consul-General at Danzig . .	Señor C. Piñeyro (1934–9)

AUSTRIA

President	Herr Wilhelm Miklas (Dec. 1928–Mar. 13, 1938)
Chancellor	Dr. Kurt von Schuschnigg (July 1934–Mar. 11, 1938)
	Dr. Artur Seyss-Inquart (Mar. 11–15, 1938)
Minister for Foreign Affairs . .	Dr. Guido Schmidt (Feb.–Mar. 11, 1938)
	Dr. Wilhelm Wolf (Mar. 12–15, 1938)
Minister of Finance . . .	Dr. Neumayr (1936–8)
Minister without Portfolio . .	Dr. E. von Glaise-Horstenau (1936–8)
State Secretary for Security . .	Dr. Skubl (1937–8)
Director of Political Department of Federal Chancellery . .	Herr Theodor Hornbostel (1934–8)

Diplomatic Representatives

Minister at Berlin	Herr Stephan Tauschitz (1933–8)
Minister at Prague . . .	Dr. Ferdinand Marek (1922–38)
Military Attaché at Berlin . .	Major-General A. Pohl

BELGIUM

King	Leopold III (1934–51)
Prime Minister	M. Paul van Zeeland (Mar. 1935–Nov. 1937)
	M. Paul E. Janson (Nov. 1937–May 1938)
	M. Paul Henri Spaak (May 1938–Feb. 1939)
	M. Hubert Pierlot (Feb. 1939; April 1939–Feb. 1945)
Minister for Foreign Affairs . .	M. Paul Henri Spaak (June 1936–Jan. 1939)
	M. Paul E. Janson (Jan.–Feb. 1939)
	M. Eugène Soudan (Feb.–Mar. 1939)
	M. Hubert Pierlot (April 1939–Jan. 1940)
Minister for National Defence .	Lt.-Gen. H. J. C. E. Denis (1936–42)
Ministry of Foreign Affairs:	
Secretary-General . . .	M. F. van Langenhove
Political Director . . .	Baron van Zuylen

BELGIUM (*cont.*)

Diplomatic Representatives

Ambassador at Berlin	Vicomte J. Davignon (1938–40)
Ambassador in China . . .	Baron Jules Guillaume (1937–44)
Ambassador at London . .	Baron E. de Cartier de Marchienne (1927–46)
Ambassador at Madrid . .	Comte C. de Romrée de Vichenet (1939–41)
Ambassador at Paris . . .	M. Pol le Tellier (1938–40)
Ambassador at Rome . . .	Comte André de Kerchove de Denterghem (1938–40)
Ambassador at Tokyo . . .	Baron Albert de Bassompierre (1921–38)
Ambassador at Warsaw . .	M. Alexandre Paternotte de la Vaillée (1936–9)
Minister at The Hague. . .	Baron Joseph Herry (1937–40)
Counsellor at Rome . . .	Comte F. de Chastel de la Howarderie
Military Attaché at Berlin . .	Lt.-Col. B. E. M. Goethals
Military Attaché at The Hague .	Lt.-Col. P. J. Diepenrykz
Consul-General at Tientsin . .	M. R. Guillaume

BRAZIL

President	Dr. G. D. Vargas (1934–45)
Minister for Foreign Affairs . .	Dr. O. Aranha (1938–44)

Diplomatic Representatives

Ambassador at Tokyo . . .	Senhor F. de Castello-Branco Clark (1939–42)

BULGARIA

King.	Boris III (1918–1943)
President of the Council and Minister for Foreign Affairs	M. Gheorgi Kiosseivanoff (1935–40)

Diplomatic Representatives

Minister at Angora	Dr. Theodore Christoff (1936–9)
Minister at London	M. Nicolas Momtchiloff (1938–41)

CHINA: National Government

President	Mr. Lin Sen (1931–43)
Commander-in-Chief of Chinese armed forces and member of Central Executive Committee of the Kuomintang . .	Generalissimo Chiang Kai-shek
President of the Executive Yuan .	Dr. H. H. Kung (1938–9)
Minister for Foreign Affairs . .	Mr. Wang Chung-hui (1937–41)
Minister for War	Mr. Ho Ying-chin (1930–44)
Minister of Finance . . .	Dr. H. H. Kung
Vice-Minister for Foreign Affairs .	Mr. Hsu Mo (1932–41)
Director of Propaganda and Publicity .	Mr. Ku Meng-yu
Maritime Customs Administration: Inspector-General	Sir Frederick Maze

Diplomatic Representatives

Ambassador at London . .	Dr. Quo Tai-chi (1935–41)
Ambassador at Paris . . .	Dr. V. K. Wellington Koo (1932–9)
Ambassador at Washington . .	Dr. C. T. Wang (1937–8)
Counsellor at London . . .	Dr. Chen Wei-cheng
Commercial Attaché at London .	Dr. P. W. Kuo

CZECHOSLOVAKIA

President of the Republic . .	Dr. Eduard Benes (Dec. 1935–Oct. 1938)
	(*ad interim*) General Jan Syrovy (Oct.–Nov. 1938)
	Dr. Emil Hacha (Nov. 1938–Mar. 1939)

President of the National Council (Prime Minister)	Dr. Milan Hodza (Nov. 1935–Sept. 1938)
	General Jan Syrovy (Sept.–Oct. and Oct.–Nov. 1938)
	Dr. Rudolf Beran (Dec. 1938–Mar. 1939)
Vice-President of the National Council .	M. Rudolf Bechyne (1935–8)
Minister for Foreign Affairs . . .	Dr. Kamil Krofta (Nov. 1935–Oct. 1938)
	M. Frantisek Chvalkovsky (Oct. 1938–Mar. 1939)
Minister of Agriculture . . .	Dr. Ladislav Feierabend (1938–9)
Minister of Commerce. . . .	M. Karvas (Sept.-Nov. 1938)
	Dr. Vlastimil Sadek (1938–9)
Minister of Education	Dr. Emil Franke (1935–8)
	Dr. Jan Kapras (1938–9)
Minister of Finance	Dr. Josef Kalfus (1938–9)
Minister of Health	Dr. Ludwig Czech (1935–8)
Minister of Health and Social Welfare .	Dr. Vladislav Klumpar (1938–9)
Minister of the Interior . . .	Dr. Josef Cerny (1935–8)
	Dr. Otakar Fischer (1938–9)
Minister of Justice and Unification .	Dr. Jaroslav Krejci (1938–9)
Minister of National Defence . .	M. Frantisek Machnik (1935–8)
	General Jan Syrovy (1938–9)
Minister of Public Works . . .	M. Dominik Cipera (1938–9)
Minister of Railways	M. Rudolf Bechyne (1935–8)
	General Alois Elias (1938–9)
Minister of Social Welfare . . .	M. Jaromir Necas (1935–8)
Minister without Portfolio . . .	Dr. Butovsky
	M. Karel Sidor
. . . . .	Dr. Jiri Havelka
Political Director, Ministry of Foreign Affairs	M. J. Krno

Diplomatic Representatives

Minister at Berlin	Dr. Vojtech Mastny (1932–9)
Minister at Budapest	M. Milos Kobr (1933–9)
Minister at London	M. Jan Masaryk (1925–38)
Minister at Moscow	M. Zdenek Fierlinger (1937–9)
Minister at Paris	M. Stefan Osusky (1921–39)
Minister at Rome	M. Frantisek Chvalkovsky (1932–8)
Minister at Tokyo	M. Frantisek Havlicek (1932–8)
Minister at Warsaw	Dr. Juraj Slavik (1936–9)
Minister at Washington . . .	M. Vladimir Hurban (1936–9)
Chargé d'Affaires at Berlin . . .	M. Schubert (Counsellor)
Counsellor at London . . .	M. Karel Lisicky
Military Attaché at Berlin . . .	Colonel A. Hron
Military Attaché at Moscow . .	Colonel F. Dastich
Military Attaché at Paris . . .	Lt.-Col V. Kalina
Military Attaché at Rome . . .	General V. Klecanda
Military Attaché at Vienna . . .	Colonel R. Kucera

DANZIG FREE STATE

President of the Senate . . .	Herr A. K. Greiser (1934–9)
Vice-President of the Senate. . .	Herr W. Huth (1936–9)
Head of Foreign Department of the Senate	Dr. V. Böttcher
Minister of Finance	Dr. J. Hoppenrath (1933–9)

DENMARK

King.	Christian X (1912–47)
President of the Council . . .	M. Th. A. M. Stauning (1929–42)
Minister for Foreign Affairs . . .	M. Peter R. Munch (1929–40)

DENMARK *(cont.)*

Diplomatic Representative

Consul-General at Shanghai.   .   .   M. Paul Scheel (1935–47)

EGYPT

King.   .   .   .   .   .   .   Farouk I (1936–52)
President of the Cabinet (Prime Minister)   Mohamed Mahmud Pasha (1938–9)
Minister for Foreign Affairs.   .   .   Abdul Fattah Yehia Pasha (1938–9)

Diplomatic Representatives

Ambassador at London   .   .   .   Dr. Hassan Nashat Pasha (1938–45)
Minister at Berlin   .   .   .   .   Dr. Hassan Nashat Pasha (1929–38)
Minister at Paris   .   .   .   .   Mahmud Fakhri Pasha (1924–40)

ESTONIA

President .   .   .   .   .   .   M. Konstantin Päts (1931–40)
Prime Minister .   .   .   .   .   M. Kaanel Eenpalu (1934–9)
Minister for Foreign Affairs .   .   .   M. Karl Selter (1938–9)
Ministry of Foreign Affairs:
     Head of Political Department .   .   Dr. Nikolai Kaasik

Diplomatic Representatives

Minister at Berlin   .   .   .   .   M. Karl Tofer (1936–9)
Minister at London   .   .   .   .   M. August Schmidt (1934–40)
Minister at Moscow   .   .   .   .   M. August Rei (1938–40)
Minister at Warsaw   .   .   .   .   M. Hans Markus (1935–9)
Military Attaché at Moscow   .   Major A. Sinka

FINLAND

President .   .   .   .   .   .   M. Kyösti Kallio (Feb. 1937–Nov. 1940)
Prime Minister .   .   .   .   .   Professor A. K. Cajander (Mar. 1937–Dec. 1939)
Minister for Foreign Affairs .   .   .   M. Eljas Erkko (Dec. 1938–Dec. 1939)

Diplomatic Representatives

Minister at London   .   .   .   .   M. G. A. Gripenberg (1933–41)
Minister at Moscow   .   .   .   .   Baron A. Yrjö-Koskinen (1930–9)
Chargé d'Affaires at Prague   .   .   Dr. E. Hiitonen (1938–9)

FRANCE

President of the Republic   .   .   .   M. Albert Lebrun (May 1932–July 1940)
President of the Council of Ministers   .   M. Camille Chautemps (June 1937–Mar. 1938)
     M. Léon Blum (Mar.–April 1938)
     M. Édouard Daladier (April 1938–Mar. 1940)
Minister for Foreign Affairs ,   .   .   M. Yvon Delbos (June 1936–Mar. 1938)
     M. Joseph Paul-Boncour (Mar.–April 1938)
     M. Georges Bonnet (April 1938–Sept. 1939)
Minister of Agriculture   .   .   .   M. G. Monnet (Mar.–April 1938)
Minister for Air .   .   .   .   .   M. Guy La Chambre (1938–40)
Minister for Colonies .   .   .   .   M. Georges Mandel (1938–40)
Minister of Education .   .   .   .   M. Jean Zay (1936–9)
Minister of Finance   .   .   .   .   M Paul Marchandeau (Jan.–Nov. 1938)
     M. Paul Reynaud (Nov. 1938–Mar. 1940)
Minister of the Interior   .   .   .   M. Albert Sarraut (1938–40)
Minister of Justice   .   .   .   .   M. Paul Reynaud (April–Nov. 1938)
     M. Paul Marchandeau (Nov. 1938–Sept. 1939)
Minister of Labour   .   .   .   .   M. Anatole de Monzie (1938–9)
Minister of Marine   .   .   .   .   M. C. Campinchi (1938–40)

Ministry of Foreign Affairs:
Secretary-General	.	.	.	.	M. Alexis Léger (1933–40)
Political Director	.	.	.	.	M. René Massigli (1937–8)
					M. Émile Charvériat (1938–40)

Diplomatic Representatives

Ambassador at Angora	.	.	M. René Massigli (1939–40)
Ambassador at Berlin .	.	.	M. André François-Poncet (Sept. 1931–Oct. 1938)
			M. Robert Coulondre (Nov. 1938–Sept. 1939)
Ambassador at Berne .	.	.	M. Charles Alphand (1936–40)
Ambassador at Brussels	.	.	M. Paul Bargeton (1937–40)
Ambassador at Bucharest	.	.	M. Adrien Thierry (April 1939–40)
Ambassador in China .	.	.	M. Paul É. Naggiar (July 1936–Nov. 1938)
			M. Henri Cosmé (Mar. 1939–43)
Ambassador at London	.	.	M. Charles Corbin (1933–40)
Ambassador at Moscow	.	.	M. Robert Coulondre (1936–8)
			M. Paul E. Naggiar (1939–40)
Ambassador at Rome	.	.	M. André François-Poncet (1938–40)
Ambassador at Tokyo .	.	.	M. Charles Arsène-Henry (1937–43)
Ambassador at The Vatican.	.	.	M. F. Charles-Roux (1932–40)
Ambassador at Warsaw	.	.	M. Léon Noël (1935–9)
Ambassador at Washington .	.	Comte R. Doynel de St. Quentin (1938–40)
Minister at Belgrade .	.	.	M. Raymond Brugère (1937–40)
Minister at Bucharest .	.	.	M. Adrien Thierry (1936–9)
Minister at Budapest .	.	.	M. Gaston Maugras (1934–8)
			M. Pierre Guerlet (1939–40)
Minister at Durazzo .	.	.	M. Louis Mercier (1935–9)
Minister at The Hague	.	.	Baron d'Arnauld de Vitrolles (1931–40)
Minister at Kovno	.	.	M. Georges Dulong (1935–40)
Minister at Prague .	.	.	M. Léopold Victor de Lacroix (1936–9)
Minister at Vienna .	.	.	M. Gabriel Puaux (1933–8)
Chargé d'Affaires at Berlin .	.	.	Comte H. Barthon de Montbas (Counsellor: Oct. 1936–Mar. 1939)
			M. Carra de Vaux Saint-Cyr (April 1939)
			M. J. Tarbé de Saint-Hardouin (Counsellor: July and Aug. 1939)
Chargé d'Affaires in China .	.	.	M. G. Georges Picot (1st Secretary: Nov. 1938–Mar. 1939)
Chargé d'Affaires at London	.	.	M. Roger Cambon (Minister Counsellor)
Chargé d'Affaires at Moscow	.	.ᐧ	M. Jean Payart
Chargé d'Affaires at Rome .	.	.	M. J. F. Blondel (Minister)
Chargé d'Affaires at Warsaw	.	.	M. J. de Seguin (Counsellor)
Counsellor at Berlin .	.	.	Comte H. Barthon de Montbas
			M. J. Tarbé de Saint-Hardouin (July–Aug. 1939)
Counsellor at London .	.	.	M. Roger Cambon
Counsellor at Rome .	.	.	M. H. Guérin
Counsellor at Tokyo .	.	.	Baron G. Fain
Secretary in China .	.	.	M. G. Georges Picot
Secretary at London .	.	.	M. Roland de Margerie
			M. Guy de Girard de Charbonnière
Secretary at Prague .	.	.	M. A. Lamarle
Secretary at Warsaw .	.	.	M. H. Gauquié
Military Attaché at Berlin .	.	.	General G. Renondeau (to Nov. 1938)
			Colonel H. Didelet
Military Attaché at Brussels .	.	.	Colonel Laurent
Military Attaché at Budapest	.	.	Colonel P. Donnat
Military Attaché at London	.	.	General A. Lelong
Military Attaché at Moscow	.	.	Colonel Palasse
Military Attaché at Rome .	.	.	General J. Toussaint

FRANCE *(cont.)*

Military Attaché at Vienna . . .	Lt.-Col. R. Salland
Military Attaché at Warsaw. . .	General F. Musse
Assistant Military Attaché at Moscow .	Lt.-Col. Abraham
Assistant Military Attaché at Rome .	Major Donati
Naval Attaché at Rome . . .	Captain G. de Lafond
Naval Attaché at Warsaw . . .	Captain G. Gruillot
Air Attaché at Moscow . . .	Lt.-Col. Luguet
Financial Attaché at Berlin . . .	M. J. Aris
Financial Attaché at London . .	M. E. Monick
Consul-General at Dresden . . .	M. A. Boissier (1933–9)
Consul-General at Munich . . .	M. Carra de Vaux Saint-Cyr (1934–8)
Consul-General at Shanghai . .	M. Marcel Baudez (1935–41)
Consul-General at Tientsin . . .	M. Charles Lépissier (1938–43)
Consul-General at Vienna . . .	M. Jean Chauvel (1938)
Consul at Amoy	M. Fernand Roy (1935–43)
Consul at Danzig	M. Guy Le Roy de la Tournelle (1934–9)

GERMANY

Head of State, Leader and Chancellor .	Herr Adolf Hitler (1934–45)
Minister for Foreign Affairs . . .	Herr Joachim von Ribbentrop (1938–45)
Minister for Air	Field-Marshal H. W. Göring (1933–45)
Minister of Economics . . .	Dr. Walther Funk (1937–45)
Minister of Finance	Count Ludwig Schwerin von Krosigk (1932–45)
Minister of Food and Agriculture . .	Dr. Walther Darré (1933–45)
Minister of the Interior . . .	Dr. Wilhelm Frick (1933–43)
Minister of Propaganda . . .	Dr. Josef Goebbels (1933–44)
Minister of War	Field-Marshal Werner von Blomberg (1935–8)
Minister and Head of Presidential Chancellery	Dr. Otto Meissner
Minister and President of Secret Cabinet Council	Baron C. von Neurath (1938–45)
Minister and Head of Government Chancellery	Dr. H. H. Lammers (1937–45)
Chief of Diplomatic Protocol . .	Baron von Dörnberg
Leader of German Labour Front . .	Dr. Robert Ley
Ministry of Foreign Affairs:	
State Secretary	Baron Ernst von Weizsäcker (1938–43)
Head of Political Department and Under State Secretary . . .	Dr. Ernst Woermann (1938–43)

Diplomatic Representatives

Ambassador at Angora . . .	Herr Franz von Papen (1939–44)
Ambassador at Brussels . . .	Herr V. von Bülow-Schwante (1938–40)
Ambassador at Buenos Aires .	Dr. E. Freiherr von Thermann (1936–41)
Ambassador at Burgos (then Madrid) .	Dr. E. von Stöhrer (1937–43)
Ambassador in China . . .	Dr. O. Trautmann (1935–8)
Ambassador at London . . .	Herr J. von Ribbentrop (1936–8)
	Dr. H. von Dirksen (1938–9)
Ambassador at Moscow . . .	Count F. W. von der Schulenberg (1934–41)
Ambassador at Paris . . .	Count J. von Welczeck (1936–9)
Ambassador at Rio de Janeiro .	Dr. Karl Ritter (1937–8)
Ambassador at Rome . . .	Herr Ulrich von Hassell (1932–8)
	Herr H. G. von Mackensen (1938–43)
Ambassador at Tokyo . . .	General Eugen Ott (1938–42)
Ambassador at The Vatican. . .	Dr. Diego von Bergen (1920–43)
Ambassador at Vienna (on Special Mission)	Herr Franz von Papen (1934–8)
Ambassador at Warsaw . . .	Herr H. A. von Moltke (1934–9)

Ambassador at Washington . . .	Dr. H. H. Dieckhoff (1937–41)
Minister at Athens	Prince V. zu Erbach-Schönberg (1936–41)
Minister at Belgrade	Herr V. von Heeren (1933–41)
Minister at Bucharest . . .	Dr. W. Fabricius (1936–41)
Minister at Budapest	Dr. Otto von Erdmannsdorff (1937–41)
Minister at Durazzo	Dr. E. von Pannwitz (1936–9)
Minister at The Hague . . .	Count J. von Zech-Burkersroda (1928–40)
Minister at Helsingfors . . .	Dr. W. von Blücher (1935–45)
Minister at Kovno	Dr. E. Zechlin (1933–40)
Minister at Oslo	Dr. H. Sahm (1936–9)
Minister at Prague	Dr. E. Eisenlohr (1936–40)
Minister at Tallinn	Dr. H. Frohwein (1936–40)
Chargé d'Affaires at Angora . .	Dr. H. Kroll (Counsellor)
Chargé d'Affaires at London . .	Dr. Th. Kordt (Counsellor)
Chargé d'Affaires at Paris . .	Dr. K. Bräuer (Counsellor)
Chargé d'Affaires at Prague .	Herr A. Hencke (Counsellor)
Chargé d'Affaires at Warsaw .	Herr J. von Wühlisch (Counsellor)
Chargé d'Affaires *ad interim* at Washington	Herr H. Thomsen
Counsellor at Helsingfors . .	Count R. Adelmann von Adelmannsfelden
Counsellor of Embassy at London .	Dr. Th. Kordt
Counsellor of Legation at London .	Dr. E. von Selzam
Counsellor at Moscow . .	Herr Werner von Tippelskirch
Counsellor at Paris . . .	Dr. K. Bräuer
Counsellor at Prague . . .	Herr A. Hencke
Secretary at London . . .	Dr. W. M. Weber
Military Attaché at Belgrade .	Herr M. von Faber du Faur
Military Attaché at London .	Lt.-Col. A. Freiherr von Bechtolsheim
Military Attaché at Moscow .	Lt.-Gen. Köstring
Military Attaché at Paris . .	Lt.-Gen. Kühlental
Military Attaché at Prague . .	Colonel Toussaint
Military Attaché at Rome . .	Colonel E. von Rintelen
Military Attaché at Vienna . .	Lt.-Gen. W. Muff
Military Attaché at Warsaw. .	Colonel K. Himer
Assistant Military Attaché at Rome .	Major Pretzell
Naval Attaché at London . .	Captain L. Siemens
Naval Attaché at Moscow . .	Captain N. von Baumbach
Air Attaché at London . .	Lt.-Gen. R. F. A. Wenninger
Commercial Counsellor at Moscow .	Herr G. Hilger
Consul-General at Bratislava .	Dr. Ernst von Drüffel (1939)
Consul-General at Danzig . .	Dr. M. von Janson (1938–9)
Consul-General at Geneva . .	Dr. W. Krauel (1932–43)
Consul-General at Tientsin . .	Dr. W. Stoller (1936–41)
Consul at Basle	Herr G. von Haeften (1939–45)
Consul at Brno	Herr V. L. R. Wolf (1939)
Consul at Lodz	Dr. Baron von Berchem-Königsfeld (1934–9)

GREECE

King.	George II (1922–4, 1935–47)
Prime Minister and Minister for Foreign Affairs	General Ioannis Metaxas (1936–41)
Under-Secretary of State for Foreign Affairs	M. Nicholas Mavroudis (1936–41)

Diplomatic Representatives

Minister at Angora	M. Raphael Raphael (1936–9)
Minister at Belgrade	M. Raoul Bibica-Rosetti (1936–41)
Minister at Berlin	M. Alexander Rizo-Rangabé (1933–41)
Minister at Berne	M. Constantin Psaroudas (1936–41)
Minister at Budapest	M. Panoyotis Pipinelis (1936–9)

GREECE (*cont.*)

Minister at Durazzo	M. Pericles Skeferis (1935–9)
Minister at London	M. Charalambos Simopoulos (1935–42)
Minister at Rome	M. Pierre Metaxas (1931–9)
Chargé d'Affaires at Rome . . .	M. J. Romanos (Counsellor)

HUNGARY

Regent	Admiral Horthy (1920–44)
Prime Minister	Dr. Bela de Imredy (May 1938–Feb. 1939)
	Count Paul Teleki (Feb. 1939–April 1941)
Minister for Foreign Affairs . .	M. Kalman de Kanya (Feb. 1933–Nov. 1938)
	Dr. Bela de Imredy (Nov.–Dec. 1938)
	Count Istvan Csaky (Dec. 1938–Jan. 1941)
Secretary-General of Ministry of Foreign Affairs	M. Jean Vörnle (1938–9)

Diplomatic Representatives

Minister at Angora	M. Zoltan de Mariassy (1935–41)
Minister at Berlin	M. Döme Sztojay (1935–44)
Minister at Bucharest	M. Ladislas de Bardossy (1934–41)
Minister at London	M. George de Barcza (1938–41)
Minister at Prague	M. Jean Wettstein de Westersheimb (1933–9)
Minister at Rome	Baron Frederic de Villani (1934–41)
Counsellor at London	M. Francis de Marosy
Counsellor at Rome	M. L. Nagy de Galantha
Military Attaché at Berlin . . .	Colonel K. Hardy
Military Attaché at Paris . . .	Colonel L. de Karatsony
Military Attaché at Prague . . .	Lt.-Col. V. de Solymossy
Consul at Bratislava	Dr. J. de Petravich

IRAQ

King.	Ghazi I (Sept. 1933–April 1939)
	Feisal II (April 1939–July 1958)
Prime Minister	General Nuri-al-Said (Dec. 1938–Mar. 1940)
Minister for Foreign Affairs . . .	General Nuri-al-Said (Dec. 1938–April 1939)
	M. Ali Jaudat (April 1939–Feb. 1940)

Diplomatic Representative

Minister at Rome	Muzahim al Pachachi (1935–9)

ITALY

King.	Victor Emmanuel III (1900–46)
Prime Minister	Signor Benito Mussolini (1922–43)
Minister for Foreign Affairs . . .	Count Galeazzo Ciano (1936–43)
Minister of Education	Signor G. Bottai (1939)
Minister of Finance	Count P. Thaon di Revel (1935–43)
Minister of Popular Culture . .	Signor Dino Alfieri (1936–9)
Minister of Trade and International Payments	Signor F. Guarneri
Minister of State	Signor Alberto Pirelli
Under-Secretary of State in Ministry of Foreign Affairs	Signor Giuseppe Bastianini

Diplomatic Representatives

Ambassador at Angora . . .	Signor Ottavio de Peppo (1938–43)
Ambassador at Berlin	Dr. Bernardo Attolico (1935–40)
Ambassador at Brussels . . .	Signor Vincenzo Lojacono (1939–40)
Ambassador at Burgos . . .	Count Guido Viola di Campalto (1937–9)
Ambassador in China . . .	Marchese F. M. Taliani de Marchio (1938–43)
Ambassador at London . . .	Count Dino Grandi (1932–9)

Ambassador at Paris . . .	Signor V. Cerruti (1935–7)
	Signor Raffaele Guariglia (Nov. 1938–40)
Ambassador at Tokyo . . .	Signor Giacinto Auriti (1933–40)
Ambassador at The Vatican . .	Count P. Morano di Custoza (1935–9)
Ambassador at Warsaw . .	Baron P. Arone di Valentino (1936–9)
Minister at Athens . . .	Signor Emanuele Grazzi (1939–40)
Minister at Belgrade . .	Signor Mario Indelli (1936–40)
Minister at Bucharest . . .	Signor Pellegrino Ghigi (1938–41)
Minister at Durazzo . . .	Signor Francesco Jacomoni (1936–9)
Minister at The Hague . .	Marchese Pasquale Diana (1938–40)
Minister at Prague . . .	Signor Domenico de Facendis (1935–8)
	Signor Francesco Fransoni (1938–9)
Minister at Vienna . . .	Signor Pellegrino Ghigi (1937–8)
Chargé d'Affaires at Athens .	Signor Giovanni Fornari (1st Secretary)
Chargé d'Affaires at Berlin . .	Count Massimo Magistrati (Counsellor)
Chargé d'Affaires at London .	Signor Guido Crolla (Counsellor)
Chargé d'Affaires at Paris .	Signor R. Prunas (Counsellor)
Counsellor at Berlin . . .	Count Massimo Magistrati
Counsellor at London . . .	Signor Guido Crolla
Counsellor at Paris . . .	Signor R. Prunas (till end 1938)
	Marchese G. Capranica del Grillo
Naval Attaché at London . .	Rear Admiral B. Brivonesi
Military Attaché at Berlin . .	Major-General E. Marras
Military Attaché at London .	Colonel C. Ruggeri Laderchi
Military Attaché at Paris . .	General Count S. Visconti Prasca
Military Attaché at Prague .	Colonel Count Valfre di Bonzo
Commercial Counsellor at Berlin .	Dr. A. Ricciardi
Press Counsellor at Paris . .	Signor Landini
Consul-General at Danzig . .	Signor A. Spechel
Consul-General at Shanghai . .	Comdr. Luigi Neyrone
Consul at Tientsin . . .	Signor F. Stefenelli
Vice-Consul at Danzig . . .	Signor Prati

JAPAN

Emperor	Hirohito (since 1926)
Prime Minister	Prince Konoye (June 1937–Jan. 1939)
	Baron Hiranuma (Jan.–Aug. 1939)
	General N. Abe (Aug. 1939–Jan. 1940)
Minister for Foreign Affairs . .	Mr. K. Hirota (June 1937–May 1938)
	General K. Ugaki (May–Sept. 1938)
	Prince Konoye (Oct. 1938)
	Mr. H. Arita (Oct. 1938–Aug. 1939)
	General N. Abe (Aug.–Sept. 1939)
Minister of Communications . .	General K. Koiso
Minister of Education . . .	Marquis K. Kido (1937–8)
	General Baron S. Araki (1938–9)
Minister of Finance . . .	Mr. S. Ikeda (June 1938–Jan. 1939)
	Mr. Y. Sakurauchi (Jan.–Aug. 1939)
Minister for Home Affairs . .	Marquis K. Kido (1939)
Minister of Justice . . .	Mr. S. Shiono (1937–9)
Minister of Marine . . .	Admiral M. Yonai (1937–9)
Minister of Overseas Affairs .	Mr. Y. Hatta (1938–9)
Minister of War . . .	General S. Itagaki (1938–9)
Vice-Minister of Finance . .	Mr. S. Ishiwata (1938–9)
Vice-Minister for Foreign Affairs .	Mr. K. Horinouchi (April 1936–Oct. 1938)
	Mr. Renzo Sawada (Oct. 1938–Sept. 1940)
Vice-Minister of Marine . .	Vice-Admiral I. Yamomoto
Vice-Minister of War . . .	Lt.-Gen. H. Tojo (May–Dec. 1938)
Director of Commercial Department, Ministry of Foreign Affairs . .	Mr. S. Matsushima

JAPAN *(cont.)*

Diplomatic Representatives

Ambassador at Berlin	General H. Oshima (1938–45)
Ambassador at Brussels . . .	Mr. S. Kurusu (1936–9)
Ambassador at London . . .	Mr. S. Yoshida (1936–8)
	Mr. M. Shigemitsu (1938–41)
Ambassador at Moscow . . .	Mr. S. Togo (1938–40)
Ambassador at Rome	Mr. T. Shiratori (1938–9)
Ambassador at Warsaw . . .	Mr. S. Sakoh (1937–9)
Ambassador at Washington . . .	Mr. H. Saito (1934–8)
	Mr. K. Horinouchi (1938–40)
Minister at Berne	Mr. E. Amau (1937–9)
Minister in charge of Embassy at Shanghai	Mr. Masayuki Tani (1938)
Minister (at large) in China . . .	Mr. S. Kato (1939–40)
Counsellor in charge of Embassy in China	Mr. Morito Morishima (1938–9)
Counsellor at London	Mr. Suemasa Okamoto (1938–40)
Naval Attaché in China . . .	Vice-Admiral N. Nomura (1938–9)
Military Attaché at Berlin . . .	Major-General T. Kawabe
Consul-General at Amoy . . .	Mr. G. Uchida
Consul-General at Canton . . .	Mr. K. Okazaki
Consul-General at Hankow . . .	Mr. Y. Hanawa
Consul-General at Shanghai . .	Mr. S. Okamoto (1937–8)
	Mr. Sh. Hidaka (Mar.–Dec. 1938)
	Mr. Y. Miura (1938–9)
Consul-General at Tientsin . . .	Mr. S. Tashiro
Consul-General at Tsingtao . . .	Mr. S. Ohtaka
Consul at Chefoo	Mr. H. Nagaoka
Consul at Tientsin	Mr. Hori
	Mr. S. Shima
Vice-Consul at Tientsin . . .	Mr. H. Tanaka

LATVIA

President and Prime Minister . .	Dr. K. Ulmanis (1936–40)
Minister for Foreign Affairs . . .	M. Vilhelms Munters (1936–40)
Secretary-General of Ministry of Foreign Affairs	M. Martins Nuksa (1939–40)

Diplomatic Representatives

Minister at Berlin	M. Edgars Kreewinsch (1938–40)
Minister at London	M. Charles Zarine (1933–40)
Minister at Moscow	M. Fricis Kocins (1937–40)
Military Attaché at Moscow . .	Lt.-Col. Zalitis

LEAGUE OF NATIONS

Secretary-General	M. Joseph Avenol (1933–40)
High Commissioner at Danzig . .	Mr. Séan Lester (1933–7)
	Professor C. J. Burckhardt (1937–9)

LITHUANIA

President	M. Antanas Smetona (1926–40)
Prime Minister	M. Vladislovas Mironas (1938–9)
Minister for Foreign Affairs . . .	M. Juozas Urbsys (1938–40)
Secretary-General of Ministry of Foreign Affairs	M. Urbsys

Diplomatic Representatives

Minister at Berlin	M. Kazys Skirpa (1938–40)
Minister at London	M. Bronius K. Balutis (1934–40)
Minister at Moscow	M. Jurgis K. Baltrusaitis (1922–40)

Minister at Paris	.	.	.	.	Dr. Petras Klimas (1925–40)
Minister at Prague	.	.	.	.	M. E. Turauskas (1934–9)
Minister at Warsaw	.	.	.	.	Dr. Jurgis Saulys (1939)
Military Attaché at Berlin	.	.	.	Colonel K. Grinius
Military Attaché at Riga	.	.	.	Colonel P. Meskaukas

MANCHUKUO

| Emperor | . | . | . | . | . | Pu Yi (1934–45) |

Prime Minister and Minister for Foreign
Affairs . . . . . Marshal Chang Ching-hui (1937–45)

Diplomatic Representative

Minister at Rome . . . . Hsu Shao-ching (1938–41)

NETHERLANDS

Queen	.	.	.	.	.	Wilhelmina (1890–1948)
Prime Minister	.	.	.	.	Dr. H. Colijn (1933–July 1939)
					Jkhr. D. J. de Geer (Aug. 1939–1940)
Minister for Foreign Affairs	.	.	Dr. J. A. N. Patijn (Oct. 1937–July 1939)
					Dr. E. N. van Kleffens (Aug. 1939–1946)
Minister of Defence	.	.	.	Dr. J. J. C. van Dijk (1937–9)

Diplomatic Representatives

Ambassador at Tokyo	.	.	.	General J. C. Pabst (1923–40)
Minister at Berlin	.	.	.	Jkhr. H. M. van Haersma de With (1938–40)
Minister at Brussels	.	.	.	Baron B. Ph. van Harinxma (1938–40)
Minister in China	.	.	.	Baron G. W. de Vos van Steenwijk (1935–40)
Minister at London	.	.	.	Count John de Limburg-Stirum (1937–9)
Minister at Paris	.	.	.	Jkhr. Dr. J. Loudon (1919–40)
Minister at Washington	.	.	Dr. Alexandre Loudon (1938–42)
Counsellor at Berlin	.	.	.	Baron C. G. W. H. van Boetzelaer van Ooster-hout
Military Attaché at Berlin	.	.	Captain B. R. P. F. Hasselman
Military Attaché at Brussels and Paris	.	Lt.-Col. D. van Voorst Evekink
Consul-General at Danzig	.	.	Jkhr. G. H. van der Maesen de Sombreff (1938–9)

NORWAY

King	.	.	.	.	.	Haakon VII (1905–57)
Prime Minister	.	.	.	.	M. Johan Nygaardsvold (1935–40)
Minister for Foreign Affairs	.	.	Professor Halvdan Koht (1935–40)
President of the Storting	.	.	M. C. J. Hambro (1927–40)

Diplomatic Representative

Consul-General at Danzig . . . M. L. Myreboe (1937–9)

PERU

| President | . | . | . | . | General Don O. R. Benavides (1933–9) |
| Minister for Foreign Affairs | . | . | Dr. C. Concha (1937–9) |

Diplomatic Representative

Minister at Rome . . . . Señor E. Gildemeister (1938–42)

POLAND

President of the Republic . . . M. Ignacy Moscicki (1926–39)
Prime Minister and Minister of the In-
terior . . . . . General F. Slawoj-Skladkowski (1936–9)
Deputy Prime Minister and Minister of
Finance . . . . . M. E. Kwiatkowski (1936–9)

POLAND (*cont.*)

Minister for Foreign Affairs . . .	Colonel Jozef Beck (1932–9)
Minister of Agriculture . . .	M. J. Poniatowski (1934–9)
Minister of Industry and Commerce .	M. A. Roman (1936–9)
Minister for War	General T. Kasprzycki (1935–9)
Vice-Minister of Commerce . . .	Dr. A. Rose (1936–9)
Under-Secretary of State in Ministry of Foreign Affairs (Vice-Minister for Foreign Affairs)	M. Miroslaw Arciszewski (1938–9)
Legal Adviser to Ministry of Foreign Affairs	M. Kulski
Chef de cabinet of Minister for Foreign Affairs	M. Lubienski

Diplomatic Representatives

Ambassador at Angora . . .	M. Michel Sokolnicki (1936–9)
Ambassador at Berlin	M. Jozef Lipski (1934–9)
Ambassador at Bucharest . . .	Count Roger Raczynski (1938–9)
Ambassador at London . . .	Count Edward Raczynski (1934–45)
Ambassador at Moscow . . .	Dr. Waclaw Grzybowski (1936–9)
Ambassador at Paris	M. Jules Lukasiewicz (1936–9)
Ambassador at Rome . . .	M. Alfredo Wysocky (1933–8)
	General B. W. Dlugoszowski (1938–9)
Ambassador at Tokyo . . .	M. Thaddée de Romer (1937–9)
Minister at Berne	M. Titus Komarnicki (1938–9)
Minister at Brussels . . .	M. Michel Moscicki (1937–9)
Minister at Budapest	M. Leon Orlowski (1936–9)
Minister at The Hague . . .	Dr. Waclaw Babinski (1934–9)
Minister at Prague . . .	M. Kazimierz Papée (1936–9)
Minister at Stockholm . . .	M. Gustave Potworowski (1936–9)
Commissioner-General at Danzig . .	M. Marjan Chodacki
Assistant Commissioner-General at Danzig	M. Perkowski
Chargé d'Affaires at Berlin . . .	Prince Lubomirski (Counsellor)
Chargé d'Affaires at London . .	M. A. Jazdzewski (Counsellor)
Secretary at The Hague . . .	M. G. Hoszard
Secretary at London . . .	Count Roman Michalowski
Military Attaché at Berlin . . .	Lt.-Col. A. Szymanski
Military Attaché at Paris . . .	Colonel G. W. Fyda
Commercial Counsellor at Berlin . .	M. Pilch
Financial Counsellor at London . .	Dr. J. Rucinski

PORTUGAL

President	General A. O. de Fragosa Carmona (1928–51)
Prime Minister	Dr. Antonio de Oliveira Salazar (since 1932)
Minister for Foreign Affairs . . .	Dr. Antonio de Oliveira Salazar (since 1936)

Diplomatic Representative

Minister at Rome	Senhor J. L. d'Avila Lima (1935–45)

ROUMANIA

King.	Carol II (1930–40)
Prime Minister	M. Armand Calinescu (Mar.–Sept. 1939)
Minister for Foreign Affairs . . .	M. Petrescu Comnène (Mar.–Dec. 1938)
	M. Grigore Gafencu (1938–40)
Secretary-General of Ministry of Foreign Affairs	M. Cretzianu
Minister of Court	M. E. Urdarianu

Diplomatic Representatives

Ambassador at Angora . . .	M. Basile Stoica (1939–41)
Ambassador at Athens. . . .	M. Radu T. Djuvara (1939–40)
Ambassador at Belgrade . . .	M. Victor Cadere (1939–40)
Ambassador at Paris	M. Georges Tatarescu (1938–9)
Ambassador at Warsaw . . .	M. Richard Franassovici (1938–9)
Minister at Berlin	M. Radu T. Djuvara (1938–9)
Minister at Budapest . . .	Dr. Raoul Bossy (1936–9)
Minister at The Hague . .	M. Vespasien V. Pella (1936–40)
Minister at London . . .	M. Basile Grigorcea (1937–9)
	M. Viorel V. Tilea (Feb. 1939–1940)
Minister at Moscow . . .	M. Nicolas Dianu (1938–9)
Minister at Prague	M. Radu Crutzescu (1938–9)
Minister at Rome . . .	M. A. D. Zamfirescu (1938–9)
Military Attaché at London .	Captain G. St. Dumitrescu
Chargé d'Affaires at London .	M. Radu Florescu (Counsellor)

SPAIN

Republican Government

President	Don Manuel Azaña (1936–Feb. 1939)
President of the Council of Ministers	Dr. Juan Negrin (May 1937–Mar. 1939)

Diplomatic Representatives

Ambassador at London . .	Don Pablo Azcarate y Florez (1936–9)
Ambassador at Paris . . .	Señor Marcelino Pascua y Martinez (1938–9)

Nationalist Government

Head of State and Prime Minister .	General Francisco Franco (since 1936)
Minister for Foreign Affairs . .	General Count de Jornada (Feb. 1938–Aug. 1939)
	Colonel Juan Beigbeder (Aug. 1939–Oct. 1940)
Minister of the Interior . .	Señor R. Serrano Suñer (Dec. 1938–Oct. 1940)

Diplomatic Representatives

Ambassador at Rome . . .	Señor D. P. Garcia Condé (1937–40)
Ambassador at The Vatican. .	Don José Maria de Yanguas y Messia (1938–42)

SWEDEN

King.	Gustav V (1907–50)
Prime Minister	M. P. A. Hansson (1936–46)
Minister for Foreign Affairs . .	M. R. J. Sandler (1932–9)

Diplomatic Representatives

Minister at Berlin . . .	M. A. G. Richert (1937–45)
Minister at London . . .	M. B. G. Prytz (1938–47)
Minister at Oslo . . .	M. C. Günther (1938–9)
Minister at Prague . . .	M. H. F. Malmar (1938–9)
Minister at Rome . . .	M. K. E. T. Wirsen (1938–40)
Minister at Warsaw . . .	M. J. Lagerberg (1938–9)
Consul at Danzig . . .	M. K. E. J. Lundberg (1938–9)

SWITZERLAND

President of the Confederation for 1939	M. Philipp Etter
Minister for Foreign Affairs . . .	Dr. Giuseppe Motta (1921–40)

Diplomatic Representatives

Minister at Berlin	Dr. Hans Frölicher (1938–45)
Minister at Prague	Dr. C. Bruggmann (1937–9)
Military Attaché at Berlin . .	Colonel H. von Werdt

TURKEY

President	Kemal Ataturk (1923–38)
	General Ismet Inönü (1938–50)
Prime Minister	Dr. Refik Saydam (1939–42)
Minister for Foreign Affairs . . .	M. Sükrü Saracoglu (1938–42)
Minister of Justice . . .	M. Fethi Okyar
Secretary-General of the Ministry of Foreign Affairs	M. Numan Rifaat Menemencioglu (1937–42)

Diplomatic Representatives

Ambassador at London . . .	Dr. Tevfik Rüstü Aras (1939–42)
Ambassador at Moscow . . .	M. Zekai Apaydin (1935–9)
	M. Ali Haydar Aktay (Aug. 1939–42)
Ambassador at Paris	M. Suat Davaz (1932–40)
Ambassador at Rome	M. Huseyin Ragip Baydur (1934–40)
Minister at Belgrade	M. Ali Haydar Aktay (1931–9)
Minister at Budapest . . .	M. Behiç Erkin (1928–39)
Minister at Durazzo . . .	M. Hulusi Fuat Togay (1938–9)
Commercial Attaché at London .	M. A. S. Ozbekkan
Military Attaché at Moscow .	Lt.-Col. B. Türkmen

UNION OF SOVIET SOCIALIST REPUBLICS (U.S.S.R.)

Chairman of the Presidium of the Supreme Council	M. Mikhail Ivanovich Kalinin (1938–46)
Chairman of the Council of People's Commissars	M. Vyacheslav Mikhailovich Molotov (1930–41)
People's Commissar for Foreign Affairs.	M. Maxim Maximovich Litvinov (1930–9)
	M. V. M. Molotov (May 1939–49)
Deputy People's Commissar for Foreign Affairs	M. Vladimir P. Potemkin (1937–9)
People's Commissar for Foreign Trade .	M. Anastas Ivanovich Mikoyan
Deputy People's Commissar for Foreign Trade	M. S. Stepanov
People's Commissar for Internal Affairs .	M. L. P. Beriya (Beria)
People's Commissar for the Navy .	Flagman N. G. Kuznetsov
People's Commissar for Transport .	M. L. M. Kaganovich
Head of Press Bureau of Commissariat for Foreign Affairs	M. E. A. Gnédine

Diplomatic Representatives

Ambassador at Angora	M. Alexei Terentiev (1938–40)
Ambassador at Berlin . . .	M. Alexej F. Merekalov (1938–9)
Ambassador at London . . .	M. Ivan Mikhailovich Maisky (1932–43)
Ambassador at Paris . . .	M. Yakov Zakharovich Suritz (1937–40)
Ambassador at Rome . . .	M. Boris E. Stein (1935–9)
Ambassador at Warsaw . . .	M. Nikoloj Sharonov (1939)
Minister at Kovno . . .	M. Pavel Krapivincev (Feb.–Oct. 1938)
Chargé d'Affaires at Berlin . .	M. Georgi Astakhov (Counsellor)
Chargé d'Affaires at Kovno . .	M. N. Posdniakoff (Secretary)
Counsellor at London . . .	M. S. B. Cahan
Counsellor at Rome . . .	M. L. Helfand
Secretary at London . . .	M. Mikhail Korj

UNITED STATES OF AMERICA

President	Mr. Franklin Delano Roosevelt (1933–45)
Secretary of State . . .	Mr. Cordell Hull (1933–44)
Under Secretary of State . .	Mr. Sumner Welles (1937–43)
Secretary of the Interior . .	Mr. Harold L. Ickes (1933–46)

Secretary of the Treasury . . .	Mr. Henry Morgenthau, Jnr. (1934–45)
Fiscal Assistant Secretary of the Treasury	Mr. Wayne C. Taylor
Chairman of Senate Standing Committee on Foreign Relations . . .	Senator K. Pittman (1933–40)

Diplomatic Representatives

Ambassador at Angora . . .	Mr. J. V. A. MacMurray (1936–42)
Ambassador at Berlin	Mr. Hugh R. Wilson (1938–40: recalled Nov. 1938; did not return to post)
Ambassador in China	Mr. Nelson T. Johnson (1935–41)
Ambassador at London ' . . .	Mr. Joseph P. Kennedy (1938–41)
Ambassador at Moscow . . .	Mr. L. A. Steinhardt (1939–41)
Ambassador at Paris . . .	Mr. William C. Bullitt (1936–40)
Ambassador at Prague . .	Mr. Wilbur J. Carr (1937–9)
Ambassador at Rome	Mr. William Phillips (1936–41)
Ambassador at Tokyo . . .	Mr. J. C. Grew (1932–41)
Ambassador at Warsaw . . .	Mr. A. J. Drexel Biddle, Jnr. (1937–9)
Minister at Durazzo . . .	Mr. H. G. Grant (1935–9)
Chargé d'Affaires at Berlin . .	Mr. R. H. Geist (1st Secretary: Feb.–May 1939) Mr. Alexander C. Kirk (Counsellor: May 1939–40)
Chargé d'Affaires in China . .	Mr. W. R. Peck (Counsellor)
Chargé d'Affaires at London .	Mr. Herschel V. Johnson (Counsellor)
Chargé d'Affaires at Moscow .	Mr. Alexander C. Kirk (Counsellor: 1938–9)
Chargé d'Affaires at Tokyo .	Mr. E. H. Dooman (Counsellor)
Secretary at London . . .	Mr. R. Schoenfeld
Military Attaché at Berlin . .	Lt.-Col. T. Smith
Military Attaché in China . .	Colonel J. W. Stilwell
Military Attaché at Moscow .	Major F. Hayne
Military Attaché at Prague . .	Major J. S. Winslow
Military Attaché at Rome . .	Colonel G. H. Paine
Military Attaché at Warsaw. .	Major W. H. Colbern
Commercial Attaché at Tokyo .	Mr. F. S. Williams
Consul-General at Shanghai. .	Mr. C. E. Gauss
Consul-General at Tientsin . .	Mr. J. K. Caldwell
Consul-General at Vienna . .	Mr. J. W. Wiley
Consul at Amoy. . . .	Mr. Karl de G. MacVitty
Consul at Danzig	Mr. C. P. Kuykendall

THE VATICAN

The Pope	Pius XI (1922–39) Pius XII (1939–58)
Cardinal Secretary of State . .	Cardinal E. Pacelli (1930–Mar. 1939) Cardinal L. Maglione (1939–44)
Under-Secretary of State . .	Mgr. Domenico Tardini

Diplomatic Representatives

Apostolic Nuncio in Germany .	Mgr. Cesare Orsenigo (1930–45)
Apostolic Nuncio in Great Britain	Mgr. William Godfrey (1938–53)
Apostolic Nuncio in France . .	Mgr. Valerio Valeri (1936–44)
Apostolic Nuncio in Poland . .	Mgr. Filippo Cortesi (1937–9)

YUGOSLAVIA

King.	Peter II (1934–41)
Senior Regent	Prince Paul (1934–41)
President of the Council and Minister for Foreign Affairs . . .	Dr. Milan Stoyadinovitch (1935–Feb. 1939)
President of the Council . . .	M. Drogisha Cvetkovitch (Feb. 1939–Mar. 1941)

YUGOSLAVIA (*cont.*)

Minister for Foreign Affairs . . .	M. A. Cinkar-Markovitch (Feb. 1939–Mar. 1941)
Minister of Court	M. Antitch

Diplomatic Representatives

Minister at Angora	M. Ilija Shumenkovitch (1939)
Minister at Berlin	M. A. Cinkar-Markovitch (1935–9)
	Dr. Ivo Andritch (1939–41)
Minister at Bucharest	M. Jovan Doutchitch (1937–Feb. 1939; then Ambassador till 1940)
Minister at London . . .	M. Ivan Soubotitch (June 1939–41)
Minister at Prague	Dr. Vasilije Protitch (1935–9)
Minister at Rome . . .	M. Bochko Christitch (1937–41)
Minister at The Vatican . .	Dr. N. M. Sorgo (1937–41)
Minister at Warsaw . . .	Dr. A. Vukchevitch (1938–9)
Counsellor at London . . .	M. V. Milanovitch
Military Attaché at Berlin . .	Colonel V. Vauhnik
Military Attaché at Budapest .	Comm. D. Michkovitch
Military Attaché at Durazzo .	Comm. V. Kalecak
Military Attaché at Rome . .	Lt.-Col. R. Trajanovitch
Press Attaché at London . .	M. P. Yevtitch

Part III: Index of Persons

Abdul Fattah Yehia Pasha (Egyptian Minister for Foreign Affairs, 1938–9), **vi** 111

Abe, Rear-Admiral (Departmental Chief of the Japanese Naval Staff), **viii** 457*n*, 469

Abe, General Nobuyuki (Prime Minister of Japan, Aug. 1939–Jan. 1940; in charge of Ministry of Foreign Affairs, Aug. and Sept. 1939), **ix** 498, 507–8, 514, 515*n*, 519, 523–4
Statement by, Sept. 4, 1939, **ix** 525–7

Abetz, Otto (Paris representative of Herr von Ribbentrop's private bureau), **vi** 213

Abraham, Lt.-Col. (French Assistant Military Attaché at Moscow), **vii** 46, 562

Adams, Squadron Leader A. A. (British Assistant Air Attaché at Berlin and Warsaw, Sept. 1938–Sept. 1939), **vii** 499

Adelmannsfelden, Count R. Adelmann von (Counsellor of German Legation, Helsingfors), **v** 253

Affleck, J. B. (H.M. Consul-General at Tientsin, Feb. 1935–Aug. 1938).
To British Embassy, Shanghai, **viii** 9

Aga Khan III (1885–1957), **i** 602

Aktay, Ali Haydar. *See* Ali Haydar Aktay

Al Pachachi, Muzahim Beg. *See* Muzahim Beg Al Pachachi

Albanesi, Lucia (Italian soprano), **iii** 536

Albedyl, Hauptmann (E) von (Acting Head of Attaché Group, Berlin), **ii** 47, 184; **v** 806
Conversation with Col. Mason-MacFarlane, **ii** 42–5, 184–5

Alephuzov, Captain (Deputy Chief of Soviet Naval Staff), **vii** 45

Alexander I, King of Yugoslavia (1921–34), **ii** 11; **iv** 617; **v** 672; **vii** 47

Alfieri, Dino (Italian Minister for Popular Culture, 1936–9), **iii** 533; **vii** 93, 335

Ali Haydar Aktay (Turkish Minister at Belgrade, 1931–9; Ambassador at Moscow, Aug. 1939–1942), **v** 596, 667; **vi** 66, 228; **vii** 384

Ali Jaudat (Iraqi Minister for Foreign Affairs, April 1939–Feb. 1940), **vi** 127*n*

Allen of Hurtwood, 1st Baron, **ii** 647, 662; **iii** 245
Conversation with Herr von Ribbentrop, **ii** 88

Allen, W. D. (Secretary, H.M. Embassy in China, Jan. 1938–Oct. 1941)
To Viscount Halifax, **viii** 153, 159–60, 166, 238, 240, 242, 255–6, 559
To Mr. Jamieson, **viii** 559

Alley, R. (a technical expert employed by the Chinese Government), **viii** 68, 257–8, 308–9, 391–2

Alness, 1st Baron (Chairman of the Chinese Bondholders Committee), **viii** 483*n*

Alphand, Charles (French Ambassador at Berne, 1936–40), **iv** 49

Alphand, Hervé (Director of Commercial Treaties Department in French Ministry of Commerce), **iv** 260

Altenburg, Dr. Günther (Head of Political Division dealing with Austria and Czechoslovakia, German Ministry of Foreign Affairs, 1938–9), **i** 328

Amau, Eiji (Japanese Minister at Berne, 1937–9), **iv** 161

Anderson, H. J. P. (Chairman of Municipal Council, International Settlement, Amoy (Kulangsu)), **ix** 256

Andorka, Colonel (Head of Military Intelligence, Hungary), **iii** 11–2, 27, 44, 239; **iv** 247; **v** 59–60, 62
Conversation with Sir G. Knox, **iv** 247–8

Andreoni, Captain (Chief clerk to British Military Attaché, Rome), **iv** 313

Andritch, Dr. Ivo (Yugoslav Assistant Minister for Foreign Affairs, 1937–9; Minister at Berlin, 1939–41), **ii** 151; **v** 80

Anfuso, Filippo (Count Ciano's *chef de cabinet*), **v** 170; **vii** 517

Angell, Sir Norman (author and lecturer), **vi** 202

Ansaldo, Giovanni (Editor of the 'Telegrafo' of Leghorn), **iii** 476

Antitch, M. (Yugoslav Minister of Court), **ii** 25*n*; **vi** 167
Conversation with Mr. Shone, **ii** 25

Apaydin, Zekai. *See* Zekai Apaydin

Apponyi, Count Albert (Head of Hungarian delegation to Paris Peace Conference, 1919–20), **iii** 227

Araki, General Baron S. (Japanese Minister of Education, 1938–9), **ix** 65, 174, 412

Aras, Dr. Tevfik Rüstü (Turkish Minister for Foreign Affairs, 1925–38; Ambassador at London, 1939–42), **iv** 425, 474, 496–7, 521, 559; **v** 180, 296; **vi** 190, 387; **ix** 213
Conversation with Sir A. Cadogan, **v** 672–3
Conversation with Viscount Halifax, **iv** 436–7, 558–60; **v** 57–8; **vi** 82–3, 567–8
Conversation with Sir L. Oliphant, **v** 346

Archer, H. A. F. B. (H.M. Consul at Peking, July 1937–Aug. 1939)
To British Embassy, Shanghai, **viii** 210, 300; **ix** 352
To Viscount Halifax, **ix** 246

Arciszewski, Miroslaw (Polish Vice-Minister for Foreign Affairs, 1938–9), **iii** 35, 46–7, 50, 53, 82, 105, 111, 121, 138, 559; **iv** 245, 431–2, 472, 506, 551; **v** 280, 415, 417, 419–20, 605; **vi** 81,

Arciszewski, M. (*cont.*)
    94, 186, 200, 204, 206, 545, 553–4, 592–3, 679;
    vii 54, 236, 297, 364
        Conversation with Sir H. Kennard, **iii** 34, 41;
        iv 80–2, 201–2, 262–3, 401–2, 428–9,
        506–7, 524–5, 543; **v** 281–2; **vi** 105–6,
        176–7, 562–3, 627–8; **vii** 22
Aris, J. (Financial Attaché, French Embassy,
    Berlin), **iii** 130–1, 177
Arita, Hachiro (Japanese Minister for Foreign
    Affairs, April 1936–Feb. 1937 and Oct. 1938–
    Aug. 1939), **v** 644; **vi** 249, 341; **viii** 175*n*,
    181–3, 192, 194, 201, 207, 209, 212, 238, 255,
    258, 269, 271, 283, 287, 292, 299–300, 324–5,
    327, 330, 334, 340–2, 349, 369, 405, 432, 452*n*,
    464, 468–9, 475–6, 478, 480, 493, 499, 501–3,
    518, 537, 539; **ix** 12, 23, 36, 56, 63–4, 69, 93,
    98*n*, 101, 109, 114, 129, 131, 133, 145–6,
    148–9, 172, 174, 181–2, 185–6, 193, 197–9,
    206, 208, 214, 222–3, 225–6, 233, 235, 252–6,
    263, 267, 269–71, 273–4, 281, 285, 289–91,
    296–301, 304–5, 309–10, 313, 315, 318–20,
    323–4, 347, 351–2, 354, 360, 368, 373, 384,
    392–3, 395, 397, 400–1, 412, 433, 437, 442–3,
    454, 459, 469–70, 473, 484, 492, 496, 512, 516–7
        Conversation with Sir R. Craigie, **viii** 202,
        211, 234–6, 238, 260, 262–7, 304–6,
        344–7, 393–4, 442–4, 460–1, 536, 537*n*;
        ix 21–2, 26, 56, 142–3, 157–8, 170–1, 199,
        207–8, 219–21, 229–30, 245, 278–80,
        282–3, 298–302, 305–8
        Conversation with Mr. Dooman, **viii** 272–6
        Conversation with Mr. Grew, **viii** 254–5, 348;
        ix 91–2, 94–5
        Memorandum by, Dec. 8, 1938, **viii** 304, 313;
        referred to, **viii** 324, 348, 353
        Speech by, on May 8, 1939, **ix** 77*n*
        Statement by, to foreign press correspondents,
        Dec. 19, 1938, **viii** 356–8; *referred to*, **viii**
        339, 355–6, 371, 403
Armengaud, General, **iv** 331–2
Arnal, Pierre (Head of League of Nations section
    of French Ministry of Foreign Affairs), **iii**
    587–8; **iv** 383; **v** 394; **vi** 17, 48, 660, 677, 689,
    697–8, 724*n*, 726
Arnhold, H. E. (Chairman of the British Resi-
    dents' Association, Shanghai), **ix** 137–8
Arsène-Henry, Charles (French Ambassador at
    Tokyo, 1937–43), **viii** 15, 23–4, 45–6, 64, 73,
    87–8, 118, 149*n*, 157*n*, 166–7, 176, 184*n*, 195,
    201, 229, 238, 244, 255*n*, 259, 269, 283, 294,
    334, 341, 352, 370, 382, 389, 392, 393*n*, 395,
    463, 477, 493, 497–8, 513, 532, 534, 538; **ix** 43,
    57, 64, 67, 78, 95, 111, 114, 145–6, 149, 151,
    163, 187, 224, 245, 251, 253–5, 258, 275, 289,
    303, 308, 331, 342, 359, 360*n*, 379–80, 392,
    395, 399, 418, 450, 488, 490–1, 496, 500,
    509–10, 521
        Conversation with Sir R. Craigie, **viii** 184
        Conversation with Mr. Sawada, **ix** 399–400

Aschmann, Gottfried (Head of the Press Depart-
    ment, German Ministry of Foreign Affairs,
    1933–9), **iii** 450; **vii** 631
        Conversation with Sir G. Ogilvie-Forbes, **iii**
        551–2, 560
Ashton-Gwatkin, Frank T. A. (Counsellor in
    the Foreign Office 1934–9; attached to Lord
    Runciman's Mission to Prague), **i** 79; **ii** 50,
    74, 82, 112, 115, 136, 142, 148–50, 152–5,
    160, 165–6, 180, 183, 189, 196, 208–9, 248,
    251, 305, 313, 321–2, 629, 634, 656; **iii** 78,
    134; **iv** 568; **vi** 271, 538; **ix** 272
        To Mr. Strang, **ii** 75, 80, 100, 121–2, 170,
        177, 199, 202, 222, 241, 243, 261, 265–6,
        273, 333; **iii** 113, 147, 151
        Conversation with Herr Frank, **ii** 177
        Conversation with Dr. Funk, **iv** 604–6
        Conversation with Field-Marshal Göring, **iv**
        606–8
        Conversation with Herr Henlein, **ii** 177, 199–
        200, 231–2, 333–4, 657–60
        Conversation with M. Maisky, **v** 208–9
        Conversation with Prince Max of Hohenlohe-
        Langenburg, **iv** 227*n*
        Conversation with Herr von Ribbentrop, **iv**
        602–3
        Conversation with Herr Ritter, **iii** 151–2
        Conversation with Dr. Schacht, **ix** 273*n*
        Conversation with Herr Wiehl, **iv** 603–4
        Conversation with Dr. Wohltat and Dr.
        Weber, **v** 791–2
        Letter to Mr. Strang, **ii** 69, 661, 663, 665,
        668, 670
        Note by, **ii** 167, 660, 670, **vii** 547
        Report on visit to Berlin, **iv** 597–608
        Visit to Berlin, Feb. 1939, **iv** 131, 134*n*, 238,
        597–610
        Visit to Switzerland, July 1939, **ix** 272*n*
Astakhov, Georgi (Counsellor of Soviet Embassy,
    Berlin: acted as Chargé d'Affaires), **v** 634
Ataturk, Kemal. *See* Kemal Ataturk
Atholl, Duchess of (M.P. for Kinross and West
    Perth), **i** 520, 529
Attlee, Clement R. (Leader of the Labour
    Party), **iii** 272; **v** 310; **viii** 178
Attolico, Dr. Bernardo (Italian Ambassador at
    Berlin, 1935–40), **i** 597, 615; **ii** 240, 297, 588,
    643; **iii** 63–4, 66, 74, 77, 92–4, 128–30, 134–5,
    150–1, 176, 204, 234–5, 242, 272, 655; **iv** 223,
    230, 232, 319, 442, 455, 461, 589–90; **v** 28*n*,
    79, 199*n*, 232, 265, 305, 318, 400, 424, 516,
    523, 570, 586, 656, 699, 733, 782, 798, 802–4;
    vi 11, 123, 330, 349, 358–9, 704, 720, 728–9,
    746; **vii** 19, 36–7, 57, 67, 81, 83–4, 100, 104,
    109, 302, 358, 367, 377, 392, 435*n*, 436, 438,
    440, 465–6, 505–8, 524
        Conversation with General von Brauchitsch,
        ii 232
        Conversation with M. Burckhardt, **vi** 44
        Conversation with Sir N. Henderson, **ii** 49,

119–20, 171–2, 242; **vi** 254–5, 348, 456, 607–8, 699–701; **vii** 7–8, 255–6, 362, 401-2, 504

Attolico, Signora, **v** 716

Auriti, Giacinto (Italian Ambassador at Tokyo, 1933–40), **viii** 180, 451

Avenol, Joseph (Secretary-General of League of Nations, 1933–40), **ii** 594; **iii** 283, 606, 613, 660; **iv** 166, 261, 383; **v** 392–3, 395, 630, 654; **vi** 45, 107, 639, 732; **vii** 261; **ix** 105, 141

Aymé, Colonel (Member of Secretariat-General of French Council of National Defence), **iv** 223

Azcarate y Florez, Pablo (Spanish Ambassador at London, 1936–9), **iii** 515; **viii** 93

Babarin, E. (Soviet Deputy Trade Representative at Berlin), **vi** 447; **vii** 99

Babinski, Dr. Waclaw (Polish Minister at The Hague, 1934–9), **vii** 349

Bacinsky, Dr. Edmund (Minister of the Interior in Ruthenian Government, 1938), **iii** 377

Badoglio, Marshal (Chief of Italian General Staff), **vi** 185; **vii** 93

Bailby, Léon (Proprietor of the 'Jour-Écho de Paris'), **ii** 606, 623

Bailly, Commandant (a member of French Air Staff), **iv** 223

Baker, Mr. Earl, **ix** 293

Baker, G. H. (H.M. Vice-Consul at Danzig, July-Sept. 1939), **vii** 544, 546

Balbo, Marshal Italo (Governor-General of Libya, 1933–40), **ii** 89, 122, 646, 691; **vii** 93

Baldwin, Stanley (1937, Earl Baldwin of Bewdley) (Prime Minister, 1935–7), **i** 75; **iii** 434*n*, 474, 478; **iv** 602

Baltrusaitis, Jurgis K. (Lithuanian Minister at Moscow, 1922–40), **iv** 286, 568
Conversation with Sir W. Seeds, **vi** 256–7

Balutis, Bronius K. (Lithuanian Minister at London, 1934–40), **iv** 378, 431
Conversation with Mr. Collier, **iv** 378*n*, 533–4, 638–9
Conversation with Viscount Halifax, **iv** 474–5

Barclay, R. E. (a member of Central Department of the Foreign Office)
Minute by, **vii** 205, 523

Barclay, Major W. P. (British Assistant Military Attaché at Rome, Nov. 1937–Mar. 1939), **iv** 311–3, 337

Barcza, George de (Hungarian Minister at London, 1938–41), **ii** 460*n*; **iii** 1, 19, 30, 48, 113, 116, 189*n*; **v** 66, 110; **vi** 452, 629, 631, 641; **vii** 58, 377
To Viscount Halifax, **iii** 10, 21
Conversation with Sir A. Cadogan, **iii** 4; **vi** 77–8
Conversation with Viscount Halifax, **iii** 9–10
Conversation with Sir O. Sargent, **iii** 19–20

Bardossy, Ladislas de (Hungarian Minister at Bucharest, 1934–41), **iv** 281

Bargeton, Paul (French Ambassador at Brussels, 1937–40), **vii** 329, 340

Barkov, M. (Chief of Protocol Department of People's Commissariat for Foreign Affairs in U.S.S.R.), **iv** 568–9; **vii** 45

Barrère, Camille (French Ambassador at Rome, 1898–1924), **iii** 472

Barter, Major A. R. (British Assistant Military Attaché at Rome, Mar. 1939–June 1940), **v** 751

Bartmann, Herr (Governmental President of the Protectorate of Bohemia and Moravia, Mar. 1939), **iv** 564

Bashford, R. F. O'N. (H.M. Vice-Consul at Breslau, May 1936–Oct. 1938; Press Attaché at Berlin, Oct. 1938–Sept. 1939), **i** 359, 580; **iii** 450, 573; **iv** 13; **v** 425
Conversation with Dr. Meissner, **vi** 286*n*

Bass, Captain G. R. (Secretary and Chief Police Officer, International Settlement, Amoy (Kulangsu)), **ix** 339, 480

Bassler, Herr (a member of German Ministry of Foreign Affairs), **iv** 80

Bassompierre, Baron Albert de (Belgian Ambassador at Tokyo, 1921–38), **viii** 138, 532, 538

Bastianini, Giuseppe (Under-Secretary of State in Italian Ministry of Foreign Affairs, 1936–9), **iv** 332–3, 335, 341; **vii** 95, 120, 185
Conversation with Sir P. Loraine, **vii** 215–6
Conversation with the Earl of Perth, **iv** 325–7

Bata, Dr. J. A., **ii** 100, 668; **iii** 377

Bata, Madame, **ii** 662

Baudez, M. (French Consul-General at Shanghai, 1935–41), **viii** 164, 465, 469; **ix** 446, 489

Baudouin, Paul (Director of the Banque de l'Indo-Chine), **iv** 323, 335; **v** 263–4, 345, 347, 480*n*; **ix** 112

Baumbach, Captain N. von (German Naval Attaché at Moscow), **ii** 299

Baydur, Huseyin Ragip. *See* Huseyin Ragip Baydur

Bayerle, M., **ii** 94–5

Beaufré, Captain (a member of French Military Delegation to Moscow, Aug. 1939), **vii** 562, 584

Bechtolsheim, Lt.-Col. A. Freiherr von (German Military Attaché at London), **ii** 101; **iv** 170; **vi** 306

Bechyne, Rudolf (Deputy Prime Minister and Minister of Railways in Dr. Hodza's Cabinet, 1935–8; leader of Czechoslovak Social Democratic party), **i** 377, 390, 440, 519; **iv** 561

Beck, Colonel Jozef (Polish Minister for Foreign Affairs, 1932–9), **i** 173, 247, 315*n*, 431, 444*n*, 464–5, 480, 512, 550–1; **ii** 68, 107, 190*n*, 317–8, 355; **iii** 8–9, 13, 16*n*, 27–8, 33–5, 48, 54, 63, 98, 101–8, 111, 120–2, 138, 179–82, 188–90, 213 229, 264, 281, 366, 378, 418–9,

Beck, Colonel Jozef (*cont.*)
    425, 430, 525, 555, 557, 559, 566*n*, 567, 572–4,
    580–2, 585, 589–91, 593–4, 596–7, 606,
    658–9; **iv** 4, 16, 38, 67, 80–1, 103, 152, 163,
    178–81, 203, 227, 231, 245, 252–3, 293, 335,
    362, 372–3, 398, 423–4, 428, 431–2, 434–5,
    458, 463–7, 469, 471, 473, 480, 486, 496,
    500–2, 506–7, 510, 519, 524, 543, 549, 554,
    572, 581–2, 616; **v**–**vii** *passim*
    To Sir H. Kennard, **iii** 23, 32
    Conversation with M. Burckhardt, **vi** 41–2,
       721, 725-6
    Conversation with Mr. Eden, **v** 36–8
    Conversation with M. Gafencu, **v** 298–300
    Conversation with Herr Hitler. *See* Subject
       Index: Berchtesgaden (meeting between
       Herr Hitler and M. Beck)
    Conversation with Sir H. Kennard, **i** 315–6,
       351, 512; **ii** 217–8; **iii** 24, 52–3, 64, 205–6,
       283–4, 419–20, 438–9, 580–1; **iv** 68–9,
       182, 362–3, 370–1, 401, 452–3, 549; **v**
       93–4, 200–1, 203, 289–90, 378–9, 466,
       475–6, 501–2; **vi** 545, 549–50, 612–3, 644,
       683–4; **vii** 11–2, 69–70, 85–6, 151, 189–
       90, 301, 355–6, 366, 370–1, 434, 450–1,
       481–2, 522, 534
    Conversation with M. Noël, **ii** 441; **vi** 292–3;
       vii 223
    Conversation with Mr. Norton, **ii** 190; **vi**
       233–5, 259, 475–6, 482
    Conversation with M. Potemkin, **v** 500–1
    Speech on May 5, 1939, *referred to*, **v** 430,
       440–2, 454–5, 467, 476, 482, 511, 513,
       579, 619, 699, 816–7; **vi** 60, 503; **vii** 30
    Visit (suggested) to Berlin, **vii** 376, 388, 395,
       451, 469
    Visit to Gdynia, July 1939, **vi** 527, 549
    Visit to London, April 1939, **v** 1–19, 30–6,
       47–9
Beck, Madame, **iv** 181
Beck, Colonel-General Ludwig (Chief of German
    General Staff, 1935–8), **ii** 242, 408, 683, 690;
    vii 415–6
Behiç Erkin (Turkish Minister at Budapest,
    1928–39), **v** 614–5
Beigbeder, Colonel Juan (Spanish Minister for
    Foreign Affairs, Aug. 1939–Oct. 1940), **v**
    144; **vii** 287
Beith, J. G. S. (a member of American Dept. of
    Foreign Office), **iv** 637
Bell, Commander L. H. (at Anglo-German
    Naval conversations, Dec. 1938), **iii** 664, 669
Benes, Dr. Eduard (President of Czechoslovakia,
    Dec. 1935–Oct. 1938), **i** 34, 67–629 *passim*;
    ii *passim*; **iii** 2, 21, 27, 34, 36, 45, 47–8, 49*n*,
    50*n*, 63, 80, 90–1, 96, 108–9, 114, 117, 123,
    125, 142–3, 182, 190, 229, 254, 304, 411, 415,
    427, 615, 625; **iv** 231–2, 252, 265; **v** 86, 310,
    388–9, 424, 546, 557, 803; **vi** 203, 331, 719,
    753–4; **vii** 38, 624–5

    resignation of, Oct. 5, 1938, **iii** 99*n*, 136
    Conversation with Dr. Eisenlohr, **ii** 37–8
    Conversation with M. de Facendis, **ii** 37
    Conversation with Mr. A. L. Kennedy, **i** 75*n*
    Conversation with Herr Kundt, **ii** 150, 222–3
    Conversation with M. de Lacroix, **ii** 1, 208,
       475
    Conversation with M. de Lacroix and Mr.
       Newton, **ii** 449–50
    Conversation with Mr. Newton, **i** 72–6, 102,
       179–82, 307–15, 442–4, 446, 469–73,
       525–6, 529–31, 569–73, 578–9, 600–1,
       604–7, 612–3; **ii** 36–8, 226–9, 329–30,
       332–3, 449–50, 582, 604–5; **iii** 21–2, 90
    Conversation with Lord Runciman, **ii** 50, 171,
       221, 254*n*
    Letter to M. Móscicki, *text*, **iii** 40, 42;
       referred to, **iii** 34–6, 38, 40, 49*n*, 50*n*
    Message to Mr. Chamberlain, **ii** 604, 606
Benes, Madame, **ii** 69
Benfield, Major K. V. B. (British Military
    Attaché at Vienna, Jan. 1935–May 1938), **i**
    67
Bentevegni, Colonel (an officer in the German
    Military Intelligence), **vi** 326*n*
Bentinck, Sir Charles (H.M. Minister and
    Consul-General at Prague, 1936–7), **ii** 244
Beran, Dr. Rudolf (President of Czechoslovak
    National Council, Dec. 1938–Mar. 1939), **ii**
    673; **iii** 214–5, 380, 410, 634; **iv** 61, 98, 126,
    242, 258–9, 469, 564–5
    Appointment as President of Council, **iii** 376–8
    Statement of policy, **iii** 384–5
Bérard, Léon (Representative in French Senate
    of the Basses-Pyrénées Département), **iv** 461;
    v 144, 508
Berchem-Königsfeld, Dr. Baron von (German
    Consul at Lodz, 1934–9), **v** 605
Bérenger, Henri (President of Foreign Affairs
    Commission of French Senate), **iii** 391, 393;
    iv 243
Bérenger, Madame, **iii** 391
Bergen, Diego von (German Ambassador at The
    Vatican, 1920–43), **vii** 448
Bergen, Lt.-Gen. E. M. Van den (Chief of
    Belgian General Staff), **iii** 583; **iv** 76–8, 105
Beriya (Beria), L. P. (People's Commissar for
    Internal Affairs in U.S.S.R.), **v** 545
Bernard, Mr. (a member of Chinese Trading
    Commission), **viii** 473
Bernus, Pierre (Foreign Editor of the 'Journal
    des Débats'), **iv** 266; **v** 413
Berthelot, Philippe (Secretary-General of
    French Ministry of Foreign Affairs, 1920–2
    and 1925–33), **v** 277
Bevan, Captain R. H. (British Naval Attaché
    at Rome, July 1936–Jan. 1939), **iii** 501
Bewley, T. K. (Financial Adviser, H.M.
    Embassy, Washington, Feb. 1933–Mar. 1937
    and Mar. 1938–May 1939), **viii** 311, 335

Bibica-Rosetti, Raoul (Greek Minister at Belgrade, 1936–41), **v** 348, 551

Biddle, A. J. Drexel, Jnr. (U.S. Ambassador at Warsaw, 1937–9), **iii** 103; **iv** 547, 550; **v** 285; **vi** 247, 337–8, 678; **vii** 49, 63, 294

Bieberstein, Baron Marschall von (at Anglo-German Naval conversations, Dec. 1938), **iii** 664

Bielfeld, Dr. (in charge of African Department of German Foreign Office), **iv** 598, 601

Bigi, Captain L., **v** 190

Bismarck, Prince Otto Christian von (Deputy Head of Political Department of the German Ministry of Foreign Affairs, 1937–9), **vi** 711
   Conversation with Sir G. Ogilvie-Forbes, **v** 244–5

Blacha, Captain, **vii** 323

Blackburn, Sir Arthur D. (Chinese Secretary, H.M. Embassy in China, Sept. 1935–Nov. 1942), **viii** 551
   To Viscount Halifax, **viii** 3, 6, 9

Blake, Lt.-Col. F. A. A. (British Military Attaché at Brussels, Feb. 1939–May 1940), **iv** 53, 450, 576–7
   Conversation with Lt.-Col. D. van Voorst Evekink, **iv** 451–2

Bland, Sir Nevile (H.M. Minister to Netherlands Government, Sept. 1938–May 1942, then Ambassador until 1948), **iv** 85; **ix** 146
   To Viscount Halifax, **iii** 592; **iv** 52; **vi** 254; **vii** 349, 464
   To Sir A. Cadogan, **iv** 27, 31
   Conversation with M. Patijn, **iv** 27–9, 31, 52–3
   Letter to Sir A. Cadogan, **iv** 36

Blaskowitz, General Johannes von (Commander-in-Chief of the Third Army Group, German Army), **iv** 258, 275, 279, 562, 564

Blomberg, Field-Marshal Werner von (German War Minister and Commander-in-Chief of the German Army, 1935–8), **i** 98–9, 112, 128, 202, 513

Blondel, J. F. (French Minister at Rome: acted as Chargé d'Affaires), **i** 14, 20, 28; **ii** 589, 591; **iii** 486, 489, 495

Blücher, Marshal V. K. *See* Blyukher, Marshal V. K.

Blücher, Dr. Wipert von (German Minister at Helsingfors, 1935–45), **v** 253

Blum, Léon (President of the French Council of Ministers, Mar.–April, 1938), **i** 35, 41*n*, 53–4, 304; **ii** 235, 535; **iii** 156, 526; **iv** 51*n*, 462; **v** 356; **vi** 495; **vii** 177
   Conversation with Viscount Halifax, **v** 507–8
   Conversation with Sir E. Phipps, **ii** 278–9, 568–9; **vii** 244–5

Blunt, A. P. (H.M. Consul-General at Canton, Feb. 1937–July 1943)
   To British Embassy, Shanghai, **viii** 214, 224

Blyukher (Blücher), Marshal V. K. (Commander-in-Chief of Soviet Far Eastern army), **i** 163

Bock, General Fedor von, **i** 129; **vii** 517

Bodenschatz, General Karl Heinrich von (Personal Chief of Staff to Field-Marshal Göring), **i** 551–2; **ii** 363, 401, 562, 597; **v** 433, 546; **vi** 749, 751, 759*n*; **vii** 66–7, 242, 395, 551

Boeck, A. (Senator for Culture and Education, Danzig), **v** 608; **vi** 136

Boetzelaer van Oosterhout, Baron C. G. W. H. van (Counsellor of Netherlands Legation at Berlin), **iii** 551

Boheman, Erik (Secretary-General, Swedish Ministry of Foreign Affairs), **iii** 445

Bohle, E. W. (Head of the Foreign Organisation of the Nationalist-Socialist Party, Germany), **iv** 54–5; **vii** 96

Böhme, Major-General Franz (Head of Intelligence Branch of Austrian War Ministry), **i** 129

Böhming, Herr (a member of Herr von Ribbentrop's private bureau), **vi** 326

Boissier, A. (French Consul-General at Dresden, 1933–9), **iv** 233

Boncour, Jean Paul. *See* Paul-Boncour, Jean

Bonnet, Georges (French Minister for Foreign Affairs, April 1938–Sept. 1939), **i** 157, 160, 198, 224, 241, 246, 253, 299, 303, 340, 343, 347, 351, 360, 363, 375, 384, 389, 402, 419, 425, 444, 452, 460, 468, 478, 491*n*, 495, 497, 500, 503, 522*n*, 523, 524*n*, 535–6, 539, 549, 578; **ii** 1, 2, 18, 20, 71, 72*n*, 95–6, 112, 159, 168, 194, 196, 198, 261–2, 270, 275, 282*n*, 292, 302–3, 305, 309, 311–2, 327, 361–2, 373, 387, 394, 409–10, 412–3, 419, 423, 436, 444, 456, 459, 463, 489, 494, 509, 512, 516, 567–8, 582–3, 585–6, 588, 591, 600–2, 612–3, 675; **iii** 36, 59, 87*n*, 99, 250, 267, 269, 273, 284, 286, 322, 343, 346, 352–3, 355, 363, 365, 390–3, 396, 421, 436, 446–7, 465, 479–80, 487, 503, 507, 555, 575, 607, 619–21, 636, 658; **iv** 17, 48–9, 51, 90–1, 108, 124, 130, 137, 167, 243, 245, 309, 328–35, 340, 343–4, 347–9, 351*n*, 353*n*, 359, 368, 371, 375–6, 382, 434–5, 531–3, 596, 603, 616, 638–9, 642; **v** 49, 55, 68, 105, 124, 126, 143–4, 146, 148, 166, 183, 216–7, 228, 252, 258, 261–3, 266, 270, 272, 274, 276, 294, 296, 312, 329, 342, 377, 385*n*, 406, 414, 432, 438, 465, 467, 522–3, 533, 535, 566, 569, 572, 578, 590, 630, 683, 693, 698, 700, 724, 737, 746, 749, 790–1, 793, 795, 799, 800–1; **vi** 2, 25, 62–3, 99, 122–3, 167, 169, 180–1, 185, 198, 213, 220, 227–8, 236, 240, 261, 302, 328–32, 337, 346–7, 353, 358, 381, 383–4, 397, 489–91, 509, 512, 519–20, 535, 664–5, 697, 729; **vii** 18–9, 25, 107, 117, 120, 129, 158, 161, 164, 167, 177, 227, 294–5, 303*n*, 333, 371, 401, 443, 471, 498, 500–3, 505–7, 520, 526, 529–31, 536, 560; **viii** 16–7, 22–3, 399; **ix** 101, 192, 312, 342, 445

Bonnet, Georges (*cont.*)
   Conversation with Mr. R. A. Butler, Captain Wallace and Mr. Stevenson, ii 293–4
   Conversation with Sir A. Cadogan, vii 513–4
   Conversation with Mr. R. I. Campbell, ii 38–9, 71–4, 194, 201–2; vi 398–9, 677–8; vii 77, 79, 130–1
   Conversation with Viscount Halifax, i 601–3; iii 530–1; iv 422–7, 487–90; v 608–11, 623–5, 638–9; vii 511–2, 525–6; *see also below, Speeches at* Anglo-French conversations
   Conversation with M. Litvinov, ii 294; iii 67
   Conversation with Sir P. Loraine, v 795–7
   Conversation with Sir E. Phipps, i 157, 197, 336–7, 357, 366–7, 476, 526–7, 577–8; ii 215–6, 219–20, 245–6, 255–6, 282, 287, 303n, 309, 310–1, 323, 336–7, 420, 451, 493, 558–9, 571–2; iii 67, 244–5, 257–8, 262–3, 389–90, 425–6, 465, 489, 493–4; iv 263, 339, 345, 640–1, 645; v 130, 148, 151–2, 160, 178, 222–3, 347, 381, 432, 737; vi 64, 146, 150–1; vii 278, 340–1; ix 192–3
   Conversation with Herr von Ribbentrop, iii 389, 396–7
   Conversation with Count Welczeck, i 384; ii 216; vi 237–8
   Letter to Viscount Halifax, vi 514
   Letter to Herr von Ribbentrop, vi 517; *referred to*, vii 18
   Memorandum handed to M. Osusky, i 523–4; *referred to*, i 476, 495, 500, 503, 522n, 527, 545
   Message to Viscount Halifax, July 19, 1939, vi 398; July 25, vi 489; *referred to* vi 491
   Note of Aug. 11, 1939 relating to China, ix 447; *referred to*, ix 456n, 463n, 467
   Note to Count Ciano, iii 494
   Note to Sir E. Phipps, ii 607
   Speech in Chamber of Deputies, Jan. 26, 1939, iv 33n, 51; vi 518
   Speech at Arcachon, June 25, 1939, ix 234n; at Gourdon, Feb. 26, 1939, iv 168n
   Speeches at Anglo-French Conversations, April 28–9, 1938, i 210–1, 222–4, 229, 231; Sept. 18, 1938, ii 391, 393, 398–9; Sept. 26, 1938, ii 538–9; Nov. 24, 1938, iii 286–7, 294–8, 300–4, 307–10; Jan. 10, 1939, iii 513–5; Mar. 21, 1939, iv 422–6; Mar. 22, 1939, iv 457–63; May 20, 1939, v 608–9, 611
   Statement on signing of Franco-German Declaration, Dec. 6, 1938, iii 396
Bonnet, Madame Georges, iii 390–2
Bono, Marshal Emilio de, vi 664
Bonzo, Colonel Count Valfre di (Italian Military Attaché at Prague), ii 143
   Conversation with Lt.-Col. H. C. T. Stronge, ii 146–7

Boris III, King of Bulgaria (1918–43), iii 314, 318, 334; vi 438
   Conversation with Sir A. Cadogan, iii 318–9
   Conversation with Field-Marshal Göring, iii 142–3
   Conversation with Herr Hitler, iii 143
   Conversation with Mr. Rendel, iii 142–5
   Conversation with Herr von Ribbentrop, iii 143–4
   Visit to Germany, iii 46, 142–4
Borman, F. W. (Archivist at H.M. Legation, Durazzo, July 1928–June 1939), v 176–7, 190
Bormann, Martin (Deputy Head of the National Socialist Party Chancellery, Berlin), vi 212
Bossy, Dr. Raoul (Roumanian Minister at Budapest, 1936–9), iii 36; iv 289, 511; v 62–3, 77
Bost-Waldeck, Count von, ii 668, 670
Bottai, G. (Italian Minister for Education), v 271
Böttcher, Dr. V. (Head of Foreign Department of Danzig Senate), iv 46; v 25–7, 211, 788; vi 7–8, 31, 164–5, 178, 223, 337, 395, 462, 487, 490, 506, 532, 593, 621–2, 653–4, 685; vii 50, 153, 217–8, 542, 545
   Conversation with Mr. E. H. G. Shepherd, vi 1, 9–10
Bouhler, Philip (Chief of Herr Hitler's Chancellery), vii 96
Bourbon-Parma, Prince Louis of, iv 42n
Bourguès, Lucien (a French journalist), i 54; v 439
Bourne, Major K. M. (Commissioner of Police, Shanghai International Settlement, 1938–9), viii 137, 365, 515, 538; ix 37
Bourne, V. H. (Deputy Treasurer, Revenue, Shanghai Municipal Council, 1939), ix 136–7
Bourquin, Maurice (Belgian substitute delegate to League of Nations), viii 111, 145
Bourragué, Rear-Admiral (Assistant to Chief of French Naval Staff), iv 223
Bova-Scoppa, Renato (Secretary of Italian Legation at Geneva), iii 486
Bowater, Sir Frank (Lord Mayor of London, 1938–9), ix 479
Bowyer-Smyth, Captain Sir Philip W., Bart. (British Naval Attaché at Rome, Jan. 1939–Jan. 1940), iv 338; v 129, 159, 174
   To Earl of Perth, v 190
Brassert, Mr., iv 608
Brauchitsch, Colonel-General Walter von (Commander-in-Chief of the German Army, 1938–41), i 44, 92; ii 44, 66, 101, 690; iii 19–20; iv 275–6, 279, 439, 565; v 292, 478, 728; vi 2, 248, 708, vii 92, 258, 316, 415–6
   Conversation with Dr. Attolico, ii 232
   Proclamation of March 15, 1939, iv 276
Bräuer, Kurt (Counsellor of German Embassy, Paris: acted as Chargé d'Affaires), iv 298–9, 363–4; vi 213

Brenan, Sir John (H.M. Consul-General at Shanghai, 1930–7; a member of Far Eastern Department of the Foreign Office, 1938–43) *Memorandum by*, **viii** 521; **ix** 536

Bressy, P. G. P. (*Chef de cabinet* to M. Bonnet), **v** 414; **vi** 63
At Anglo-French conversations, Mar. 21, 1939, **iv** 422; Mar. 22, 1939, **iv** 457

Briand, Aristide (French Minister for Foreign Affairs, 1925–32), **i** 218; **ii** 383, 386

Bridges, E. E. (1939 Sir Edward) (Secretary of the Cabinet, 1938–46)
At Anglo-French conversations, Sept. 1938, **ii** 373, 520, 536

Brinkmann, R. (Vice-President of the Reichsbank), **iv** 24

Brinon, Fernand de (Foreign Editor of 'l'Information'), **i** 324, 460

Brisson, Pierre, (Managing Director of 'Le Figaro', 1932–42), **iv** 61

British Military Mission (Moscow). *See under* Drax, Admiral

Brivonesi, Rear-Admiral B. (Italian Naval Attaché at London), **vii** 367n

Broadmead, P. M. (Counsellor of H.M. Embassy in China, Dec. 1938–April 1941), **ix** 104n
To Sir A. Cadogan, **ix** 96–7
To Sir A. Clark Kerr, **ix** 24, 79
To Viscount Halifax, **viii** 445; **ix** 18, 30, 54, 66, 72, 74, 103

Brocket, 2nd Baron (Chairman of the Anglo-German Fellowship), **iv** 238; **v** 292; **vii** 631

Brody, Andrej (Head of Ruthenian Government, Oct. 1938), **iii** 217; **iv** 249

Brooks, Mr., **iii** 675

Brown, Constantine (Editor of the Washington 'Evening Star'), **iii** 516; **iv** 305
Conversation with Count Ciano, **iii** 516–7

Bruce, Stanley M. (High Commissioner for Australia in London, 1933–45), **ii** 593; **vi** 588, 633; **vii** 49; **viii** 550
Conversation with Viscount Halifax (with Mr. te Water), **vi** 588–90

Brugère, Raymond (French Minister at Belgrade, 1937–40), **ii** 137; **vii** 248, 379
Conversation with Mr. Shone, **ii** 135–6

Bruggmann, Dr. Charles (Swiss Minister at Prague, 1937–9), **ii** 669–71, 673

Bruggmann, Madame, **ii** 671

Bruner, Professor, **ii** 674–5

Bryant, Group Captain W. E. G. (British Air Attaché, Tokyo, Dec. 1937–Dec. 1941), **viii** 168, 174n; **ix** 287n

Buchan, Sir John. *See* Tweedsmuir, 1st Baron

Buday, Father (Vice-Marshal of Czechoslovak Senate), **i** 429

Budenni (Budyonny), Marshal S. M. (Commander of the Moscow Military District), **i** 422; **vii** 46

Bukharin, N. I. (Editor-in-chief of 'Isvestiya' and 'Pravda'; executed Mar. 1938), **iv** 414–5

Bullitt, William C. (U.S. Ambassador at Paris, 1936–40), **ii** 220, 546; **iii** 59, 89; **iv** 51, 423–4, 499; **v** 250, 356, 505, 775–6, 791; **vii** 136, 177, 202, 244–5
Conversation with Mr. R. I. Campbell, **vii** 78, 164–6
Conversation with Sir E. Phipps, **ii** 218–9; **v** 251–2; **vii** 202–3

Bülow-Schwante, V. von (German Ambassador at Brussels, 1938–40), **v** 256, 269, 271; **vii** 270, 312, 340

Bumke, Dr. (a German medical doctor), **vii** 416

Bürckel, Josef (Gauleiter of the Saar Palatinate; Head of civil administration in Moravia, Mar. 1939), **i** 67, 136, 147–8; **iv** 276, 279, 438, 564

Burckhardt, Professor C. J. (League of Nations High Commissioner at Danzig), **ii** 683, 689; **iii** 280n, 281n, 283–4, 401–5, 431, 438–9, 441–2, 542–3, 552–5, 558–9, 561, 567, 572–4, 580–1, 585–9, 593–603, 610–4, 657; **iv** 46–7, 68, 81, 146–7, 166–7, 169–70, 186–7, 261, 265, 281, 383; **v** 17–8, 24–5, 52, 391–3, 431, 466, 477, 514, 525, 527, 582, 629, 637, 654, 667, 731, 739, 782, 811–4; **vi** 1, 10, 42, 44, 48, 107, 178, 223, 337–8, 364–5, 395, 401, 419–21, 431, 433, 448, 475–7, 480, 490–1, 495, 506–7, 530, 532, 546–9, 560, 565, 569, 577, 594–5, 597, 610–1, 613–4, 620–2, 624, 640, 642–4, 652–3, 660–2, 675, 683, 689, 698, 703–5, 707, 714, 716, 718, 760n; **vii** 6, 8–12, 18, 24–5, 32, 49, 55, 66, 68, 89, 100–2, 109–10, 123, 129, 152–3, 200, 214, 219, 222, 224, 261, 269, 296, 318, 450–1, 458, 470, 542–5; departure from Danzig, **vii** 483, 510
Conversation with Dr. Attolico, **vi** 44
Conversation with M. Beck, **vi** 41–2, 721, 725–6
Conversation with Herr Forster, **ii** 689; **iii** 660–1, **vi** 42, 388–9, 420–1, 507, 726, 733
Conversation with Herr Greiser, **ii** 689–90; **vi** 42, 726
Conversation with Viscount Halifax, **iii** 595–6; **v** 627–30
Conversation with Herr Hitler, **vi** 691–6
Conversation with Sir H. Kennard, **iii** 280–1, 558; **v** 709–10
Conversation with Gauleiter Koch, **iii** 659–60; **vi** 729–31
Conversation with Dr. Krauel, **v** 561–2
Conversation with M. Lipski, **vi** 44, 723–4, 728
Conversation with Mr. Makins, **iii** 610–1; **v** 395; **vi** 41–7, 689–98
Conversation with Herr von Ribbentrop, **iii** 658–9; **vi** 43, 721–3, 727–8
Conversation with Mr. E. H. G. Shepherd, 441–2, 442n; **vi** 187

Burckhardt, Professor (*cont.*)
  Conversation with Mr. F. M. Shepherd, **vi** 451–2, 454–5
  Conversation with Mr. Skrine Stevenson, **ii** 689–91
  Conversation with Mr. Walters, **v** 561–2
  Conversation with Baron von Weizsäcker, **ii** 690–1; **vi** 43–4, 727
  Letter to Mr. Makins, **vi** 728, 732
  Letter to Mr. Walters, **iii** 657
  Visit to Berchtesgaden, Aug. 1939. *See* Berchtesgaden in Subject Index
  Visits to Warsaw, Danzig and Berlin, May–June, 1939, **v** 709, 752; **vi** 41–7, 107, 721–35
  At Meetings of Committee of Three, Jan. 1939, **iii** 598–603, 613–4
Burgin, Dr. E. Leslie (Minister of Supply, July 1939–May 1940), **vii** 37
Burnett, Air Marshal Sir Charles (a member of British Military Mission to Moscow), **vi** 527; **vii** 34, 562, 581–2, 585, 587
  Letter to Air Chief Marshal Sir C. L. N. Newall, **vii** 597
Burrows, Colonel M. B. (British Military Attaché at Rome, May 1938–May 1940), **ii** 131, 356; **iii** 334, 501; **iv** 170, 299–301, 304–5, 308, 311, 328, 337, 339, 355–6; **v** 117, 159, 170, 193, 420–1, 426, 774; **vi** 31, 549, 664*n*; **vii** 240
  Conversation with General Toussaint, **v** 172–4
  Conversation with Colonel Tripiccione, **v** 118–9
Bushati, Malik (Albanian Minister of the Interior), **v** 383
Buti, Signor (Head of European and Mediterranean Section, Italian Ministry of Foreign Affairs)
  Conversation with Mr. Yencken, **v** 250–1
Butler, R. A. (Parliamentary Under-Secretary of State for Foreign Affairs, Feb. 1938–July 1941; substitute U.K. delegate to League of Nations), **ii** 489*n*; **iii** 530, 589; **iv** 110, 112–3, 132; **v** 678; **vi** 325; **ix** 104*n*, 508
  Conversation with M. Bonnet, **ii** 293–4
  Conversation with Mr. Edwardes, **ix** 511
  Conversation with M. Komarnicki, **iii** 592–4
  Conversation with Dr. Wellington Koo and Dr. Quo Tai-chi, **viii** 93–4, 104–5
  Conversation with M. Litvinov and M. Maisky, **ii** 497–8
  Conversation with M. Maisky, **iv** 106–7, 208–9; **vi** 594–5
  Conversation with M. Prytz, **vi** 107
  Conversation with M. Shigemitsu, **ix** 513–4
  Conversation with M. de Velics, **iii** 5
  Minute by, **iv** 208; **ix** 513
  Speeches and Statements in House of Commons, June 13, 1938, **ix** 498; July 26, **viii** 1*n*; Nov. 2, **viii** 193–4, 222; Nov. 9, **viii** 210, 212, 244; Feb. 13, 1939, **iv** 108; Mar. 20, **iv** 345*n*; Mar. 27, **iv** 534; July 3, **ix** 241*n*;

July 31, **vi** 559, 571, 574, 578, 594–5; **ix** 388, 459*n*
  at League of Nations meeting, Jan. 1939, **iii** 587
  at Meetings of Committee of Three, Jan. 1939, **iii** 598–603, 612–4
  See also United Kingdom Delegation (Geneva).
Butovsky, Dr. (Czechoslovak Minister without Portfolio in General Syrovy's Cabinet, Sept. 1938), **iii** 21

Cadere, Victor (Roumanian Ambassador at Belgrade, 1939–40), **v** 333–4, 481, 491, 597, 660, 676; **vi** 70
Cadogan, Sir Alexander (Permanent Under-Secretary of State for Foreign Affairs, Jan. 1938–Feb. 1946), **i** 21, 62*n*, 261, 322, 339, 439, 498, 536, 563, 584, 628; **ii** 314*n*, 409, 411, 422; **iii** 31, 78, 113–4, 145, 189*n*, 314, 361, 422*n*, 433, 435, 444, 447, 450, 463, 502, 510*n*, 511, 532, 534, 536, 671; **iv** 260, 293, 367, 377*n*, 473, 546*n*, 556, 559; **v** 47, 74, 289, 384–5, 685*n*; **vi** 22, 25, 122, 125*n*; **vii** 2*n*, 36*n*, 58, 108*n*, 282, 357, 359, 424*n*, 442, 529, 538, 632*n*; **viii** 198*n*, 257*n*, 301–2, 367, 455, 468, 482*n*; **ix** 272*n*, 528*n*
  To Sir N. Bland, **iv** 16
  To Sir A. Clark Kerr, **ix** 97
  To Sir R. Craigie, **ix** 98
  To Sir H. Kennard, **iii** 29; **v** 653
  To Sir H. Knatchbull-Hugessen, **v** 606
  To Sir G. Knox, **iii** 29
  To Earl of Perth, **iv** 547
  To Sir E. Phipps, **ii** 535
  To U.K. Delegation (Geneva), **v** 622
  Conversation with M. Aras, **v** 672–3
  Conversation with M. de Barcza, **iii** 4; **vi** 77–8
  Conversation with M. Bonnet, **vii** 513–4
  Conversation with King Boris of Bulgaria, **iii** 318–9
  Conversation with Mr. Campbell, **v** 279*n*
  Conversation with M. Corbin, **i** 339, 498–500, 551–3; **iii** 330; **iv** 70–1, 90–1, 170–1, 266–8, 334, 377, 486–7, 519–20; **v** 113–5, 225, 260, 452, 683*n*; **vi** 3–4, 95
  Conversation with M. Cretzianu, **v** 111–3
  Conversation with M. Dahlerus, **vii** 479–80
  Conversation with Dr. von Dirksen, **i** 598–9; **iv** 583
  Conversation with Herr Forster and Professor Noe, **i** 653–5
  Conversation with Sir N. Henderson, **ii** 421, 592–4
  Conversation with Dr. Wellington Koo, **ix** 238
  Conversation with Dr. Kordt, **iii** 671–2
  Conversation with M. Maisky, **iv** 530–2; **v** 21–3, 235
  Conversation with M. Jan Masaryk, **i** 142*n*, 289–90, 292; **ii** 443

Conversation with Count Raczynski, **vi** 132, 679–80
Conversation with M. Tilea, **iv** 389, 520; **v** 65–6, 207
Conversation with Dr. Woermann, **i** 80–2
Letter to Mr. Campbell, **vii** 32
Letter to Sir R. Clive, **iv** 104
Letter to M. Corbin, **v** 683
Letter to Mr. Norton, **vi** 282
Letter to Earl of Perth, **iii** 473; *referred to* 477–8
Letter to Sir E. Phipps, **v** 356n
Letter to Mr. Quo Tai-chi, **viii** 422
Letter to Captain Wiedemann, **i** 589
Minute by, **iii** 502n; **iv** 70, 141, 334; **v** 527, 693; **vi** 33, 95; **vii** 441, 479–80, 511, 518, 524-5, 537, 552n, 553–4; **ix** 238, 539
At Anglo-French conversations, April 1938, **i** 198; Sept. 1938, **ii** 373, 520, 536; Nov. 1938, **iii** 285; Jan. 1939, **iii** 513–5; Mar. 1939, **iv** 457
At Anglo-Polish conversations, April 1939, **v** 1, 9, 30; Aug. 1939, **vii** 64–6
At Anglo-Roumanian conversations, April 1939, **v** 295, 306, 309, 321–2, 342–4
Caha, M. (a ·senior official in Czechoslovak Prime Minister's Office), **ii** 448, 672
Cahan, Samuel B. (Counsellor of Soviet Embassy, London), **iv** 635
Cahill, J. R. (1932 Sir Robert) (Commercial Counsellor, H.M. Embassy, Paris, Feb. 1921–July 1939), **ii** 535, 558
Caillaux, Joseph (President of Finance Commission of French Senate), **i** 477–8; **ii** 305, 509, 559, 579; **v** 130; **vii** 177
Conversation with Sir E. Phipps, **ii** 513–4
Caldwell, J. K. (U.S. Consul-General at Tientsin), **viii** 72, 83-4, 248, 314, 323, 328, 527; **ix** 161, 165, 167–9, 185–6
Caldwell, Mrs., **viii** 248
Calinescu, Armand (Roumanian Prime Minister, Mar.–Sept. 1939), **iv** 580; **v** 74, 77, 111, 382; **vi** 660, 687
Conversation with Sir R. Hoare, **v** 239
Cambon, Roger (Minister Counsellor, French Embassy at London: acted as Chargé d'Affaires), **i** 336, 343; **ii** 101, 125, 137; **iii** 494n, 503–4; **v** 396n, 496, 724; **vi** 528; **vii** 2n, 5n, 32, 105–6, 121, 131–2, 287, 423, 478, 529; **viii** 495, 497; **ix** 7–8, 421–2
To Viscount Halifax, **iv** 633
Conversation with Viscount Halifax, **ii** 158–60; **vii** 167–8
Conversation with Mr. Roberts, **iii** 77–8
Conversation with Sir O. Sargent, **ii** 167–8; **v** 778
Conversation with Mr. Strang, **iii** 553–4; **v** 565–6; **vii** 106–8
Letter to Sir O. Sargent, **ii** 168; **vi** 167, 169
Campbell, Sir Ronald Hugh (H.M. Minister at Belgrade, Aug. 1935–Oct. 1939), **iv** 470, 621;

v 92, 294, 314, 348n; **vi** 11–2, 51, 69, 463–4; **vii** 152n
To Viscount Halifax, **iv** 102, 352, 384, 388, 399, 494; **v** 275, 563, 588, 596, 676–7; **vi** 66, 166, 242, 421–2
Conversation with M. Cinkar-Markovitch, **v** 596–7
Conversation with Prince Paul of Yugoslavia, **iv** 352, 384, 388; **v** 79–80
Letter to Sir A. Cadogan, **v** 79; **vii** 16, 177
Campbell, Ronald Ian (H.M. Minister at Paris, May 1938–Dec. 1939: acted as Chargé d'Affaires), **ii** 18n, 96n, 201n, 235, 261; **iii** 447, 482; **iv** 138, 274, 353n, 371, 381; **v** 123n; **vi** 519; **vii** 523, 560; **viii** 16; **ix** 331, 360n, 491n
To Viscount Halifax, **i** 554; **ii** 38, 71, 124-5, '190, 192, 194, 197n, 201; **iii** 159; **iv** 395-6, 409, 434, 457, 467–8, 490; **vi** 25, 464, 480, 495, 509, 528, 534-5, 561, 611, 617-8, 646, 667, 677, 687; **vii** 14, 25, 77-8, 96, 102–3, 117, 119–20, 123, 128, 130-1, 136-7, 158, 163-4, 166, 194; **viii** 16, 22; **ix** 342, 359, 379, 418, 446
Conversation with M. Bonnet, **ii** 38–9, 71-4, 194, 201–2; **vi** 398–9, 677–8; **vii** 77, 79, 130–1
Conversation with Mr. Bullitt, **vii** 78, 164–6
Conversation with Sir A. Cadogan, **v** 279n
Conversation with M. Charvériat, **iv** 298–9, 363–4; **vi** 25
Conversation with M. Daladier, **vii** 163–4
Conversation with M. Léger, **i** 554–5; **iv** 335-7, 373, 382, 468–9; **v** 143–4, 250, 260–2; **vi** 561–2, 618–9; **vii** 119–20, 378–9
Conversation with M. Massigli, **ii** 95-7, 124–5; **viii** 17, 23
Conversation with Signor Prunas, **iii** 487–8
Letter to Viscount Halifax, **vi** 397–8, 489
Letter to Sir O. Sargent, **ii** 95
Minute by, **iv** 335
Campinchi, C. (French Minister of Marine, 1938–40), **iv** 359; **v** 799
Camrose, 1st Baron (newspaper proprietor and editor), **ii** 257
Canaris, Vice-Admiral (Head of German Military Intelligence Staff), **vi** 282, 326n
Capek, Dr. Karel (Czech. writer and dramatist), **i** 521; **iii** 412
Capelle, Baron (*Chef de cabinet* to King Leopold III of the Belgians, 1937–9), **iv** 58, 66, 70; **v** 256
Capranica del Grillo, Marchese G. (Counsellor of Italian Embassy, Paris), **v** 144; **vi** 220
Caquot, Albert (President of the Société des Ingénieurs de France, Nov. 1938), **iii** 289–91
Carnogursky, P. (Chief of Slovak Press Bureau), **v** 87
Carol II, King of Roumania (1930–40), **i** 217; **iii** 45–6, 300–1, 385, 565; **iv** 284, 336, 370,

Carol II (*cont.*)
388, 390, 396, 398–9, 433, 465, 494, 556, 578, 581, 619; **v** 91, 113, 298, 301, 310, 313–5, 325, 327–8, 333, 481, 483; **vi** 146, 661, 673–4; **vii** 259

　Conversation with Mr. N. Chamberlain and Viscount Halifax, **iii** 231–3, 243
　Conversation with Sir R. Hoare, **iv** 398–9, 419, 578–9
　Conversation with M. Saracoglu, **vi** 673–4
　Visit to Great Britain, **iii** 231*n*
　Visit to Istanbul, **vi** 673*n*

Carolet, Commandant (a member of German Section of the Deuxième Bureau, Paris), **v** 72

Carr, Wilbur John (U.S. Ambassador at Prague, 1937–9), **i** 381; **iv** 233

Carter, Edward C. (General Secretary of Institute of Pacific Relations), **ix** 134

Cartier de Marchienne, Baron E. de (Belgian Ambassador at London, 1927–46), **vii** 271
　Conversation with Viscount Halifax, **iv** 44

Carton de Wiart, Major-General A. (Head of British Military Mission to Poland, Aug. 1939) **vii** 236, 294, 309, 364, 371, 374, 533

Carvell, J. E. M. (H.M. Consul-General at Munich, April 1938–Aug. 1939), **i** 318*n*; **ii** 89*n*; **vi** 640
　To Viscount Halifax, **ii** 89
　To Sir N. Henderson, **iv** 229

Catchpole, T. C. P. (a relief worker in the Sudeten areas), **ii** 662

Cavan, 10th Earl of, Field-Marshal, **vii** 97

Cavendish-Bentinck, V. F. W. (a member of Egyptian Dept. of the Foreign Office), **iv** 302*n*

Cazalet, Captain V. A. (M.P. for Chippenham), **i** 169–70, 181, 401*n*, 520

Cecil of Chelwood, 1st Viscount (President, League of Nations Union), **i** 34

Cermak, M., **ii** 670

Cernak, Professor Matus (Slovak Minister of Education, 1938; Minister at Berlin, April 1939), **iii** 377; **v** 87

Cerny, Dr. Josef (Czechoslovak Minister of the Interior in Dr. Hodza's Cabinets, 1935–8), **i** 74, 126, 195, 278, 316, 349, 367, 387, 441*n*; **ii** 448

Cerruti, V. (Italian Ambassador at Paris, 1935–7), **iii** 483, 486

Chamberlain, Sir Austen (Secretary of State for Foreign Affairs, 1924–9), **v** 132

Chamberlain, A. Neville (Prime Minister and First Lord of the Treasury, May 1937–May 1940), **i** 29, 35, 42–3, 49, 52*n*, 53, 75, 82–3, 85, 112*n*, 128, 175, 198, 283, 285, 584*n*, 586, 591, 618*n*, 630; **ii** 10, 19, 38, 41*n*, 59, 60, 111, 112*n*, 148, 153, 172, 174, 240, 242, 268–9, 293, 296, 318, 323–5, 352, 358*n*, 359–60, 362, 364, 371, 400, 409–11, 421–2, 427–8, 430–1, 452, 458, 510–2, 515, 546–7, 562, 565, 567, 580, 600–1, 614–5, 624, 654–5, 673, 675*n*, 683, 688; **iii** 1,

19, 59, 65*n*, 87–8, 93*n*, 100, 127, 143–6, 149, 161, 172, 244*n*, 250, 259, 261–2, 278, 284, 293, 311, 313–4, 316, 319–22, 325–7, 330, 336–7, 339, 348, 351, 360–1, 371, 389–90, 392, 425–6, 428, 433–4, 462, 468, 488, 490–1, 493, 500, 560, 566, 615; **iv** 12, 13*n*, 17, 82, 92, 111, 120–2, 124, 130, 137, 171, 208–9, 237, 240, 261, 267, 294, 306, 309–11, 314, 320, 324, 326–7, 361, 364, 367, 409, 420, 427, 486, 532, 546*n*, 547, 557–8, 602; **v** 27, 47, 49–50, 71, 96, 105, 107, 139, 149–50, 154, 156–7, 158*n*, 181–2, 184, 218, 227–8, 237, 240, 245, 270, 277, 337–8, 342, 403, 416, 435, 439, 456, 469, 474, 503, 539, 593, 614, 617, 648, 651, 653*n*, 664, 684, 691, 704, 706, 713, 715, 721, 729, 748–9, 752*n*, 801, 804–5; **vi** 6, 13–4, 63–4, 122, 151, 172, 180, 185–6, 197, 199, 238, 252, 262, 297, 302–3, 317, 327, 331, 353, 363, 442, 463, 481, 489–91, 514, 556*n*, 589–90, 633, 659, 677, 700, 712, 718–20, 724, 739, 742, 744–8, 750, 752, 754, 758; **vii** 31, 36, 56–7, 60, 99, 109, 124*n*, 158, 202, 247, 258–9, 277, 281, 285, 299, 308, 351–3, 384, 392, 417*n*, 426, 441–3, 449, 465, 506, 508, 518–9, 529–30, 550, 552*n*, 553, 627; **viii** 121, 158, 247, 257*n*, 381–2; **ix** 13, 262

　To Sir N. Henderson, **iv** 591
　To Signor Mussolini, **iii** 458*n*, 539; **v** 157*n*
　To Mr. Newton, **ii** 491, 497, 629
　To Sir E. Phipps, **ii** 488
　To Lord Runciman, **ii** 328–9
　To Sir H. Wilson, **ii** 550, 559
　Communications with Herr Hitler
　　message of Sept. 13, 1938, **ii** 314
　　message of Sept. 16, **ii** 354
　　message of Sept. 19, **ii** 406
　　message of Sept. 20, **ii** 424
　　letter of Sept. 23 a.m., **ii** 482; *referred to*, **ii** 481; 484, 488, 493, 521
　　letter of Sept. 23 p.m., **ii** 489–90
　　letter of Sept. 26, **ii** 541; *referred to*, **ii** 537, 553–6, 576
　　message of Sept. 28, **ii** 587
　　letter of Aug. 22, 1939, *text of*, **vii** 127, 170; *draft of*, **vii** 110; *referred to*, **vii** 81, 126, 129, 139, 147–51, 156, 162, 165, 168, 174, 177, 181, 185, 331–2
　　proposed reply to Herr Hitler's proposals of Aug. 25, **vii** 310–2, 319–21, 323–4, 328
　　reply of H.M. Govt., Aug. 28, *text of*, **vii** 330, 344; *referred to*, **vii** 333–4, 342–3, 348, 351, 355, 357–9, 362, 367, 371, 380, 387, 396, 457, 508
　　reply of H.M. Govt. to Herr Hitler's communication of Aug. 29, *text of*, **vii** 413, 417; *referred to*, **vii** 406, 410–2, 423, 427, 429, 434, 438, 448
　　message of Aug. 30, 1939, **vii** 403
　　communication of H.M. Govt. of Sept. 1,

1939, **vii** 488. *See also* Germany (Great Britain) in Subject Index

Communications with Signor Mussolini

message of Sept. 28, 1938, **ii** 587, 643–4; *referred to,* **ii** 600, 624

letter of Mar. 20, 1939, **iv** 402; *referred to,* **iv** 507, 547, 556, 573

message of Mar. 31, 1939, **iv** 551–2; *referred to,* **iv** 554

message of July 6, 1939, **vi** 257–8; *referred to,* **vi** 288, 290, 588; **vii** 59

Conversation with King Carol of Roumania, **iii** 231–3, 243

Conversation with M. Dahlerus, **vii** 282n, 395–8

Conversation with M. Daladier, **ii** 537n; **vii** 524–5

Conversation with Dr. von Dirksen, **i** 618–20; *referred to,* **ii** 10, 41, 59, 106

Conversation with Gen. Gamelin, **ii** 575n, 610

Conversation with Viscount Halifax, **ii** 477

Conversation with Herr Hitler, at Berchtesgaden, **ii** 338–51; *at* Godesberg, **ii** 463–73, 499–508; *at* Munich, **ii** 635–40

Conversation with Mr. J. Kennedy, **ii** 212–3

Conversation with Signor Mussolini, **ii** 636; **iii** 517–21, 524–30

Conversation with Mr. Montagu Norman, **ix** 271–2

Conversation with Count Raczynski, **v** 778–9

Conversation with Herr von Ribbentrop, **i** 21–3; *referred to,* **i** 46, 81–2

Conversation with M. Shigemitsu, **viii** 262–3

Conversation with M. Wenner-Gren, **vi** 736–8

Declaration at Munich (the Hitler–Chamberlain Declaration, Sept. 30, 1938), **ii** 640; *referred to,* **iii** 60n, 159, 172, 252, 268, 273, 282, 286, 293, 389, 525; **iv** 241, 267, 602, 641; **v** 361; **vii** 621

Letter to M. Daladier, **vi** 350, 587

Letter to Dr. von Dirksen, **ii** 41, *referred to,* **ii** 60, 105–6

Letter to Lord Halifax, **ii** 686

Letter to M. Wenner-Gren, **vi** 741

Message to M. Beck, **iii** 59–60

Message to Dr. Benes, **ii** 570

Messages to M. Daladier, **ii** 318; **iii** 90n

Minute by, **vii** 554n, 555n

Speech at Albert Hall, May 11, 1939, **v** 546n, 549, 805

Speech at Birmingham, Jan. 28, 1939, **iv** 6, 51, 306

Speech at annual meeting of Birmingham Unionist Association, March 17, 1939, **iv** 291n, 350, 365, 367, 372, 379–80, 402; **vi** 114

Speech at Cardiff, June 24, 1939, **ix** 237n

Speech at Foreign Press Association dinner, Dec. 13, 1938, **iii** 426, 434n

Speech at Rome, Jan. 1939, **iii** 538

Speeches at Anglo-French conversations, April 28–9, 1938, **i** 198, 203–5, 207–12, 219–22, 226–7, 230–2; Sept. 18, 1938, **ii** 373–82, 386–99; Sept. 25, 1938, **ii** 520–35; Sept. 26, 1938, **ii** 536–40; Nov. 1938, **iii** 285–310; Jan. 1939, **iii** 512–5; Mar. 1939, **iv** 457–63

Speeches at Anglo-Italian conversations, Jan. 1939. *See above, Conversation with* Signor Mussolini

Speeches at Anglo-Polish conversations, April, 1939, **v** 9–19, 30–5

Speeches at Anglo-Roumanian conversations, April 1939, **v** 309–15

Speeches and statements in House of Commons, March 14, 1938, **i** 44–8, 41–3, 49–52, 54; Mar. 24, **i** 95–7; **ii** 689; *referred to,* **i** 88, 94, 112, 141, 142n, 143–5, 150–1, 180, 195, 213–4, 227, 229, 231–2, 236–7, 242, 263, 264n, 268, 273, 284, 314, 325, 332, 335, 345, 353, 356, 379, 399, 409, 602, 629; **ii** 56, 86–7, 107, 159, 174, 198, 211, 262, 286, 295, 302, 394, 681, 683, 688; **vii** 623; May 11, **viii** 12n; May 23, **i** 370n, 440; June 21, **viii** 25n; July 26, **ii** 2n, 7–8; **iii** 662; **viii** 1n, 12n, 19, 24, 27, 29, 31, 36, 48, 54, 57, 60; Sept. 28, **ii** 624; Oct. 3, **iii** 249–50, 324; **vii** 550; Oct. 5, **iii** 119, 147; Oct. 6, **iii** 160; Nov. 1, **iii** 257; **viii** 178, 185, 198–9, 210; Nov. 28, **iii** 415; Dec. 5, **iii** 426;

Jan. 31, 1939, **iv** 90, 306; Feb. 6, **iv** 90n, 101, 114, 160, 308–9, 311, 317, 319, 329–30, 343, 345; Mar. 15, **iv** 277; Mar. 23, **iv** 488n, 509, 527, 615; Mar. 28, **iv** 544; **v** 21; Mar. 31, **iv** 359, 545–6, 552–5, 557, 571, 575, 578; **v** 11, 21, 27, 29, 44, 49, 51, 68–9, 76, 101, 116; April 6, **v** 50, 53, 57, 64–5, 68, 129, 290; April 13, **v** 197–8, 200, 219, 236, 548n; April 19, **ix** 25; April 26, **v** 320–1, 798; May 3, **v** 413; May 10, **v** 506, 521; May 19, **v** 606–7, 707–8, 763, 774; **vi** 17; May 24, **v** 668–70, 787; June 5, **v** 767n; June 7, **v** 787–8; **vi** 5–6, 121, 264; June 15, **vi** 59n; **ix** 181–2; June 19, **ix** 215n, 228; June 21, **ix** 228; June 22, **ix** 217; June 23, **ix** 218, 228; June 28, **ix** 232n; July 3, **vi** 261; **vii** 30; July 10, **vi** 255–6, 259–60, 274, 321, 327, 337, 342, 381–2, 399, 414, 448, 486, 647, 713; **vii** 111; July 13, **vi** 353; July 17, **ix** 311n, 327; July 24, **vi** 465n, 480–1; **ix** 323, 333–4, 367, 374, 472; July 31, **vi** 529; **ix** 388, 459n; Aug. 4, **ix** 404, 438, 459n; Aug. 24, **vii** 194, 216, 228, 245, 247, 250; Aug. 29, **vii** 368, 403; Sept. 2, **vii** 501–2, 520–1, 524, 539

Statement to press, Sept. 11, 1938, **ii** 680–2; *referred to,* **ii** 268–9, 297–9, 302, 653; **vii**

Chamberlain, A. Neville (*cont.*)
68; Sept. 27, 1938, **ii** 559; *referred to* 561, 565, 567–8, 571–2, 602–3, 641–2; **viii** 107n
Visits to France, Nov. 1938 and Jan. 1939. *See Speeches at* Anglo-French conversations
Visits to Germany. *See above, Conversation with* Herr Hitler, *and also* Berchtesgaden, Godesberg, and Munich Conference in Subject Index
Visit to Italy, Jan. 1939, **iii** 321, 356–8, 362, 458–540 *passim; referred to,* **iv** 87, 292–4, 306, 346–7, 402; **vi** 257; **viii** 437n
Chamberlain, Mrs. Neville, **iii** 466
Chang Chun (Secretary-General of Military Affairs Commission of Chinese Govt.), **viii** 186
Chao Hung, **ix** 362
Chapelain, Mr. (Head of the 'special bureau' at Shanghai), **ix** 418
Charbonnière, Guy de Girard de (2nd Secretary, French Embassy at London), **iv** 368n; **v** 273–4; **vii** 132, 205
To Sir O. Sargent, **iv** 368
Charles, Sir Noel H. H., Bart. (Counsellor of H.M. Embassy, Rome, Oct. 1937–Oct. 1939; acted as Chargé d'Affaires in 1938), **iii** 327, 532, 534; **iv** 206, 281–2, 340, 353, 492, 554; **v** 121, 126, 237, 429; **vii** 72, 424, 488
To Sir A. Cadogan, **iv** 358, 556
To Viscount Halifax, **ii** 101, 130–1, 221, 315, 331, 356; **v** 342, 375; **vi** 31
Conversation with Count Ciano, **ii** 101–2, 130–1, 331–2; **iv** 348–9, 358–9
Conversation with Comte de Kerchove, **v** 566–7
Charles-Roux, François (French Ambassador at The Vatican, 1932–40), **v** 222, 718; **vi** 316; **vii** 448, 495
Charvériat, Émile (Political Director, French Ministry of Foreign Affairs, 1938–40; member of League of Nations Committee of Three), **iii** 438, 447, 530; **iv** 138, 156, 169, 274, 397; **v** 54, 71, 123n, 405–6, 654; **vi** 535, 611; **vii** 16
Conversation with Mr. Campbell, **iv** 298–9, 363–4; **vi** 25
Conversation with Sir E. Phipps, **iv** 48–9
At Anglo-French conversations, Nov. 1938, **iii** 285
At Meetings of the Committee of Three, Jan. 1939, **iii** 591, 598–603, 612–4
Chastel de la Howarderie, Comte F. de (Counsellor of the Belgian Embassy at Rome: acted as Chargé d'Affaires), **iv** 294, 297
Chastenet, Jacques (Editor of 'Le Temps'), **vi** 63
Chatfield, 1st Baron, Admiral of the Fleet, (Minister for Co-ordination of Defence, Jan. 1939–April 1940), **vi** 485, 534, 674; **vii** 3
To Admiral Drax, **vii** 9
Chautemps, Camille (President of the French Council of Ministers, June 1937–Mar. 1938;

Vice-President, April 1938–9), **i** 83, 85; **ii** 535; **iii** 288, 391
Conversation with Sir E. Phipps, **vii** 279–80
Chauvel, Jean (French Consul-General at Vienna, 1938; then Head of Far Eastern Department, French Ministry of Foreign Affairs), **iv** 42; **ix** 247, 251, 342, 359, 379, 446n
Chen, General (Chief of Chinese Air Staff), **viii** 102
Chen Chi-tang (a Chinese military leader), **viii** 160n, 364n
Chen, K. P. (Head of Chinese Mission to the United States, Dec. 1938), **viii** 302
Chen Lu (Minister for Foreign Affairs in 'Reformed' Chinese Government), **viii** 431, 464, 466, 506–7
Chen Wei-cheng, Dr. (Counsellor of Chinese Embassy, London), **ix** 209
Cheng Hsiang-mao (Principal of the Far East Middle School, Tientsin), **viii** 354
Cheng Lien-shih (Superintendent of Customs, Tientsin), *assassination of,* **ix** 1, 3, 211; the four men arrested as suspects, **ix** 66–7, 72, 83–4, 97, 106, 116, 118–23, 126–7, 139, 145, 155–237 *passim,* 325, 338, 356–535 *passim*
Chi Nien-hua, **ix** 111, 118, 122–4, 126–7, 180
Chiang Kai-shek, Generalissimo (Commander-in-Chief of Chinese armed forces, member of Central Executive Committee of the Kuomintang), **viii** 2n, 4, 6n, 7–8, 12n, 21, 27, 74–5, 86–7, 89, 98, 102, 108, 119, 130, 132n, 146, 148, 150, 156, 158–60, 190, 202–3, 219, 225, 249–50, 263, 277, 284, 292–3, 295–6, 306, 309, 345, 352n, 363–4, 369, 377, 408–10, 415, 417, 429–30, 433, 435, 437, 445, 455, 466–7, 469–70, 474, 485–6, 503, 510, 519, 524; **ix** 13, 17, 31, 33, 92–3, 95, 158–9, 174–5, 183, 198, 201, 209, 211–2, 220, 228, 231, 235, 240, 243, 252, 254, 259–61, 264, 276, 286, 288, 293, 295, 307, 316, 318, 326, 340, 372–3, 385–6, 392, 411–2, 427n, 428–9, 432, 442, 476n, 481, 490, 495, 523, 527
To Sir A. Clark Kerr, **viii** 477
Conversation with Sir A. Clark Kerr, **viii** 4, 195–6, 216–8; **ix** 52–3, 99–100
Conversation with Mr. Greenway, **viii** 136–7
Chiang Kai-shek, Madame, **viii** 219, 249; **ix** 33, 67, 295
Chibisov, General (Chief of Staff of Leningrad Military District), **vii** 45
Chichery, M. (President of Socialist Radical Group in French Chamber of Deputies), **ii** 605
Chichibu, Prince (Brother of the Emperor of Japan), **viii** 276, 334
Conversation with Sir R. Craigie, **viii** 276–7
Chichibu, Princess, **viii** 276
Chilston, 2nd Viscount (H.M. Ambassador at Moscow, Oct. 1933–Nov. 1938), **i** 346, 419; **iii** 280n; **iv** 45, 629n; **v** 542; **viii** 40n

To Viscount Halifax, **i** 54, 65, 161, 172; **ii**
179, 229, 266, 298, 617; **iii** 192, 280, 629,
631; **viii** 38
Conversation with M. Fierlinger, **ii** 229
Conversation with M. Litvinov, **i** 54; **iii** 280
Letter to Mr. Collier, **ii** 140, 141*n*
Note to M. Litvinov, **iv** 629

Chodacki, Marjan (Polish Commissioner-Gen-
eral at Danzig), **ii** 689; **iii** 442, 558–9; **iv** 156,
159, 181, 280–1; **v** 25, 466, 476, 514, 538, 561,
576, 623, 626, 733–4, 764; **vi** 7, 9, 26, 44, 148,
214, 293, 337–8, 364–5, 386–7, 401, 452, 455,
461, 491, 505, 527, 568, 577, 594, 597, 610–4,
621–2, 624, 640, 647, 650, 652, 668, 683, 685,
689–91, 696–7, 717; **vii** 6–7, 9, 11–2, 31, 129,
152, 190, 219, 240, 269, 296, 355–6, 363,
543

Cholerton, Mr. (Correspondent of 'Daily
Telegraph' in Moscow), **ii** 142

Chou En-lai (Vice-Chairman of Executive
Committee of Chinese Communists), **viii** 198

Christie, Colonel M. G., **i** 556, 630

Christitch, Bochko (Yugoslav Minister at Rome,
1937–41), **iii** 358; **v** 129, 551; **vi** 166
Conversation with Earl of Perth, **iv** 333

Christoff, Dr. Theodore (Bulgarian Minister at
Angora, 1936–9), **v** 464; **vi** 30, 53, 68, 84, 147,
169, 263

Chu Min-yi (Chief Secretary of Chinese Executive Yuan, 1932–5), **ix** 368–9

Churchill, Winston Spencer (M.P. for Epping),
i 630; **ii** 683, 685; **iii** 158, 172, 261, 272, 526;
iv 59; **vi** 297, 305, 752; **vii** 550
Conversation with Herr Henlein, **i** 297–8,
633–5
Conversation with Herr von Kleist, **ii** 687–8
Letter to Herr von Kleist, **ii** 688
Speech in House of Commons, May 19, 1939,
vi 54
Statement to the press, Nov. 7, 1938, **iii** 259,
263

Chvalkovsky, Frantisek (Czechoslovak Minister
at Rome, 1932–8; Minister for Foreign
Affairs, Oct. 1938–Mar. 1939), **i** 439; **iii** 96,
114, 124*n*, 150–1, 170, 187–8, 212, 220, 234,
376–7, 380, 384, 408, 411, 418, 420–1, 428,
448, 559; **iv** 126–7, 180, 204, 233, 239, 242–3,
246, 368, 441, 566
Conversation with Mr. Newton, **iii** 140–1,
221–2, 423–4; **iv** 220–1
Conversation with the Earl of Perth, **iii** 126–7
Conversation with Mr. Troutbeck, **iv** 129–30
Visits to Berlin, Oct. 1938, **iii** 174, 190–2,
222; **iv** 3; Jan. 1939, **iv** 7–8, 61–3;
referred to, **iii** 378, 386, 446, 610; **iv** 1–3,
32, 54–6, 86, 180, 227; Mar. 1939, **iv**
403–5, 443–4; *referred to,* **iv** 246–7,
255–6, 258–9, 270

Ciano di Cortellazzo, Admiral Count Costanza
(President of Italian Chamber of Deputies,
1934–9), **iii** 464–5, 469–70; *death of,* **vi** 252;
vii 336

Ciano di Cortellazzo, Count Galeazzo (Italian
Minister for Foreign Affairs, 1936–43), **i** 14,
20, 23, 27, 33, 261–2, 291, 322*n*, 366–7; **ii** 101,
561, 588, 591, 600, 608; **iii** 62*n*, 63, 174, 220,
222, 245, 297, 312–8, 322–4, 328–42, 353–4,
356–8, 362, 385, 463–9, 471–2, 474, 476, 480,
486, 488–9, 497–8, 502, 506, 511–2, 516–7,
533; **iv** 17, 61, 87, 171, 227, 281, 292, 296–7,
302–3, 305, 313, 315, 317, 321–4, 326–7,
331–3, 339–40, 343, 346–9, 353, 359, 401, 507,
547, 556; **v** 2, 124–6, 131, 132*n*, 135–7, 139,
142–3, 145–7, 152–4, 159–60, 169, 171, 173,
175–6, 181–2, 195, 222*n*, 230, 263–4, 277, 342,
346, 348, 376–7, 386, 400, 426, 428–9, 432,
442, 474, 477, 551, 566–7, 611, 613, 654–5,
703, 706–7, 732, 737, 774, 780, 799, 800–3;
vi 19, 21, 115, 127, 146, 166, 220–1, 240–1,
273–4, 284, 290, 324, 358, 439, 443, 472, 556,
588, 596, 628, 658–9, 665–6, 701, 723; **vii**
52–3, 55–6, 62, 76, 81, 83, 93, 95, 120, 139–40,
145, 148, 156, 159, 165, 168, 185–6, 191, 199,
244, 247–8, 263, 266, 302–4, 311, 322–3, 326,
329–30, 333, 335–6, 349–51, 362, 369–70, 373,
386–7, 391–2, 395, 405, 411, 424, 427, 444–5,
477–8, 481, 483, 489, 491–2, 497–8, 511,
516–7, 524–6, 530–1; **viii** 179, 239, 269, 437*n*
To Viscount Halifax, **iii** 540
Conversation with Mr. C. Brown, **iii** 516–7
Conversation with Sir N. Charles, **ii** 101–2,
130–1, 331–2; **iv** 348–9, 358–9
Conversation with M. François-Poncet, **v** 347,
759
Conversation with M. François-Poncet and
Sir P. Loraine, **vii** 505–6
Conversation with Viscount Halifax, **iii** 521–3;
vii 302, 310, 358, 436–7, 442, 465, 507–8,
518–9
Conversation with Sir P. Loraine, **v** 442–3,
599, 754–6; **vi** 15–7, 21, 252–4, 450, 453,
578–9; **vii** 59–61, 144–5, 157–8, 181–2,
299, 302, 307, 336–7, 339, 366–7, 392–3,
438–9, 459, 483, 491–2, 520–1
Conversation with Earl of Perth, **i** 27–9,
261–2, 342–3, 353; **ii** 600, 602–3, 642–4;
iii 319–21, 324–7, 329, 336–9, 344–6,
356–7, 458–9, 467–70, 478, 490–1; **iv** 298,
306–8, 316–7, 319–20, 340; **v** 120–2,
128–9, 149–51, 172
Conversation with Herr von Ribbentrop. *See
below, Visit to* Germany, Aug. 1939, *and
also* Ribbentrop, Joachim von (*Visit to*
Milan, Rome)
Note to M. François-Poncet, Dec. 17, 1938;
iii 491
Note to Earl of Perth, Jan. 1939, **iv** 634
Speech on Nov. 30, 1938, **iii** 462
Speech on April 15, 1939, **v** 219; *referred to,* **v**
229, 258

Ciano, Count (*cont.*)
  Visit to Germany, May 1939, **v** 598, 656;
    Aug. 1939, **vi** 643, 658, 667, 675, 678,
    699–700, 720; **vii** 13, 19–20, 23, 55, 62,
    71–2, 79–80, 103, 110, 123, 138–9, 491–2
  Visit to Spain, July 1939, **vi** 284, 453
  Visit to Tirana, April 1939, **v** 149, 187, 193
  Visit to Warsaw, Feb. 1939, **iv** 177–9,
    182; *referred to*, **iii** 459n, 572; **iv** 143, 152,
    163, 201–2, 206, 335
  At Anglo-Italian conversations, 1939, **iii**
    517, 520, 534–5
  At Munich Conference, **ii** 631, 633
Ciano, Countess Galeazzo, **iii** 540; **iv** 177, 179
Cinkar-Markovitch, Aleksander (Yugoslav Min-
  ister at Berlin, Dec. 1935–Feb. 1939; Minister
  for Foreign Affairs, Feb. 1939–Mar. 1941), **i**
  614–5; **iv** 333, 384–5, 388; **v** 79, 275, 348, 481,
  490–1, 498, 551, 597, 672, 681–2, 708, 729,
  739–40, 798; **vi** 66, 69–70, 167, 228–9
  Conversation with Sir R. Campbell, **v** 596–7
  Conversation with M. Gafencu, **v** 659–62,
    676, 686–7, 725
  Conversation with Sir N. Henderson, **ii** 241
  Visit to Germany, **v** 287, 395, 551, 660, 662,
    681, 740; **vi** 18
  Visit to Italy, **v** 287, 294, 348, 551, 588–9,
    660, 686
Cipera, Dominik (Czechoslovak Minister of
  Public Works in Dr. Beran's Cabinet, 1938–9),
  iii 377
Clanchy, Captain H. (British Naval Attaché at
  Moscow, Oct. 1936–Jan. 1942), **vii** 45, 562
Clark, F. de Castello-Branco (Brazilian Ambassador at Tokyo, 1939–42), **ix** 31
Clark, H. H. (H.M. Acting Consul at Palermo,
  1936–8), **iii** 347
Clark Kerr, Sir Archibald (H.M. Ambassador
  in China, Feb. 1938–Feb. 1942), **viii** 6n, 12,
  15–7, 23, 48, 67, 84, 87, 89, 97, 105, 106n, 109,
  113n, 117, 123n, 132n, 133n, 137n, 138n, 139,
  150n, 158, 165, 210, 224–5, 227, 231, 233n,
  242, 258, 293, 297n, 322n, 337n, 338n, 388,
  390, 407, 410n, 453, 467n, 483n, 532n, 533,
  537n, 539n, 542–3, 549, 551; **ix** 7, 17, 67,
  70, 85, 96–7, 103n, 106, 122–3, 126, 158, 160–2,
  174–5, 190, 196, 204, 250, 262, 275, 314n,
  354n, 361n, 365, 379, 381, 412–3, 416–7, 424,
  427, 431n, 432, 434, 436–7, 485, 500, 535
  To British Embassy, Shanghai, **ix** 37
  To Sir A. Cadogan, **ix** 92, 95, 99
  To Sir R. Craigie, **viii** 330; **ix** 164, 461, 478
  To Mr. Fitzmaurice, **ix** 266
  To Mr. Greenway, **viii** 388, 409, 466, 510,
    523
  To Viscount Halifax, **viii** 2, 4, 6, 10, 15,
    17–9, 21, 24, 41–2, 49, 50, 55, 81, 101,
    103, 106, 111, 123, 131–2, 137, 156, 160,
    195, 202, 216, 218, 246, 249, 251, 283,
    310, 332, 337, 361, 363, 369, 375, 379,

414, 427, 429, 431, 433, 439, 447, 451,
    463, 469, 474, 490, 506, 511, 514, 525,
    531, 533, 535, 537, 552, 556; **ix** 18, 31,
    33–4, 43, 52, 72, 78, 119, 132, 140, 156–7,
    169, 177, 203, 228, 230, 250, 255, 259,
    268, 275, 285, 288, 292, 295, 312, 316–7,
    326, 340–1, 343, 347, 366–72, 382, 386,
    423, 428, 444, 452, 456, 466, 504, 519
  To Mr. Howe, **viii** 130; **ix** 82
  To Mr. Jamieson, **viii** 322, 417, 462, 479,
    523, 554–5; **ix** 106, 139, 167
  To Mr. Prideaux-Brune, **ix** 242, 316
  To Sir J. Simon, **viii** 385, 392, 399
  To Mr. Stark Toller, **viii** 524
  Conversation with Generalissimo Chiang Kai-
    shek, **viii** 4, 195–6, 216–8; **ix** 52–3,
    99–100
  Message to General Chiang Kai-shek, Jan.
    1939, **viii** 410–1; March 1939, **viii** 523–4;
    July 1939, **ix** 242
  Movements of, **viii** 2n, 27n, 44, 130, 142n,
    249n, 433n; **ix** 18n, 19n, 92n, 106n
  Views on British policy in the Far East, **viii**
    8, 41, 50, 103, 196, 251–2, 332, 379; **ix**
    201, 228–9, 231–2, 428–30
Clary-Aldringen, Prince and Princess (Hosts of
  Lord Runciman in Czechoslovakia), **ii** 670
Clauzel, M. (a member of French Ministry of
  Foreign Affairs), **iii** 285
Clerk, Sir George (H.M. Minister at Prague,
  1919–26), **i** 520, 529
Cleverly, O. S. (Principal Private Secretary to
  the Prime Minister, 1936–9), **iii** 532, 534
Clive, Sir Robert H. (H.M. Ambassador at
  Brussels, July 1937–Nov. 1939), **viii** 289; **ix**
  146
  To Viscount Halifax, **iv** 48, 58, 67, 69, 75,
    106, 450, 508; **v** 256, 269, 271; **vii** 270,
    312, 329, 338, 340
  To Sir J. Simon, **iii** 583
  Conversation with M. Janson, **iv** 69–70
  Conversation with King Leopold III, **vii** 312
  Conversation with M. Soudan, **iv** 508–9
  Letter to Sir O. Sargent, **iv** 66; **vi** 221
Coburg, Duke of. *See* Saxe-Coburg-Gotha,
  Duke Leopold of
Cochrane, Commander Hon. Sir Archibald D.
  (Governor of Burma, 1936–41), **viii** 160
Codreanu, M. (Chief of Roumanian Iron
  Guard), **i** 217
Colbern, Major W. H. (U.S. Military Attaché
  at Warsaw), **v** 247–8
Colijn, Dr. H. (Netherlands Prime Minister,
  1925–6 and 1933–9), **iii** 388; **iv** 16–7, 28, 48
Collier, Group Captain A. C. (a member of
  British Military Delegation to Moscow, Aug.
  1939), **vii** 562, 607
Collier, Laurence (Counsellor in the Foreign
  Office: Head of Northern Department), **ii**
  140, 141n, 179; **iv** 14, 639

Conversation with M. Balutis, **iv** 378n, 533–4, 638–9
Minute by, **iv** 638
Colson, General L. A., **iv** 75
Coltman, Captain T. A. H. (a member of British Military Delegation to Moscow, Aug. 1939), **vii** 562, 602
Colvin, Ian (Correspondent in Berlin of the 'News Chronicle'), **iii** 366
Colyer, Wing Commander D. (British Air Attaché at Paris, 1936–40), **iv** 237
Conversation with Lt.-Col. de Vitrolles, **iii** 583–5; **v** 488–9
Comnène, Petrescu (Roumanian Minister for Foreign Affairs, Aug.–Dec. 1938), **ii** 135, 137, 151, 157, 179, 204, 235; **iii** 47, 97n, 112n, 233; **v** 333
Conversation with Dr. Fabricius, **ii** 179–80
Conversation with Sir M. Palairet, **iii** 45–6, 197
Conversation with Lord de la Warr, **ii** 354–5; **iii** 18–9
Condé, D. P. Garcia (Spanish Ambassador at Rome, 1937–40), **iii** 358
Conwell-Evans, T. P. (Joint Honorary Secretary of the Anglo-German Fellowship), **iv** 18
Cooper, Alfred Duff. *See* Duff Cooper, Alfred
Corbin, André Charles (French Ambassador at London, 1933–40), **i** 50n, 322, 339, 404, 523, 563, 577; **ii** 72, 160, 246, 292–3, 306, 477, 570, 590; **iii** 59, 78, 97, 203, 444, 447, 468, 502–3, 505, 510n, 554, 637; **iv** 3, 368, 473, 510, 628n; **v** 124, 127, 178, 273–4, 480, 502, 508–9, 527–8, 551–2, 565–6, 640n, 680n, 693, 778, 790, 800; **vi** 22, 25, 33, 167, 169, 180, 208, 239–40, 310, 340n, 398, 493; **vii** 79, 167, 245, 333, 341, 371, 398n, 406, 417n, 423, 443, 449, 501–2; **viii** 256; **ix** 145, 313
To Sir A. Cadogan, **ii** 427
To Viscount Halifax, **ii** 359, 584; **v** 96, 396
Conversation with Sir A. Cadogan, **i** 339, 498–500, 551–3; **iii** 330; **iv** 70–1, 90–1, 170–1, 266–8, 334, 377, 486–7, 519–20; **v** 113–5, 225, 260, 452, 683n, **vi** 3–4, 95
Conversation with Viscount Halifax, **i** 35–6, 52–3, 88–90, 356–7, 477, 531–2, 563–5; **ii** 19–20, 196–8, 246–8, 262–4, 275–7, 326–8; **iii** 99–100, 258–9, 427–8, 436–7, 507–8, 511–2, 567; **iv** 42–4, 272–3, 344–5, 378–9, 532–3; **v** 49–51, 67–8, 95–6, 136–8, 234, 344–6, 385–7, 504, 507, 577–8, 772–3, 793–4; **vi** 106, 512–3; **vii** 246–9, 288–9, 342–3, 509–10; **ix** 207
Conversation with Sir O. Sargent, **iii** 634–5; **vi** 180–1, 242–3, 511–2
Letter to Sir A. Cadogan, **v** 683; **vi** 27, 98
Letter to Viscount Halifax, **v** 569, 698
Letter to Sir O. Sargent, **vi** 181–2, 328
At Anglo-French conversations, April 1938, **i** 198, 205; Sept. 1938, **ii** 373, 520, 536;

Nov. 1938, **iii** 285; Mar. 22, 1939, **iv** 457, 459–60
Cordell Hull. *See* Hull, Cordell
Cortesi, Mgr. Filippo (Apostolic Nuncio in Poland, 1937–9), **v** 466; **vi** 371; **vii** 301, 402–3
Cosmé, Henri (French Ambassador in China, Mar. 1939–1943), **ix** 57, 97, 119, 125, 141, 312, 353, 361, 418, 444, 462, 478
Cot, Pierre (French Minister for Air, 1933–4, 1936–7), **i** 581n, 617; **ii** 508
Coulondre, Robert (French Ambassador at Moscow, 1936–8; at Berlin, Nov. 1938–Sept. 1939), **iii** 193, 234–5, 242, 296, 310, 390–1, 446, 465, 489, 493, 586, 607; **iv** 41, 86, 167–8, 223, 232, 246, 260, 263, 268–9, 371, 376, 442–3, 461, 594–5, 601, 641–6; **v** 724, 770, 778, 791, 802; **vi** 2, 17, 150, 192, 198, 235–7, 318, 331, 368, 396, 399; **vii** 68, 78, 109, 132, 145, 192, 277–8, 286–7, 289, 295, 316n, 317, 341, 376, 443, 454, 485, 492–3, 500, 525, 535, 538–9
recall to Paris, Mar. 1939, **iv** 376, 382, 394, 461, 468, 490, 595–6; *return to* Berlin, June 1939, **v** 790
Conversation with Sir N. Henderson, **vi** 348
Conversation with Herr Hitler, **vii** 288
Conversation with Sir G. Ogilvie-Forbes, **iv** 41
Conversation with Mr. Vereker and Col. Firebrace, **i** 303–7, 402
Conversation with Baron von Weizsäcker, **iv** 264–5; **v** 527–8
Coulondre, Madame, **iii** 391
Craigie, Sir Robert L. (H.M. Ambassador at Tokyo, Sept. 1937–Dec. 1941), **iii** 668; **vii** 482; **viii** 5n, 6n, 17, 19, 21, 23, 30, 40n, 41, 48, 50, 70n, 77, 79n, 82, 111, 124, 126n, 133, 137, 151n, 156, 157n, 164, 167, 168n, 170n, 176n, 195n, 206n, 211, 226n, 232n, 234, 246n, 247n, 249, 251, 255n, 257n, 265n, 298n, 301, 307n, 311, 312n, 313n, 319, 324n, 332n, 341, 370, 377n, 379, 392, 408, 413–5, 419, 433–4, 436, 448–9, 452, 457–8, 474, 542–3, 549; **ix** 3n, 31, 49–50, 53–4, 58n, 74, 98n, 103, 145–6, 151, 160–1, 172, 176–7, 182–3, 187, 201, 210, 218n, 223, 228, 231, 245–7, 249, 251–5, 258, 260–1, 272, 283, 285, 288, 311n, 316, 323, 326, 330, 342, 344, 359–60, 366–8, 372, 381, 388, 390, 411, 418, 420–1, 428–30, 432, 438, 444, 447, 450, 464, 466–7, 484–5, 487–8, 503–5, 514, 521, 528–30, 532–3
To Mr. Arita, **viii** 200, 206, 367, 403
To British Embassy, Shanghai, **viii** 125, 434; **ix** 168
To Sir A. Cadogan, **ix** 91, 93–5, 101–2
To Sir A. Clark Kerr, **ix** 431, 454, 487
To Mr. J. C. Grew, **viii** 316
To Viscount Halifax, **viii** 1, 13–4, 22–3, 26, 29, 31, 34, 36–7, 43, 46, 51, 53, 55, 57, 62, 64–5, 69, 73–5, 77, 79, 82, 84–8, 91, 96–7,

Craigie, Sir R. (*cont.*)

To Viscount Halifax (*cont.*)

105, 107–8, 110, 114–7, 120, 122, 124–9, 131, 133–4, 136, 138–9, 141, 151–2, 154, 158, 161–2, 166, 168, 170, 172, 174–7, 179–81, 183–5, 187, 190, 199, 201–2, 204–7, 209, 211, 214, 219, 224, 226, 228, 231, 234, 236–7, 240, 243, 247, 253–5, 266, 269–71, 276–81, 283–4, 289–90, 294–6, 298–9, 302–4, 307, 311, 313, 316, 320, 324, 327, 334, 339–40, 342, 344, 346–9, 353, 355, 359, 362, 367–9, 377, 382, 403, 405, 419, 425, 432, 439, 442, 446, 451–2, 460, 470, 475–6, 479, 482, 485, 488, 493, 499, 501–3, 505, 513, 518, 532, 536–8, 551, 553; **ix** 5, 12, 17, 21, 23, 26, 35, 42–5, 49, 56–9, 64, 69, 78–80, 85, 88, 106–9, 114, 127–8, 134, 138–9, 142, 148, 152, 157–8, 161, 163, 170, 173, 176, 178, 185–6, 189–90, 195–6, 198–9, 207–9, 211, 214–5, 217, 219–23, 226, 229, 232–4, 239, 241–2, 245, 249, 255, 261, 263, 265, 267, 273–4, 276–8, 280–2, 285, 287, 291, 296–8, 300–5, 308, 310–1, 313–5, 318–21, 323–4, 337–8, 342, 344, 346, 349, 351, 353, 355–6, 358, 361, 363–4, 369–70, 376, 378–9, 381, 385–7, 392, 394–7, 399, 400–1, 403, 405–6, 409, 411, 415, 424–7, 431, 433, 436, 441, 443, 445, 451–3, 457, 459, 461, 468–70, 473–5, 478, 480–1, 489, 492, 495, 497, 500–3, 515, 518–9, 522–3, 525–6

To Mr. Jamieson, **ix** 256, 494

To Mr. Sawada, **viii** 171, 221, 420

To Sir J. Simon, **viii** 387, 389–91, 393, 399

Conversation with Mr. Arita, **viii** 202, 211, 234–6, 260, 262–7, 304–6, 344–7, 393–4, 442–4, 460–1, 536, 537n; **ix** 21–2, 26, 56, 142–3, 157–8, 170–1, 199, 207–8, 219–21, 229–30, 245, 278–80, 282–3, 298–302, 305–8

Conversation with M. Arsène-Henry, **viii** 184

Conversation with Prince Chichibu, **viii** 276–7

Conversation with Mr. Dooman, **ix** 148, 185–6, 394–5

Conversation with Mr. Grew, **viii** 183–4, 264

Conversation with the Emperor Hirohito, **viii** 276–7

Conversation with Mr. Horinouchi, **viii** 64–5, 91–2, 107–8, 115–6, 125–6

Conversation with Mr. Kato, **ix** 255, 392–3, 400–1, 433–4, 443, 453–4, 469–70, 473–4, 502–3

Conversation with General Koiso, **ix** 173–6

Conversation with Prince Konoye, **viii** 128–9, 175–7

Conversation with General Ott, **viii** 31

Conversation with Mr. Sawada, **viii** 279–80, 281–2, 344, 476, 502–4; **ix** 44–5, 91n, 214, 226, 526–7

Conversation with General Ugaki, **viii** 5n, 12n, 13n, 26–8, 34–5, 73–7, 86–7, 91, 96–101

Letter to Sir A. Cadogan, **viii** 528

Letter to Mr. Howe, **viii** 492

Letter to Mr. Ikeda, **viii** 530

Views and suggestions, on British policy in Far East, **vii** 29, 36, 53–4, 62, 105, 117–8, 122–3, 141, 161–2, 180, 189–93, 209, 215–6, 291–3, 312, 453; **ix** 235, 277, 286–7, 382, 411–3, 437, 495–6, 500, 504; on treatment of terrorists in China, **ix** 5, 59, 85, 106, 127, 143, 161–2, 168, 170, 190, 363–4, 386, 427, 431–4, 443, 497, 523

Craigie, Lady, **viii** 276, 529

Crawley, Mr. (an employee of Customs Administration, Hankow), **viii** 3

Cretzianu, M. (Secretary–General of Roumanian Ministry of Foreign Affairs), **v** 91, 207, 358, 687, 708, 723; **vi** 118

Conversation with Sir A. Cadogan, **v** 111–3

Conversation with Viscount Halifax, **v** 74–7, 657–63

Crolla, Guido (Counsellor of Italian Embassy at London; acted as Chargé d'Affaires), **ii** 119, 172; **iii** 174, 327; **iv** 637; **v** 125, 131–5, 145–6, 149–50, 152–3, 157–9, 163, 181, 196; **vii** 517

Conversation with Viscount Halifax, **v** 127–8, 140–3, 146–7, 151, 153–7, 164, 343

Cromer, 2nd Earl of, **iii** 89–90

Crosby, Sir J. (H.M. Minister at Bangkok, Aug. 1934–Feb. 1942), **viii** 320, 549

Crowe, Sir Eyre (Permanent Under-Secretary of State for Foreign Affairs, 1920–5), 'the Crowe tradition', **ii** 131; **vi** 14

Crutzescu, Radu (Roumanian Minister at Prague, 1938–9), **iii** 51, 112, 222

Csaky, Count Istvan (Private Secretary to Hungarian Minister for Foreign Affairs, 1935–8; Minister for Foreign Affairs, Dec. 1938–Jan. 1941), **ii** 233, 239; **iii** 6, 111, 121; **iv** 8, 163, 202, 434, 511; **v** 2, 62–3, 78, 300, 302, 309, 332–3, 614–5; **vi** 583, 585, 660n, **vii** 350, 361

Conversation with Sir G. Knox, **iv** 55–6, 395–6

Visits to Germany, **iv** 55; **v** 210n; **vi** 720; **vii** 83, 92, 377

Visit to Italy, **vii** 71, 83

Cummings, A. J. (Political Editor of the 'News Chronicle'), **viii** 457

Cunningham, Vice-Admiral Sir A. B. (Deputy Chief of Naval Staff, 1938–9)

Conversation with Admiral Raeder, **iii** 671

Speeches at Anglo-German Naval conversations, Dec. 30, 1938, **iii** 664–71

Custoza, Count P. Morano di (Italian Ambassador at The Vatican, 1935–9), **vi** 304, 316, 372; **vii** 20, 448

Cvetkovitch, Drogisha (Yugoslav Prime Minister, Feb. 1939–Mar. 1941), **v** 34n

Czech, Dr. Ludwig (Czechoslovak Minister of Health, 1935–8), **i** 69

Czernin, Count (Host of Lord Runciman in Czechoslovakia), ii 671–3
Czerny, M., ii 672–3

Dahlerus, Birger, vi 216, 759n; vii 66, 176, 194–5, 242, 281–6, 318n, 321–2, 325, 327, 337n, 356–7, 362n, 368, 393, 405, 410n, 417n, 440, 443, 453, 466–7, 537, 551–5
  Conversation with Sir A. Cadogan, vii 479–80
  Conversation with Mr. Chamberlain, vii 282n, 395–8
  Conversation with Field-Marshal Göring, vi 744–51, 759n; vii 194, 220, 231–4, 282–5, 360–1, 396–7, 399–400
  Conversation with Field-Marshal Göring and Herr Hitler, vii 284–5
  Conversation with Viscount Halifax, vi 483–4; vii 234n, 281–3, 395–8
  Conversation with Sir N. Henderson, vii 512–3
  Conversation with M. Lipski, vii 445–6
  Conversation with Mr. Mensforth, vii 551
  Conversation with Sir G. Ogilvie-Forbes, vii 319–20
  Conversation with Mr. Roberts, vii 537n
  Conversation with Mr. Spencer, vii 219–20, 356–7, 368, 474–5, 485
  Conversation with Sir H. Wernher, vii 320n
  Conversation with Sir H. Wilson, vii 441–2
  Meeting in London with British business men, vi 743, 751–8
  Proposed visit to London, Sept. 1, 1939, vii 474–5, 480, 485
Daladier, Édouard (President of the French Council of Ministers and Minister of War, April 1938–Mar. 1940), i 198, 236, 257, 324, 357, 484, 460, 477, 554–5, 561, 591; ii 2, 275–6, 278, 292, 311, 361–2, 373, 409, 444n, 452, 459, 481, 508–9, 512, 514, 516, 546–7, 559, 566, 568, 583, 588, 594, 599–601, 605–6, 613, 629–32, 641, 675; iii 87, 89, 93n, 127, 151, 157, 249–50, 257, 259, 262, 322, 346, 352, 355, 391–2, 396, 421, 427, 462, 479, 483, 507, 524, 569, 579, 619; iv 48–9, 336, 342, 353–4, 372, 382, 395, 434, 457, 462, 469, 532, 596, 603; v 49, 92, 105, 107–8, 113–5, 126, 130, 146, 148, 166, 178, 217, 252, 259, 263, 272, 279, 302, 342, 347, 356, 395, 403, 411, 414, 432, 456, 523, 663–5, 691, 693, 698, 703, 763, 799, 800; vi 62, 64, 150, 185, 212–3, 215, 236–7, 301–3, 317, 330, 398, 489–91, 562–3, 674, 678, 752, 754; vii 15, 18, 21, 78–9, 96n, 103, 107, 117, 131, 165–6, 245–8, 277–80, 289, 295, 314, 379, 406, 439, 443, 489, 503, 506, 508, 511, 515, 518, 520, 523, 529–30, 558, 563, 604
  Conversation with Mr. Campbell, vii 163–4
  Conversation with Mr. Chamberlain, ii 537n; vii 524–5
  Conversation with Viscount Halifax, i 601–3; v 608–14, 623–5
  Conversation with Sir E. Phipps, ii 269–70,

311–2, 329; iii 257–8; iv 50–1, 354–5; v 148, 151–2, 239–40, 276–8; vi 2, 357–8; vii 449, 463–4
  Letter to Mr. Chamberlain, vi 471
  Message to Mr. Chamberlain, Sept. 13, 1938, ii 313
  Message to Herr Hitler, vii 278, 287
  Speech on July 12, 1938, i 554, 561, 578; Jan. 26, 1939, iv 50n; March 29, iv 355n, 358; *referred to,* v 119, 124; vi 471; June 27, vi 213
  Speeches at Anglo–French conversations, April 1938, i 198, 202–3, 205–7, 209, 211, 216–9, 225–7, 229–30, 232; Sept. 18, ii 373, 379–84, 386–99; Sept. 25, ii 522–35; Sept. 26, ii 537–40; Nov. 1938, iii 285, 287–94, 298–306, 310; Jan. 1939, iii 512–5
  Statement to the press, May 4, 1939, v 438–9; Sept. 27, 1939, ii 574
  suggested visit to Great Britain, Aug. 1939, vii 167, 401, 404, 406
Dalton, Dr. Hugh (M.P. for Bishop Auckland), v 21, 310; vi 577
Daly, Colonel T. D. (British Military Attaché at Berlin, May–Sept. 1939), vii 16, 97, 266, 309, 337, 415–6, 419, 454, 514, 517
  Memorandum by, vi 698
Damm, General (French military representative on a sub-committee of International Commission set up in Oct. 1938), iii 163
Danckwerts, Captain V. H. (Director of Plans, Admiralty), iv 237
  Letter to Mr. Perowne, iii 451n
  Speeches at Anglo-German Naval conversations, Dec. 30, 1938, iii 666–70
Daranyi, Dr. Kalman (Hungarian Prime Minister, Oct. 1936–May 1938), iii 188
Darré, Dr. Walther (German Minister of Food and Agriculture, 1933–45), ii 691; v 805; vi 47, 705
Dastich, Colonel F. (Czechoslovak Military Attaché at Moscow, 1936–9), i 165, 172–3, 419, 423–4
  Conversation with Col. Firebrace, i 420–1
Dautry, Raoul (Director of State Railways, France), iii 258
Davaz, Suat. *See* Suat Davaz
Davidov, M. (Soviet Trade Commissioner at Berlin), iv 134
Davidson, Colonel F. H. N. (a member of British Military Delegation to Moscow, Aug. 1939), vii 562, 602, 606–8
Davies, Mr. (President of the 'Canadian Press'), vi 720
Davignon, Vicomte J. (Belgian Ambassador at Berlin, 1938–40), ii 59; iv 230, 442; v 232, 244, 265, 423; vi 349, 412, 634
  Conversation with Sir N. Henderson, vi 348

Davis, Wing Commander E. P. M. (British Air Attaché at Brussels, July 1937–May 1940), **iv** 78

Déat, Marcel (French Minister for Air, 1936), **v** 414, 438–9

Decoux, Vice-Admiral J. (Commander-in-Chief, French Naval Forces in the Far East), **ix** 361

Dekanozov, V. G. (a member of Soviet Commissariat for Foreign Affairs), **v** 545

De la Baume, Comte (Head of Economic Dept., French Foreign Office), **iv** 598, 601

Delacroix, L. V. *See* Lacroix, Léopold Victor de

De la Howarderie, Comte F. de Chastel. *See* Chastel de la Howarderie, Comte F. de

Delamain, Major C. B. H. (Brigade Major at Tientsin), **viii** 504, 512

De la Rocque, Colonel (Proprietor of the 'Petit Journal'), **v** 439

De la Tournelle, Guy Le Roy (French Consul at Danzig, 1934–9), **iii** 553–4, 561; **vi** 10, 401, 419, 657, 659, 697

De la Vaillée, A. Paternotte. *See* Paternotte de la Vaillée, A.

De la Warr, 9th Earl (Lord Privy Seal, May 1937–Oct. 1938), **ii** 625; **iii** 434; **viii** 83
  Conversation with M. Comnène, **ii** 354–5; **iii** 18–9
  Conversation (with Mr. Butler) with M. Litvinov and M. Maisky, **ii** 497–8

Delbos, Yvon (French Minister for Foreign Affairs, 1936–8), **i** 35, 41, 51–2, 83, 85, 144, 199, 216, 277; **iii** 485–6; **v** 356
  Declaration of Dec. 4, 1936 *re* French assistance to Great Britain, **iii** 260, 288, 426, 446

Delebecque, J. (a French journalist), **v** 414

Dembinski, M. (a Polish journalist), **v** 425

Denain, General (French Minister for Air, 1934–6), **iii** 289

Denis, Lt.-Gen. H. J. C. E. (Belgian Minister for National Defence, 1936–42), **iv** 66, 76–7

Denisov, Major (Military Commandant of the city of Leningrad), **vii** 45

Dennis, R. H. (Chief of Municipal Police, British Concession, Tientsin), **viii** 383, 504; **ix** 66, 72. 160, 161n, 166, 179, 216, 322, 346, 370, 377

Dentz, General (Deputy Chief of French General Staff), **ii** 453; **iii** 570; **iv** 330n; **vi** 88; **vii** 206
  Conversation with Colonel Fraser, **ii** 473–4; **iii** 159–60; **iv** 221–2

Derby, 17th Earl of, **vi** 723

Dew, A. R. (Secretary, H.M. Embassy, Moscow, Sept. 1938–Feb. 1940), **vii** 190

Diana, Marchese Pasquali (Italian Minister at The Hague, 1938–40), **vii** 349

Dianu, Nicolas (Roumanian Minister at Moscow, 1938–9), **ii** 229

Dickson, A. G. (a member of Corps of Observers in Czechoslovakia, Oct. 1938), **iii** 74, 84

Didelet, Colonel H. (French Military Attaché at Berlin, 1939), **v** 240; **vii** 309

Dié, Henri, **v** 439

Dieckhoff, Dr. H. H. (German Ambassador at Washington, 1937–41), **ii** 651; **iii** 279

Diepenrykx, Lt.-Col. P. J. (Belgian Military Attaché at The Hague, 1937–40), **iv** 52

Dietrich, Dr. Otto (Head of German Press Bureau, 1934–45), **i** 178; **ii** 103; **iii** 261; **iv** 280; **vi** 585

Dijk, Dr. J. J. C. van (Netherlands Minister of Defence, 1937–9), **iv** 452

Dirksen, Dr. H. von (German Ambassador at London, May 1938–Sept. 1939), **i** 240, 247, 253, 282, 388, 440, 475, 587, 589, 591, 596; **ii** 41n, 141, 143, 297, 651–2; **iii** 435, 445, 450, 620; **iv** 143n, 273, 381n, 583, 593; **v** 245, 469, 728; **vi** 61, 76, 172, 238, 287, 337, 399, 412–3, 650; **vii** 79
  To Viscount Halifax, **iii** 422; **iv** 583, 636
  Conversation with Sir A. Cadogan, **i** 598–9; **iv** 583
  Conversation with Mr. N. Chamberlain, **i** 618–20
  Conversation with Viscount Halifax, **i** 239–40, 355–6, 369–71, 454–8; **iii** 127–8, 433–5, 439–40, 566–7; **iv** 138–41, 270–2, 272n, 380–1; **v** 600–3; **vi** 88–9, 647–8
  Conversation with Sir N. Henderson, **ii** 48–9, 59; **v** 429–30
  Conversation with Sir H. Wilson, **ii** 351–3; **vi** 579–82
  Letter to Mr. Chamberlain, **ii** 60; **iv** 143

Dixon, P. J. (Secretary, H.M. Embassy, Rome, Feb. 1938–Jan. 1940)
  Minute by, **vii** 517

Djuvanni, Mgr. Vissarion, **v** 176

Djuvara, Radu T. (Roumanian Minister at Berlin, 1938–9; Ambassador at Athens, 1939–40), **i** 614; **v** 264, 395; **vi** 127–8, 130

Dlugoszowski, General B. W. (Polish Ambassador at Rome, 1938–9), **vi** 19, 665–6; **vii** 52

Dodds, J. L. (Counsellor of H.M. Embassy, Tokyo, March 1936–Sept. 1940), **viii** 64, 71, 348; **ix** 189, 480–1, 487
  To Viscount Halifax, **ix** 3

Doihara, Lt.-Gen. K. (General Officer Commanding 14th Division, Japanese army in North China), **viii** 338, 535

Dollfuss, Dr. Engelbert (Federal Chancellor of Austria, 1932–4), **i** 2, 127, 129; **vi** 506

Domaniewski, M. (a member of the Polish economic delegation in London, July–Aug. 1939), **vi** 545, 570

Domanski, Father (Leader of the Association of Poles in Germany), **v** 408

Donald, W. H. (an adviser to Generalissimo

Chiang Kai-shek), **viii** 198, 202, 249, 364, 410–1, 435, 467, 469

Donati, Major (French Assistant Military Attaché at Rome), **iv** 311–3

Donnat, Colonel P. (French Military Attaché at Budapest), **iii** 11

Dooman, E. H. (Counsellor of the U.S. Embassy, Tokyo; acted as Chargé d'Affaires), **viii** 255, 265, 271; **ix** 107–9, 124, 149, 161, 167–8, 178, 234, 240*n*, 247, 258, 303, 372, 380–1, 396, 450, 488, 490–1, 496, 500–1, 509–10, 521
   Conversation with Mr. Arita, **viii** 272–6
   Conversation with Sir R. Craigie, **ix** 148, 185–6, 394–5

Doriot, Jacques (Proprietor of 'La Liberté'), **ii** 622

Dormer, Sir Cecil (H.M. Minister to Norwegian Government, June 1934–May 1941)
   To Viscount Halifax, **vii** 422

Dörnberg, Baron von (German Chief of Diplomatic Protocol), **iv** 241

Doumenc, General (Head of French Military Delegation to Moscow, Aug. 1939), **vi** 511, 534–5, 674, 682; **vii** 2*n*, 8, 21, 34, 46, 107, 117, 121, 130, 141, 143, 150, 158, 161, 166–7, 187, 225, 560, 562–5, 567–73, 581, 583–4, 587, 594, 598, 600, 602, 604–6, 608, 613
   Conversation with Marshal Voroshilov, **vii** 609–13

Doutchitch, Jovan (Yugoslav Minister at Bucharest, 1937–9; then Ambassador, Feb. 1939 till 1940), **iii** 358; **v** 106

Dragun, Major (a member of External Relations Bureau of the Defence Commissariat of U.S.S.R.), **vii** 45

Drax, Admiral Sir Reginald A. R. Plunkett-Ernle-Erle- (Head of British Military Delegation to Moscow, 1939), **vi** 527, 641, 674; **vii** 8, 46, 108*n*, 161, 166–7, 187–8, 237, 385, 558–614 *passim*
   To Lord Chatfield, **vi** 674, 683; **vii** 3, 22, 41, 101, 114, 119, 141, 184, 225
   Letter to Admiral Lord Chatfield, **vii** 32

Drüffel, Dr. Ernst von (German Consul-General at Bratislava, Mar. 1939), **iv** 241

Duff Cooper, Alfred (First Lord of the Admiralty, May 1937–Oct. 1938), **ii** 190; **iii** 158, 172, 272; **iv** 59; **vi** 752; **vii** 550
   Speech in House of Commons, Mar. 1939, **iv** 455*n*

Dulong, Georges (French Minister at Kovno, 1935–40), **iv** 455

Dumitrescu, Captain G. St. (Roumanian Military Attaché at London) **iv** 520; **v** 343

Dunglass, Lord (Parliamentary Private Secretary to the Prime Minister), **iii** 532

Dunlop, Charles (Translator in H.M. Embassy, Moscow, 1935–44), **iv** 569

Dupree, Mr. (Director of the Municipal Bureau,

Third Special Administrative District, Hankow), **ix** 73, 79, 81–2, 96

Durcansky, Dr. Ferdinand (Minister for Railways, Posts and Public Works in Province of Slovakia, Dec. 2, 1938–Mar. 10, 1939; appointed Minister for Foreign Affairs of Republic of Slovakia, Mar. 14, 1939), **iii** 377; **iv** 63, 98, 158, 184, 219–20, 225, 227, 239–42, 246, 406, 408, 455; **v** 78, 85

Duvivier, Lt.-Gen. E. F. L. (Chief of the Belgian Air Staff), **iv** 78

Dyott, H. F. (Chairman of British Chamber of Commerce, Tientsin), **ix** 180*n*

Eberhardt, Major-General (Commanding Officer of troops in Danzig), **vi** 478, 532, 547, 689

Eckhardt, Dr. (Leader of the Hungarian Smallholders' party), **iii** 44*n*; **iv** 248

Eden, Anthony (Secretary of State for Foreign Affairs, Dec. 1935–Feb. 1938; M.P. for Warwick and Leamington), **i** 83, 130, 151; **iii** 158, 172, 594; **iv** 12, 59, 309, 600, 602; **vi** 466, 752; **vii** 255, 550
   Conversation with M. Beck, **v** 37–8
   Letter to Viscount Halifax, **v** 36
   Speech at Leamington, Nov. 20, 1936, **i** 84, 91, 96
   Visit to Berlin and Moscow, 1935, *referred to*, **iv** 106; **vi** 7, 753

Edmonds, W. S. (H.M. Consul-General at Milan, Oct. 1938–Aug. 1939), **iii** 346; **iv** 300, 355–7

Edward VIII, H.M. King (Jan.–Dec. 1936), **vi** 750

Edwardes, A. (Adviser to Japanese Embassy, London), **ix** 509, 514
   Conversation with Mr. R. A. Butler, **ix** 511

Eisenlohr, Dr. Ernst (German Minister at Prague, 1936–40), **i** 34, 62, 72, 117*n*, 186, 321, 333, 337–8, 340, 349, 359, 390*n*, 396, 400, 438*n*, 541, 568, 571–2, 574, 576, 591; **ii** 144, 204, 261, 369, 428, 569, 593, 673; **iv** 54, 564
   Conversation with Dr. Benes, **ii** 37–8
   Conversation with Mr. Newton, **i** 116–7, 277–80, 541, 543–4, 559–61

Elias, General Alois (Czechoslovak Minister of Railways and Posts, Dec. 1938–Mar. 1939; appointed Premier of Protectorate of Bohemia and Moravia, April 1939), **iii** 377; **v** 554

Elibank, 2nd Viscount
   Speech in House of Lords, Dec. 6, 1938, **viii** 306, 325

Elliott, S. P. (H.M. Vice-Consul at Liberec, 1923–39: in charge of post, 1936–9) **i** 435

Engliš, Dr. (President of the National Bank, Prague), **ii** 671

Epp, General Ritter von (Head of German Colonial Policy Office), **ii** 652; **iii** 256

Erbach-Schönberg, Prince Viktor zu (German Minister at Athens, 1936–41), **v** 186; **vi** 128

Erdmannsdorff, Dr. Otto von (German Minister at Budapest, 1937–41), **iii** 243; **iv** 289–90; **v** 60, 63

Erkin, Behiç. *See* Behiç Erkin

Erkko, Eljas (Finnish Minister for Foreign Affairs, Dec. 1938–Dec. 1939), **v** 253; **vi** 35, 55, 118, 120–1, 266, 413, 415
Conversation with Mr. Snow, **v** 495–6

Esterhazy, János (Leader of Hungarian minority in Slovakia), **iv** 246

Etter, Philipp (President of Switzerland, 1939), **vii** 67

Evekink, Lt.-Col. D. van Voorst. *See* Voorst Evekink, Lt.-Col. D. van

Faber du Faur, M. von (German Military Attaché at Belgrade), **ii** 268; **v** 80

Fabricius, Dr. Wilhelm (German Minister at Bucharest, 1936–41), **ii** 135, 152; **iii** 197, 236; **iv** 580*n*, 581; **vi** 17–8, 101, 585
Conversation with M. Comnène, **ii** 179–80

Facendis, Domenico de (Italian Minister at Prague, 1935–8), **i** 409; **ii** 29
Conversation with Dr. Benes, **ii** 37

Faifr, General (Czechoslovak Chief of Air Staff), **ii** 320

Fain, Baron Guy (Counsellor of French Embassy, Tokyo), **viii** 475; **ix** 185*n*, 189, 487

Farinacci, Roberto (Italian journalist), **ii** 332

Farouk I, King of Egypt (1936–52), **vi** 579

Farquhar, H. L. (Secretary, H.M. Legation, Bucharest, Dec. 1935–Jan. 1939: acted as Chargé d'Affaires, 1936–8)
To Viscount Halifax, **ii** 179

Faucher, General Eugène (Head of French Military Mission in Prague, 1926–38), **i** 302, 338–9, 495*n*, 496, 503, 543, 577; **ii** 357

Faur, M. von Faber du. *See* Faber du Faur, M. von

Faurice, General, **vii** 102

Fawzia, Princess, of Egypt, **v** 460*n*

Feierabend, Dr. Ladislav (Czechoslovak Minister of Agriculture, 1938–9), **iii** 151, 377

Feldmans, Jules (Latvian Minister at Berne and Permanent Delegate to League of Nations), **viii** 111, 145

Fessenden, Stirling (Secretary-General, Shanghai Municipal Council), **viii** 431; **ix** 137

Fethi, Okyar (Turkish Minister of Justice)
Conversation with Herr von Papen, **vi** 74–5

Fierlinger, Zdenek (Czechoslovak Minister at Moscow, 1937–9), **iv** 447
Conversation with Viscount Chilston, **ii** 229

Filliter, D. F. S. (H.M. Consul-General at Naples, Nov. 1937–June 1940), **iii** 347; **iv** 301, 304–5

Firebrace, Colonel R. C. W. G. (British Military Attaché at Moscow, April 1937–Dec. 1939), **i** 161–2, 402, 419; **iv** 188; **v** 463*n*; **vi** 426; **vii** 45, 562, 602, 608, 613–4
To Viscount Chilston, **i** 162, 172–3
To Mr. Vereker, **i** 420
Conversation with Colonel Dastich, **i** 420–1
Conversation with General Köstring, **i** 421–3
Conversation with Mr. Vereker and M. Coulondre, **i** 303–7, 402
Conversation with Marshal Voroshilov, **v** 471
Memorandum by, **iv** 194

Firkusny, Rudolf (Czechoslovak pianist), **ii** 662, 668

Fischböck, Dr. Hans (Minister of Commerce in the Cabinet of Dr. Seyss-Inquart, Austria), **i** 129

Fischer, Dr. Otakar (Czechoslovak Minister of the Interior in Dr. Beran's Cabinet, 1938–9), **iii** 376

Fish, Hamilton (U.S. Congressman), **vii** 67

Fisher, H. A. L. (British historian), **vi** 718; **vii** 36, 257

Fitzmaurice, G. G. (a Legal Adviser in the Foreign Office), **vii** 64, 66; **viii** 455, 549
Memorandum by, **viii** 543

Fitzmaurice, Nicholas (H.M. Consul-General at Amoy, April 1938–June 1943), **ix** 361, 371, 433
To British Embassy, Shanghai, **ix** 70, 339, 480

Flandin, Pierre Étienne (French Prime Minister, Nov. 1934–June 1935; Minister for Foreign Affairs, Jan.–June 1936; President of the 'Alliance Démocratique'), **i** 140, 153; **ii** 218, 220, 509, 568, 622–3; **iii** 157–8, 420, 484, 490; **vi** 212; **vii** 18

Florescu, Radu (Counsellor of Roumanian Legation, London; acted as Chargé d'Affaires), **iv** 519–20; **v** 29
Conversation with Sir O. Sargent, **iv** 576

Florez, Pablo Azcarate y. *See* Azcarate y Florez, Pablo

Foch, Marshal (1851–1929), **iii** 660

Forbes, Sir G. A. D. Ogilvie. *See* Ogilvie-Forbes, Sir George Arthur D.

Fornari, Giovanni (Secretary, Italian Legation at Athens: acted as Chargé d'Affaires), **v** 151, 155, 160–1, 163

Forsche, Herr (Leader of the Reichenberg section of Sudeten German party), **i** 434–5

Forster, Albert (Nazi Gauleiter of Danzig), **ii** 689–90; **iii** 281*n*, 402, 442, 552–4, 558–9, 573, 581, 586–7, 596, 598, 601, 613, 657–60; **iv** 68, 80–1, 147, 383; **v** 25, 291, 512, 515, 561, 812; **vi** 42, 45, 66, 107, 212, 216, 338, 381, 395, 402, 433, 452, 454–6, 476–7, 480, 490–1, 495, 506–7, 513, 533, 546–9, 551, 557, 561, 563, 577, 594, 610–1, 614, 620–2, 627, 635–8, 640, 644, 652–3, 659, 661–2, 667, 677, 683, 689–91, 694–6, 703, 714, 718, 728–9, 732; **vii** 10–1, 17–8, 25, 32, 55, 66, 96, 153, 222, 237, 363, 450, 510, 542–5, 552*n*, 553

appointed Head of Free City of Danzig, **vii** 199, 217, 219, 224*n*
Conversation with M. Burckhardt, **ii** 689; **iii** 660–1; **vi** 42, 388–9, 420–1, 507, 726, 733
Conversation with Sir A. Cadogan and Professor Noe, **i** 653–5
Article by, **vi** 480*n*; referred to, **vi** 388, 401, 420–1, 433, 448, 480, 527, 718
Speech by, **vi** 178; **vii** 104–5
Visit to Berchtesgaden, July 1939, **vi** 364, 369, 388, 689
Four Men arrested as suspects in connection with assassination of Cheng Lien-shih. *See* Cheng Lien-shih
Foury, General (Head of French Military Mission to Poland, Aug. 1939), **vii** 236
Franassovici, Richard (Roumanian Ambassador at Warsaw, 1938–9), **iii** 47, 111, 120, 138, 242; **iv** 142, 370, 551; **v** 66, 94, 200, 211, 218
Franco, General Francisco (Head of Spanish Nationalist Government), **ii** 66, 124*n*, 220, 235, 240, 528, 636; **iii** 270, 297–300, 314, 319–20, 324–5, 327, 329, 331–2, 337, 340–2, 345, 357, 462, 479, 483, 487–8, 506, 509, 514, 518, 521–4, 530, 619; **iv** 104, 292, 296, 318, 319*n*, 461–2; **v** 71, 143–4, 173, 222–3, 508, 643; **vi** 284; **vii** 624, 631
    Government recognized by Great Britain and France, **iv** 318*n*
    Proposed military parade in Madrid, **v** 150, 153, 155, 171, 219, 258
François-Poncet, André (French Ambassador at Berlin, Sept. 1931–Oct. 1938; at Rome, Nov. 1938–June 1940), **i** 12, 24–5, 32, 58, 111, 197, 238, 274, 285–6, 303, 304*n*, 318, 336, 344, 348–9, 359, 364, 415, 427, 452, 458, 460–1, 531, 534*n*, 535*n*, 539, 552, 563–4, 604, 613; **ii** 61, 67–8, 96, 171, 217, 270, 291*n*, 297, 423, 571, 583, 586–7, 589–91, 595, 609, 646, 650–1; **iii** 63, 77–8, 91–4, 99, 128–30, 134–5, 176–8, 234, 244*n*, 250, 257, 286, 296, 298, 310, 355, 390, 436, 465, 467–8, 470, 480, 483, 489–92, 502, 510, 511*n*, 513, 536, 572; **iv** 41, 90, 298, 305, 335, 340, 345, 359, 487; **v** 122, 126, 130, 172, 222, 237, 252, 263, 277, 347, 429, 432, 475, 477, 586, 611, 613, 651, 737, 795, 799, 800; **vi** 146, 193, 220–1, 303, 358, 396, 471–2, 587; **vii** 84, 248, 303*n*, 442, 445, 479, 488–9, 511, 516–7, 520
    Conversation with Count Ciano, **v** 347, 759; **vii** 505–6
    Conversation with Sir N. Henderson, **i** 12, 460–1, 535; **ii** 68–9
    Conversation with Herr Hitler, **ii** 600–1, 607–8; **iii** 244, 618–20
    Conversation with Sir P. Loraine, **v** 428–9; **vii** 349–50
    Conversation with Signor Mussolini, **iii** 461–2
    Conversation with Sir G. Ogilvie-Forbes, **ii** 479
    Conversation with Earl of Perth, **iii** 470–3,

488–9, 510–1; **iv** 296–7, 308, 325, 332–3; **v** 124
    Conversation with Sir E. Phipps, **i** 452; **iii** 619–21
    Views on need for Franco-Italian conversations, **v** 124, 428, 663–4; **vi** 330
François-Poncet, Madame, **iii** 619
Frank, Karl Hermann (Deputy leader of the Sudeten German party), **i** 117, 125, 275, 278–9, 338, 349, 365, 395, 510, 522, 529–31, 544; **ii** 95, 167, 171, 176, 183, 243, 274, 279, 313, 316, 321–2, 332–3, 336, 658, 660, 662, 666–7, 669, 671–4, 676; **vii** 96, 101, 153, 543; *position in* Protectorate of Bohemia and Moravia, **iv** 564; **v** 556
    Conversation with Mr. Ashton-Gwatkin, **ii** 177
    Conversation with Herr Hitler, **ii** 177; referred to, **ii** 180, 182
    Conversation with Mr. Newton, **i** 517–8
    Conversation with Observers attached to H.M. Legation, Prague, **i** 555–7
    Conversation with Lord Runciman, **ii** 82
    Speech at Oberläutensdorf, **ii** 183
Franke, Dr. Emil (Czechoslovak Minister of Education in Dr. Hodza's Cabinet, 1935–8), **i** 519, 524; **ii** 93
Franklin, C. S. (Chairman, Shanghai Municipal Council, 1938–9), **viii** 375, 431, 453–4, 464–7, 471, 476, 480–1, 483, 489, 501, 538; **ix** 54, 68*n*, 489
Fransoni, Francesco (Italian Minister at Prague, 1938–9), **ii** 171
Fraser, Colonel William (British Military Attaché at Paris, Aug. 1938–Nov. 1939), **ii** 427, 452, 473, 484, 509; **iii** 568–9, 578; **iv** 236–7, 243, 261, 274, 330, 333–4, 337; **vi** 87; **vii** 14, 123, 136–7, 341, 463, 489, 503
    To Sir E. Phipps, **ii** 453, 473, 609; **iii** 159, 556, 569, 579, 608; **iv** 74, 221; **vii** 136–7, 206
    Conversation with General Dentz, **ii** 473–4; **iii** 159–60; **iv** 221–2
    Conversation with General Gamelin, **vii** 420
    Conversation with Colonel Gauché, **ii** 190–1, 454, 610; **iii** 556–7, 608–9; **iv** 535
    Conversation with Colonel Petitbon, **ii** 609–10
    Conversation with Colonel de Vitrolles, **iv** 74–5
Frasheri, Mehdi (Permanent Albanian representative to the League of Nations), **v** 175–6
Frick, Dr. Wilhelm (German Minister of the Interior, 1933–43), **iii** 270, 381; **iv** 280; **vii** 464*n*
Fricke, Captain (at Anglo-German Naval conversations, Dec. 1938), **iii** 664
Fritsch, Col.-Gen. Werner (Commander-in-Chief of the German Army, 1934–8), **ii** 44; **v** 594
Fritz, Dr. Gejza (Slovak Minister of Justice), **iv** 230

Froböss, M. (Chief of Police, Danzig Free State), **vi** 452, 454, 729

Frohwein, Dr. Hans (German Minister at Tallinn, 1936–40), **v** 697, 775

Frölicher, Dr. Hans (Swiss Minister at Berlin, 1938–45), **i** 494; **v** 232

Frolov, Captain (a member of External Relations Bureau of U.S.S.R. Defence Commissariat), **vii** 45

Fu Siao-en (Fu Tsung-yao) (Mayor of Shanghai appointed by Japanese-sponsored Reformed Government of Nanking), **viii** 376, 431; **ix** 489

Fuller, Major-General, **v** 292

Funk, Dr. Walther (German Minister of Economics, 1937–45; President of the Reichsbank, 1939–45), **iii** 246, 270; **iv** 5*n*, 10, 24, 111, 138*n*, 559, 598–600, 604–5, 608–10; **v** 673; **vi** 171, 202, 238, 359, 710–1, 717; **vii** 17, 464*n*
  Conversation with Mr. Ashton-Gwatkin, **iv** 604–6
  Proposed visit to London, **v** 717, 728

Fyda, Colonel G. W. (Polish Military Attaché at Paris), **iii** 159

Gafencu, Grigore (Roumanian Minister for Foreign Affairs, Dec. 1938–1940; President of the Balkan Entente), **iv** 178, 281, 389, 391, 395, 398, 401, 580; **v** 8, 15, 29, 68, 74, 94, 105–6, 207, 211, 217–8, 233, 296, 382, 387, 404, 480, 491, 501, 575, 597, 607, 657, 663, 670, 672, 681–2, 685, 687, 708–9, 729, 739–40, 761, 801; **vi** 23–4, 29*n*, 36, 78–9, 93, 101, 103, 228–9, 261, 263, 320–1, 437, 583, 585, 629, 687; **vii** 57–8, 152*n*; **ix** 28
  Conversation with Col. Beck, **v** 298–300
  Conversation with M. Cincar-Markovitch, **v** 659–62, 676, 686–7, 725
  Conversation with Sir R. Hoare, **iv** 580–1; **v** 81, 91–2; **vi** 17–9, 146–7
  Conversation with Sir H. Kennard, **iv** 182–3
  Conversation with Sir H. Knatchbull-Hugessen, **vi** 29–30, 51–2, 68–71
  Conversation with Sir P. Loraine, **v** 426–8
  Conversation with Sir M. Palairet, **vi** 84
  Conversation with Mr. le Rougetel, **vi** 294–5, 641–2
  Statement on March 27, 1939, **v** 111
  Visit to Angora, April 1939, **v** 92, 222, 296, 323; June, **vi** 18, 24, 53–4, 78, 84, 146–7, 169–70, 188, 263
  Visit to Athens, June, **vi** 84, 128, 130, 147
  Visit to Berlin, April, **iv** 580–1; **v** 264–5, 271–2, 289, 300–6, 309–11
  Visit to London, April, **iv** 581*n*; **v** 295–315, 321–34, 342–4, 358, 374
  Visit to Paris, April, **v** 395–6, 403
  Visit to Rome, April–May, **v** 481, 551
  Visit to Warsaw, March, **iv** 182–3, 202; **v** 62, 298, 657

Gainer, D. St. Clair (H.M. Consul-General at Munich, Oct. 1932–Mar. 1938; at Vienna, Mar. 1938–Sept. 1939), **i** 7, 9, 57, 321*n*, 327*n*; **iii** 367
  To Sir N. Henderson, **i** 19, 119; **ii** 615

Galantha, L. Nagy de (Counsellor of Hungarian Legation at Rome), **iv** 282

Gallienne, W. H. (H.M. Consul at Tallinn, Sept. 1935–June 1941), **v** 349
  To Viscount Halifax, **v** 696; **vi** 325
  To Mr. Orde, **v** 349, 410, 560, 696, 775
  Conversation with M. Kaasik, **v** 349–50
  Conversation with M. Selter, **v** 697–8; **vi** 325–7

Gamble, F. H. (H.M. Vice-Consul at Durazzo, June 1938–June 1939), **v** 176–7, 751

Gamelin, General M. G. (Generalissimo and Chief of the French General Staff), **i** 445; **ii** 192, 234*n*, 269, 509, 514, 527, 535, 539, 541, 575, 600; **iii** 365, 569, 579; **iv** 75, 146, 155, 236, 243, 274, 339, 373; **v** 797; **vi** 297, 419, 528, 534–5, 678; **vii** 96, 103, 105, 136, 247, 249, 489, 569–72
  Conversation with Mr. Chamberlain, **ii** 575*n*, 610
  Conversation with Colonel Fraser, **vii** 420
  Conversation with Mr. Hore-Belisha, **vii** 102–3

Garcia Condé, D. P. *See* Condé, D. P. Garcia

Garvin, J. L. (Editor of 'The Observer', 1908–42), **iv** 310

Gascoigne, A. D. F. (1st Secretary, H.M. Legation, Budapest, April 1936–Aug. 1939; acted as Chargé d'Affaires), **ii** 239; **iii** 11, 236; **vi** 630*n*
  To Viscount Halifax, **iii** 5

Gauché, Colonel (Head of French Deuxième Bureau), **ii** 453; **iii** 571, 578; **iv** 261; **v** 56
  Conversation with Colonel William Fraser, **ii** 190–1, 454, 610; **iii** 556–7, 608–9; **iv** 535
  Views on probability of outbreak of war in Europe in 1939, **v** 70–1

Gauquié, H. (First Secretary, French Embassy, Warsaw), **vi** 501–2, 506
  Memorandum by, **vi** 504

Gaus, Dr. Friedrich (Director of Legal Department of German Ministry of Foreign Affairs), **ii** 352; **iii** 390, 649, 652; **v** 803

Gauss, C. E. (U.S. Consul-General at Shanghai), **viii** 124, 164, 186*n*, 432, 465, 471; **ix** 37, 54, 60, 71, 74, 97, 312, 353, 444, 446, 450–1, 461–2, 489

Gayda, General Rudolf (Chairman of Fascist party, Czechoslovakia), **iv** 280, 470, 565

Gayda, Dr. Virginio (Italian journalist and editor of 'Giornale d'Italia'), **i** 37; **iii** 322, 475–6; **iv** 318, 327, 350, 355; **v** 443, 473, 654, 707; **vi** 347, 444

Geist, R. H. (1st Secretary, U.S. Embassy at

Berlin: acted as Chargé d'Affaires, Feb.–May 1939), **iv** 176; **v** 107, 423
Conversation with General Halder, **v** 107

George II, King of the Hellenes (1922–4, 1935–47), **iv** 499

George VI, H.M. King (Dec. 1936–Feb. 1952), **ii** 673; **iii** 566; **v** 411
Visit of Their Majesties King George VI and Queen Elizabeth to Paris, **i** 569, 591; to Washington, **v** 775

George, A. H. (Commercial Secretary, H.M. Embassy, China, Oct. 1935–July 1940), **ix** 30, 347

Georges, General A. J. (Deputy Chief of the French General Staff, 1935–9), **vi** 63

Georges-Picot, G. *See* Picot, G. G.

Geraldine, Queen of Albania, **v** 119, 175–7

Géraud, André. *See* 'Pertinax'

Ghigi, Pellegrino (Italian Minister at Vienna, 1937–8; at Bucharest, 1938–41), **i** 11, 132; **vi** 17–8, 263

Gie, Dr. S. F. N. (South African Minister at Berlin, 1934–9), **i** 348, 617; **v** 423; **vii** 192

Gignoux, C. J. (French journalist and Editor of 'La Journée Industrielle'), **vi** 495

Gilbert, Ernest (H.M. Vice-Consul at Lodz, Feb. 1924–Sept. 1939), **vii** 203–4

Gildemeister, E. (Peruvian Minister at Berlin, 1938–42), **vii** 322

Girling, C. J. (H.M. Vice-Consul at Dresden, July 1936–Dec. 1938, Mar.–Sept. 1939; Acting Consul there in 1936, 1937 and 1938), **i** 317; **iv** 218

Giro, Signor (Italian Youth Organiser in Albania), **v** 195

Gjoni, Gjon Marko (Chief of the Merdite tribe, Albania), **v** 196

Glaise-Horstenau, Dr. Edmund von (Austrian Minister without Portfolio, 1936–8), **i** 9, 11, 24, 45, 132–5

Glauser, M., **ix** 1

Globke, Dr. Hans (Ministerial Counsellor in German Ministry of the Interior), **iii** 649, 652

Gnédine, E. A. (Head of Press Bureau, U.S.S.R. Commissariat for Foreign Affairs), **v** 545

Godfrey, Rear-Admiral J. H. (Director of Naval Intelligence, 1939–42), **vi** 295, 305–6; **vii** 367n

Godfrey, Lt.-Col. J. T. (British Military Attaché at Warsaw, Oct. 1935–June 1938), **i** 445
Conversation with Gen. Stachiewicz, **i** 480–4

Godfrey, Mgr. William (Apostolic Delegate in Great Britain, 1938–53), **iii** 535; **v** 435, 482
To Viscount Halifax, **v** 420
Conversation with Viscount Halifax, **v** 435–6, 439–40, 452

Goebbels, Dr. Josef (German Minister of Propaganda, 1933–44), **i** 26–7, 100, 155–6, 160, 187n, 195, 223, 370, 388, 399, 426, 474; **ii** 44, 77, 103, 118, 130, 163, 225, 231, 280, 297,

300, 329–30, 647, 650, 652–3, 659, 684; **iii** 249, 257, 268, 270–1, 276–7, 281, 493–4, 563, 625; **iv** 9, 589, 596; **v** 360, 608, 617; **vi** 1, 32, 42, 44, 113–4, 184, 197, 248, 298, 307, 470, 504, 551, 619–20, 634, 638, 723, 729, 734, 736; **vii** 48, 203, 631, 632n
Conversation with Sir N. Henderson, **ii** 283
Speech at Berlin, June 27, 1939, **vi** 175–6
Speech at Danzig, June 17, 1939, **vi** 108, 123, 200
Speech at Hamburg, Oct. 21, 1938, **iii** 245n
Visit to Danzig, **vi** 108, 136–7; *referred to,* **vi** 60, 223, 357

Goerdeler, Dr., **v** 433n

Goethals, Lt.-Col. B. E. M. (Belgian Military Attaché at Berlin), **ii** 309

Goetz, Dr. Carl (President of the Dresdner Bank, Germany), **iv** 597

Gömbös, General (Prime Minister of Hungary, 1932–6), **iii** 6

Göring, Field-Marshal Hermann Wilhelm (German Minister, for Air and Commander-in-Chief of German Air Force: Commissioner for the Four-Year Plan), **i** 23–4, 26, 29, 32, 33n, 34n, 36, 39–41, 43–4, 47, 51, 58–61, 66, 95, 104, 112, 156, 173–6, 187n, 197, 223, 229–30, 245–6, 252–7, 260, 287, 295–6, 311, 324, 369, 485, 512, 527–8, 551, 568n, 580, 585, 587–8, 591, 610–1, 614, 618n, 626; **ii** 15, 46, 49, 59, 64, 66, 76, 96, 103, 122–4, 178, 217, 231, 278, 280, 289, 297, 322, 329–30, 352, 354, 358n, 367, 371, 378–9, 388, 423, 428, 441, 597, 646–51, 653, 659, 684, 687, 691; **iii** 9n, 79, 123, 145, 150, 198, 236, 265, 270, 281, 361, 388, 435, 545, 562–4, 580, 586, 615–6, 619, 626, 657–60, 662–3; **iv** 10, 80, 111, 115, 117, 123, 160, 210–1, 242, 404, 443, 445, 455, 567, 589, 595–6, 598, 600–1, 608–9; **v** 292, 301, 304, 309, 400, 433, 455, 546, 656, 792, 801–2, 805, 812; **vi** 11–2, 28, 43–4, 75, 193, 208, 216, 236, 238, 248, 331, 345, 359, 390, 408–10, 412, 496, 500, 508, 620, 702–4, 711, 723–4, 729, 734, 736–43; **vii** 13, 36, 59, 62, 66–7, 86, 104, 129, 151, 176n, 207, 222, 230, 242, 258–9, 281–6, 316, 319–20, 322, 327, 337–8, 353, 356–7, 368, 387, 405, 437, 440–1, 464n, 469, 474, 477, 479, 485, 512–3, 517, 537, 547–8, 552–5, 631–2
Conversation with Mr. Ashton-Gwatkin, **iv** 606–8
Conversation with King Boris III of Bulgaria, **iii** 142–3
Conversation with M. Dahlerus, **vi** 744–51, 759n; **vii** 194, 220, 231–4, 282, 283–5, 360–1, 396–7, 399–400
Conversation with M. Dahlerus and Messrs. Spencer, Holden, Rawson, Mensforth, McLaren, Mountain and Sir Robert Renwick, **vi** 751–9; *referred to,* **vi** 483, 745–6, 760n; **vii** 231, 551, 553–4

Göring, Field-Marshal (*cont.*)
    Conversation with Sir N. Henderson, i 23–4, 39, 58–9, 173–6, 513–4; ii 283, 362–4, 378, 410, 543, 561–2, 589; iv 120–1, 123, 592; v 713–7; vi 13–4; vii 453–4, 476
    Conversation with M. Lipski, vii 216
    Conversation with Mr. L. Runciman, vii 548–50
    Conversation with M. Wenner-Gren, vi 738–9
    Statements at Nuremburg Congress, Sept. 1938, ii 289, 300
    Speech on Mar. 1, 1938, i 296; May 23, 1939, v 671
    Suggested visit to London, i 585–90; vii 537
Göring, Frau, i 513; vi 746
Gort, 6th Viscount, General (Chief of Imperial General Staff, 1937–9), vi 297; vii 249
Gottwald, Dr. Klement (Chairman of Communist party, Czechoslovakia), ii 167
Grandi, Count Dino (Italian Ambassador at London, 1932–9), i 233, 247; iii 361, 533; iv 308, 324, 340; v 127, 790; vi 445, 556; vii 93
    appointed Italian Minister of Justice, July 1939, vi 450n
    Conversation with Viscount Halifax, ii 626–7; iii 360–1; iv 346–7; v 779–81, 800–1
    Speech at celebration of Italo–German alliance, v 780–1
Grant, H. G. (U.S. Minister at Durazzo, 1935–9), v 123, 127, 169, 176, 229–30
Grasett, Major-General A. E. (General Officer Commanding British Troops in China, 1938–41), viii 9n, 103, 106, 427, 431, 465, 557; ix 178, 372–3
Grayburn, Mr. (Chief Manager, Hongkong and Shanghai Banking Corporation, Hongkong), ix 167
Grazynski, Dr. M. (the Voivode of Upper Silesia), iii 251; iv 162; v 246, 407
Grazzi, Emanuele (Italian Minister at Athens, 1939–40), v 444
Greenway, J. D. (1st Secretary, H.M. Embassy in China, Nov. 1937–April 1940: Head of British Diplomatic Mission at Hankow), viii 2n, 16, 131n, 150, 158n, 410n, 430, 435n, 540n; ix 240n
    To British Embassy, Shanghai, viii 136, 294, 364, 409–10, 441, 467, 469, 477–8, 510, 539
    To Sir A. Clark Kerr, viii 197
    To Viscount Halifax, viii 185; ix 8, 19
    Conversation with General Chiang Kai-shek, viii 136–7
    Conversation with Dr. Kung, viii 410–1, 441–2
    Conversation with Wang Chung-hui, viii 294–5
Greenwood, A. (M.P. for Wakefield), iii 261; v 21

Greiser, Arthur Karl (President of the Danzig Senate, Nov. 1934–Sept. 1939), iii 402, 558, 561, 572–3, 586, 598, 613; iv 47, 181, 383; v 25–7, 512, 514–5, 561–2, 764, 812; vi 1, 7, 9, 26, 42, 107, 148, 178, 365, 386, 395, 452, 476, 490–1, 532, 577, 594, 610–4, 621, 649, 652–3, 668, 685, 690–1; vii 12
    To M. Chodacki, vi 8
    Conversation with M. Burckhardt, ii 689–90; vi 42, 726
    Conversation with Mr. Shepherd, iii 552–3
Grew, Joseph C. (U.S. Ambassador at Tokyo, 1932–41), viii 12–5, 19, 43, 45–6, 51, 64–5, 69n, 82, 107–8, 116, 118, 135–6, 151, 166–8, 176, 185, 189, 193–4, 195n, 201, 205, 224–5, 228–9, 236, 238, 243–4, 247, 249, 255n, 258, 260–2, 265–6, 268–9, 271–2, 275–6, 281, 283, 295–6, 298n, 300, 306, 313, 316, 326–7, 334, 340–2, 345–6, 348–9, 352–3, 359, 363, 370, 382, 389, 434, 436, 446, 458, 461, 463, 475, 477, 497, 501, 513, 528, 530–2, 538; ix 45, 64, 67, 69–71, 74, 77–8, 101–2, 109, 120, 139, 148, 159, 187–8, 224, 240, 245, 247, 289, 308, 418
    To Sir R. Craigie, viii 317
    Conversation with Mr. Arita, viii 254–5, 348; ix 91–2, 94–5
    Conversation with Sir R. Craigie, viii 183–4, 264
Grey, Sir Edward (1st Viscount Grey of Fallodon) (Secretary of State for Foreign Affairs, Dec. 1905–Dec. 1916), ii 644; vi 364; vii 609
Grey, P. F. (Secretary, H.M. Embassy, Rome, Oct. 1938–Sept. 1939), iv 338–9
Grigorcea, Basile (Roumanian Minister at London, 1937–9), iii 97n, 114
Grillo, Marchese G. Capranica del. *See* Capranica del Grillo, Marchese G.
Grimsdale, Colonel, ix 373
Grinius, Colonel K. (Lithuanian Military Attaché at Berlin), i 10; iii 548; iv 397
Gripenberg, Georg Achates (Finnish Minister at London, 1933–41), v 462n, 522; vi 281, 413–4
    Conversation with Viscount Halifax, v 522; vi 264–6; 307–8
Gritzbach, Dr. Erich (Personal assistant to Field-Marshal Göring), iv 606
Grover, B., iv 24n
Grübner, Herr, v 625, 636; vi 149
Gruillot, Captain G. (French Naval Attaché at Warsaw), v 205, 248–9
Grynszpan, Herschell, iii 275, 277, 383
Grzybowski, Dr. Waclaw (Polish Ambassador at Moscow, 1936–9), iii 364; iv 509; v 476, 571, 657; vi 3
Guariglia, Raffaele (Italian Ambassador at Paris, Nov. 1938–1940), iii 392, 465; v 127, 144, 278, 790; vi 146, 185, 220–1; vii 340

Guarneri, F. (Italian Minister of Trade and International Payments), **vi** 556; **vii** 93

Guattari-Stafford, R. A. (H.M. Vice-Consul at Spezia, June 1924–Nov. 1939; Acting Consul there, 1936–8), **iii** 346; **iv** 338

Gubbins, Lt.-Col. (British military representative on a Sub-Commission of International Commission set up in Oct. 1938), **iii** 163

Guérin, H. (Counsellor of French Embassy, Rome), **iv** 359

Guerlet, Pierre (French Minister at Budapest, 1939–40), **iv** 423; **v** 63; **vii** 350, 361

Guillaume, Baron Jules (Belgian Ambassador in China, 1937–44), **ix** 125

Guillaume, R. (Belgian Consul-General at Tientsin), **viii** 248; **ix** 493

Guinness, Arthur (of Messrs. Guinness, Mahon & Company), **viii** 472

Günther, Christian (Swedish Minister at Oslo, 1938–9), **vii** 422

Gustav V, King of Sweden (1907–50), **i** 626; **vi** 759; **vii** 327

Gustav Adolf, Duke of Skåne (Crown Prince of Sweden), **vi** 736

Gustloff, Herr, **iii** 261

Gwatkin, Mr. Ashton. *See* Ashton-Gwatkin, Frank T. A.

Gwiazdowski, M. (Head of League of Nations section, Polish Ministry of Foreign Affairs), **iii** 558–9; **iv** 32; **vi** 206

Gwiźdź, Senator (Head of the 'Friends of Slovakia' association in Poland), **i** 429, 479

Haakon VII, King of Norway (1905–57), **vii** 67

Hacha, Dr. Emil (President of Czechoslovakia, Nov. 1938–Mar. 1939), **i** 452, 461, 466, 530; **iii** 377, 380; **iv** 98, 219, 221, 241–2, 246, 260, 368, 447, 469–70, 565, 583; **v** 33, 291–2, 325, 616–7, 699, 726; **vi** 161, 231, 280, 375, 522, 572–4; **vii** 428, 451

Visit to Berlin, Mar. 14–5, 1939, **iv** 247, 255–6, 258–9, 289, 403–5, 444; *referred to*, **iv** 270, 562, 595; **v** 616, 713; **vi** 754

Hadow, R. H. (a member of Northern Department of the Foreign Office)

Minute by, **vii** 315

Haeften, G. von (German Consul at Basle, 1939–45), **v** 709

Haersma de With, Jonkheer H. M. van (Netherlands Minister at Berlin, Dec. 1938–40), **v** 423

Conversation with Sir N. Henderson, **iv** 137

Hai Te-mou (a member of Mr. K. P. Chen's Mission to the United States), **viii** 302

Haig, 1st Earl, Field-Marshal, **iii** 660

Hajek, Colonel (Chief of Czechoslovak Military Intelligence), **i** 432–3; **ii** 176n

Conversation with Colonel Stronge, **ii** 90–1

Hajek, Jean (Head of Propaganda Department in Czechoslovak Ministry of Foreign Affairs, 1935–8), **iv** 561

Halder, General Franz (Chief of German General Staff, Sept. 1938–Aug. 1939), **iv** 455; **v** 478, 728; **vi** 282, 708; **vii** 417n

resignation of, **vii** 415

Conversation with Mr. Geist, **v** 107

Halfeld, Herr (Berlin correspondent of the 'Hamburger Fremdenblatt'), **iii** 256n; **iv** 222; **v** 425

Halifax, 3rd Viscount (Secretary of State for Foreign Affairs, Feb. 1938–Dec. 1940), **i** 81–3, 269, 282, 285, 299, 309n, 321n, 333n, 401n, 403–4, 410, 412, 503n, 516n, 520n, 526, 571n, 584n, 589, 592, 601n, 614n, 628, 630; **ii** 70, 76n, 112n, 168, 172, 174, 240, 373, 379, 431, 536, 550n, 606–7, 683, 688; **iii** 4, 15, 16n, 93n, 145–6, 244n, 287, 298, 311, 314, 318, 327, 392, 397n, 447–8, 493, 554, 558, 600, 636; **iv** 16, 26, 31, 36, 82, 105, 171, 285, 296, 309–10, 320, 350n, 409, 473–4, 519, 545n, 546n, 585, 597, 639; **v** 47, 163, 218, 495, 506, 509, 564, 565n, 566, 606n, 640n, 668, 682–3, 763, 804–5; **vi** 3, 70, 113–4, 122, 167, 169, 206, 297, 328, 384, 410, 466, 519–20, 695, 754; **vii** 2n, 17, 36n, 108, 110, 132, 234n, 281, 285, 351, 386, 400–1, 421n, 441–2, 488, 506, 510, 517, 520, 530–1, 535, 537, 548, 552n, 553, 555n; **viii** 201, 257n, 308–9, 447n, 542–3, 549; **ix** 79, 90n, 101, 141, 180, 294, 513, 533, 535

To Mr. Allen, **viii** 164, 213, 233, 556–7

To M. de Barcza, **iii** 11, 30

To Sir N. Bland, **iv** 48, 73; **v** 252; **vi** 226; **vii** 447

To Mr. Broadmead, **viii** 452, 455; **ix** 29

To Sir Reader Bullard, **iii** 341

To Mr. R. A. Butler, **ii** 480; **iii** 605

To Sir R. Campbell, **iii** 341; **iv** 351, 361, 386, 521; **v** 56, 110, 129, 132, 148, 252, 595, 762; **vi** 166, 170, 175, 534; **vii** 180, 201, 492

To Mr. R. I. Campbell, **i** 551, 563; **ii** 18–9, 71, 158, 194, 196; **iv** 486–7, 519; **vi** 464, 491, 512, 527, 545, 598, 601, 603–4, 606, 664, 676, 688; **vii** 114, 147–8, 161, 192; **viii** 30, 67, 532; **ix** 467

To Mr. Chamberlain (*at* Godesberg), **ii** 475, 490

To Sir N. Charles, **v** 320; **vi** 115

To Viscount Chilston, **ii** 107, 271, 623; **iii** 153–4, 331, 453; **viii** 40n

To Count Ciano, **iii** 540

To Sir A. Clark Kerr, **viii** 4, 16, 18–9, 24, 30, 38, 48, 50, 58, 114, 123, 133, 145, 150, 173, 203, 244, 270, 303, 308–9, 312, 315, 336, 341–2, 376, 381, 401, 418, 430, 436, 440–1, 470, 472, 485–6, 495, 508, 516, 533; **ix** 5, 12, 23, 46, 55, 116, 121, 123–4, 140, 143–4, 147, 162, 165, 184, 209, 225, 236, 246, 248, 288, 292, 307, 323, 326–7, 332, 353, 361, 388–9, 410,

Halifax, Viscount (*cont.*)
  To Sir A. Clark Kerr (*cont.*)
  417, 419, 432-3, 438, 456-8, 466, 469, 476, 506, 524-5
  To Sir R. Clive, **iii** 172; **iv** 37, 44, 102, 109; **v** 252; **vii** 303, 447, 532
  To M. Corbin, **ii** 452
  To Sir R. Craigie, **v**, 56; **viii** 5, 11, 16, 25, 41-2, 45, 48, 56-7, 70, 78, 95, 109, 118, 127, 135, 138, 140, 143, 151, 156, 163, 169, 178, 193-4, 212-3, 227, 229, 238-9, 280, 283, 303, 324, 326, 330, 352, 370-1, 401, 407, 422, 468, 475, 477-8, 487, 494, 497-8, 505, 520, 532-3; **ix** 22, 25, 27, 45, 57, 61-3, 67, 77, 86, 103, 120, 124, 133, 148, 155, 162-3, 181, 193-4, 202, 205, 217-8, 225, 227, 239, 241, 243, 256, 258, 264, 267-9, 274, 289, 291, 303, 307-9, 315, 323, 327-8, 331, 365, 373, 379, 384, 388-9, 399, 413-4, 416-7, 419, 422-3, 427, 431-2, 434-5, 437, 439, 444, 460, 463-4, 466-7, 471, 476, 482, 487, 490-1, 494, 504, 507, 509, 511
  To Dr. von Dirksen, **iii** 432, 628
  To Mr. Dodds, **viii** 539
  To Sir Cecil Dormer, **iii** 453; **v** 252; **vii** 180, 201
  To Mr. Gallienne, **v** 572, 590; **vii** 180, 201
  To Mr. Gascoigne, **iii** 12, 389; **vi** 452
  To Mr. Greenway, **viii** 210, 435, 540
  To Sir N. Henderson, **i** 4, 5, 8, 14, 18, 21, 29, 32-3, 40, 42, 80, 95, 160, 235, 239, 243, 245, 253, 256, 264, 281, 322-3, 331, 341, 352, 355, 365, 369, 374, 382, 386, 388, 393, 399, 438, 440, 453-5, 458, 484, 528, 537, 598, 618; **ii** 3, 17, 25*n*, 41*n*, 61, 71, 76, 78, 100, 105, 118, 148, 165, 205, 236, 249, 273, 285-6, 290*n*, 314, 327, 372, 401, 406, 417, 421, 424, 455, 462, 475, 483, 517, 550, 559-60, 572, 587, 591; **iii** 57, 75, 77, 85-6, 93, 95, 98, 112, 127, 167, 169, 172, 185, 630, 662; **iv** 109, 115, 138, 250, 270, 291, 592; **v** 320, 360, 402, 437, 478, 517, 525, 549, 600, 603; **vi** 88, 153, 533, 647; **vii** 72, 125, 127-8, 243, 391, 403, 405-6, 410, 413, 415, 417, 443, 455, 458, 485, 488, 496, 521-3, 528, 533-5
  To Sir R. Hoare, **iv** 283, 366, 375, 389-90, 484, 515, 520, 540-1, 547, 553; **v** 46, 56, 65, 74, 109, 111, 148, 208, 252, 357, 395, 403, 480, 531, 597, 670, 689, 701, 752; **vi** 109, 166, 263; **vii** 180, 201
  To Mr. Hutchison (includes 'from Treasury to Mr. Rogers'), **viii** 379; **ix** 104, 110, 112, 128, 150, 167, 213
  To Mr. Jamieson, **viii** 560; **ix** 70, 133, 155, 166, 212, 493, 524
  To Sir H. Kennard, **i** 247; **ii** 317, 459, 545; **iii** 3, 13, 28-9, 47, 53, 59, 97, 186, 189,

  401, 430, 453, 574; **iv** 11, 110, 144, 204, 253, 290, 361, 386, 389, 400, 434, 500, 510, 515, 524, 540-1, 543, 546-7, 554, 575; **v** 23, 51, 56, 73, 97, 108, 110, 148, 208, 224, 234, 254, 257, 265, 357, 401, 430, 451, 490, 492, 525, 539, 597, 599, 604, 670, 682, 689-90, 731, 747, 776, 778, 786; **vi** 85, 132, 192, 198, 211, 564, 627, 649, 663, 669, 675, 679; **vii** 6, 28, 39-40, 58, 88, 122, 124, 130, 146, 150, 168, 214, 223, 226, 241, 244, 249, 271, 290, 304, 310, 324, 326, 333-4, 337, 375, 377, 380, 392, 405, 410, 419, 427, 438, 445, 449, 455, 469, 489, 496, 526, 532
  To Mr. Kirkpatrick, **ii** 277
  To Sir H. Knatchbull-Hugessen, **iv** 361, 386, 436, 558; **v** 56-7, 108, 129, 148, 166-7, 179, 190, 199, 206-7, 221, 240, 252, 279, 293, 320, 346, 364, 367, 471, 494, 498, 502, 523, 534, 559, 574, 589, 614, 672, 738, 740, 743, 785; **vi** 23, 82, 93, 145, 165, 187-9, 228-9, 279, 303, 336, 355, 403, 429, 463, 560, 567, 596, 670, 688; **vii** 26, 180, 183, 218, 225, 242-3, 273-4, 306, 320, 325, 327, 356, 359, 372, 407, 412, 418, 431, 446, 449, 471, 484, 487, 490, 503
  To Sir G. Knox, **i** 95; **ii** 459; **iii** 2*n*, 9, 29, 115, 484-5; **v** 56, 110
  To Sir M. Lampson, **iii** 341; **iv** 399, 432, 552; **v** 56
  To Sir R. Lindsay, **i** 95; **ii** 149, 209, 212, 252, 284, 295, 625; **iii** 34*n*, 343; **iv** 159, 364, 380, 420, 465, 495, 499, 526, 528, 555; **v** 56, 169, 793; **vii** 151, 295, 333-4, 357, 630; **viii** 66, 94, 152, 165, 167, 297, 301, 488, 494, 496, 532; **ix** 84, 142, 165, 172, 183, 233, 258, 330, 353, 360, 464, 491, 493, 503
  To Sir P. Loraine, **iii** 341; **v** 451, 475, 478, 499, 518, 536, 765, 779; **vi** 127, 240, 257, 295, 628; **vii** 62, 75, 113, 146, 156, 159, 186, 191, 199, 224, 240, 263, 265, 267, 295, 310-1, 323, 332, 334, 343, 348, 369, 391-2, 394-5, 399, 405, 411, 427, 444, 448, 455, 462, 477, 489, 497
  To Marquess of Lothian, **vii** 398, 412, 473, 489; **ix** 514
  To Mr. Mack, **iii** 172; **vi** 22
  To M. Maisky, **i** 101
  To Mr. Mallet, **iii** 452-3, **iv** 4, 40, 83-4, 114; **viii** 329, 353, 373, 411, 416, 433, 437
  To Sir E. Monson, **iii** 406*n*, 453; **v** 252; **vi** 107, 668; **vii** 180, 201
  To Mr. Newton, **i** 33, 90, 95, 113, 137, 149-50, 159, 235, 241, 272, 289, 292, 297, 299, 324, 340, 350, 362, 365, 375, 378, 383, 388, 400-1, 418, 428, 441, 444, 453, 454*n*, 467, 491, 493, 498, 501, 506, 508, 516, 529, 532, 562, 567, 581, 595,

608; **ii** 4–5, 7, 17, 23, 53, 77, 110, 136, 153, 155, 172, 180, 188, 193, 195, 202, 206, 230–1, 244, 264, 267–8, 308, 325, 328, 373, 403–4, 406–7, 409–10, 419, 437, 446, 460–1, 477, 483, 511, 544, 561, 570, 599, 601, 614; **iii** 18–9, 35, 40, 42, 54, 57, 74, 76, 97, 113, 153, 173, 195n, 398, 631–3; **iv** 277

To Mr. Norton, **ii** 82, 190n; **iii** 12; **vi** 226, 244, 255, 274, 321, 339, 365, 378–400, 404, 431–2, 451, 463, 479, 494, 597

To Sir G. Ogilvie-Forbes, **iii** 200, 205, 230, 268, 429, 433, 435, 439, 445, 450–1, 453, 508, 566, 671; **iv** 17, 380, 547, 583, 641, 643, 647; **v** 56, 265; **vii** 269, 328, 330

To Mr. O'Malley, **v** 786; **vi** 77; **vii** 151, 180, 201, 377

To Mr. Orde, **iv** 474, 533, 669, 689; **v** 252, 689; **vi** 48, 95, 158, 281, 382; **vii** 180, 201, 426

To Mr. Osborne, **v** 435, 439, 524, 685; **vi** 32, 290, 550; **vii** 23, 61, 117, 149, 153, 227, 325, 455

To Sir M. Palairet, **i** 13, 30, 40; **iii** 126, 231, 243; **vi** 166; **vii** 180, 201

To Earl of Perth, **i** 14, 27, 33, 259, 366; **ii** 587, 590, 596, 626; **iii** 62, 202, 316, 325, 328, 330–1, 333, 340–2, 353–4, 356, 360–2, 453, 460, 463, 467–8; **iv** 302–3, 315, 317, 324, 333, 346–7, 494, 551; **v** 56, 125, 127, 129, 131–2, 135, 140, 145–6, 153, 155, 164, 181, 252, 255; **viii** 268

To Sir M. Peterson, **iii** 341; **iv** 399, 432

To Sir E. Phipps, **i** 32, 35–6, 50, 52, 82, 86, 88, 95, 140, 246, 325, 339, 346, 351, 356, 361, 383, 389, 401, 419, 468, 477, 495–6, 498, 527, 531, 578; **ii** 230, 246, 261–2, 275, 282n, 301, 318, 323, 325–6, 362, 410, 436, 456–7, 460–2, 477, 479, 484, 489n, 511, 535, 570, 575, 586, 602; **iii** 99, 203, 258, 260, 267, 282, 284, 341, 343, 353, 401n, 406, 426–7, 436, 440, 446, 452–3, 460, 502–3, 507, 509, 511, 567–8, 629–32; **iv** 18, 37, 42, 79, 90, 100, 133, 135, 152, 166, 170, 236, 266, 272, 328–9, 342, 344, 349, 353, 360, 377–9, 400, 514, 532, 545, 552, 642; **v** 49, 56, 67, 95, 107, 113, 126, 136, 146, 160, 166, 179, 183, 189, 207, 225, 243, 254, 257, 260, 265–6, 287, 344, 385–6, 451, 459, 480, 496, 504, 507, 522, 527, 534, 551, 577, 670, 691, 703, 772, 793; **vi** 106, 165, 194, 196, 215, 260, 295, 315, 337; **vii** 167, 187, 225, 241, 244, 246, 276, 288, 305, 333–4, 342, 369, 408, 423, 439, 447, 455, 498, 501, 509, 523; **viii** 165, 167, 419, 424, 488, 494, 497, 517; **ix** 7, 82, 145, 149, 191, 207, 245, 260–1, 353, 420–1

To Mr. Preston, **vii** 180, 201

To Dr. Quo Tai-chi, **ix** 498, 512

To Count Raczynski, **iii** 14; **vii** 531

To Sir Patrick W. Ramsay, **iii** 453; **v** 252; **vii** 180, 201

To Mr. Rendel, **v** 56, 129, 148, 529; **vi** 496; **vii** 180, 201

To Mr. Le Rougetel, **vi** 320, 582, 629, 631, 687; **vii** 42, 57

To Lord Runciman, **ii** 180, 193, 202, 206, 244, 264, 267, 308

To Sir A. Ryan, **v** 138, 412

To Sir W. Seeds, **iv** 35, 106, 360, 391–2, 400, 508, 512, 530, 544, 556; **v** 20–1, 53, 56, 82, 201, 205, 209, 235, 368, 373, 443, 448, 453, 461, 479, 528, 595, 668, 678–80, 688, 719, 773, 776–7, 787; **vi** 5, 22, 50, 91–2, 103, 109, 128, 142, 144, 152, 173, 193, 212, 225, 232, 257, 275–7, 279, 310, 319, 333, 336–7, 339, 355–6, 360, 386, 427, 429–30, 448, 456, 476, 478, 484, 492–3, 525–6, 533, 543–4, 548, 577, 591–2, 594–5; **vii** 8–9, 27, 42, 44, 121, 126, 161, 187, 224; **ix** 334

To Sir W. Selby, **iv** 399, 432

To Mr. E. H. G. Shepherd, **vi** 226

To Mr. F. M. Shepherd, **vi** 431, 435, 447, 462, 595, 642; **vii** 5, 8, 129, 261, 318

To Mr. Shone, **ii** 137; **vi** 437

To Sir J. Simon, **iii** 530

To Mr. Snow, **iii** 453; **v** 252, 522, 669, 689; **vi** 264, 307, 413; **vii** 180, 201

To Mr. Troutbeck, **iv** 14, 25, 109

To U.K. Delegation (Geneva), **viii** 83, 102, 104

To U.K. Delegation (Munich), **ii** 614, 616, 620; **iii** 48

To Mr. Vereker, **i** 256, 389

To Sir G. R. Warner, **v** 252

To Sir S. Waterlow, **iii** 341; **iv** 361, 386, 497; **v** 56, 129, 132, 138, 148, 151, 157–8, 161, 165, 179, 185, 236, 348, 615

Conversation with M. Aras, **iv** 436–7, 558–60; **v** 57–8; **vi** 82–3, 567–8

Conversation with M. Balutis, **iv** 474–5

Conversation with M. de Barcza, **iii** 9–10

Conversation with M. Blum, **v** 507–8

Conversation with M. Bonnet, **iii** 530–1; **iv** 422–7, 487–90; **v** 638–9; **vii** 511–2, 525–6; *see also* Anglo-French conversations in Subject Index

Conversation with M. Bonnet and M. Daladier, **i** 601–3; **v** 608–14, 623–5

Conversation with Mr. Bruce and Mr. te Water, **vi** 588–90

Conversation with M. Burckhardt, **iii** 595–6; **v** 627–30

Conversation with M. Cambon, **ii** 158–60; **vii** 167–8

Conversation with King Carol of Roumania, **iii** 231–3, 243

Halifax, Viscount (*cont.*)
Conversation with Baron de Cartier de Marchienne, iv 44
Conversation with Mr. Chamberlain (*at Godesberg*), ii 477
Conversation with Count Ciano, iii 521–3; vii 302, 310, 358, 436–7, 442, 465, 507–8, 518–9
Conversation with M. Charles Corbin, i 35–6, 52–3, 88–90, 356–7, 477, 531–2, 563–5; ii 19–20, 196–8, 246–8, 262–4, 275–7, 326–8; iii 99–100, 258–9, 427–8, 436–7, 507–8, 511–2, 567; iv 42–4, 272–3, 344–5, 378–9, 532–3; v 49–51, 67–8, 95–6, 136–8, 234, 344–6, 385–7, 504, 507, 577–8, 772–3, 793–4; vi 106, 512–3; vii 246–9, 288–9, 342–3, 509–10; ix 207
Conversation with M. Cretzianu, v 74–7, 657–63
Conversation with Signor Crolla, v 127–8, 140–3, 146–7, 151, 153–7, 164, 343
Conversation with M. Dahlerus, vi 483–4; vii 234n, 281–3, 395–8
Conversation with M. Daladier, i 601–3; v 608–14, 623–5
Conversation with Dr. von Dirksen, i 239–40, 355–6, 369–71, 454–8; iii 127–8, 433–5, 439–40, 566–7; iv 138–41, 270–2, 272n, 380–1; v 600–3; vi 88–9, 647–8
Conversation with Mgr. W. Godfrey, v 435–6, 439–40, 452
Conversation with Count Grandi, ii 626–7; iii 360–1; iv 346–7; v 779–81, 800–1
Conversation with M. Gripenberg, v 522; vi 264–6, 307–8
Conversation with Mr. Herschel Johnson, ii 149
Conversation with Mr. J. Kennedy, ii 213, 284–5, 295–6, 625; iv 364–6, 380, 499–500; v 169, 793; ix 233–4, 493–4
Conversation with M. Komarnicki, iii 597; v 637
Conversation with Dr. Wellington Koo, viii 398–9
Conversation with Dr. Th. Kordt, ii 105–6; vii 496–7
Conversation with M. Kurti, v 138–9
Conversation with M. Maisky, i 256; ii 107, 271–2, 623–5; iii 153–4, 331; iv 35–6, 391–2, 544, 556–8; v 53–4, 82–4, 201–2, 209–10, 373–5, 453–4, 479–80, 528–9, 630–4; vi 5–7, 50–1, 152–3, 279–81, 339, 484–6; ix 334–5
Conversation with M. Jan Masaryk, i 33–4, 235–8, 324–5, 378–9, 493–4, 571n
Conversation with M. Milanovitch, iv 521–3; v 762
Conversation with M. Momtchiloff, v 529–31
Conversation with M. Munters, v 648–9
Conversation with Mr. Okamoto, ix 487–8

Conversation with Prince Paul, Regent of Yugoslavia, vi 437–9
Conversation with Sir E. Phipps, vii 518
Conversation with Dr. Quo Tai-chi, viii 4–5, 58–9, 145–7, 173–4, 203–4, 244–5, 308–9, 336–7, 381–2; ix 5–7, 12–4, 46–7, 144, 209–11, 236–8, 248–9, 292–3, 332–4, 389–92, 506–7
Conversation with Count Raczynski, i 247–8; ii 317–8; iii 3, 13, 189–90, 430–2; iv 11, 434–6, 500–3, 510–1, 575; v 51–2, 97–9, 539–40, 747–9; vi 198–201, 244–6, 321–5, 365–6, 378, 564–6, 649–50, 669–70; vii 168–70, 249–50, 290–2, 310–1, 380, 496, 532
Conversation with M. Paul Reynaud, i 325–7
Conversation with Herr von Ribbentrop, i 4–6, 13, 21–3
Conversation with M. Sandler, iii 594–5
Conversation with M. A. Schmidt, vi 281–2, 382
Conversation with Mr. Shigemitsu, viii 422–4; ix 27–9, 57–8, 86–8, 202–3, 205–6, 507–8
Conversation with M. Simopoulas, iv 497–9; v 157–8, 185
Conversation with M. Tilea, iv 283–4, 360–1, 366–7, 375–6; v 395–6, 480–3; vi 263, 582–5
Conversation with Captain Wiedemann, i 584–9; *referred to,* i 601–2, 613, 618; ii 78–9; vii 626
Conversation with Mr. Yoshida, viii 78–9
Letter to Mr. Chamberlain, vii 80, 553
Letter to Sir N. Henderson, i 622, 627; ii 54, 256; v 802; vi 75, 219, 353, 441, 529; vii 632
Letter to Sir P. Loraine, vi 487, 588; vii 49
Letter to Prince Paul, Regent of Yugoslavia, vii 421n, 492
Letter to Earl of Perth, iii 459
Letter to Sir E. Phipps, ii 303; iii 249, 251; v 800; vi 301, 317
Letter to Count Raczynski, vi 699
Letter to Herr von Ribbentrop, ii 18; *referred to,* ii 41, 127
Letter to Viscount Runciman, ii 111
Memorandum communicated to M. Bonnet, i 545; *referred to,* i 563, 577
Memorandum communicated to Herr Hitler, ii 78; *referred to,* ii 87, 91–3, 101, 105–6, 109, 115, 117, 119, 121, 128, 134, 153, 249
Message to President Benes, ii 443
Message to M. Burckhardt, vii 5–6
Message to M. Comnène, iii 45n
Message to Field-Marshal Göring, vii 283; *referred to,* vii 284, 286n, 314
Message to Signor Mussolini, Aug. 20, 1939, vii 75–6; *referred to,* ii 95, 113, 120, 144, 167; Aug. 28, vii 323
Message to Herr von Ribbentrop, May 22,

1938, **i** 341; *referred to,* **i** 348, 355, 475; Sept. 9, 1938, **ii** 277; *referred to,* **ii** 273, 285, 295; **vi** 707n
Minute by, **v** 286n; **vi** 483; **vii** 354n, 355n, 436, 442, 465; **viii** 398
Speech at Hull, Feb. 3, 1939, **iv** 90
Speech at 1900 Club dinner, June 21, 1939, **vi** 202
Speech at Royal Institute of International Affairs, June 29, 1939, **vi** 213, 216, 220, 235, 245, 273, 296, 318, 390, 442, 554, 648, 713, 744; **vii** 30, 48, 111
Speeches at Anglo-French conversations, April 1938, **i** 199–201, 209–16, 224–5, 227–9, 232–3; Sept. 18, 1938, **ii** 384–5, 394; Sept. 26, 1938, **ii** 538–40; Nov. 1938, **iii** 300–2, 304–5, 307; Jan. 10, 1939, **iii** 513–5; Mar. 21, 1939, **iv** 422, 424–7; Mar. 22, 1939, **iv** 457–61
Speeches at Anglo–Italian conversations, Jan. 1939, **iii** 519–20
Speeches at Anglo-Polish conversations, April 1939, **v** 3–9, 15, 17–8
Speeches at Anglo-Roumanian conversations, April 1939, **v** 295–315, 321–33, 343
Speeches and statements in House of Lords, Mar. 16, 1938, **i** 52n, 75; May 18, **i** 345n; May 20, **i** 339; May 23, **i** 370; July 27, **i** 584n; **ii** 17–20, 37, 53, 94; **viii** 1n, 31, 48, 54, 57, 60; Oct. 3, **iii** 128; Feb. 23, 1939, **iv** 329; Mar. 20, **iv** 431n, 436, 472; April 13, **v** 236; April 19, **ix** 25; June 8, **vi** 15, 51, 59, 71, 73, 77, 739–40; June 12, **vi** 126; June 20, **ix** 228, 499; July 24, **vi** 465n; **ix** 334, 374; Aug. 3, **vi** 529, 591–2, 595; **ix** 459n, 506; Aug. 24, **vii** 245n, 247, 250; Sept. 2, **vii** 523–4, 526, 534
Proposed speech on Czechoslovak question, Sept. 1938, **ii** 205, 211–2, 214–5, 239, 247, 256
Proposed statement to press, Sept. 1938, **ii** 268–9, 272
Visits to France, Nov. 1938 and Mar. 1939. *See Speeches at* Anglo-French conversations
Visit to Italy, Jan. 1939. *See* Chamberlain, Mr. N. (*visit to* Italy)
Halifax, Lady, **iii** 466
Halit Nazmi Kesmir (Under-Secretary of Turkish Ministry of Commerce), **vii** 321
Hall, Mr. (Commissioner of Customs, Canton), **viii**, 238, 240
Hallawell, Wing Commander C. (British Air Attaché at Moscow, Mar. 1937–Nov. 1941), **iv** 188; **vii** 45, 562
Memorandum by, **iv** 196
Haller, General Joseph, **vi** 262
Hall-Patch, E. L. (Financial Adviser to H.M. Embassies in China and Japan, June 1936–Sept. 1939), **viii** 125, 231, 237 301–2

Hambro, C. J. (President of the Norwegian Storting, 1927–40), **iv** 622
Hamilton, General Sir Ian (President of the British Legion, Scotland)
Conversation with Herr Hitler, **ii** 57–8
Hamilton, Maxwell M. (Head of Far Eastern Division, U.S. Department of State), **ix** 263, 372
Hammerstein-Equord, Colonel-General Baron Kurt von, **v** 460; **vii** 416, 417n
Han Li-wu (a member of the Chinese National People's Political Council), **viii** 295; **ix** 340, 341n
Hanawa, Y. (Japanese Consul-General at Hankow), **ix** 73–4, 81, 157, 225
Hankey, Sir Maurice (1939 1st Baron) (Secretary to the Cabinet, 1919–38), **iii** 87
Memorandum by, Oct. 3, 1938, **iii** 88
Hankey, R. M. A. (Secretary, H.M. Embassy, Warsaw, Nov. 1936–Sept. 1939), **v** 538; **vi** 405, 487
Conversation with M. Wszelaki, **vi** 405–7
Hansen, Generalmajor (German representative on Military Sub-Committee of International Commission set up in Oct. 1938), **iii** 162
Harada, Baron Kumao (Private Secretary to Prince Saionji), **viii** 528
Hardy, Colonel K. (Hungarian Military Attaché at Berlin), **ii** 309
Harinxma, Baron B. Ph. van (Netherlands Minister at Brussels, 1938–40), **iv** 450, 452
Harvey, O. C. (Counsellor in the Foreign Office; Principal Private Secretary to Secretary of State for Foreign Affairs, 1936–9), **ii** 411, 463, 606n, 691; **iii** 532, 534, 536; **iv** 209; **vii** 166, 315
To Sir F. Leith-Ross, **iii** 636
Minute by, **vii** 286, 507
Hasbach, Senator (Chairman of Council of Germans in Poland), **iv** 87–8
Hassan Nashat Pasha (Egyptian Minister at Berlin, 1929–38; Ambassador at London, June 1938–45), **i** 494; **vi** 412
Hassell, Ulrich von (German Ambassador at Rome, Nov. 1932–Feb. 1938), **iii** 659; **vii** 435n, 437n, 466
Conversation with Sir N. Henderson, **ii** 330–1; **vii** 47–8
Hasselman, Captain B. R. P. F. (Netherlands Military Attaché at Berlin), **iii** 551
Hata, General S. (a member of Japanese Supreme War Council), **viii** 535
Hatta, Yoshiaki (Japanese Minister for Overseas Affairs, 1938–9), **viii** 181, 183
Havelka, Dr. Jiri (Czechoslovak Minister without Portfolio in Dr. Beran's Cabinet, 1938–9), **iii** 377; **iv** 565
Havliçek, Dr. Frantisek (Czechoslovak Minister at Tokyo, 1932–8), **viii** 1, 451, 498

Havrankova, Madame (Host of Lord Runciman in Czechoslovakia), **ii** 667
Hayne, Major F. (U.S. Military Attaché at Moscow), **i** 306
Hearson, Commander Glyn (British Assistant Naval Attaché for Europe, Sept. 1937–Sept. 1939), **vi** 454
Heeren, Viktor von (German Minister at Belgrade, 1933–41), **ii** 135–6, 151–2, 260; **vi** 166
Heiderich, A. (Czechoslovak Permanent Delegate to League of Nations), **iii** 132, 176, 207–8
Heidrich, Dr. (Legal Adviser to Czechoslovak Ministry of Foreign Affairs), **ii** 663
Helen, Princess of Montenegro, Queen of Italy, **iii** 535
Helfand, L. (Counsellor of Soviet Embassy at Rome: acted as Chargé d'Affaires), **iv** 292; **v** 429; **vi** 293–4, 596; **vii** 72n
   Conversation with Sir P. Loraine, **vi** 283–5
Hemming, Francis (Secretary of Non-Intervention Committee), **iii** 297, 332, 337, 341
Henchman, Mr. (Shanghai Manager of the Hongkong and Shanghai Banking Corporation), **ix** 55
Hencke, A. (Counsellor of German Legation, Czechoslovakia: acted as Chargé d'Affaires), **ii** 82, 662; **iv** 63, 243, 270, 403
Henderson, Arthur (M.P. for Kingswinford), **i** 520; **v** 310; **ix** 12, 25n
Henderson, Ian Leslie (attached to Lord Runciman's Mission to Prague, 1938), **ii** 305, 662, 665, 667, 672; **iii** 83, 142
Henderson, Sir Nevile (H.M. Ambassador at Berlin, April 1937–Sept. 1939), **i** 32, 46, 56n, 115, 152–3, 241, 243, 246, 253, 259, 277, 290n, 303–4, 317n, 318n, 321n, 323n, 330n, 336, 343, 353–4, 358, 387, 400, 402, 409, 412, 414–5, 424, 463n, 469, 476, 491, 498n, 499, 504, 516, 522, 525–6, 533n, 539–40, 552n, 553, 560, 561n, 564, 568n, 577, 581, 586–8, 614n, 647; **ii** 5, 18–9, 41n, 54n, 59n, 77, 88, 105–6, 108, 136, 142, 148–9, 151, 172n, 195, 206n, 211, 217n, 260, 279, 290n, 291n, 295–6, 314n, 324, 352, 354, 378, 388, 409, 411, 421–2, 569n, 583, 593–4, 596–7, 605, 608–9, 620, 681, 683, 686; **iii** 60n, 78, 109, 128–30, 134–5, 147, 167n, 296, 414, 607, 620; **iv** 160, 218n, 260–1, 267–8, 287n, 376, 441–5, 591n, 597–8; **v** 415, 417–9, 497; **vi** 137–8, 208, 358, 399, 412, 534, 661, 707n, 753–4; **vii** 73, 78, 89, 123, 129, 144, 147–9, 156, 164, 177n, 214, 247, 249, 257, 269, 278–9, 284, 294–5, 299, 301, 310–1, 316n, 317, 323, 334, 355n, 357, 367–8, 373, 380, 388, 392, 396, 417n, 435, 437, 441–2, 457, 474, 489, 492, 500–1, 505, 507, 519, 521, 525, 538–9; **viii** 11n, 12n, 179, 239; **ix** 507
   To Sir A. Cadogan, **v** 635; **vii** 393, 435, 438

To Mr. Chamberlain, **iv** 594
To Viscount Halifax, **i** 3, 7–9, 12, 15–6, 18–9, 23, 25–6, 30–2, 39, 43–4, 48, 56, 59, 65, 92, 97, 103, 108, 115, 118, 155, 173, 176, 238–9, 252, 255, 257, 260, 262, 265, 271, 273, 284, 286–7, 290, 294, 310, 317–20, 329, 333–5, 343–5, 348–9, 358–9, 362, 364, 376, 380, 382, 384–5, 391–3, 417, 426–7, 447, 458, 460, 474–5, 485, 503, 511, 513, 520, 527, 533–4, 536–7, 542, 561, 568, 580, 584, 596–8, 609, 613; **ii** 2, 6, 13, 23, 26–7, 39, 41, 46–8, 51–2, 57, 61, 65, 67–8, 76n, 77, 87, 91–2, 97, 101–3, 108–9, 116, 119–20, 122–3, 125–7, 129, 137, 156, 160, 169–71, 203, 205, 214, 216, 224, 232–3, 241–2, 244, 250, 272, 283, 296, 298, 300, 306, 309–10, 322, 330, 334, 357–8, 360, 362, 364, 367, 370, 402, 407–8, 410, 413–4, 417, 423, 425, 428, 430, 436, 439, 481, 512, 515, 543, 545, 551–3, 561, 563, 569, 574, 576, 578, 584, 586, 589, 597–8, 601, 603; **iii** 9n, 56, 63–6, 73, 79, 91–3, 99, 108–9, 119–20, 122, 125, 128, 148–9, 151, 158, 160–1, 169–71, 174–5, 186, 191, 630, 639; **iv** 110, 116, 120, 122–3, 131, 134–5, 137, 162–3, 165, 168–9, 171, 173, 200, 210, 218, 222–3, 230–4, 237, 242, 244–5, 249–51, 255–60, 263–4, 275–6, 278, 319, 371, 589–90, 592–3, 595; **v** 318, 337, 369, 387–90, 398–400, 403, 429, 433, 437, 462–3, 517, 523, 562, 584, 616, 656, 671, 673–4, 692, 713, 723, 732, 768; **vi** 59, 80, 93, 113, 132, 175, 197, 211, 215, 235, 238, 348, 355, 359, 362, 368, 381, 432, 434, 465, 481, 497, 543, 559, 606, 609, 611, 615, 626, 628, 632, 636, 662, 667, 698; **vii** 7, 12, 29, 47, 56, 62, 75, 90, 97, 100, 104, 108–9, 118, 124, 132, 145, 150, 161, 173, 177, 181, 184, 191–2, 198, 201, 207, 222, 227, 229, 235–6, 239, 251, 292, 343, 348, 351, 360, 362–3, 368, 372, 374, 376, 380, 388, 393–4, 400–2, 409, 415, 419, 429–30, 432–4, 437, 440, 445, 453–4, 457, 459, 468, 475–7, 483, 487, 493–4, 504, 510, 512, 514, 517, 522, 533, 536
To Sir P. Loraine, **v** 516
To Mr. Newton, **iii** 73
Conversation with Dr. Attolico, **ii** 49, 119–20, 171–2, 242; **vi** 254–5, 348, 456, 607–8, 699–701; **vii** 7–8, 255–6, 362, 401–2, 504
Conversation with Sir A. Cadogan, **ii** 421, 592–4
Conversation with M. Cincar-Markovitch, **ii** 241
Conversation with M. Coulondre, **vi** 348
Conversation with M. Dahlerus, **vii** 512–3
Conversation with Vicomte Davignon, **vi** 348
Conversation with Dr. von Dirksen, **ii** 48–9, 59; **v** 429–30

Conversation with M. François-Poncet, **i** 12, 460–1, 535; **ii** 68–9
Conversation with Dr. Goebbels, **ii** 283
Conversation with Field-Marshal Göring, **i** 23–4, 39, 58–9, 173–6, 513–4; **ii** 283, 362–4, 378, 410, 543, 561–2, 589, 648; **iv** 120–1, 123, 592; **v** 713–7; **vi** 13–4; **vii** 453–4, 476
Conversation with M. van Haersma de With, **iv** 137
Conversation with Herr von Hassell, **ii** 330–1; **vii** 47–8
Conversation with Herr Hitler, Mar. 3, 1938, *referred to*, **i** 26, 98, 109, 111, 175–6, 232, 244, 252, 255, 260, 285, 287, 296, 427, 622, 624; **vii** 363, 387, 624
Conversation with Herr Hitler, **ii** 592, 596–8; **iv** 165–6; **vii** 162–3, 201–2, 227–31, 236, 251–3, 288, 290, 348, 351–4, 363–4, 374–7, 387–8, 393, 426–7
Conversation with Herr von Kühlmann, **vi** 28–9
Conversation with M. Lipski, **iv** 263–4; **vi** 238–9; **vii** 13, 62–3, 192, 239, 394, 433
Conversation with Prince Lubomirski, **vi** 636–7
Conversation with M. Mastny, **i** 65–6, 262, 319, 503–4; **iv** 245–6
Conversation with Baron von Neurath, **i** 15–6, 44, 57–8, 384–5; **ii** 224–6, 283, 413
Conversation with Herr von Papen, **v** 674–5
Conversation with Prince Paul of Yugoslavia, **vi** 11–2
Conversation with Herr von Ribbentrop, **i** 284–6, 286–7, 290, 329–30, 334–5, 542–3; **ii** 205–6, 216–7, 283; **iv** 110–1; **v** 387–90; **vii** 429–30, 432–3, 493–4, 511
Conversation with Dr. Schacht, **ii** 23–4
Conversation with M. Schubert, **ii** 428–30, 578–9
Conversation with Herr Tauschitz, **i** 12
Conversation with Baron von Weizsäcker, **i** 335, 344–6, 348, 393–4, 426–8, 485–6, 537–8, 568–9, 596–7; **ii** 6, 11, 24, 109–10, 123, 203–4, 216, 283, 325–6, 417–8, 584–5; **iii** 149–50; **iv** 122–3, 244, 250, 590–1; **v** 337–9, 562–3, 807; **vi** 28, 59–62, 75–6, 359, 362–4, 381–2, 609–12; **vii** 29–31
Conversation with Herr Woermann, **i** 260, 304*n*; **ii** 87–8, 91–3
Letter to Sir A. Cadogan, **i** 603, 616; **ii** 239, 257; **v** 424, 468, 526*n*, 546, 594, 665, 781, 804, 807; **vi** 124, 201, 634, 702, 720; **vii** 16, 37, 69, 110, 257, 467, 623–5, 630, 632
Letter to Viscount Halifax, **i** 494, 590–1, 621–4, 626, 628; **ii** 10, 45, 58, 63, 83, 108*n*, 131, 134, 138, 238, 646, 651, 654; **iii** 615–6; **v** 422, 455, 586, 716, 728, 798–9, 801–2; **vi** 11–2, 28, 75, 123, 171,

184, 254, 329, 372, 385, 456, 657, 699, 706, 709–11, 713–8; **vii** 36, 67, 82, 137–8, 212, 255, 386, 426, 465
Letter to Mr. Harvey, **vi** 519
Letter to Sir H. Kennard, **v** 699
Letter to Mr. Kirkpatrick, **v** 666, 720
Letter to Baron von Neurath, **i** 24
Letter to Mr. Newton, **ii** 112*n*
Letter to Sir G. Ogilvie-Forbes, **ii** 280
Letter to Herr von Ribbentrop, **ii** 431; **vii** 292
Letter to Sir O. Sargent, **i** 592; **v** 425; **vi** 703, 709; **vii** 51
Letter to Mr. Strang, **i** 450; **ii** 13, 21, 35; **v** 817; **vii** 37
Letter to Sir H. Wilson, **ii** 283, 647–9
Message to Mr. Strang, **ii** 419
Movements of, **i** 553*n*; **ii** 149*n*, 178*n*, 240, 296, 686*n*; **iii** 196*n*; **iv** 109*n*; **vi** 201*n*; **vii** 145, 266*n*, 328; *recall to* London, Mar. 17, 1939, **iv** 291*n*; *referred to*, **iv** 364, 379–81, 461, 490, 533, 595–6; **v** 245; *return to* Berlin, **v** 318*n*
At Meeting at Berlin between Sir H. Wilson and Herr Hitler, **ii** 554–7
At Meeting at Godesberg between Mr. Chamberlain and Herr Hitler, **ii** 472, 499
At Munich Conference, **ii** 631
Note on Nuremberg Congress, Sept. 1938, **ii** 650
Views on Dr. von Schuschnigg's decision to hold plebiscite, **i** 8, 24–5, 29, 39
Views on character and objectives of Herr Hitler, **i** 98–100, 108–12; **ii** 257, 296–7, 299; **iv** 121–2, 210–6; **v** 369–70; **vi** 501
Views on effect on Herr Hitler of British démarche of May 21–2, 1938, **i** 450, 533; **ii** 240, 280, 647
Views on Sudeten German question. *See* Sudeten German question (in Subject Index)
Views on German action towards Czechoslovakia, Mar. 15, 1939, **iv** 278–9, 595; **v** 617–8; **vi** 498
Views on Danzig question in relation to possible outbreak of war, **v** 422–4, 584–7, 619–21, 665–6, 721, 768–71, 798, 817–8; **vi** 329, 359, 372, 498, 558, 637, 657, 703, 713–20; **vii** 16, 36, 56, 257, 409, 476, 483
Views on German-Soviet Non-Aggression Pact, **vii** 125, 137–8, 185, 256
Henlein, Konrad (Leader of Sudeten German party), **i** 55, 64, 69, 77, 118, 122–3, 125, 140, 142, 149, 170, 174, 187, 212, 238, 243–5, 248–629 *passim*; **ii** 1, 4–6, 12, 23, 70, 75, 80, 81, 95, 102, 121, 135, 142, 144, 153–5, 164, 166, 170–1, 177–8, 183, 189, 192–3, 200–2, 205, 215, 248, 250–1, 255, 263, 267, 274,

Henlein, Konrad (*cont.*)
283, 292, 300, 305, 313, 320–2, 327, 335–6, 357n, 369, 383–4, 403, 440, 647–8, 650, 652 660, 662–4, 666–9, 672–4, 676; iii 214; iv 562; vii 624
  appointed Head of Civil Administration in Bohemia, iv 272, 275, 279, 564
  Communications with Sir R. Vansittart, i 416, 418n; ii 4n, 5
  Conversation with Mr. Ashton-Gwatkin, ii 177, 199–200, 231–2, 333–4, 657–60
  Conversation with Mr. Churchill and Sir A. Sinclair, i 297–8, 633–5
  Conversation with Herr Hitler, ii 231–2, 659
  Conversation with Lord Runciman, ii 122, 333–4, 656–7
  Conversation with Sir R. Vansittart, i 298–9, 630–3
  Proclamation by, Sept. 1938, ii 335, 357n, 415
  Speech at Breslau, Aug. 11, 1938, ii 95
  Speech at Carlsbad, April 24, 1938, i 182–6; *referred to*, i 186, 195–6, 215–6, 219, 221, 230, 238, 243, 262, 269, 279, 388, 395, 630, 633–4; iii 214; *see also* Carlsbad Programme in Subject Index
  Visit to Herr Hitler, i 568n; ii 177, 180–1, 199–201, 208–9, 212, 215, 221, 231, 233, 238, 242–4, 246–7, 250, 252–3, 255–6, 659, 661, 668–70
  Visit to London, May 1938, i 292, 297–9, 364, 372–3, 416n, 418, 459, 468, 630–5
Henlein, Frau, ii 669
Henniker-Major, J. P. E. C. (a member of Far Eastern Dept. of the Foreign Office)
  Minute by, vii 435
Henry, Charles Arsène. *See* Arsène-Henry, Charles
Henry, Jules (a member of French Ministry of Foreign Affairs), iv 639
  At Anglo-French conversations, Sept. 1938, ii 373, 520, 536; Nov. 1938, iii 285
Herbert, Major G. A. (H.M. Consul at Tientsin, Oct. 1938–Nov. 1939), viii 233, 314, 323, 350, 427, 504, 511, 527n, 558; ix 2, 66, 72, 126, 160, 161n, 166, 179, 186, 196, 216, 221, 324, 355, 357–8, 361, 363–5, 369, 409, 424, 470, 481, 497, 504–5
  To British Embassy, Shanghai, viii 452, 468, 489, 491
  Conversation with General Homma, viii 491–2
Héring, General (Governor of Strasbourg), iii 569, 579
Herriot, Édouard (President of French Chamber of Deputies, 1936–40), ii 219–20, 337, 355, 535, 547, 560, 622; vii 515
  Conversation with Sir E. Phipps, ii 337
Herry, Baron Joseph (Belgian Minister at The Hague, 1937–40), iv 28, 52–3
Heske, Herr, ii 672

Hess, Rudolf (German Minister without Portfolio, Herr Hitler's deputy, 1933–41), i 223, 611; ii 89, 652; iv 80; vii 464n
  Speech, June 12, 1938, i 485n, 494, 499; Aug. 28, 1938, ii 178–9
Hesse, Prince Christopher of, vii 422
Hesse, Dr. Fritz ("Deutsches Nachrichten Buro' correspondent and press adviser to German Embassy, London)
  Conversation with Sir H. Wilson, ix 539
Hesse, Prince Philip of (Son-in-law of King of Italy, special envoy between Herr Hitler and Signor Mussolini), v 801–2; vii 421–2
Hewel, Walther (Herr von Ribbentrop's personal secretary), ii 351, 353–4; iv 602–4; vii 212, 325
Heymans, Dr. Albèrt (South African Minister at Rome, 1934–40), iii 533–4
Heywood, Major-General T. G. G. (a member of British Military Delegation to Moscow, Aug. 1939), vii 34, 562, 568–9, 573, 595
  Letter to Major-General H. R. Pownall, vii 600, 604
Hidaka, Shinrokuro (Japanese Consul-General at Shanghai, viii 3n, 53, 99, 481, 485
Higuchi, General (Japanese Director of Military Intelligence), viii 439; ix 174
Hiitonen, Dr. E. (Finnish Chargé d'Affaires at Prague, 1938–9), i 549–50
Hilgenreiner, Dr. (Chairman of German Christian Socialist party, Czechoslovakia), i 69
Hilger, G. (Commercial Counsellor, German Embassy, Moscow), vi 22, 77
Hill, Sir T. St. Quintin (Comptroller-General, Department of Overseas Trade), iv 568
Himer, Colonel K. (German Military Attaché at Warsaw), v 58
Himmelmann, E. P., v 245
Himmler, Heinrich (Leader of S.S. and Chief of German Police), i 131, 286, 527, 531; ii 64, 66, 103, 108n, 297, 329, 653, 684, 690; iii 383, 388, 563, 615, 625; iv 4, 10, 19, 38, 154, 201, 280, 596, 665; vi 12, 44, 164, 178, 248, 420, 703, 724, 734, 736; vii 419, 517
Hiranuma, Baron Keiichiro (Prime Minister of Japan, Jan.–Aug. 1939), viii 369, 464; ix 23, 64, 109, 129–31, 186, 209, 233, 239, 261–2, 264–6, 311, 316–20, 385, 412, 415, 431, 437, 442, 458, 489, 496–8, 501, 517–8
Hiraoka, Colonel, viii 32
Hirohito, Emperor of Japan (since 1926), vii 259; viii 122, 334, 482; ix 130
  Conversation with Sir R. Craigie, viii 276–7
Hirota, Koki (Japanese Prime Minister, Feb. 1936–Jan. 1937; Minister for Foreign Affairs, June 1937–May 1938), viii 121, 155, 170, 355; ix 498, 517
Hitler, Adolf (Head of State, Leader and Chancellor of Germany, 1934–45), i–vii *passim*; ix 240, 277, 412, 415, 506–7, 539

Communications *with* Mr. Chamberlain
  letter of Sept. 23, 1938, **ii** 485; *referred to,*
    ii 494, 488–9, 521–2
  memorandum handed to Mr. Chamberlain,
    Sept. 23, **ii** 495–6; *referred to,* **ii** 49¹,
    499–508, 511–2, 519, 521–6, 541, 547–
    9, 551, 553–4, 556–7, 560, 564–6, 576,
    580–1, 583, 585, 612, 616, 627; **iii**
    49*n*, 104
  letter of Sept. 27, 1938, **ii** 576–8; *referred to,*
    ii 587; **v** 337, 617, 666, 684, 713
  letter of Aug. 23, 1939, **vii** 174, 177, 193;
    referred to, **vii** 181, 191–2, 193*n*, 221,
    265, 269, 302
  proposals of Aug. 25, 1939, **vii** 227–9, 251;
    referred to, **vii** 230, 235, 239, 267, 278–
    9, 284, 288, 290, 292, 322, 330, 350;
    ix 508
  note of Aug. 29, 1939, **vii** 374–5, 381,
    388–90; *referred to,* **vii** 376–7, 391–6,
    398–9, 403, 406, 413, 457, 511
Conversation *with* King Boris III of Bulgaria,
  iii 143
Conversation *with* M. Burkhardt, **vi** 691–6
Conversation *with* Mr. Chamberlain, **ii** 338–
  51, 463–73, 499–508, 635–40
Conversation *with* M. Chvalkovsky, **iii** 174,
  190–2, 222; **iv** 3
Conversation *with* M. Coulondre, **vii** 288
Conversation *with* M. Dahlerus, **vii** 284–5
Conversation *with* M. François-Poncet, **ii** 600,
  607–8; **iii** 244, 618–20
Conversation *with* Herr Frank, **ii** 177; *referred
  to,* **ii** 180, 182
Conversation *with* M. Gafencu, **v** 302–6, 309–
  11.
Conversation *with* President Hacha and M.
  Chvalkovsky, Mar. 1939. *See* Hacha,
  President (*visit to* Berlin)
Conversation *with* General Sir Ian Hamilton,
  ii 57–8
Conversation *with* Sir N. Henderson, Mar. 3,
  1938. *See* Henderson, Sir N. (*Conversation
  with* Herr Hitler, Mar. 3, 1938)
Conversation *with* Sir N. Henderson, **ii** 592,
  596–8; **iv** 165–6; **vii** 162–3, 201–2, 227–
  31, 236, 251–3, 288, 290, 348, 351–4,
  363–4, 374–7, 387–8, 393, 426–7
Conversation *with* Herr Henlein, **ii** 231–2,
  659
Conversation *with* Sir H. Wilson, **ii** 552–7,
  563–7
Conversation *with* M. Wysocky, **i** 274
Message *to* Signor Mussolini, **vii** 486
Message *to* M. Stalin, Aug. 17, 1939, **vii**
  41
Order *to* armed forces, Mar. 15, 1939, **iv**
  256
Proclamation *of* Mar. 12, 1938, on invasion of
  Austria, **i** 26

Proclamation *of* Mar. 15, 1939, on invasion of
  Bohemia and Moravia, **iv** 257
Reply *to* President Roosevelt's peace appeal
  of April 14, 19⁰ ., **v** 360, 372
Speeches *of*, Feb. 20, 1938, **i** 130, 296; Feb.
  22, **ii** 485; Mar. 18, **i** 100, 296; Mar. 28,
  i 103, 113; April, **i** 156, 177–9; May 7,
  ii 147*n*; Sept. 9, **ii** 279; Sept. 12, *see*
  Nuremberg in Subject Index; Sept. 26,
  ii 559, 562*n*, 565, 569, 572, 577–8, 584;
  iii 388; **vi** 517; Oct. 9, **iii** 157–8, 244,
  336; **vi** 744, 751–2; **vii** 550; Nov. 6, **iii**
  259, 263; *in* Reichstag on Jan 30, 1939,
  extracts from, **iv** 59, 304*n*; *referred to,* **iii** 590;
  iv 5–6, 22, 58–60, 64–5, 107, 111*n*, 160,
  164, 304, 310, 440, 591*n*, 601; **vi** 518; *at*
  Memel, Mar. 24, **iv** 495; *at* Wilhelms-
  haven, April 1, **iv** 582*n*; *referred to,* **iv**
  571, 582; **v** 28*n*, 319*n*; **vi** 715; *in* Reichstag, April 28, 1939, **v** 359–60, 370–2;
  forward references to, **v** 239, 250–3, 256,
  262, 279, 287, 304–5, 311, 337, 798–9;
  referred to, **v** 356, 360, 369–70, 372–3,
  378, 381, 391–3, 395–6, 410–1, 418, 441,
  462, 511–3, 520, 556, 584, 586, 602, 610,
  619, 628, 665, 716, 728, 792, 803, 814,
  817; **vi** 13, 61, 108, 388, 401; **vii** 331;
  ix 23; *at* Kassel, June 4, **v** 771, 782; *at*
  Munich, June 25, **vi** 176; *at* Obersalzberg, Aug. 22, 1939, **vii** 258, 260*n*, 316;
  in Reichstag, Sept. 1, **vii** 484, 497
Visit *to* Italy, May 1938, **i** 239, 274, 627; **iii**
  532
Visit *to* Memel, Mar. 1939, **iv** 482; **v** 26
  birthday celebrations in Berlin, April 20,
    1939, **v** 204, 290–3
  his motto, **vi** 5
Hletko, M. (leader of American Slovak delegation to Poland, June 1938), **i** 430
Hlinka, Mgr. Andrej (Chairman of Slovak
  People's party—died Aug. 1938), **i** 166–7,
  429–30, 465; **iv** 94, 98
Ho Ying-chin (Chinese Minister for War, 1930–
  44), **viii** 197
Hoare, Sir Reginald H. (H.M. Minister at
  Bucharest, Feb. 1935–Feb. 1941), **iv** 385,
  435, 457, 465, 510, 567, 576*n*, 580*n*, 581*n*;
  v 74*n*, 658–9; **vi** 68, 93; **vii** 152
  To Sir A. Cadogan, **iv** 542; **v** 652
  To Viscount Halifax, **iv** 35, 281, 291, 369,
    391, 396, 398–9, 419, 421, 431, 433, 546,
    555, 577–80; **v** 64, 80–1, 91, 105–6, 217,
    239, 382, 501, 607, 708, 723; **vi** 17–8, 78,
    146
  To Sir O. Sargent, **v** 29
  Conversation *with* M. Calinescu, **v** 239
  Conversation *with* King Carol II of Rou-
    mania, **iv** 398–9, 419, 578–9
  Conversation *with* M. Gafencu, **iv** 580–1; **v**
    81, 91–2; **vi** 17–9, 146–7

Hoare, Sir Samuel, Bt. (Secretary of State for Home Dept., May 1937–Sept. 1939), i 112n, 151; iii 426, 484; vi 155, 466
  Conversation with M. Masaryk, i 113–4
  At Anglo-French conversations, Sept. 1938, ii 373, 520, 536
  Speech at Anglo-French conversations, Sept. 25, 1938, ii 531, 533
  Statement in House of Commons, Mar. 22, 1939, iv 493
Hodgson, Sir Robert (Agent of H.M. Government to General Franco's Administration, Dec. 1937–Feb. 1939; Chargé d'Affaires, Feb.–April 1939), iii 297, 314, 332
Hodza, Dr. Milan (Prime Minister of Czechoslovakia, Nov. 1935–Sept. 1938), i 16, 76–80, 113, 116, 118, 121–3, 125–6, 150, 159, 169, 195–6, 241, 263–4, 269–70, 272, 275, 278–9, 284, 291, 308–9, 312–3, 322, 324, 331, 338, 349–620 *passim*; ii 4–8, 23, 28n, 29, 36, 49–50, 57, 69, 74–7, 80, 82, 93, 100, 115, 121–2, 142, 150, 153, 165–6, 183, 209, 211, 220–1, 241, 249, 253–4, 261, 264–5, 283, 304, 313, 319, 321, 332, 336, 358n, 369, 438–40, 448, 450, 650, 656, 662–5, 669–74, 679; iii 96
  Conversation with M. de Lacroix, i 390–1
  Conversation with Mr. Newton, i 76–80, 113, 125–6, 195–6, 282–3, 350, 354, 372–4, 394–7, 424–5, 466–7, 519–20, 521–2, 607–9; ii 220
  Conversation with Lord Runciman, ii 304
Hohenlohe-Langenburg, Prince Max Egon von (unofficial intermediary for the Sudeten Germans and, in Aug. 1939, for Field-Marshal Göring), ii 142, 243, 656, 660, 663–4, 666, 668–73; iv 608n; vii 66, 547–8
  Conversation with Mr. Ashton-Gwatkin, iv 227n
Hohenlohe-Langenburg, Princess Max Egon von, ii 666
Hoiden, M., ii 94n
Holburn, Mr. (correspondent of 'The Times' in Berlin), v 425; vi 136
Holden, A., vi 745–7, 751n, 756; vii 176
Holland, Captain C. S. (British Naval Attaché at Paris, Jan. 1938–June 1940), iv 237; v 55, 189
Holman, A. (1st Secretary, H.M. Embassy, Berlin, Dec. 1938–Sept. 1939), iii 451; iv 149, 597, 635n, 637; vi 235; vii 110, 417n, 435
  To Herr Schlitter, iv 631
  Conversation with Mr. Gladwyn Jebb, vii 538
  Conversation with Dr. E. Kordt, vi 285–7
  Letter to Mr. Kirkpatrick, vi 208, 558
  Letter to Sir O. Sargent, vi 285
  Letter to Mr. Strang, iv 180
  At Anglo-German Naval conversations, Dec. 30, 1938, iii 664

Holt, Rear-Admiral R. V. (Senior Naval Officer, Yangtze, 1937–9), viii 351, 361, 394, 406; ix 61, 462, 480
Homma, Lt.-Gen. M. (in charge of Japanese troops in Tientsin), viii 427, 439, 490, 511–2, 516–7, 520, 532; ix 2, 121–2
  Conversation with Major Herbert, viii 491–2
Hopkinson, H. L. d'A. (1st Secretary, H.M. Embassy, Athens, Feb. 1938–June 1939), v 777
Hoppenot, M. (Head of European Department, French Foreign Office), vi 646–7; vii 19, 102, 493
Hoppenrath, J. (Minister of Finance, Danzig Free State, 1933–9), ii 690
Hopwood, Brigadier A. H. (Commander, Tientsin Area, British Troops in China, 1935–9), viii 15, 61, 83, 106, 211, 248, 334, 351, 533, 552
Hore-Belisha, Leslie (Secretary of State for War, May 1937–Jan. 1940), vii 96, 103
  Conversation with General Gamelin, vii 102–3
  Speech in Paris, July 4, 1939, vi 297
Hori, Mr. (Japanese Consul at Tientsin), viii 61, 63, 72
Horinouchi, Kensuke (Japanese Vice-Minister for Foreign Affairs, April 1936–Oct. 1938; Ambassador at Washington, 1938–40), viii 42, 69, 76, 87, 90–1, 114, 126n, 128, 139, 151, 170–1, 176, 200, 378, 420, 443; ix 284, 342, 417, 518
  Conversation with Sir R. Craigie, viii 64–5, 91–2, 107–8, 115–6, 125–6
Hornbeck, Dr. Stanley K. (Adviser on Political Relations, U.S. Department of State, 1937–44), viii 301, 310, 341, 367, 428–9, 461, 522; ix 514
  Conversation with Mr. Mallet, ix 381, 520–1
Hornbostel, Theodor (Director of Political Department of Austrian Federal Chancellery), i 4, 6, 11
Horstenau, Dr. *See* Glaise-Horstenau, Dr.
Horthy de Nagybanya, Admiral Miklos (Regent of Hungary, 1920–44), ii 423, 441, 690; iii 9n, 224; vi 437, 585; vii 83, 92–3, 141, 152
  Visit to Germany, Aug. 1938, ii 54n, 60, 117, 123, 134, 140, 246
Hoszard, G. (Secretary of Polish Legation, The Hague), iii 592
Houdek, Dr. F. (a Slovak: Minister of Food in Czechoslovak Government, 1920), iv 98
Hough, William (Commercial Secretary, H.M. Legation, Prague), i 79; iii 560
Howe, R. G. (Counsellor in Foreign Office; Head of Far Eastern Department), viii 497, 548; ix 5, 209, 293
  To Sir A. Clark Kerr, viii 142; ix 117
  Conversation with Mr. Okamoto, ix 151–2

Conversation with Dr. Quo Tai-chi, **ix** 47*n*, 58–9
Letter to Sir R. Craigie, **viii** 267, 455
Minute by, **ix** 58, 151
Hrabcik, General, **iv** 162
Hrnciar, Dr. Alexander (Slovak Minister of Finance), **iv** 229–30
Hron, Colonel A. (Czechoslovak Military Attaché at Berlin, 1938–9), **i** 271; **ii** 309; **iii** 162; **iv** 218, 441
Hruby, M. (President of Committee of the National Community, Czechoslovakia), **iv** 566
Hsi Shih-tai, Dr. (Chief Secretary, Public Safety Bureau of the Special Municipality of Shanghai), **ix** 4
Hsu Mo (Chinese Vice-Minister for Foreign Affairs, 1932–41), **viii** 198
Hsu Shao-ching (Manchukuo Minister at Rome, 1938–41), **iii** 358
Hudson, Robert Spear (Parliamentary Secretary, Department of Overseas Trade, May 1937–April 1940), **iv** 208; **v** 209; **ix** 294, 373
Conversation with M. Litvinov, **iv** 485, 584–5
Conversation with M. Maisky, **iv** 207
Conversation with Herr Wohltat, **vi** 407–10; *referred to*, **vi** 464–6, 480–3, 495, 555, 580, 607, 648; **vii** 548
Letter to Viscount Halifax, **iv** 206
Visit to Germany, proposed, **iv** 131, 134; postponed, **iv** 260, 261*n*, 273, 364, 595; **v** 717; **vi** 497
Visit to Poland, **iv** 142, 203, 401, 453
Visit to U.S.S.R., **iv** 132–4, 207, 209, 503–4, 509, 511–2, 524, 568–71, 584–5, 621; **v** 45, 208, 235, 349–50; **vi** 533
Hudson, Mrs. R. S., **iv** 568–9
Huet, Captain (*Aide-de-camp* to General Gamelin), **v** 55, 71
Hull, Cordell (U.S. Secretary of State, 1933–44), **ii** 149, 174, 209; **iii** 343; **iv** 29, 530; **vii** 151, 333, 398, 412, 473; **viii** 146, 199, 208, 212, 461; **ix** 109, 193, 205, 223, 284, 342, 371
Conversation with Sir R. Lindsay, **ix** 348
Conversation with Mr. Mallet, **iv** 27
Message to Signor Mussolini, April 14, 1939, **v** 212
Statement to press, Nov. 4, 1938, **viii** 199*n*, 212, 246
Statement at press conference, June 19, 1939, **ix** 202*n*; *referred to*, 204*n*, 205, 210, 216*n*
Hulusi Fuat Togay (Turkish Minister at Durazzo, 1938–9), **v** 229–30, 383
Hung Li-hsiun (Chairman of Amoy Chamber of Commerce), **ix** 66*n*, 79
Huntziger, General (Head of French military mission to Angora, July 1939), **vi** 434–5, 603, 618, 625; **vii** 102
Hurban, Vladimir (Czechoslovak Minister at Washington, 1936–9), **v** 86

Husarek, General (Czechoslovak representative on Sub-Committees of International Commission set up in Oct. 1938), **iii** 132–3, 162, 240
Huseyin Ragip Baydur (Turkish Ambassador at Rome, 1934–40), **iii** 536; **v** 376, 429, 442
Hutchison, John Colville (Commercial Secretary in China; H.M. Trade Commissioner at Hong Kong, Nov. 1938–Jan. 1940)
To Viscount Halifax, **viii** 377, 379; **ix** 105, 114, 117, 163, 188, 490
Hutchison, 1st Baron, of Montrose, Major-General, **ii** 683, 686
Huth, W. (Vice-President of the Danzig Senate, 1936–9) **v** 512; **vi** 577; **vii** 510

Ibn Saud, King of Saudi Arabia (1932–53), **vi** 126–7
Ickes, Harold L. (U.S. Secretary of the Interior, 1933–46), **iv** 59
Ikeda, Seihin (Governor of Bank of Japan, 1937; Japanese Minister of Finance, June 1938–Jan. 1939), **viii** 79, 81, 493, 528; **ix** 129
Letter to Sir R. Craigie, **viii** 529
Imredy, Dr. Bela de (Hungarian Prime Minister, May 1938–Feb. 1939), **ii** 423*n*; **iii** 191
Conversation with Sir G. Knox, **iii** 3–4
Speeches by, **iii** 223–4
Indelli, Mario (Italian Minister at Belgrade, 1936–40), **vi** 166
Ingram, E. M. B. (Counsellor in the Foreign Office; Head of Southern Department), **iii** 3, 328, 480, 532; **iv** 293
Conversation with M. Marosy, **iii** 1–2
Conversation with M. Simopoulos, **v** 163, 550–1
Letter to the Earl of Perth, **iv** 295
At Anglo-Roumanian conversations, April 1939, **v** 296, 307, 309, 321, 342
Minute by, **v** 163, 468, 550; **vii** 423
Innitzer, Cardinal Theodor (Archbishop of Vienna), **i** 148; **vii** 623
Inönü, General Ismet (President of Turkey, 1938–50), **iv** 437; **v** 399, 434, 452, 530, 532, 607, 672; **vi** 241; **vii** 272–3, 384
Conversation with Herr von Papen, **vii** 299*n*, 308
Inskip, Sir Thomas W. H. (Minister for Co-ordination of Defence, March 1936–Jan. 1939), **i** 202; **ii** 537, 541, 575*n*
Statement in House of Commons, Oct. 4, 1938, **iii** 116*n*; *referred to*, **iii** 120, 186, 303, 414
Ironside, General Sir W. Edmund (Inspector-General of Overseas Forces, July–Sept. 1939), **vi** 274, 373, 381, 386, 426–7, 476, 485–6, 502, 523, 696; **vii** 56, 73, 75, 81, 90, 109–10, 113, 139, 223, 232*n*, 475
Visit to Warsaw, **vi** 353, 378*n*, 400, 415–9, 445–6

Ishiwata, Sotaro (Japanese Vice-Minister of Finance, 1938–9), **viii** 369
Ismay, Major-General H. L. (Secretary, Committee of Imperial Defence), **vi** 509, 528, 534–5, 564; **vii** 167
Ismet Inönü, General. *See* Inönü, General Ismet
Itagaki, General S. (Japanese Minister of War, June 1938–Aug. 1939), **viii** 77, 79, 81, 369*n*, 464, 476, 480; **ix** 43, 65, 186, 398, 441, 489, 516
    Statement of Feb. 21, 1939, **viii** 480
Ito, Mr. (a member of Japanese mission to Berlin, Feb. 1939), **viii** 457*n*

Jäckh, Dr. (Director of the periodical 'New Commonwealth'), **vi** 413
Jackson, Sir Wilfrid E. F. (Governor of British Guiana, 1937–41), **v** 343
Jacob, Colonel E. I. C. (Assistant Secretary to the Committee of Imperial Defence), **vii** 190
Jacomoni di San Savino, Francesco (Italian Minister at Durazzo, 1936–9), **iv** 358, 498; **v** 116, 119, 122, 176, 195, 383
Jaksch, Dr. Wenzel (a leader of Sudeten German Social Democratic party), **i** 64*n*, 69, 187; **ii** 69, 404*n*, 450–1; **iii** 208
James, Captain P. H. G. (Naval Liaison Officer, Shanghai), **viii** 159, 370; **ix** 154
Jamet, General (Secretary-General of the French Conseil Supérieur de la Guerre), **vi** 528, 534–5
Jamieson, Edgar George (H.M. Consul-General at Tientsin, Aug. 1938–Oct. 1939), **viii** 9, 125, 256, 259, 308*n*, 310, 337–8, 351, 388–9, 421*n*, 491–2, 504*n*, 507*n*, 512*n*, 551, 553, 556–7, 559; **ix** 5, 18, 29, 33–4, 56, 59–60, 83–5, 98, 116–7, 123–4, 127, 133, 142, 144, 158, 162, 164–5, 169, 186, 191, 205, 208, 218*n*, 221*n*, 243, 250, 314*n*, 364, 410, 416–7, 424, 456, 483, 519–20, 524, 533, 535
    To British Embassy, Shanghai, **viii** 35, 60, 63, 66, 71, 83, 119, 186, 225, 230, 232, 247, 308, 314–5, 323, 327–8, 333, 335, 338, 350–1, 354, 380, 383, 421, 427, 445, 447, 458–9, 504, 507, 509, 511–2, 516, 519, 526–7, 534, 554–5; **ix** 1, 19, 32, 109, 144, 151, 322, 479, 498, 505, 515
    To Sir R. Craigie, **ix** 322
    To Viscount Halifax, **viii** 243, 252, 416, 557; **ix** 66, 111, 118–9, 121–2, 125, 132, 154, 159, 164, 179, 182, 216, 236, 277, 419, 493
    Conversation with Major Ohta, **ix** 479
    Conversation with M. Tashiro, **viii** 338–9
    Letter to General Homma, **viii** 511
Jansa, Lt.-Gen. A. (Chief of Staff of Austrian Federal Army), **i** 129
Janson, Dr. M. von (German Consul-General at Danzig, 1938–9), **iii** 443; **iv** 47, 383; **v** 25–6,

511, 577; **vi** 1, 44, 164, 223, 395, 490, 533, 653; **vii** 11, 89, 101, 123, 153, 543
Janson, Frau von, **v** 26; **vi** 224
Janson, Paul E. (Belgian Foreign Minister, Jan.–Feb. 1939), **iv** 48, 58, 66–7, 75–6, 84
    To Sir R. Clive, **iv** 77
    Conversation with Sir R. Clive, **iv** 69–70
Jarostowski, Karnitz (a Polish Customs Inspector in Danzig Free City), **vi** 148
Jarrett, C. G. (Private Secretary of Parliamentary Secretary to the Admiralty), **iii** 664
Jazdzewski, Antoni (Polish Counsellor at London: acted as Chargé d'Affaires), **vi** 339–40; **vii** 359
    Conversation with Sir O. Sargent, **ii** 82–3
Jeanneney, Jules (President of the French Senate 1932–40)
    Conversation with Sir E. Phipps, **ii** 560
Jebb, Gladwyn (Private Secretary to the Permanent Under-Secretary of State in the Foreign Office, Dec. 1937–Aug. 1940), **v** 716
    Conversation with Mr. Holman, **vii** 538
    Conversation with Dr. Theodor Kordt, **vii** 555–6
    Conversation with M. Masaryk, **ii** 369
    Memorandum by, **vii** 555
    Minute by, **vi** 305, 359; **vii** 518, 538
Jeffrey, C. H. (H.M. Vice-Consul at Gdynia, Mar. 1931–Sept. 1939), **v** 538
Jezek, F. (a leader of the National Alliance party in Czechoslovakia), **iii** 96
Johnson, Herschel V. (Counsellor of U.S. Embassy, London; acted as Chargé d'Affaires), **iv** 628*n*; **vi** 678; **vii** 539; **viii** 19, 297–8
    Conversation with Viscount Halifax, **ii** 149
    Conversation with Mr. Ronald, **viii** 456–8
Johnson, Nelson T. (U.S. Ambassador in China, 1935–41), **viii** 3, 16–7, 20, 133, 154, 165, 315, 367; **ix** 100, 125, 236, 260, 288
Jonak, Dr. (a leader of the Sudeten German Socialist group), **i** 69, 250
Jones, P. Grant (Assistant Judge of H.B.M. Supreme Court for China, 1931–45), **ix** 369, 410, 456, 466, 519
Jordan, Mr. (Berlin representative of the Federation of British Industries), **iv** 598
Jordan, S. R. (Commercial Secretary at H.M. Embassy, Angora, Aug. 1938–July 1943), **vi** 361–2; **vii** 300
Jordan, William Joseph (High Commissioner for New Zealand in London, 1936–51), **viii** 104; **ix** 101
Jouhaux, Léon (Secretary-General of the Confédération Générale du Travail), **iii** 157

Kaasik, Dr. Nikolai (Head of Political Department, Ministry of Foreign Affairs, Estonia), **v** 775
    Conversation with Mr. Gallienne, **v** 349–50
Kabayama, Count A., **viii** 528

Kaganovich, Lazar Moiseivich (People's Commissar for Transport in U.S.S.R., 1935–7, reappointed April 1938), **i** 483

Kalecak, Comm. V. (Yugoslav Military Attaché at Durazzo), **v** 383, 412, 751

Kalfus, Dr. Josef (Czechoslovak Minister of Finance, Sept. 1938–Mar. 1939), **i** 608; **iii** 376–7; **iv** 14

Kalina, Lt.-Col. V. (Czechoslovak Military Attaché at Paris), **ii** 459, 461, 610

Kalinin, Mikhail Ivanovich (Chairman of Presidium of the Supreme Council·in U.S.S.R., 1938–46), **i** 288–9, 346
  Conversation with Sir W. Seeds, **iv** 45–6

Kalinowski, Jerzy (a Polish Customs Inspector in Danzig Free City), **vi** 148

Kamenev, L. B. (a former Soviet leader; shot for alleged conspiracy in Aug. 1936), **iv** 414

Kano, Viscount (a Japanese banker in London branch of the Yokohama Specie Bank), **viii** 163–4; **ix** 510n

Kanya, Kalman de (Hungarian Minister for Foreign Affairs, Feb. 1933–Nov. 1938), **i** 2; **ii** 423n; **iii** 3, 9, 47, 86, 116, 127, 138–9, 155, 188, 220, 225, 242–3; **v** 300; *resignation of,* **iii** 364
  Conversation with Sir G. Knox, **iii** 1–2, 18, 25–6, 37–8, 125
  Speech by, **iii** 237–8

Kao Tsung-wu, **viii** 364

Kapras, Dr. Jan (Czechoslovak Minister of Education, Dec. 1938–Mar. 1939), **iii** 376

Karatsony, Colonel L. de (Hungarian Military Attaché at Paris), **iii** 159

Karletan, Herr (a member of the 'Jungdeutsche Partei' in Poland), **vii** 203

Karlowa, O., **v** 245

Karmasin, Dr. (State Secretary for German Affairs in Province of Slovakia, 1938–9; leader of the 'German Party' in Slovakia), **iii** 410, 413; **iv** 63, 95–6, 233–5, 242, 406–7, 440; **v** 91

Karvas, M. (Czechoslovak Minister of Commerce, Sept.–Nov. 1938), **iii** 151

Kaspar, Cardinal (Archbishop of Prague), **ii** 74, 249, 669

Kasper, Herr (a leader of the Sudeten German Socialist group), **i** 69

Kasprzycki, General T. (Polish Minister for War, 1935–9), **v** 757

Kato, Sotomatsu (Japanese Minister-at-large in China, 1939–40; Japanese representative at Anglo-Japanese negotiations in Tokyo, July and Aug. 1939), **ix** 221, 324–5, 337–8, 342–4, 347, 349–50, 357, 361, 364, 379, 385, 395, 398, 410, 412, 427, 430n, 434, 438, 447, 457, 461, 468, 470, 478, 480–2, 487, 497, 503, 511–2
  Conversation with Sir R. Craigie, **ix** 255, 392–3, 400–1, 433–4, 443, 453–4, 469–70, 473–4, 502–3

Katzer, Dr. (a member of the Reichenberg section of the Sudeten German party), **i** 434–5

Kawabe, Major-General T. (Japanese Military Attaché at Berlin), **vii** 309

Kawai, Tatsuo (Director of the Information Bureau of Japanese Ministry of Foreign Affairs), **ix** 176

Kayser, Jacques (*homme de confiance* of M. Daladier: attached to French Cabinet), **iii** 483

Kazami, Akira (Chief Secretary of Japanese Cabinet, 1937–9), **viii** 30, 271

Keitel, General Wilhelm (Chief of the High Command of German Armed Forces, 1938–45), **i** 44, 323, 342, 610; **ii** 66, 101, 331, 473, 521; **iii** 190; **iv** 279, 404, 482; **v** 292, 478, 728, 769; **vi** 2, 296, 708; **vii** 464n

Kemal Ataturk (President of Turkey, 1923–38), **v** 607; **vii** 259

Kemsley, 1st Baron (Newspaper proprietor and editor), **vi** 717–8, 720; **vii** 98

Kennard, Sir Howard W. (H.M. Ambassador to Polish Government, Jan. 1935–May 1941: left Warsaw, Sept. 1939), **i** 315n, 364, 430n; **iii** 13n, 16n, 54, 59n, 206n, 378, 438, 445, 576–7, 582, 589–90, 660; **iv** 181n, 362n, 458, 473, 496, 502, 567; **v** 1–2, 52n, 383–4, 415–20, 539, 609–10; **vi** 214, 274, 538, 548n, 624, 679; **vii** 2n, 3n, 88n, 105, 117, 121, 167, 235n, 558–60
  To M. Beck, **iii** 31, 39
  To Sir A. Cadogan, **iii** 97; **iv** 466; **v** 231, 626, 634, 636
  To Viscount Halifax, **i** 315, 351, 429, 444, 464, 478, 481, 512; **ii** 217, 287, 409n, 441, 459n; **iii** 3, 7–8, 12, 16–7, 22–5, 27–8, 34–5, 38–9, 41, 46–7, 50, 52, 60, 63, 82, 97, 100, 110–1, 120–1, 138, 178, 188, 198–9, 205–6, 212, 218, 227–8, 242, 250, 273, 280, 283, 364–5, 418–9, 425, 438, 542, 558, 566; **iv** 15, 31–3, 67–8, 80–2, 87, 111, 145–6, 151–2, 163, 177, 181–2, 201, 205, 217, 224, 245, 252, 262, 362, 370, 398, 401, 428, 430–1, 452–3, 463–4, 476, 497, 506, 513–4, 524, 539, 543, 548–51, 572, 581; **v** 38, 58, 68, 93–4, 198, 200, 203–4, 211, 217, 233, 238, 243–5, 280–1, 289, 339, 364, 372, 378–9, 391, 406, 410, 440, 454, 466, 475–6, 500–1, 538, 547, 557, 579, 605–6, 622, 667, 689, 691, 702, 709, 730, 732–3, 739, 757, 767; **vi** 19, 25, 30, 56, 80–1, 94, 105, 176, 545–6, 549, 551, 562, 592, 609, 612, 617, 621, 627, 638, 644–5, 650, 657, 668, 678, 683–4; **vii** 11, 22, 25, 53–4, 61, 63, 69, 73, 79, 84–7, 91, 101, 115–6, 119, 126, 129, 133, 146, 149, 151, 159, 186, 189–90, 195, 199, 203–4, 208, 216–8, 221, 223, 236, 240, 267, 280–1, 296–7, 300–1, 309, 311, 318, 321, 323, 328–9, 339, 355, 358, 364, 366, 370, 373–5, 395, 399, 404, 414, 434, 447,

Kennard Sir H. (*cont.*)
  To Viscount Halifax (*cont.*)
    450–1, 453, 455, 474, 479, 481, 484,
    490–1, 498–9, 502–3, 515, 522, 533–4
  To Sir J. Simon, iii 580, 585
  Conversation with M. Arciszewski, iii 34, 41;
    iv 80–2, 201–2, 262–3, 401–2, 428–9,
    506–7, 524–5, 543; v 281–2; vi 105–6,
    176–7, 562–3, 627–8; vii 22
  Conversation with M. Beck, i 315–6, 351, 512;
    ii 217–8; iii 24, 52–3; 64, 205–6, 283–4,
    419–20, 438–9, 580–1; iv 68–9, 182,
    362–3, 370–1, 401, 452–3, 549; v 93–4,
    200–1, 203, 378–9, 466, 475–6, 501–2;
    vi 545, 549–50, 612–3, 644, 683–4; vii
    11–2, 69–70, 77, 85–6, 151, 189–90, 218–
    9, 301, 355–6, 366, 370–1, 434, 450–1,
    481–2, 522, 534
  Conversation with M. Burckhardt, iii 280–1,
    558; v 709–10
  Conversation with M. Gafencu, iv 182–3
  Conversation with M. Lubienski, iii 60
  Conversation with Herr von Moltke, iv 146–7,
    152–4, 513; v 58, 466–7; vi 81, 204–5
  Conversation with M. Noël, iii 365–6; v 72–3
  Conversation with M. Slavik, i 464–5; iii
    188–9, 199
  Letter to Sir A. Cadogan, iv 202; v 236, 283,
    397, 570, 587, 734; vi 185; vii 49, 112,
    213, 294
  Letter to Sir O. Sargent, i 444*n*; iii 32, 106,
    373; iv 142; v 72, 285; vi 29, 137, 186,
    204, 206, 557, 591, 635, 665
  Letter to Mr. Strang, iii 30
  Views on Polish claim to Teschen area, iii
    28, 32–4
  Views on Polish-German disputes, v 579–82;
    635, 667; vi 56–8
Kennedy, Brigadier (British representative at
  Anglo-French Staff conversations), iv 237
Kennedy, A. L. (British press representative in
  Czechoslovakia, Mar. 1938), i 75, 268
Kennedy, Joseph P. (U.S. Ambassador at
  London, 1938–41), ii 301; iv 124, 547, 550,
  555; v 356*n*; vii 295, 630
  To Viscount Halifax, vii 539
  Conversation with Mr. Chamberlain, ii
    212–3
  Conversation with Viscount Halifax, ii 213,
    284–5, 295–6, 625; iv 364–6, 380, 499–
    500; v 169, 793; ix 233–4, 493–4
Kent, T.R.H. the Duke and Duchess of, ix 496*n*
Kent, Mr. (Legal adviser to Municipal Council,
  British Concession, Tientsin), viii 416; ix 112,
  126, 145, 159, 364
Keppler, Dr. (an Under-Secretary at German
  Ministry of Foreign Affairs), vi 363, 412
Kerby, Wing Commander H. S. (British
  Air Attaché in China, Sept. 1936–Nov. 1938),
  viii 101

Kerchove de Denterghem, Comte André de
  (Belgian Ambassador at Rome, 1938–40), iv
  89, 335; v 238
  Conversation with Sir N. Charles, v 566–7
  Conversation with Earl of Perth, iv 297,
    322–3
Kérillis, Henri de (French deputy and journa-
  list; editor of 'L'Époque'), iii 157, 393;
  vi 55
Kerr, Sir Archibald Clark. *See* Clark Kerr, Sir
  Archibald
Kerran, F. L. (Labour candidate for Luton),
  iii 256–7
Kessel, Herr (a member of the German Foreign
  Office), vii 123
Kesselring, General Albrecht (a German General
  of Aviation), iv 258
Keswick, W. J. (Manager of Jardine Matheson
  & Co., China), ix 82, 96, 157
Khatyantsev, Regt. Kommissar (Soviet steno-
  grapher at Anglo-Franco-Soviet military
  conversations), vii 562
Khmelnitski, Corps Commander (at Anglo-
  Franco-Soviet conversations, Aug. 1939), vii
  613
Khuen-Lützow, Count (Host of Mr. Ashton-
  Gwatkin in Czechoslovakia), ii 670
Kidd, Mr. (Correspondent in Danzig of the
  Associated Press, Sept. 1939), vii 544
Kido, Marquis Koichi (Japanese Minister of
  Education, 1937–8; Minister of Welfare,
  1938–9; Minister for Home Affairs, 1939),
  viii 155, 369; ix 56
Kier, Dr. (Sudeten German party's legal ad-
  viser), ii 671
King-Hall, Commander Stephen (Editor, and
  Proprietor of the King-Hall News-Letter
  Service), vii 541
  King-Hall news-letters, vi 374, 442, 734;
    vii 47, 213
Kinsky, Prince Ulrich, ii 80, 552, 663
Kiosseivanoff, G. (President of the Council and
  Minister for Foreign Affairs in Bulgaria,
  1935–40), iv 375, 387, 620; v 110, 342, 380,
  411, 530; vi 438
  Conversation with Mr. Rendel, iii 145–6; v
    756–7; vi 344–5
  Visit to Berlin, vi 496–7, 216, 255, 344–5,
    412, 745–6
Kircher, Rudolf (Editor of the 'Frankfurter
  Zeitung'), iii 359
Kirk, Alexander C. (Counsellor of U.S. Em-
  bassy at Moscow, 1938–9; at Berlin, May
  1939–40; acted as Chargé d'Affaires at
  Moscow and Berlin), ii 617; v 802, 808; vii
  51, 100, 165, 192, 202, 287, 372
Kirke, General Sir Walter (Director-General
  of Territorial Army), vi 120–2
Kirkpatrick, Ivone A. (First Secretary at H.M.
  Embassy, Berlin, 1933–8; transferred to

Foreign Office, Dec. 1938), **i** 25, 412, 621; **ii** 138, 214; **iii** 109*n*; **iv** 66; **vi** 235; **vii** 419
  To Viscount Halifax, **ii** 178, 189
  To Sir N. Henderson, **v** 684
  Conversation with Gen. von Reichenau, **vi** 5
  Conversation with Mr. Strang, **iii** 93*n*
  Letter to Sir N. Bland, **vii** 293
  Letter to Sir R. Clive, **vii** 293
  Letter to Mr. Norton, **vi** 569
  Letter to Sir G. Ogilvie-Forbes, **iv** 13*n*
  Minute by, **v** 724; **vi** 437, 512; **vii** 314, 316*n*, 354*n*, 416*n*
  Notes on conversation between Mr. Chamberlain and Herr Hitler at Godesberg, **ii** 463, 499; between Sir H. Wilson and Herr Hitler at Berlin, **ii** 554, 564
Kirschbaum, Dr. Josef (Secretary of the Hlinka party in Province of Slovakia), **v** 85–6
Kirscher, Dr. (Representative at Rome of the 'Frankfurter Zeitung'), **vi** 610
Kishimoto, Mr. (Chief Secretary of the Chinese Maritime Customs Administration), **viii** 167
Kishinami, Major, **viii** 77
Kistler, General von (General Officer Commanding, East Prussia), **ii** 691·
Kita, General (Supreme Japanese Adviser to the Provisional Government, Peking), **viii** 535
Kitson, G. V. (H.M. Consul, Shanghai, Jan. 1939–April 1941), **ix** 337
Klapka, M. (a member of Czechoslovak Parliamentary Committee of Six), **ii** 663
Klecanda, General V. (Czechoslovak Military Attaché at Rome), **ii** 356; **v** 117
Kleffens, Dr. E. N. van (Netherlands Minister for Foreign Affairs, Aug. 1939–1946), **vii** 464
Kleist, Peter (a member of Herr Ribbentrop's bureau), **v** 561; **vi** 326
Kleist-Schmenzin, Major Ewald von (Herr von Kleist) (a retired German army officer), **ii** 125*n*, 126, 242, 683, 686; **iii** 366–7; **vii** 419*n*
  Conversation with Mr. W. Churchill, **ii** 687–8
  Conversation with Sir R. Vansittart, **ii** 683–6
Klemp, M., **vi** 149–50
Klimas, Dr. Petras (Lithuanian Minister at Paris, 1925–40), **iv** 638–9
Klinovski, Karol (Chief of police, Province of Slovakia), **iv** 438
Klumpar, Dr. Vladislav (Czechoslovak Minister of Health and Social Welfare, Dec. 1938–Mar. 1939), **iii** 377
Knatchbull-Hugessen, Sir Hughe M. (H.M. Ambassador at Angora, Feb. 1939–Sept. 1944), **v** 183, 189, 231*n*, 344, 510, 522*n*, 552–4; **vi** 299, 300, 600, 676, 688; **vii** 305, 313, 320, 423–4, 494
  To Sir A. Cadogan, **v** 652
  To Viscount Halifax, **iv** 374, 386, 399; **v** 109–10, 162–4, 187–9, 194, 219–20, 225, 227, 230, 238, 259, 278–9, 287–8, 334, 336, 340, 354, 362, 380, 387, 389, 399,

411, 433–4, 442, 444–8, 463, 465, 490, 493–4, 499, 516, 518–9, 526, 532, 535–7, 547, 549, 552, 573–4, 591–2, 666, 681, 686, 693, 720, 729, 739, 760–1, 766, 789; **vi** 29, 51, 53, 67, 71, 97, 100–1, 111, 151, 164, 169, 188, 241, 272, 313, 321, 341, 353, 360–1, 387, 434, 449, 467, 574, 619, 622–3, 625–6, 636, 661, 673, 686; **vii** 10, 140, 155, 198, 200, 214, 238, 264, 268, 271–3, 276, 299, 308, 360, 364, 444, 454, 470, 500, 508, 527, 536
  Conversation with M. Gafencu, **vi** 29–30, 51–2, 68–71
  Conversation with M. Menemencioglu, **v** 490–1, 532–3
  Conversation with Herr von Papen, **vi** 71–5, 467–70
  Conversation with M. Saracoglu, **v** 109–10, 162, 188, 194, 220, 259–60, 288, 340–1, 389, 433–5, 463–6, 519, 729–30; **vi** 229, 387, 449, 622–3; **vii** 198–9, 273
  Letter to Sir A. Cadogan, **v** 165*n*
  Letter to Mr. Ingram, **vi** 159
Knight, W. L. C. (H.M. Consul-General at Tunis, April 1937–July 1940), **iv** 325*n*
Knox, Sir Geoffrey George (H.M. Minister at Budapest, Oct. 1935–May 1939), **i** 196; **ii** 409*n*; **iii** 114, 376*n*; **iv** 305, 433, 457, 496*n*, 511*n*
  To Viscount Halifax, **ii** 423*n*, 459*n*; **iii** 1, 3, 6, 9, 11–2, 18, 25, 27, 36–7, 44, 125, 138–9, 171, 173, 194, 197, 209, 223, 236–9, 243; **iv** 55, 247–8, 253–4, 265, 277, 289–90, 395, 434, 511; **v** 59, 61, 77
  Conversation with Col. Andorka, **iv** 247–8
  Conversation with Count Csaky, **iv** 55–6, 395–6
  Conversation with Dr. Bela de Imredy, **iii** 3–4
  Conversation with M. de Kanya, **iii** 1–2, 18, 25–6, 37–8, 125
  Letter to Sir O. Sargent, **iii** 516
Kobr, Milos, (Czechoslovak Minister at Budapest, 1933–9), **iv** 248, 254
Kobylanski, M. (Head of Eastern Section of Polish Ministry of Foreign Affairs), **vi** 19
Koc, Colonel A. (Head of Polish financial and economic mission to Great Britain, June 1939), **vi** 198–9, 226, 244–5, 323, 342, 366–7, 378, 380, 401, 404, 406, 410, 451, 479, 486, 508
Koch, E. (Gauleiter of East Prussia), **iii** 442, 658–9; **vi** 395, 402, 490, 507, 689, 733–4
  Conversation with M. Burckhardt, **iii** 659–60; **vi** 729–31
Kocins, Fricis (Latvian Minister at Moscow, 1937–40), **i** 165; **iv** 568; **v** 214
Kodama, Kenji (President of Central China Development Company), **viii** 400, 493
Koerber, Dr. von, **v** 511

Koerber, Rittmeister a. D. Viktor von
Conversation with Colonel Mason-Mac-
Farlane, **ii** 65–7
Kohnert, Dr., **iv** 153
Koiso, General K. (Japanese Minister of Com-
munications), **ix** 65, 173, 412
Conversation with Sir R. Craigie, **ix** 173–6
Kollner, Herr, **ii** 167, 171
Komarnicki, Titus (Polish Minister at Berne,
1938–9; permanent Polish delegate to League
of Nations, 1934–9), **iii** 47, 591, 595–6, 600,
602–3, 606, 612–3; **iv** 11; **v** 392, 630; **vi** 726
Conversation with Mr. R. A. Butler, **iii**
592–4
Conversation with Viscount Halifax, **iii** 597;
v 637
Conversation with Mr. Makins, **iii** 604–5
Konoye, Prince Fumimaro (Japanese Prime
Minister, June 1937–Jan. 1939; in charge of
Ministry of Foreign Affairs in Oct. 1938),
viii 1, 34, 79, 81, 110n, 115–6, 118–9, 122–3,
135, 139, 141, 152, 159, 163–4, 180, 183–4,
253, 263, 283–4, 348, 443; **ix** 498, 517
position and character of, **viii** 154–6
resignation of, **viii** 369n
Conversation with Sir R. Craigie, **viii** 128–9,
175–7
Speech by, Nov. 3, 1938, **iii** 308; **viii** 214–5,
221–2, 225, 246, 251, 254, 356, 371, 403
Statement to press, Sept. 15, 1938, **viii** 90n,
92; Oct. 2, 1938, **viii** 114
Statement in Privy Council, Dec. 1, 1938,
viii 283, 294, 296
Statement by, Dec. 22, 1938, **viii** 343–4;
referred to, **viii** 347, 349, 355, 363, 371–2,
403, 405, 461; **ix** 176, 368
Koo, Dr. V. K. Wellington (Chinese Ambassa-
dor at Paris, 1932–9), **viii** 17, 23, 67, 93, 111,
257, 402–3, 418; **ix** 7, 46, 58, 78, 100–1, 113
Conversation with Mr. R. A. Butler, **viii**
93–4, 104–5
Conversation with Sir A. Cadogan, **ix** 238
Conversation with Viscount Halifax, **viii** 398–9
Kordt, Dr. Erich (Herr von Ribbentrop's private
secretary, 1938–41), **vi** 488
Conversation with Mr. Holman, **vi** 285–7
Visit to London, **vi** 705–6
Kordt, Dr. Theodor (Counsellor of German
Embassy, London, April 1938–Sept. 1939;
acted as Charge d'Affaires), **i** 235, 239, 245,
626; **iii** 671; **v** 245, 360; **vi** 579–80, 582,
707n; **vii** 557
To Viscount Halifax, **iii** 672
Conversation with Sir A. Cadogan, **iii** 671–2
Conversation with Viscount Halifax, **ii** 105–
6; **vii** 496–7
Conversation with Mr. Jebb, **vii** 555–6
Korj, Mikhail (1st Secretary, Soviet Embassy,
London)
Letter to Mr. Perowne, **iv** 635

Kostka, Senator (Mayor of Reichenberg), **i** 70–
1, 125
Köstring, Lt.-Gen. (German Military Attaché
at Moscow), **i** 419–20; **ii** 298; **iv** 185; **vi** 77
Conversation with Colonel Firebrace, **i** 421–4
Kotta, Constantine (Albanian Prime Minister,
1936–9), **v** 136
Koukal, Dr. Antonin (of the Czechoslovak
Ministry of Justice), **iii** 649, 652–3; **iv**
135
Kovalev, Army Commander (Officer Com-
manding the White Russian Special Military
District), **i** 422; **vii** 46
Kowalski, M. (a leader of the Polish National
Democrat party), **v** 69
Krapivincev, Pavel (Soviet Minister at Kovno,
Feb.–Oct. 1938), **iv** 286
Krauel, Dr. W. (German Consul-General at
Geneva, 1932–43), **v** 630
Conversation with M. Burckhardt, **v** 561–2
Krebs, Commandant (a member of French
Military Delegation to Moscow, Aug. 1939),
vii 562
Krebs, Gauleiter (a member of the Sudeten
German party), **i** 250, 449, 454, 466, 476,
632; **iii** 132+3
Kreewinsch, Edgars (Latvian Minister at Berlin,
1938–40), **v** 782
Krejci, Dr. Jaroslav (Czechoslovak Minister of
Justice and Unification, Dec. 1938–Mar.
1939), **iii** 376
Krejci, General Ludvik (Chief of Czechoslovak
General Staff), **i** 268, 328, 349, 367, 392, 417,
439, 462–3, 471, 519, 530; **ii** 145, 147, 336,
412, 641; **iii** 140, 147
resignation of, **iv** 125, 147
Conversation with Wing Commander A. H. H.
MacDonald, **iv** 148
Conversation with Colonel Stronge, **i** 462–3;
ii 370
Krno, J. (Political Director, Czechoslovak
Ministry of Foreign Affairs), **ii** 66, 454; **iii** 67,
108–9, 118, 140–1, 146, 380, 559–60, 633–4;
iv 259
Conversation with Mr. Newton, **iii** 108–9,
184–5, 239; **iv** 242–3
Krofta, Dr. Kamil (Czechoslovak Minister for
Foreign Affairs, Nov. 1935–Oct. 1938), **i** 55,
72, 76, 91, 95, 102, 114, 117, 158–9, 167, 181–
2, 186–7, 195, 197, 215, 241, 243, 252, 261–5,
270, 272, 277, 279, 282, 284, 308, 312–3, 322,
331–2, 337, 340, 350, 354, 358–61, 365–6,
377–8, 381, 390, 397–8, 400, 409, 411n,
428, 503, 507n, 510, 526, 548, 550–1, 559–60,
568, 590, 599, 600, 643n; **ii** 36, 50, 57, 69,
76–7, 89, 93–4, 135, 137, 151–2, 157–8, 163,
235, 241, 260, 316, 368, 411, 415, 439, 444,
450, 493n, 512, 519, 604, 609, 621, 662; **iii**
35–6, 43, 51–2, 54, 61, 64, 66–8, 76, 79, 118,
123

To M. Papée, **iii** 69, 72
Conversation with Mr. Newton, **i** 55, 117–8,
158–9, 186–7, 197, 263–4, 266–70, 329,
332–4, 338, 350, 354, 397–8, 508–10;
ii 94–5, 189–90, 319–20, 371–2, 426–7,
583, 621–2; **iii** 29, 41, 51–2, 80–1
Note verbale handed to Mr. Newton, July
23, 1938, **i** 620; **ii** 10
Kroll, Dr. H. (Counsellor of German Embassy
at Angora: acted as Chargé d'Affaires), **v**
110, 652
Krosigk, Count Schwerin von. *See* Schwerin
von Krosigk, Count Ludwig
Kruliš-Randa, M. and Madame (Hosts to
members of Lord Runciman's Mission,
Czechoslovakia), **ii** 668, 671
Kucera, Colonel R. (Czechoslovak Military
Attaché at Vienna), **i** 67
Küchler, General von, **vii** 517
Kühlental, Lt.-Gen. E. (German Military
Attaché at Paris), **ii** 234*n*, 454
Kühlmann, Herr von (German Minister for
Foreign Affairs, 1917–8)
Conversation with Sir N. Henderson, **vi** 28–9
Kulesza, M., **iv** 525
Kulski, M. (Legal Adviser to Polish Ministry of
Foreign Affairs), **vi** 650, 699; **vii** 63, 66,
169
Ku Meng-yu (Director of Propaganda and
Publicity in Chinese Government), **viii** 364
Kundt, Dr. Ernst (a Sudeten German leader),
i 113, 126, 311, 418, 444, 461, 493, 501, 508,
521, 543*n*, 557, 559, 617; **ii** 6–7, 18, 49, 69–70,
100, 110–1, 136*n*, 153, 165–6, 171, 178, 183,
199, 202–3, 207–8, 210, 221, 244, 253–4, 261,
265–6, 305, 333, 404, 448, 552, 657–8, 662,
664–5, 667–8, 669–73; **iii** 216, 379, 409–10;
iv 54, 63, 86, 126–8, 243
Conversation with President Benes, **ii** 150,
222–3
Conversation with Mr. Newton, **ii** 8
Conversation with Mr. Stopford, **ii** 674–5
Speech by, Aug. 1938, **ii** 110–1, 116; Feb.
1939, **iv** 126–7
Kung, Dr. H. H. (President of the Executive
Yuan, National Government of China, 1938–
9; Minister of Finance, 1938–44), **viii** 197,
250, 408–10, 429–30, 435, 451, 467, 516,
524–6, 537, 539, 540*n*; **ix** 8, 24, 37, 93, 150,
240, 276, 341
Conversation with Mr. Greenway, **viii** 410–1,
441–2
Kuo, Dr. P. W. (Commercial Attaché at Chinese
Embassy, London), **viii** 472
Kuo Tai-chi. *See* Quo Tai-chi
Kurti, Lec (Albanian Minister at London, May
1936–April 1939)
Conversation with Viscount Halifax, **v** 138–9
Kurusu, Saburo (Japanese Ambassador at
Brussels, 1936–9), **iv** 161

Kusumoto, Colonel, **viii** 173
Kuwaki, General (in command of Japanese
troops in Tientsin until Jan. 1939), **viii**
427
Kuykendall, C. P. (U.S. Consul at Danzig), **iii**
558; **iv** 47, 80; **v** 211, 538, 576–7; **vi** 1, 165,
223–4, 419; **vii** 541–2, 545–6
Kuykendall, Mrs., **vi** 224
Kuznetsov, Colonel, **iv** 128
Kuznetsov, Flagman N. G. (People's Commissar
for the Navy, U.S.S.R.), **vii** 46
At Meetings of Anglo-Franco-Soviet Military Delegations, **vii** 561, 563, 587, 591
Kwiatkowski, E. (Polish Deputy Prime Minister
and Minister of Finance, 1936–9), **iii** 103;
v 748; **vi** 322–3, 359, 366, 406, 427, 436, 508;
vii 54

Labougle, Dr. Eduardo (Argentine Ambassador
at Berlin, 1936–9), **vi** 172
La Chambre, Guy (French Minister for Air,
1938–40), **i** 205; **iii** 250*n*, 392; **iv** 532
La Chambre, Madame Guy, **iii** 392
Lacroix, Léopold Victor de (French Minister at
Prague, 1936–9), **i** 157, 160, 241, 243, 246,
251, 259, 261, 264*n*, 338, 343, 363, 366, 375,
383, 387, 390, 400, 418–9, 425, 441, 454, 459,
468, 476, 491*n*, 499, 503, 507*n*, 509, 519, 524,
526, 534*n*, 536, 545, 548–50, 558–9, 574, 577;
ii 1, 28, 57, 77–8, 125, 194, 196, 201, 230,
245–6, 251, 255, 321, 409–12, 416, 419, 436–8,
440–1, 444, 463, 546, 549, 595, 612, 620, 630,
668–71, 673; **iii** 35–6, 112, 192, 212, 234, 401*n*,
428, 444, 607, 631, 634; **iv** 130–1; **v** 93
Conversation with Dr. Benes, **ii** 1, 208, 449–50,
475
Conversation with M. Hodza, **i** 390–1
Conversation with Mr. Newton, **i** 459
Laderchi, Colonel C. Ruggeri (Italian Military
Attaché at London), **vi** 549; **vii** 315
Lafond, Captain G. de (French Naval Attaché
at Rome), **iv** 359
Lagerberg, J. (Swedish Minister at Warsaw,
1938–9), **iii** 104; **iv** 202
Laidoner, General J. (Commander-in-Chief,
Estonian army), **vi** 326
Lamarle, A. (1st Secretary, French Legation at
Prague), **ii** 549, 552
Lambert, M. (M. Burckhardt's *chef de cabinet*),
iii 613; **vii** 544
Laming, R. V. (Commercial Secretary, H.M.
Embassy, The Hague, April 1920–May 1940),
iii 592
Lammers, Dr. Hans Heinrich (Head of Chan-
cellery of German Government, 1934–45),
i 527; **ii** 87, 101, 108, 119, 123; **iv** 280; **vi**
171–2, 184, 219, 331, 359; **vii** 464*n*
Lampson, Sir Miles W. (1943 Baron Killearn)
(H.M. Ambassador at Cairo, Dec. 1936–
Mar. 1946), **iv** 528*n*

Landini, Signor (Press Counsellor of Italian Embassy, Paris), **iv** 321–2

Lang, The Most Rev. Cosmo Gordon (Archbishop of Canterbury, 1928–42), **vii** 256*n*; **viii** 43

Langenhove, F. van (Secretary-General of Belgian Ministry of Foreign Affairs), **iv** 109; **vii** 329

Lansdale, Captain R. S. (Staff Officer to Admiral Drax during his mission to Moscow, Aug. 1939), **vii** 35

Lany, Dr. (Chief Justice of Bohemia), **iv** 561

Lanyon, Mr. (Agent for Messrs. Butterfield and Swire, Tientsin), **viii** 528

Larisch, Count and Countess (Hosts of Mr. Ashton-Gwatkin in Czechoslovakia), **ii** 69

Laurent, Colonel (French Military Attaché at Brussels, 1937–40), **iii** 583; **iv** 77–8

Laurent, General, **vi** 509; **vii** 15

Laurie, Brigadier Sir John E. (Commander, Tientsin Area, British Troops in China, 1939–40), **ix** 519–20, 524–5

Laval, Pierre (French Minister for Foreign Affairs, 1934–5; President of the Council, 1935–6), **ii** 535; **iii** 366*n*, 437, 475, 490, 495; **v** 7, 613; **vi** 212

Lawford, V. G. (Secretary, H.M. Embassy, Paris, Mar. 1937–Sept. 1939), **iii** 285

Layton, Sir Walter, **i** 520, 529; **iii** 411

Lebrun, Albert (President of the French Republic, May 1932–July 1940), **ii** 588, 606, 622; **iv** 243; **v** 114; **vii** 515, 523
Visit to Great Britain, **iv** 347, 422*n*, 467*n*

Ledebourg, Count, **i** 290; **ii** 671

Ledochowski, Rev. Wladimir (General of the Jesuits, 1915–42), **v** 685, 719

Lee, Mr. (a member of Chinese Trading Commission), **viii** 472

Leeb, Field-Marshal Ritter Wilhelm von, **vii** 517

Léger, Alexis (Secretary-General of French Ministry of Foreign Affairs, 1933–40), **i** 14, 337, 476, 535; **ii** 234*n*, 255, 270, 301–2, 305, 337, 456–7, 459, 463, 481, 599; **iii** 346, 352, 389, 392, 441, 480, 506, 621, 636; **iv** 17, 49, 353, 371–2, 381, 423, 434, 457, 467–8, 639; **v** 252, 272, 427, 432, 467, 523, 526, 533, 611, 774; **vi** 25, 358, 562–3, 617; **vii** 128, 131, 523; **viii** 309; **ix** 446*n*
Conversation with Mr. R. I. Campbell, **i** 554–5; **iv** 335–7, 373, 382, 468–9; **v** 143–4, 250, 260–2; **vi** 561–2, 618–9; **vii** 119–20, 378–9
Conversation with Sir E. Phipps, **ii** 234–5, 291–3; **iii** 421
Aide-mémoire by, **iv** 154
Speeches at Anglo-French conversations, April 1938, **i** 211–2
At Anglo-French conversations, Sept. 1938,

ii 373, 520, 536; Nov. 1938, **iii** 285, 305; Jan. 10, 1939, **iii** 513–5
At Munich Conference, **ii** 630

Legmanowski, M., **v** 765

Lehmann-Heinecke, Major (of the German War Censorship Department), **vii** 419

Leith-Ross, Sir Frederick (Chief Economic Adviser to H.M. Government, 1932–9), **iii** 631, 634–5, 637; **v** 272, 303, 309, 311; **vi** 244, 269*n*, 323, 342, 381, 386, 557, 605, 635; **viii** 93, 247, 260, 401, 410, 435, 495, 519; **ix** 112
To Mr. Harvey, **iii** 635
Conversation with Dr. Schacht, **iii** 675–7

Lelong, General A. (French Military Attaché at London), **iv** 223; **vi** 511

Lenin (Vladimir Ilyich Ulyanov) (1870–1924), **vii** 619

Leopold III, King of the Belgians (1934–51), **iii** 287*n*; **iv** 48, 66–7, 76, 130, 450; **v** 314–5; **vi** 222*n*; **vii** 67, 259, 270, 303, 329, 340, 349, 447
Appeal for peace, Aug. 23, 1939, **vii** 213
Conversation with Sir R. Clive, **vii** 312

Lépissier, C. (French Consul-General at Tientsin, 1938–43), **viii** 35, 61, 63, 71–2, 83–4, 119–20, 186, 225–6, 230–1, 248, 253, 259, 308, 314, 322, 327–8, 333, 335, 351, 388–9, 418, 421, 459, 474*n*, 490, 507, 511–2, 517, 527; **ix** 3, 493
Conversation with Mr. Tashiro, **viii** 338–9

Le Rougetel, John Helier (Secretary, H.M. Legation, Bucharest, Jan.–Nov. 1939: acted as Chargé d'Affaires), **vi** 463–4; **vii** 559
To Viscount Halifax, **vi** 294, 641, 660
Conversation with M. Gafencu, **vi** 294–5, 641–2

Lester, Séan (League of Nations High Commissioner at Danzig, 1933–7), **i** 505; **iii** 401, 542; **v** 811

Le Tellier, Pol (Belgian Ambassador at Paris, 1938–40), **vii** 271

Ley, Dr. Robert (Leader of the German Labour Front), **ii** 652; **iv** 111*n*; **vi** 175, 749
Speech at Potsdam, June 1939, **vi** 176

Li, Marquis, **ix** 4

Libohova, Ekrem (Albanian Minister for Foreign Affairs, Nov. 1936–April 1939), **iv** 357; **v** 119, 168, 175

Lichner, Dr., **iii** 377

Liddell Hart, B. H. (Writer and military correspondent of 'The Times'), **iii** 660

Liebieg, Baron (President of the Czechoslovak textile manufacturers), **i** 594; **ii** 664

Lien Yu (Acting Minister for Foreign Affairs, 'Reformed Government' at Nanking)
To Sir A. Clark Kerr, **viii** 506

Li Han-yuan (Deputy Chief of British Municipal Police, Tientsin), **viii** 383–4, 421, 459–60, 504; **ix** 122, 180, 363–5, 369–70, 376, 386, 409, 416–7, 424, 427

Lima, José Lobo d'Avila (Portuguese Minister at Rome, 1935–45), **iii** 536

Limburg-Stirum, Count John de (Netherlands Minister at London, 1937–9), **iv** 577; **vi** 226–7, 240; **vii** 464

Li Ming (a Chinese banker), **viii** 526

Lindbergh, Colonel C. A. (U.S. aviator), **ii** 310, 312, 454, 474, 533, 669

Lindbergh, Mrs., **ii** 669

Linde, Major C. A. de (British Assistant Military Attaché at Paris, Aug. 1936–June 1940), **v** 55–6, 70; **vii** 15, 96
   Memorandum by, **v** 70–1

Lindsay, Sir Ronald C. (H.M. Ambassador at Washington, Mar. 1930–Aug. 1939), **ii** 541n; **vii** 261n; **viii** 66n, 193, 195n, 239n, 425, 498; **ix** 38, 120, 135, 141, 146, 148, 204n, 216n, 226n, 243, 261, 396n, 422–3, 429, 447
   To Sir A. Cadogan, **ix** 90
   To Viscount Halifax, **ii** 301; **iii** 279, 344; **iv** 124, 481; **v** 212; **vii** 41, 154, 261–2, 627, 629; **viii** 168, 185, 208, 278, 461; **ix** 86, 187, 189, 204, 223, 227, 235, 263, 283–4, 348, 370, 372, 381, 395, 404, 443, 450, 492
   Conversation with Mr. Cordell Hull, **ix** 348
   Conversation with President Roosevelt, **vii** 261–2, 627–9
   Conversation with Mr. Sumner Welles, **iv** 124–5; **vi** 41–2, 154; **viii** 278–9; **ix** 187–8, 235, 284, 443–4

Ling, Mr., **viii** 225

Lipinski, Jan von (a Polish Customs Inspector), **vi** 149

Lippmann, Walter (U.S. editor and author), **viii** 450

Lipski, Jozef (Polish Ambassador at Berlin, 1934–9), **i** 364; **ii** 297, 423; **iii** 63, 198, 442n, 586, 657; **iv** 168, 262, 453, 504, 514, 528, 543; **v** 93–4, 233, 290, 305, 379, 389–90, 410, 415–9, 425, 752, 808; **vi** 138, 236, 607–8, 634, 636–7, 662, 678, 692, 704; **vii** 29, 36, 59, 68, 86, 104, 118, 129, 151, 159, 185–6, 190, 198–9, 213–7, 221–2, 230, 233, 286, 289, 294, 311, 318n, 363, 387, 410, 432–3, 436–8, 440–2, 445, 447, 451, 454, 458, 465–6, 468, 474, 476, 495
   Conversation with M. Burckhardt, **vi** 44, 723–4, 728
   Conversation with M. Dahlerus, **vii** 445–6
   Conversation with Field-Marshal Göring, **vii** 216
   Conversation with Sir N. Henderson, **iv** 263–4; **vi** 238–9; **vii** 13, 62–3, 192, 239, 394, 433
   Conversation with Sir G. Ogilvie-Forbes, **iii** 582; **iv** 548; **v** 275–6

Li Sen-hsiang, **ix** 362

Lisicky, Karel (Counsellor of Czechoslovak Legation in London, 1938–9), **ii** 614, 623

List, General (Commander-in-Chief of German Fifth Army Group), **iv** 258, 275, 279, 564

Litauer, Dr. (President of the Foreign Press Association), **vi** 508

Litvinov, Maxim Maximovich (People's Commissar for Foreign Affairs in U.S.S.R., 1930–May 1939), **i** 54, 65, 304, 306, 390–1; **ii** 140–1, 168, 179, 219–20, 229–30, 235, 255–6, 266, 271–2, 323, 480, 489n, 595, 625; **iii** 153, 193, 364, 419, 430, 575, 586; **iv** 14, 45–6, 115, 132, 286, 391–2, 426, 446, 450, 459, 471–2, 504, 511–2, 523, 568–70, 622, 629, 631; **v** 20–1, 202, 206, 214, 217, 224, 228–9, 319, 349, 368, 373, 396, 404, 412–3, 469, 568, 595, 624, 726; **vi** 138, 150, 331; **vii** 46, 185, 594, 608; **ix** 28, 58
   Conversation with M. Bonnet, **ii** 294; **iii** 67
   Conversation with Viscount Chilston, **i** 54; **iii** 280
   Conversation with Mr. Hudson and Sir W. Seeds, **iv** 485, 584–5
   Conversation with Count Schulenberg, **ii** 140–1, 179
   Conversation with Sir W. Seeds, **iv** 24–5, 123–4, 128, 372, 385, 429, 509, 574–5; **v** 215, 221–2, 400
   Conversation (with M. Maisky) *with* Lord de la Warr and Mr. Butler, **ii** 497–8
   Note to Viscount Chilston, **iv** 631
   Note to Count Schulenberg, **iv** 447
   Statement to press, Mar. 17, 1938, **i** 62–4, 101
   resignation of, **v** 410, 542; **vi** 780; significance of, **v** 412–3, 429, 432, 451, 453, 460, 462, 484, 505, 542–5, 571, 625; **vi** 423; **ix** 58

Litvinov, Madame, **v** 546

Livingston, H. B. (H.M. Consul at Dresden, July 1936–April 1938), **i** 10

Li Wen-yu, **ix** 357, 362

Lloyd of Dolobran, 1st Baron, **ii** 683–5; **iv** 498–9

Lloyd, G. W. (Parliamentary Secretary, Mines Department, 1939–40), **vi** 244n

Lloyd George, David (Prime Minister, 1916–22), **i** 237; **v** 648; **vi** 692

Lobkowicz, Prince Max (Host of Mr. Ashton-Gwatkin in Czechoslovakia), **ii** 671–2

Lochner, Mr. (of the Associated Press of America), **vii** 257, 316

Loesch, Herr von (a German interpreter), **vii** 213

Lohr, General A. (an officer of the former Austrian Air Force), **iv** 258, 587

Lojacono, Vincenzo (Italian Ambassador at Brussels, 1939–40), **vii** 340

Loktionov, Army Commander A. D. (Chief of Soviet Air Force), **vii** 46
   At Meetings of Anglo-Franco-Soviet Military Delegations, **vii** 561, 563, 570, 585

Long, Lt.-Col. W. H. B., **vi** 487, 554

Loraine, Sir Percy L., Bart. (H.M. Ambassador at Rome, May 1939–June 1940), v 222n, 223, 432, 490, 526n, 612, 733, 737, 779, 795; vi 19, 229, 255n, 324, 589–90, 701; vii 81, 167, 247, 302, 358, 424, 498, 507, 511, 517
To Sir A. Cadogan, v 429, 650
To Viscount Halifax, v 420, 426, 428–9, 442, 461, 473, 477, 497, 503, 566, 598, 654, 663, 703–4, 707, 718, 752, 754, 756, 759; vi 15, 21, 126, 252, 273, 287–8, 293, 346–7, 450, 453, 466, 528, 549, 578–9, 596, 633, 643, 658, 664–5; vii 24, 28, 53, 55, 59, 71–2, 83–4, 93–5, 97, 120, 144–5, 147, 157, 181–2, 185, 215, 220, 240, 263, 296, 299, 303–4, 307, 326, 329–30, 335–6, 339, 349–50, 359, 366, 370, 373, 386, 392, 438–9, 444, 452, 459, 481–3, 486, 488, 491–2, 494, 508, 516, 520, 523, 526; ix 213
To Sir N. Henderson, v 495
Conversation with Signor Bastianini, vii 215–6
Conversation with M. Bonnet, v 795–7
Conversation with Count Ciano, v 442–3, 599, 754–6; vi 15–7, 21, 252–4, 450, 453, 578–9; vii 59–61, 144–5, 157–8, 181–2, 299, 302, 307, 336–7, 339, 366–7, 373, 392–3, 438–9, 459, 483, 491–2, 505–6, 520–1
Conversation with M. François-Poncet, v 428–9; vii 349–50
Conversation with M. Gafencu, v 426–8
Conversation with M. Helfand, vi 284–5
Conversation with Signor Mussolini, v 703–6, 718; vi 287–90
Letter to Sir A. Cadogan, vi 283
Letter to Viscount Halifax, vi 443, 554; vii 139
Letter to Sir O. Sargent, v 774, 784; vii 52
Views on German-Soviet Non-Aggression Pact, vii 181–2
Lothian, 11th Marquess of (H.M. Ambassador at Washington, Aug. 1939–Dec. 1940), iii 245n; vii 261n; ix 102, 120, 503n
To Viscount Halifax, vii 428–9; ix 518, 520
Conversation with President Roosevelt, vii 428–9
Conversation with Mr. Sumner Welles, ix 518
Lötschberg, Major von, iii 132–3
Loudon, Dr. Alexandre (Netherlands Minister at Washington, 1938–42, Ambassador there 1942–7), iv 27, 53, 85
To M. Patijn, iv 37
Loudon, Jonkheer Dr. J. (Netherlands Minister at Paris, 1919–40), vi 227, 240
Lozé, M. (*Chef du Protocol*, France), iii 390
Lubelski, Senator (a member of the Polish Diet), iv 88

Lubienski, M. (*Chef de cabinet* of Polish Minister for Foreign Affairs), iii 31, 58, 63, 106–7, 199; iv 32, 125, 163, 217, 245, 252, 453, 513; v 198, 238, 285, 391, 417, 626–7, 634–5, 677, 731, 767; vi 20, 30, 213, 235, 246, 270, 293, 318, 446, 448, 535, 591, 597, 683; vii 115–6, 159, 296–7, 373
Conversation with Sir H. Kennard, iii 60
Conversation with Mr. Norton, v 243; vi 214, 239
Lubomirski, Prince (Counsellor of Polish Embassy, Berlin: acted as Chargé d'Affaires), v 808; vi 634–5, 644–5, 651, 679, 697; vii 12
Conversation with Sir N. Henderson, vi 636–7
Lu Chung-lin (Chairman of the Hopei Provincial Government), viii 33
Lüdecke, Kurt G. W., v 665
Ludendorff, General Erich (1865–1937), v 270
Luguet, Lt.-Col. (French Air Attaché at Moscow), vii 45, 562
Lukasiewicz, Jules (Polish Ambassador at Paris, 1936–9), i 444; ii 317; iv 245, 423, 425, 435, 458, 469, 471; v 329, 609, 638; vi 213, 411, 518, 562; vii 2n, 25, 28, 164, 514–5, 529–30, 559
Lund, Brigadier (Head of British Military Mission in Turkey, June 1939), vi 112, 188–9
Lundberg, K. E. J. (Swedish Consul at Danzig, 1938–9), iii 561; vi 48, 165, 659–60
Lutz, General (German army mechanisation expert), iv 302n
Lutze, V. (Chief of Staff of the S.A.), iv 20–1, 302, 304, 306; v 803; vi 137, 171, 185, 238–9, 359, 710–1
Lyal, D. H. (a member of the Department of Overseas Trade), iv 568
Lyushkov, General, viii 38

Macartney, C. A. (a British historian), iii 185
MacDonald, Mr. ('The Times' correspondent in Far East), viii 474
MacDonald, Wing Commander A. H. H. (British Air Attaché at Vienna, Feb.–Mar. 1938; at Prague, Feb. 1938–May 1939), i 4, 62, 417, 566–7; ii 320; iv 62, 64–5, 126, 147, 275; v 93
To Mr. Troutbeck, iv 148
Conversation with General Faifr, ii 320
Conversation with General Krejci, iv 148
MacDonald, Malcolm (Secretary of State for the Dominions, June 1935–May 1938, Nov. 1938–Jan. 1939), iii 563
Maček, Dr. Vladimir (Leader of Croat Peasant party in Yugoslavia), iv 352; vi 285
MacFarlane, Colonel F. N. Mason. *See* Mason-MacFarlane, Colonel F. N.
Mach, Dr. Sano (Head of the Slovak Propaganda Service), iii 412; iv 220, 226, 246, 406–8; v 85, 87, 91

Machaty, M. (Leader of Czechoslovak delegation on Sub-Committee 'B' of the Inter-
national Commission set up in Oct. 1938),
iii 645, 648
Machnik, Frantisek (Czechoslovak Minister of
National Defence, Nov. 1935–Sept. 1938),
i 347–8, 367; **ii** 146
Mack, W. H. B. (1st Secretary, H.M. Embassy,
Vienna, Dec. 1934–April 1938: acted as
Chargé d'Affaires; at Rome, April–Aug.
1938; at Paris, Aug. 1938–June 1940), **iv**
330; **v** 468
    To Viscount Halifax, **i** 67, 126, 146; **vi** 17;
    ix 151
Mackensen, H. G. von (German Ambassador at
Rome, 1938–43), **i** 37, 41, 622; **ii** 59; **iii** 335;
iv 89, 293–4, 297; **v** 120; **vii** 71
McLaren, Mr., **vi** 751*n*
Maclean, F. H. R. (Secretary, H.M. Embassy at
Moscow, Feb. 1937–April 1939), **ii** 140; **iv**
188–9
    Memorandum by, **iv** 190
MacMurray, J. V. A. (U.S. Ambassador at
Angora, 1936–42), **v** 593; **vi** 30
Macnab, Major G. A. C. (British Military
Attaché at Prague, Oct. 1938–May 1939), **iii**
411, 415
    Memorandum by, **iii** 416
Macrae, H. A. (Commercial Secretary, H.M.
Embassy, Tokyo, Nov. 1929–Sept. 1940),
viii 317, 359
MacVitty, Karl de G. (U.S. Consul at Amoy),
ix 267, 288, 339, 361*n*, 371
MacWhite, Michael (Eire Minister at Rome,
1938–50), **iii** 533–4
Maesen de Sombreff, Jonkheer G. H. van der
(Netherlands Consul-General at Danzig,
1938–9), **v** 25, 27
Mafalda, Princess (daughter of King of Italy:
wife of Prince Philip of Hesse), **iii** 535
Magistrati, Count Massimo (Counsellor of
Italian Embassy at Berlin: acted as Chargé
d'Affaires), **i** 342, 353; **ii** 119; **iii** 132; **vii**
104
Maglione, Cardinal Luigi (Cardinal Secretary
of State, The Vatican, 1939–44), **v** 467, 524;
vi 32, 291, 303–4, 316, 369–70, 550; **vii** 14,
23–4, 62, 117, 182, 227, 265, 325, 350, 399,
448, 455
    To Mr. Osborne, **vi** 371
    Conversation with Mr. Osborne, **vi** 674–5;
    vii 20, 63, 403–4, 495
Magowan, J. H. (Commercial Counsellor, H.M.
Embassy at Berlin, Nov. 1937–Sept. 1939),
iii 130, 177, 644–5; **vi** 132–4
Mahmud Fakhri Pasha (Egyptian Minister at
Paris, 1924–40), **v** 143
Maillaud, M. (of the Havas Agency), **vi** 705
Maisky, Ivan Mikhailovich (Soviet Ambassador
at London, 1932–43), **iii** 194; **iv** 132, 385,

424, 429, 448, 574; **v** 20–1, 91, 98, 104, 199,
215, 224–5, 266–7, 269, 368, 385, 400, 484,
508, 542, 544, 565*n*, 578, 596, 622–5, 639–40,
659, 668, 678, 784, 787; **vi** 118, 461, 780; **vii**
594; **ix** 28, 101, 105, 141
    To Viscount Halifax, **i** 62
    Conversation with Mr. Ashton-Gwatkin, **v**
    208–9
    Conversation with Mr. R. A. Butler, **iv** 106–7,
    208–9; **vi** 594–5
    Conversation with Sir A. Cadogan, **iv** 530–2;
    v 21–3, 235
    Conversation with Viscount Halifax, **i** 256;
    ii 107, 271–2, 623–5; **iii** 153–4, 331; **iv**
    35–6, 391–2, 544, 556–8; **v** 53–4, 82–4,
    201–2, 209–10, 373–5, 453–4, 479–80,
    528–9, 630–4; **vi** 5–7, 50–1, 152–3,
    279–81, 339, 484–6; **ix** 334–5
    Conversation with Mr. Hudson, **iv** 207
    Conversation with Sir L. Oliphant, **v** 773–4
    Conversation with Mr. Strang, **v** 506–7
    Conversation with Sir R. Vansittart, **v** 564–5,
    639*n*
Major, A. G. (H.M. Consul-General at Genoa,
Jan. 1935–Aug. 1939), **iii** 346, 533
Makins, Roger Mellor (a member of Central
Department of Foreign Office), **v** 629, 710,
732*n*, 752; **vi** 402, 490, 677, 703, 707; **vii** 19,
311
    Conversation with M. Burckhardt, **iii** 610–1;
    v 395; **vi** 41–7, 689–98
    Conversation with M. Komarnicki, **iii** 604–5
    Conversation with Mr. Walters, **iv** 383*n*
    Letter to M. Burckhardt, **vi** 639
    Letter to Mr. Strang, **iii** 116
    Memorandum by, **vii** 246
    Minute by, **v** 286*n*, 391, 395; **vi** 624, 688;
    vii 66, 132, 302, 424, 492, 495, 530,
    551*n*, 552*n*, 555*n*
Makowski, W. (President of Polish Diet, 1938–
9), **iv** 543
Malik, M. (of the Czechoslovak National Bank),
ii 669
Malinowski, General (Deputy Chief of Polish
General Staff), **iv** 514; **vi** 684–5
Malkin, Sir William (Legal Adviser, Foreign
Office, 1929–45), **vi** 110, 112, 681–2
    At Munich Conference, **ii** 631–3
Mallet, Victor A. L. (Counsellor of H.M.
Embassy, Washington, Jan. 1936–Dec. 1939),
viii 336*n*, 373*n*, 461; **ix** 263–4, 370–2
    To Viscount Halifax, **iv** 9, 27, 29, 51;
    viii 301, 310, 335, 341, 366–7, 428,
    435, 447
    To Sir J. Simon, **viii** 384
    Conversation with Dr. Hornbeck, **ix** 381,
    520–1
    Conversation with Mr. Cordell Hull, **iv** 27
    Conversation with Mr. Sumner Welles, **viii**
    384–5; **ix** 395–6

Mallet, William Ivo (a member of Central Dept. of Foreign Office; appointed Assistant Private Secretary (Diplomatic) to Secretary of State, Jan. 1939), ii 143; iii 28, 77
To Mr. Steel, ii 71
Note by, ii 400; vii 520
Malmar, H. F. (Swedish Minister at Prague, 1938–9), iv 561
Malypetr, Jan (Czechoslovak Prime Minister, 1932–5), ii 663, 673
Mandel, Georges (French Minister for Colonies, 1938–40), i 617; ii 220; iii 392–3, 636; v 240, 799; vi 150
Mannerheim, Field-Marshal Baron K. G. (Finnish soldier and diplomat; Regent of Finland, Dec. 1918–July 1919)
Conversation with Mr. Snow, vi 120–2
Marchandeau, Paul (French Minister of Finance, Jan.–Nov. 1938; of Justice, Nov. 1938–Sept. 1939), iii 257, 392; iv 263
Marchandeau, Madame, iii 392
Marchienne, Baron E. de Cartier de. *See* Cartier de Marchienne, Baron E. de
Marek, Dr. Ferdinand (Austrian Minister at Prague, 1922–38), i 116n
Margerie, Roland de (1st Secretary, French Embassy, London), iii 590; iv 41; vii 166–7, 424, 530, 538
At Anglo-French conversations, April 1938, i 198; Sept. 1938, ii 373, 520, 536
Margesson, Captain H. D. (Parliamentary Secretary to the Treasury and Government Chief Whip), vi 736
Letter to M. Wenner-Gren, vi 740
Maria of Savoy, Princess, iv 42
Mariassy, Zoltan de (Hungarian Minister at Angora, 1935–41), vi 53
Marin, Louis (President of Right-wing group of the Union Républicaine Démocratique in France), ii 535, 606, 622; vii 177
Conversation with Sir E. Phipps, ii 579–80; vii 313–4
Marinkovitch, Dr. V. (Yugoslav Minister for Foreign Affairs, 1927–32), vi 498
Markovic, Dr. (Chairman of Czechoslovak Officers' Association), ii 90
Markovitch, Cinkar. *See* Cinkar-Markovitch
Markus, Hans (Estonian Minister at Warsaw, 1935–9), ii 68
Marosy, Francis de (Counsellor of Hungarian Legation, London: acted as Chargé d'Affaires), iii 3, 48
Conversation with Mr. Ingram, iii 1–2
Marras, Major-General E. (Italian Military Attaché at Berlin), ii 49, 306; iii 162; iv 461
Marshall-Cornwall, Lt.-Gen. J. H.
Report by, vi 295
Martius, Herr (a member of German Ministry of Foreign Affairs), ii 158

Masarik, Dr. (Private Secretary of Czechoslovak Minister for Foreign Affairs), ii 632; iv 56, 61–2, 129–30
Conversation with Mr. Troutbeck, iv 7–9, 13
Masaryk, Jan (Czechoslovak Minister at London, 1925–38), i 40–1, 112–5, 118, 137, 142n, 151, 159, 180–1, 243, 263, 266, 298–300, 309, 312–3, 331, 373, 404, 410, 416n, 498–9, 510, 520, 525, 529, 546, 563–4, 571–2, 630, 633, 635; ii 248, 271n, 373, 440, 517–8, 536, 540, 555–7, 561–3, 609, 675; iii 19, 49n, 50n, 54, 78, 81, 86–7, 142–3, 202–3, 629; v 86
To Viscount Halifax, i 36; ii 400, 518, 550, 609, 623
To Mr. Harvey, ii 606
Conversation with Sir A. Cadogan, i 142n, 289–90, 292; ii 443
Conversation with Viscount Halifax, i 33–4, 235–8, 324–5, 378–9, 493–4, 571n
Conversation with Sir S. Hoare, i 113–4
Conversation with Mr. Gladwyn Jebb, ii 369
Conversation with Mr. Strang, ii 536
Masaryk, Dr. T. G. (President of Czechoslovakia, 1918–35), i 237, 314; ii 81, 132, 145; iii 101, 411, 416n; iv 219n
Mason-MacFarlane, Colonel F. N. (British Military Attaché at Berlin, Dec. 1937–May 1939), i 9, 10, 17–8, 57, 317n, 323n, 335, 344, 352, 358–9, 363, 412–3, 448, 535, 552n, 561, 610; ii 13–4, 21–2, 27–8, 40–1, 47–8, 51, 61, 65, 67–8, 71, 76, 79, 87, 92, 101, 103–4, 106, 108, 117, 127–8, 137, 161, 169, 184, 236, 238, 258, 281, 285, 290, 309, 408, 512, 516, 563, 575, 581, 683; iii 57n, 162, 254, 367, 446; iv 19, 22, 102, 162, 173, 218, 232, 234–5, 393, 441, 623; v 67, 99, 199, 200, 210, 516–7, 526n, 549, 594, 805; vi 434, 632n, 699n; vii 626
To Sir N. Henderson, i 92, 271, 380–1, 450; ii 14–5, 24, 42, 61, 65, 104, 161, 169, 236, 455; iv 184, 393; v 594, 806
To Sir G. Ogilvie-Forbes, iii 368, 545, 564, 622; iv 19, 22, 623
To War Office, ii 46, 551, 615; iv 505
Conversation with Hauptmann (E) von Albedyl, ii 42–5, 184–5
Conversation with Acting Chief of Intelligence at German War Office, ii 47
Conversation with Rittmeister a. D. Viktor von Koerber, ii 65–7
Conversation with Major von Mellenthin, ii 169–70, 232–3, 290–1
Conversation with Colonel Szymanski, iv 184–6, 504
Conversation with General Tippelskirch, ii 120–1, 616
Conversation with Colonel Vauhnik, iii 564–5
Conversation with unnamed informant, ii 125–6
Memorandum by, iv 174, 624

Massigli, René (Political Director, French Ministry of Foreign Affairs, 1937–8; Ambassador at Angora, 1939–40), **i** 42, 337, 343; **ii** 158, 192, 365, 595; **v** 115, 162–3, 183, 220, 230–1, 238, 278–9, 288, 397, 399, 448, 465, 509–10, 518–9, 523, 526, 532–3, 535–6, 550, 724, 786, 796; **vi** 261, 299, 300, 341, 434–5, 600, 625, 636, 670, 676, 687–8; **vii** 155–6, 183*n*, 238, 248, 264, 287, 299*n*, 305, 313, 320, 364, 372, 379, 423, 487–8, 494
  Conversation with Mr. R. I. Campbell, **ii** 95–7, 124–5; **viii** 17, 23
  Conversation with M. Potemkin, **v** 380
Mastny, Dr. Vojtech (Czechoslovak Minister at Berlin, 1932–9 and representative on International Commission set up in Oct. 1938), **i** 24, 33*n*, 34*n*, 36–7, 47, 51, 59, 65–6, 76, 323, 328, 330, 337, 354, 361, 363, 521, 540, 568, 581, 616; **ii** 68, 171, 234, 428–9, 614, 623, 629, 632–3, 651; **iii** 123, 129–30, 134–5, 150–1, 169, 234–6, 240–1, 610, 615, 654–6; **iv** 3, 180, 204, 218, 232, 244, 441–3, 624; **v** 713
  Conversation with Sir N. Henderson, **i** 65–6, 262, 319, 503–4; **iv** 245
  Conversation with Herr von Ribbentrop, **i** 332–3
Matchek, Dr. V. *See* Maček, Dr. V.
Matsudaira, Tsuneo (Minister of Japanese Imperial Household), **viii** 528
Matsuoka, Yosuke (President of the South Manchuria Railway Company), **viii** 181–2
Matsushima, S. (Director of Commercial Department of Japanese Ministry of Foreign Affairs), **ix** 36
Matthews, The Very Reverend W. R. (Dean of St. Paul's Cathedral), **ii** 114
Maugham, Lord (Lord Chancellor, Mar. 1938–Sept. 1939), **ix** 410
Maugras, Gaston (French Minister at Budapest, 1934–8), **iii** 36, 116, 243
Maurice, Major-General Sir Frederick (President of the British Legion, 1932–47), **iii** 65*n*, 98, 551
Mavroudis, Nicholas (Greek Under-Secretary of State for Foreign Affairs, 1936–41), **iv** 374; **v** 186
  Conversation with Sir M. Palairet, **vi** 130
Maze, Sir Frederick (Inspector-General of Chinese Maritime Customs), **viii** 153–4, 160, 165–7, 214, 231, 238, 240, 242–3, 315, 397, 399, 430, 516, 524–6, 533, 537, 539*n*, 540; **ix** 24, 312, 353, 450–1
Medhurst, Group Captain C. E. H. (British Air Attaché at Rome, Aug. 1937–June 1940), **ii** 131; **iii** 501; **iv** 338–9; **v** 159
Megerle, Dr., **vi** 331
Meissner, Dr. (Head of English section of Press Department of German Ministry of Propaganda)
  Conversation with Mr. Bashford, **vi** 286*n*

Meissner, Dr. Alfred (leading member of Czechoslovak Committee of Six), **ii** 70, 93, 267, 662–3, 668
Meissner, Dr. Otto (German Minister of State and Head of the Presidential Chancellery), **vi** 171; **vii** 388
Mekhlis, L. Z. (Head of Political Directorate of Soviet Army), **i** 164
Melas, M. (Director of Political section, Greek Ministry of Foreign Affairs), **v** 777
Mellenthin, Major von (Head of Attaché Gruppe, German General Staff), **ii** 309; **v** 806
  Conversation with Col. Mason-MacFarlane, **ii** 169–70, 232–3, 290–1
  Conversation with Major Strong, **ii** 126–7
Mendl, Sir Charles (British Press Attaché at Paris, June 1926–May 1940), **vii** 19
Menemencioglu, Numan Rifaat (Secretary-General of Turkish Ministry of Foreign Affairs, 1937–42), **v** 238, 399, 464, 532, 536, 549–50, 552, 574, 592, 667, 687; **vi** 53, 97, 101, 111, 169–70, 188, 321, 360–1, 434–5; **vii** 198, 501, 527–8, 536
  Conversation with Sir H. Knatchbull-Hugessen, **v** 490–1, 532–3
Mensforth, Mr., **vi** 751*n*; **vii** 552
  Conversation with M. Dahlerus, **vii** 551
Menthan, M. de (French representative on Sub-Committee 'C' of International Commission set up in Oct. 1938), **iii** 132
Mercier, Louis (French Minister at Durazzo, 1935–9), **iv** 357; **v** 120, 175, 229–30, 383
Merekalov, Alexej Fedorovich (Soviet Ambassador at Berlin, 1938–9), **iv** 34; **v** 232; **vi** 705
Merry, A. F. (Commercial Secretary at H.M. Embassy, Berlin, Jan. 1938–Sept. 1939), **vii** 207
  Report by, **iv** 537
Meskaukas, Colonel P. (Lithuanian Military Attaché at Riga), **iv** 369, 390
Metaxas, General Ioannis (Greek Prime Minister and Minister for Foreign Affairs, 1936–41), **iv** 374, 465, 470, 499; **v** 151, 161, 163, 182, 185–6, 236, 327, 436, 444, 729; **vi** 101, 147
  Conversation with Sir S. Waterlow, **v** 145
  Message to Viscount Halifax, **v** 185
Metaxas, Pierre (Greek Minister at Rome, 1931–9), **v** 136, 158, 182, 550–1
Michalowski, Count Roman (1st Secretary, Polish Embassy at London)
  Conversation with Mr. Strang, **iii** 15
Michkovitch, Comm. D. (Yugoslav Military Attaché at Budapest), **iii** 12
Miedzinski, B. (a leader of the Polish Camp of National Unity group), **i** 429
Mierry, Lt.-Col. de (Acting Head of the French Deuxième Bureau), **vii** 15

Miklas, Wilhelm (President of Austria, Dec. 1928–Mar. 1938), **i** 2, 16–8, 130, 132, 134–5, 137, 150

Mikoyan, Anastas Ivanovich: (People's Commissar for Foreign Trade in U.S.S.R.), **iv** 503, 511–2, 568–70; **v** 208

Milanovitch, Vladimir (Counsellor of Yugoslav Legation, London: acted as Chargé d'Affaires), **vi** 170–1, 175
  Conversation with Viscount Halifax, **iv** 521–3; **v** 762

Milch, General Erhard (Inspector-General of the German air force), **ii** 289; **iii** 608; **iv** 1.3; **vi** 305, 413

Millerand, Alexandre (President of French Republic, 1920–4), **ii** 337; **iii** 227

Milojevitch, M. (Yugoslav Press correspondent in London), **v** 563

Mironas, Vladislovas (Lithuanian Prime Minister, 1938–9), **iv** 397, 643
  Conversation with Mr. Preston, **iv** 285–7

Mistler, Jean (Chairman of Foreign Affairs Commission of the French Chamber), **i** 478; **iii** 391

Mistler, Madame, **iii** 391

Mitchell, Mr. (of Messrs. Butterfield and Swire), **ix** 157

Mitford, Unity, **ii** 654

Miura, Y. (Japanese Consul-General at Shanghai, Dec. 1938–Oct. 1939), **viii** 365, 375, 453–5, 464, 466–7, 476, 480–1, 483–4, 489, 501–2, 507, 538–9; **ix** 16, 49, 53–4, 60, 62, 152–4, 446
  To the Municipal Council, Shanghai, **viii** 484

Molotov, Vyacheslav Mikhailovich (Chairman of the Council of People's Commissars in U.S.S.R., 1930–41: appointed People's Commissar for Foreign Affairs, May 1939), **iii** 193; **iv** 123, 411, 417–8, 511–2, 569, 571; **v** 429, 443–4, 450, 460, 463, 471, 476, 505, 542–4, 571, 596, 698, 707–8, 719–20, 753–4, 773, 777, 787; **vi** 6–7, 24, 33–4, 37, 49, 54, 65, 84–5, 91, 98–9, 103–4, 109, 122–3, 128–9, 134–5, 138–9, 144–5, 152, 161–3, 169, 173–4, 179–80, 182–4, 193–4, 209–10, 212, 225, 232, 242–3, 257, 265–8, 272, 275–81, 307, 324, 328, 331–5, 340, 349–50, 352, 383–4, 386, 396–7, 423–4, 426–30, 437, 448, 450–1, 456, 477–8, 484–5, 491–4, 525, 539, 544, 548, 565, 575, 681, 703, 780–1; **vii** 41–4, 46, 122, 127, 154, 164, 187–8, 225, 268, 276, 278, 384–5, 594, 604, 606–7; **ix** 58*n*
  appointed Commissar for Foreign Affairs, **v** 410, 542
  description of, **v** 544, 722; **vi** 138–9
  Conversation with M. Naggiar, **v** 737
  Conversation with Sir W. Seeds, **v** 469–71, 483–7, 558–9, 567–8, 701–2, 722, 726–7; **vii** 142–3

  Conversation with Sir W. Seeds and M. Naggiar, **vi** 79, 89–91, 116–20, 140–3, 230–2, 249–51, 308–12, 375–9, 456–60, 509–10, 521–5, 570–4; **vii** 237
  Conversation with Sir W. Seeds and M. Payart, **v** 710–2
  Speech to Supreme Council of U.S.S.R., May 31, 1939, *extracts from*, **v** 743–6; *referred to*, **v** 736, 746, 767, 785; **vi** 48–9, 781; **vii** 383
  Speech on ratification of Soviet-German Pact, Aug. 31, 1939, **vii** 430–1, 615–22

Moltke, Hans Adolf von (German Ambassador at Warsaw, 1934–9), **i** 445, 512; **ii** 651; **iii** 243, 581, 586; **iv** 16, 67, 163, 178, 252, 362, 548; **v** 37, 94, 203–4, 233–4, 281, 290, 318, 379, 415–6, 501, 605, 739; **vi** 20, 239, 530, 552
  Conversation with Sir H. Kennard, **iv** 146–7, 152–4, 513; **v** 58, 466–7; **vi** 81, 204–5

Momtchiloff, Nicolas (Bulgarian Minister at London, 1938–41), **iv** 498; **v** 346, 348; **vi** 496
  Conversation with Viscount Halifax, **v** 529–31

Monick, Emmanuel (French Financial Attaché at London, 1934–40), **iii** 634, 637

Monnet, Georges (French Minister of Agriculture, June 1936, June 1937, Mar.–April 1938)
  Conversation with Mr. Newton, **i** 549

Monson, Sir Edmund St. J. D. J., Bart. (H.M. Minister at Stockholm, Jan. 1938–Jan. 1940)
  To Viscount Halifax, **iii** 445, 505

Montague, F. (M.P. for West Islington), **ii** 24*n*

Montbas, Comte H. Barthon de (Counsellor of French Embassy, Berlin: acted as Chargé d'Affaires), **iii** 655; **iv** 394, 487, 490, 644

Monzie, Anatole de (French Minister of Labour, 1938–9), **vi** 303; **vii** 166

Morgan, J. (Counsellor of H.M. Embassy, Angora, Oct. 1930–Sept. 1940), **vi** 360

Morgas, M., **iv** 234

Morgenthau, Henry, Jr. (Secretary of U.S. Treasury, 1934–45), **iv** 366

Morioka, General, **ix** 73–4

Morishima, Morito (Counsellor in charge of Japanese Embassy in China, Jan. 1938–Sept. 1939), **viii** 300, 310; **ix** 30–1, 37, 266–7, 538

Morrison, W. S. (Minister of Agriculture & Fisheries, Oct. 1936–Dec. 1938; Chancellor of the Duchy of Lancaster, Jan. 1939–April 1940), **iv** 209

Móscicki, Ignacy (President of Poland, 1926–39), **i** 431; **ii** 538; **iii** 35, 103–4; **iv** 154, 543, 549, 572, 581; **v** 19, 411; **vi** 234, 247, 322–3, 400, 406, 419, 434–5, 445; **vii** 159, 216, 356, 404
  Letter to Dr. Benes, **iii** 43

Reply to President Roosevelt, Aug. 26, 1939, *text of*, **vii** 280; *referred to*, **vii** 261, 324, 372

Moscicki, Michel (Polish Minister at Brussels, 1937–9), **vii** 340

Moshanov, S. (President of the Bulgarian Parliament), **vi** 438, 583

Mossop, A. (1937 Sir Allan) (Judge of H.B.M. Supreme Court for China, Shanghai, 1933–43), **viii** 558; **ix** 156, 369

Mounsey, Sir George A. (Assistant Under-Secretary of State for Foreign Affairs, July 1929–June 1940), **viii** 30; **ix** 13, 210

Mountain, Mr., **vi** 751*n*

Mozzoni, Mgr. U. (Italian Secretary to the Apostolic Delegation in Great Britain), **vi** 304, 316

Muff, Lt.-Gen. W. (German Military Attaché at Vienna), **i** 4

Mufti of Jerusalem, The, (Amin al Husseini), **iii** 308

Munakata, Mr., **ix** 36

Munch, Peter R. (Danish Minister for Foreign Affairs, 1929–40), **v** 462

Munster, 5th Earl of (Under-Secretary of State for War, Jan.–Sept. 1939), **ix** 287

Munters, Vilhelms (Latvian Minister for Foreign Affairs, 1936–40), **iii** 591; **v** 394, 669, 680, 688, 697, 700, 767, 775; **vi** 45, 47, 118, 159, 161, 301, 327
  Conversation with Viscount Halifax, **v** 648–9
  Conversation with Mr. Orde, **v** 214–5, 461–2, 767

Murgas, General (Slovak Chief of Staff), **iv** 96, 226, 406, 408

Musse, General F. (French Military Attaché at Warsaw), **ii** 441; **v** 757; **vi** 262, 292; **vii** 2*n*, 21, 26–8, 41, 54, 61, 70, 84, 91, 105, 107, 158–9, 208, 210–1, 503, 559–60
  Conversation with Lt.-Col. Sword, **v** 757–9

Mussolini, Benito (Italian Prime Minister and Minister of Interior, War, Navy, Air and for Italian Africa), **i** 14, 20, 23, 27–9, 33, 42*n*, 127–8, 132, 210, 239, 265, 325, 353, 626–7; **ii** 20, 191, 197, 220, 233*n*, 235, 239, 359, 414, 556, 561, 580, 586, 588, 590, 594, 596–603, 608, 614, 624, 626–7, 641–5, 691; **iii** 104, 127, 140, 157, 160–1, 203, 222, 224, 253, 259, 280, 287, 297–9, 309, 313–5, 318–628 *passim*; **iv** 10, 17–8, 60–1, 64–5, 87, 92, 107, 124, 130, 161, 171, 177, 185–6, 215, 241–2, 273, 293–359 *passim*, 402*n*, 455, 461, 488, 507, 531, 547, 554, 556, 559, 589–90; **v** 70, 82, 84, 119, 125, 128, 139–808 *passim*; **vi** 15–7, 19, 21, 44, 115, 124, 127, 166, 214, 221, 252, 301–2, 324, 358–9, 370–1, 443–5, 471–2, 474, 488, 502, 554–6, 579, 588–90, 596, 641, 664, 667, 675, 701, 704–5, 708, 710, 723–5, 728, 731, 746, 752; **vii** 7–8, 13, 36, 49, 53, 57, 71–586 *passim*; **viii** 239, 437*n*, 438

To Mr. Chamberlain, **iii** 458*n*, 540; **iv** 572*n*, 573
Conversation with Mr. Chamberlain, **ii** 636; **iii** 517–21, 524–30
Conversation with M. François-Poncet, **iii** 461–2
Conversation with Sir P. Loraine, **v** 703–6, 718; **vi** 287–90
Conversation with Earl of Perth, **v** 262–4
Message to Mr. Chamberlain, **v** 129; *referred to*, **v** 127, 131, 136
Message to Viscount Halifax, **iii** 318
Message to Herr Hitler, Aug. 29, 1939, **vii** 367
Message to M. Metaxas, **v** 160–1
Message to Prince Paul of Yugoslavia, **iv** 352
Speech by, at Milan, Nov. 1936, **iv** 620; at Rome, Jan. 11, 1939, **iii** 537; at Rome, Jan. 22, **iv** 299*n*; at Rome, Mar. 26, **iv** 353*n*; *referred to*, **iv** 358, 532, 573–4, 797; **vi** 471; at Reggio, Mar. 31, **iv** 358*n*; at Rome, April 20, **v** 263; at Turin, May 14, **v** 567*n*, 578, 650–1, 664, 762, 766; at Cuneo, May 20, **v** 650–1, 664
At Munich Conference, **ii** 631, 633
Proposal for international conference, Sept. 1939, **vii** 442

Muti, Ettore (appointed Secretary of Fascist party, Oct. 1939), **vii** 335

Muto, General (a Japanese representative at Anglo-Japanese negotiations in Tokyo, July–Aug. 1939), **ix** 361, 363–4, 369, 386, 424, 427, 439*n*, 441

Muzahim al Pachachi (Iraqi Minister at Rome, 1935–9), **iii** 536

Myers, W. R. (Commissioner of Customs at Tientsin), **viii** 243, 388; **ix** 314, 315*n*

Myreboe, L. (Norwegian Consul-General at Danzig, 1937–9), **vi** 165

Nagaoka, H. (Japanese Consul at Chefoo), **viii** 287

Naggiar, Paul Émile (French Ambassador in China, July 1936–Nov. 1938; at Moscow, Feb. 1939–1940), **iv** 115, 123; **v** 216–7, 678, 684; 753–4, 778; **vi** 3, 33, 56, 65, 84–5, 95, 98, 104, 109–10, 115–6, 120, 122–3, 134, 138–40, 163, 167, 174, 179, 194, 208–10, 225, 233, 240, 243, 277–8, 310, 332, 345, 349*n*, 352, 383–4, 437, 449–50, 456, 475, 491, 493–4, 526, 535, 539, 576, 595, 606, 611–2, 615, 641, 674, 681–2, 780–2; **vii** 1–2, 3*n*, 21, 34, 40, 42, 46, 74, 107, 121, 127, 129, 154–5, 164, 187–8, 194, 205–6, 227, 268, 276, 278, 384, 604, 606–7; **viii** 16–8, 25, 55, 137*n*, 154, 165, 186, 231, 256, 300
  Conversation (with Sir W. Seeds) *with* M. Molotov, **v** 737; **vi** 79, 89–91, 116–20, 140–3, 230–2, 249–51, 308–12, 375–9, 456–60, 509–10, 521–5, 570–4; **vii** 237

Nakagawa, Mr. (Japanese Adviser to the Municipal Council, Tientsin), **viii** 421; **ix** 155*n*, 164

Nakamura, Lt.-Gen. K. (Japanese Commander-in-Chief, Korea), **ix** 155

Napier, Alan (H.M. Consul at Venice, Nov. 1924–June 1940), **iii** 346

Nasse, Pandeli (Albanian Chargé d'Affaires at Bucharest, 1937–9), **v** 120

Nathan, Mr., **ix** 112

Nečas, Jaromir (Czechoslovak Minister of Social Welfare, Nov. 1935–Sept. 1938), **i** 70; **ii** 667

Negrin, Dr. Juan (President of the Council of Ministers, Republican Government of Spain, May 1937–Mar. 1939), **iii** 298–9, 514; **iv** 590

Neubauer, Captain (a member of German delegation at Anglo-German Naval conversations, Dec. 30, 1938), **iii** 664

Neumann, Dr. E. (Leader of the Memel National Socialist party), **iv** 390

Neumann, Herr (Statistician of the German Four-Year Plan), **iv** 606

Neumark, Otto (H.M. Pro-Consul at Brno, Nov. 1935–Sept. 1939; acted as Vice-Consul, 1936 and 1938–9), **iv** 235

Neumayr, Dr. (Austrian Minister of Finance, 1936–8), **i** 135

Neurath, Baron Constantin von (German Minister and President of the Secret Cabinet Council, Feb, 1938–May 1945; Protector of Bohemia and Moravia, Mar. 1939–Aug. 1943), **i** 8, 12, 15, 23–4, 26, 37, 40–1, 51, 60, 66, 112, 531, 587, 589; **ii** 59, 66, 217, 251, 280, 284, 297, 300, 410, 428, 597, 647–9, 652–3; **iii** 619; **iv** 122, 439; Protector of Bohemia and Moravia, **iv** 564–5; **v** 291–2, 554, 556, 782; **vi** 704
  Conversation with Sir N. Henderson, **i** 15–6, 44, 57–8, 384–5; **ii** 224–6, 283, 413
  Letter to Sir N. Henderson, **i** 30–2; *referred to*, **i** 46, 80

Neuwirth, Dr. Hans (a leader of the Sudeten German party), **i** 121, 349, 365; **ii** 673; **iii** 216

Newall, Air Chief Marshal Sir Cyril L. N. (Chief of Air Staff, 1937–40), **iii** 435; **iv** 115*n*, 123; **vii** 293

Newton, Basil Cochrane (Jan. 1939, Sir Basil) (H.M. Minister at Prague, Mar. 1937–April 1939), **i** and **ii** *passim*; **iii** 65, 77, 116, 118*n*, 125–6, 169*n*, 195*n*, 376*n*, 380*n*, 448, 607; **iv** 9, 278, 596
  To Sir A. Cadogan, **i** 112*n*
  To Viscount Halifax, **i** and **ii** *passim*; **iii** 21–2, 29, 35, 41–5, 49, 51, 54, 59, 61–2, 64, 66–8, 74, 76, 79–82, 86, 90–1, 96, 108, 112, 114–5, 118, 123–4, 136, 140–1, 146, 152, 155–6, 170, 184, 187, 190, 192, 195, 197*n*, 209–13, 219, 221–2, 239–40, 253,

368, 375–6, 378, 380, 384, 386, 407, 414, 418, 423, 428, 559, 632–3; **iv** 183, 200, 204, 219–20, 224–6, 229, 233–5, 241–2, 246–7, 249, 255, 258–9, 275, 279–80, 282, 287–9, 403, 438, 460, 469, 560
  Conversation with Dr. Benes, **i** 72–6, 102, 179–82, 307–15, 442–4, 446, 469–73, 525–6, 529–31, 569–73, 578–9, 600–1, 604–7, 612–3; **ii** 36–8, 226–9, 245–7, 329–30, 332–3, 449–50, 582, 604–5; **iii** 21–2, 90
  Conversation with M. Chvalkovsky, **iii** 140–1, 221–2, 423–4; **iv** 220–1
  Conversation with Dr. Eisenlohr, **i** 116–7, 277–80, 541, 543–4, 559–61
  Conversation with Herr Frank, **i** 517–8
  Conversation with Dr. Hodza, **i** 76–80, 113, 125–6, 195–6, 282–3, 350, 354, 372–4, 394–7, 424–5, 466–7, 519–22, 607–9; **ii** 220
  Conversation with M. Krno, **iii** 108–9, 184–5, 239; **iv** 242–3
  Conversation with Dr. Krofta, **i** 55, 117–8, 158–9, 186–7, 197, 263–4, 266–70, 329, 332–4, 338, 350, 354, 397–8, 508–10; **ii** 94–5, 189–90, 319–20, 371–2, 426–7, 583, 621–2; **iii** 29, 41, 51–2, 80–1
  Conversation with Herr Kundt, **ii** 8
  Conversation with M. de Lacroix, **i** 459
  Conversation with M. Monnet, **i** 549
  Conversation with Mr. Strang, **i** 403–12

Neyrone, Comdr. Luigi (Italian Consul-General at Shanghai), **viii** 459, 469

Nicholl, Captain A. D. (Assistant Secretary, Committee of Imperial Defence), **vii** 2*n*

Nicolai, Colonel, **v** 594

Nicolson, Harold (author and critic: Secretary, H.M. Embassy, Berlin, 1927–8; Counsellor, 1928–9), **i** 630

Nidda, Krug von (Correspondent in Paris of the 'Deutsche Allgemeine Zeitung'), **vi** 728

Niemöller, Dr. (Leader of Confessional Movement in the German Evangelical Church), **vi** 741; **vii** 256

Noble, Sir Andrew Napier, Bart. (Secretary, H.M. Embassy, Rome, Nov. 1933–Jan. 1938; transferred to Foreign Office, Jan. 1938)
  Note by, **iii** 328

Noble, Vice-Admiral (1939 Admiral) Sir Percy L. H. (Commander-in-Chief, China Squadron, 1938–40), **viii** 106, 234, 278, 324, 338*n*, 441; **ix** 119, 140, 156, 178, 361, 433

Noe, Professor (Director of the International Shipbuilding and Engineering Company of Danzig)
  Conversation with Sir A. Cadogan and Herr Forster, **i** 653–5

Noël, Léon (French Ambassador at Warsaw, 1935–9), **i** 444*n*, 445, 480; **ii** 289, 545; **iii** 17, 22, 27–8, 33, 35, 38, 104, 110, 120, 122, 138,

282, 590; **iv** 32, 51, 69, 142, 203, 205, 515,
549–50, 567; **v** 205, 211, 734; **vi** 185, 213,
317, 501, 638, 644, 657, 668, 676, 679, 724;
vii 3*n*, 7, 25–6, 28, 40, 53–4, 70, 77, 79, 85–6,
105–6, 112, 116–7, 119, 130, 149, 164, 190,
213–4, 236, 267, 269, 289, 294, 297, 364, 371,
375, 438, 476, 482, 498, 522, 559
  Conversation with M. Beck, **ii** 441; **vi** 292–3;
  vii 223
  Conversation with Sir H. Kennard, **iii** 365–6;
  v 72–3
  Conversation with Mr. Norton, **vi** 262
  Conversation with Herr von Ribbentrop, **iv** 33
Noel-Baker, Philip J. (M.P. for Derby), **i** 386,
409
Noel-Buxton, 1st Baron, **ii** 114
Noguès, General Auguste (French Resident-
General, Morocco), **v** 144
Noiret, Major, **iv** 223
Nomura, Vice-Admiral N. (Japanese Naval
Attaché in China, 1938–9), **viii** 157, 370
Norman, Montagu (Governor of Bank of Eng-
land, 1920–44), **iii** 675
  Conversation with Mr. Chamberlain, **ix** 271–2
Northcliffe, 1st Viscount (Newspaper proprietor
and editor), **vi** 94
Northcote, Sir Geoffrey Alexander Stafford
(Governor and Commander-in-Chief, Hong
Kong, 1937–41), **viii** 137; **ix** 19, 33, 84, 97,
370
Norton, Clifford John (Counsellor of H.M.
Embassy, Warsaw, Dec. 1937–Oct. 1939;
acted as Chargé d'Affaires), **ii** 190*n*; **iii** 31,
101, 206*n*; **iv** 217, 252, 290, 513; **v** 238, 286*n*,
391, 417, 419, 677, 731, 767; **vi** 30, 207; **vii**
2*n*, 296, 358*n*
  To Viscount Halifax, **ii** 190; **iii** 58; **vi**
  213–4, 233–4, 239, 242, 259, 262, 274,
  292, 337–8, 358, 378, 386–7, 399, 400, 402,
  404–5, 415, 427, 436, 439, 447, 475–6,
  482, 486, 501, 526–7, 536, 597
  Conversation with M. Beck, **ii** 190; **vi** 233–5,
  259, 475–6, 482
  Conversation with M. Lubienski, **v** 243; **vi**
  214, 239
  Conversation with M. Noël, **vi** 262
  Letter to Sir A. Cadogan, **vi** 246, 317, 342
  Letter to Sir L. Oliphant, **vi** 445
  Letter to Sir O. Sargent, **vi** 248, 269, 530,
  536
  Letter to Mr. Strang, **v** 352
  Views on Poland's attitude towards Danzig
  question, **vi** 247–8
  Views on Anglo-Polish financial negotiations,
  vi 537–8
Nosworthy, R. L. (Commercial Counsellor,
H.M. Embassy, Rome, Oct. 1934–June 1940),
iii 346, 496, 501, 532; **iv** 292, 338, **v** 171; **vi**
555
  Memorandum by, **vi** 556

Nothomb, Baron (a member of the Belgian
Senate), **iv** 78
Nuksa, Martins (Secretary-General, Latvian
Ministry of Foreign Affairs, 1939–40), **v** 700
Numan, M. *See* Menemencioglu, Numan
Rifaat

Ogilvie-Forbes, Sir George Arthur D. (Counsellor of H.M. Embassy, Berlin, Mar. 1937–
Sept. 1939; acted as Chargé d'Affaires), **i** 295,
450; **ii** 60, 290*n*, 455*n*, 569*n*; **iii** 131, 196*n*,
242*n*, 269*n*, 273–4, 436, 445*n*, 451*n*, 582*n*, 589,
655; **iv** 3*n*, 180, 582*n*; **v** 217, 388*n*, 462; **vi**
125*n*, 208, 702; **vii** 51, 402, 440–2, 445–6, 453,
474–5, 480, 495–6
  To Sir A. Cadogan, **ii** 280; **iv** 18; **vii** 318,
  321–2, 324, 327
  To Viscount Halifax, **ii** 184, 279, 281, 285,
  289–91, 479, 615; **iii** 196, 200, 203–4,
  207–8, 211, 213, 218, 220–1, 230, 234–6,
  241–2, 245, 247, 256, 259–64, 267*n*,
  269–72, 275, 278–9, 282, 363, 365–8, 375,
  378, 381, 386, 446, 449, 455, 457, 544,
  551, 560–1, 564, 568, 573, 610, 622, 642,
  644, 647, 649, 653–4; **iv** 1, 3, 18–9, 22,
  30, 34, 41, 54, 58–9, 86, 91, 303, 393–4,
  397, 421, 440, 455, 482–3, 493, 495,
  504–5, 523, 525, 528, 536, 540, 548, 551,
  571, 582, 586, 640, 643–6; **v** 28, 46, 67,
  107, 199, 210, 216, 231–2, 244, 264, 275,
  286, 290; **vi** 261, 265–6, 270, 297, 309,
  318, 322, 324, 327, 337
  To Sir J. Simon, **iii** 582
  To Mr. Strang, **iii** 266, 581
  Conversation with Herr Aschmann, **iii** 551–2,
  560
  Conversation with Prince Bismarck, **v** 244–5
  Conversation with M. Coulondre, **iv** 41
  Conversation with M. Dahlerus, **vii** 319–20
  Conversation with M. François-Poncet, **ii**
  479
  Conversation with M. Lipski, **iii** 582; **iv** 548;
  v 275–6
  Conversation with Dr. Ritter, **iii** 235, 242
  Conversation with Baron von Weizsäcker, **iii**
  203–4
  Conversation with Herr Woermann, **iii** 271
  Letter to Mr. Kirkpatrick, **vii** 257, 316
  Letter to Mr. Strang, **iii** 279*n*, 379; **iv** 12,
  623; **v** 99
Ohnishi, Major, **ix** 216
Ohta, Major (Head of Japanese gendarmerie in
Tientsin), **ix** 324, 357, 361–2, 364, 377, 387
  Conversation with Mr. Jamieson, **ix** 479
Ohtaka, S. (Japanese Consul-General at Tsing-
tao), **viii** 289, 331, 353
Oikawa, Admiral (Commander-in-Chief of the
Japanese China Fleet), **viii** 278, 321, 324*n*
Okamoto, Suemasa (Japanese Consul-General
at Shanghai, 1937–8; Counsellor of Japanese

Okamoto, S. (*cont.*)
Embassy, London, 1938–40), **viii** 95, 99; **ix** 62–3, 165, 215, 513; **viii** 99
Conversation with Viscount Halifax, **ix** 487–8
Conversation with Mr. Howe, **ix** 151–2
Okazaki, K. (Japanese Consul-General at Canton), **viii** 214, 224
Okyar, Fethi. *See* Fethi Okyar
Olga, Princess Paul of Yugoslavia, **vi** 11
Oliphant, Sir Lancelot (Deputy Under-Secretary of State for Foreign Affairs, Mar. 1936–Dec. 1939), **iii** 450n, **ix** 272n
Conversation with M. Aras, **v** 346
Conversation with M. Maisky, **v** 773–4
O'Malley, Owen St. Clair (H.M. Minister at Budapest, May 1939–April 1941), **vi** 19; **vii** 350
To Viscount Halifax, **vii** 92, 140–1, 361
Oosterhout, Baron C. G. W. H. van Boetzelaer van. *See* Boetzelaer van Oosterhout, Baron
Orbay, General Kazim (Head of Turkish military mission to Great Britain, June 1939), **vi** 191, 435
Orde, C. W. (H.M. Minister at Riga, Tallinn and Kovno, April 1938–July 1940)
To Viscount Halifax, **iv** 285, 369; **v** 214, 349, 461, 700, 730, 767; **vi** 301
Conversation with M. Munters, **v** 214–5, 461–2, 767
Orlowski, Leon (Polish Minister at Budapest, 1936–9), **iii** 36; **iv** 428, 433; **v** 63, 94; **vi** 19
d'Ormesson, Comte Wladimir (Foreign Editor of the 'Figaro'), **iii** 393; **iv** 61; **vi** 495
Orr, Sir John Boyd (Nutritional expert), **i** 155
Orsenigo, Mgr. Cesare (Apostolic Nuncio in Germany, 1930–45), **v** 291, 338, 462–3; **vi** 370, 372; **vii** 402
Osborne, F. D'A. G. (H.M. Minister at The Vatican, Feb. 1936–June 1947), **iii** 358, 533, 535; **iv** 308; **vi** 294; **vii** 265, 333, 399, 448, 452
To Viscount Halifax, **v** 411, 458, 489, 498, 718; **vi** 303, 316, 369, 674; **vii** 13, 20, 63, 182, 196, 253, 308, 350, 403, 448, 452, 495
Conversation with Cardinal Maglione, **vi** 674–5; **vii** 20, 63, 403–4, 495
Conversation with Mgr. Tardini, **vii** 183, 196
Osetrov, Colonel (Chief of External Relations Department of People's Commissariat of Defence in U.S.S.R.), **vii** 45, 613
Oshima, General Hiroshi (Japanese Ambassador at Berlin, 1938–45), **viii** 309, 316; **viii** 179, 182, 482, 485, 492; **ix** 42, 64
Osusky, Stefan (Czechoslovak Minister at Paris, 1921–39), **i** 53, 113, 336, 343, 366, 460, 476, 495, 500, 503, 522n, 523, 526–7, 545, 634; **ii** 387–8, 415, 419–20, 422, 425–6, 440, 444, 518, 572, 609; **iii** 81, 392, 424, 444–5, 447; **iv** 364
Conversation with M. Paul-Boncour, **i** 53–4
Ott, General Eugen (German Ambassador at

Tokyo, 1938–42), **viii** 12, 15, 17, 23, 89, 90, 162–3, 451
Conversation with Sir R. Craigie, **viii** 31
Overstraeten, Major-General R. F. C. van (*aide-de-camp* to King Leopold III of the Belgians), **iv** 451
Ozbekkan, A. S. (Commercial Attaché, Turkish Embassy, London), **vi** 362

Pabst, General J. C. (Netherlands Ambassador at Tokyo, 1923–40), **viii** 88
Pacelli, Cardinal Eugenio (Cardinal Secretary of State, The Vatican, 1930–9; elected Pope, Mar. 2, 1939; *see* Pius XII), **v** 222
Conversation with Mr. Torr, **ii** 136–7
Pack, A. J. (Commercial Counsellor, H.M. Embassy at Warsaw, Aug. 1937–May 1939), **iv** 142; **vi** 538
Pahlavi, Prince Mohammed Reza (Crown Prince of Iran), **v** 460n
Paine, Colonel G. H. (U.S. Military Attaché at Rome,) **iv** 304–5; **v** 171
Palairet, C. M. (June 1938, Sir Michael) (H.M. Minister at Vienna, Dec. 1937–Mar. 1938; acted as Chargé d'Affaires at Bucharest, Sept.– Dec. 1938; H.M. Minister to Greek Government, June 1939–May 1942), **i** 1n, 129, 131, 134; **iii** 45n, 112n; **vi** 463–4
To Viscount Halifax, **i** 1–2, 4, 6–7, 9–11, 13, 15–9, 27, 38, 40, 42–3; **iii** 45, 97n, 197; **v** 777; **vi** 84, 127, 130
Conversation with M. Comnène, **iii** 45–6, 197
Conversation with M. Gafencu, **vi** 84
Conversation with M. Mavroudis, **vi** 130
Palasse, Colonel (French Military Attaché at Moscow), **i** 162, 164, 172–3, 307; **vii** 45, 562, 613
Pannwitz, Dr. Eberhard von (German Minister at Durazzo, 1936–9), **v** 169, 192
Papée, Kazimierz (Polish Minister at Prague, 1936–9), **i** 351; **ii** 217, 671; **iii** 36, 39, 49n, 50n, 51
To M. Krofta, **iii** 70
Papen, Franz von (German Ambassador on Special Mission at Vienna, Aug. 1934–Mar. 1938; Ambassador at Angora, 1939–44), **i** 7, 128–9; **ii** 428; **v** 322, 354, 442, 464, 550, 592–4, 777–8, 789–90; **vi** 241, 321, 497, 506, 619–20; **vii** 48, 200, 214–5, 242, 248, 264, 272–3, 422
Conversation with Sir N. Henderson, **v** 674–5
Conversation with President Inönü, **vii** 299n, 308
Conversation with Sir H. Knatchbull-Hugessen, **vi** 71–5, 467–70
Conversation with M. Fethi Okyar, **vi** 74–5
Conversation with M. Saracoglu, **v** 354–5, 442, 574; **vii** 214–5
Pares, Peter (H.M. Consul at Bratislava, Dec. 1938–Sept. 1939), **i** 121, 248, 354, 396, 406,

411*n*, 434–5; **ii** 9, 29*n*, 91, 265*n*, 304, 664; **iv** 92–3, 226, 233–4, 246, 280, 287
To Viscount Halifax, **iv** 406; **v** 84
To Mr. Newton, **i** 68, 123, 249, 396*n*, 436, 487; **ii** 30; **iv** 406
To Mr. Troutbeck, **iv** 92, 94, 157
Conversation with Dr. Tiso, **iv** 92–3
Paris, Lt.-Col. D. K. (British Military Attaché at Brussels, Feb. 1935–Feb. 1939), **iii** 583; **iv** 66, 76
To Sir R. Clive, **iv** 77
Parkanyi, Dr. (Ruthenian member of Gen. Syrovy's Government, Oct.–Nov. 1938), **iii** 140–1
Pascua y Martinez, Marcelino (Spanish Ambassador at Paris, 1938–9), **iii** 514–5
Paternotte de la Vaillée, A. (Belgian Ambassador at Warsaw, 1936–9), **iv** 205
Patijn, Dr. J. A. N. (Netherlands Minister for Foreign Affairs, Oct. 1937–July 1939), **iii** 592; **iv** 31*n*, 36, 73, 85; **vi** 254*n*; **vii** 349
Conversation with Sir N. Bland, **iv** 27–9, 31, 52–3
Paul, Prince (Senior Regent of Yugoslavia, 1934–41), **ii** 25*n*, 241, 260–1; **iv** 351, 465, 495, 523, 620; **v** 80, 309, 314, 321, 328, 333–4, 346, 659–60; **vi** 69, 167, 637, 727; **vii** 152*n*, 379, 421*n*
Conversation with Sir R. Campbell, **iv** 352, 384, 388; **v** 79–80
Conversation with Viscount Halifax, **vi** 437–9
Conversation with Sir N. Henderson, **vi** 11–2
Letter to Lord Halifax, **vii** 421*n*
Visit to Germany, **v** 287, 586, 656, 660, 662, 677, 717, 725, 728, 740, 756; **vi** 14, 66, 75
Visit to Great Britain, *question of,* **v** 309, 321–2, 481, 662; **vi** 52, 69, 70; *referred to,* **vi** 437*n*, 463–4, 513, 583, 630, 748–9; *see also Conversation with* Viscount Halifax
Visit to Italy, **v** 588, 660, 676, 686, 756; **vi** 66
Paul-Boncour, Joseph (French Minister for Foreign Affairs, Mar.–April 1938), **i** 41, 51, 88, 140, 143, 149, 197
Conversation with M. Osusky, **i** 53–4
Conversation with Sir E. Phipps, **i** 50, 94–5
Pauliny-Toth, Dr. Jan (Leader of the Slovak National party), **iv** 158; **v** 85
Payart, Jean (French Chargé d'Affaires at Moscow), **v** 198, 224, 229, 566, 572, 688, 693, 698, 710
Conversation with Mr. Vereker, **ii** 229
Peake, C. B. P. (a member of News Department of the Foreign Office), **iii** 532; **v** 385
Peck, W. R. (Counsellor of U.S. Embassy in China; acted as Chargé d'Affaires), **viii** 478; **ix** 97
Pelevaynski, Colonel (Chief of the Deuxième Bureau, Poland)
Conversation with Lt.-Col. E. R. Sword, **iii** 17

Pelham, George Clinton (Commercial Secretary, H.M. Embassy in China, Oct. 1933–Aug. 1942), **ix** 493
Pella, Vespasien V. (Roumanian Minister at The Hague, 1936–40), **iii** 592
Pennell, W. V. (Editor of the 'Peking and Tientsin Times'), **viii** 504
Pennington, Squadron Leader, **vii** 565
Pennington, Mrs. R. V., **v** 176
Peppo, Ottavio de (Italian Ambassador at Angora, 1938–43), **v** 355–6
Péri, Gabriel (a member of the Foreign Affairs Committee of French Chamber), **v** 439; **vi** 146
Perkowski, M. (Polish Assistant Commissioner-General at Danzig), **v** 538, 576, 625, 734, 764; **vi** 569, 622–4, 724–5; **vii** 152
Peroutka, Dr. (Director-General of Czechoslovak National Bank), **iii** 130–1
Peroutka, M. (a Czechoslovak journalist), **iv** 561
Perowne, J. V. T. W. T. (a member of American Dept. of the Foreign Office)
Letter to Mr. Holman, **iii** 451*n*
Letter to Dr. von Selzam, **iv** 637
Perth, 16th Earl of (Sir Eric Drummond) (H.M. Ambassador at Rome, Oct. 1933–April 1939), **i** 42*n*, 246*n*, 322*n*, 439; **ii** 240, 561*n*; **iii** 62*n*, 174*n*, 203, 312–5, 329–31, 480, 488, 511*n*, 524, 528, 533, 536; **iv** 273, 317*n*, 319, 331, 335, 339, 341, 343, 345, 349, 353*n*; **v** 136–7, 138*n*, 139, 143, 159, 161, 173, 195–6, 230, 257, 259, 277, 345, 386, 612, 763, 766, 798; **vi** 94; **vii** 179, 239, 269*n*
To Sir A. Cadogan, **iii** 170, 477–8; **iv** 307, 359, 507
To Viscount Halifax, **i** 20, 23, 27, 37, 42*n*, 261, 274, 291, 342, 353, 367; **ii** 561, 588, 590–1, 600–2, 641; **iii** 126, 174–5, 319–20, 322–6, 329, 334, 336–9, 341, 344, 346, 356–8, 362, 400, 461–2, 464–5, 467, 469–70, 474, 488, 490, 492, 496, 505, 510, 531, 572; **iv** 89, 206, 281, 292, 296, 298–301, 304, 306–9, 311, 316, 318–9, 321–3, 325–8, 337, 340, 346, 348–51, 355, 492, 554, 572, 634; **v** 117–8, 120–1, 123–4, 128, 135, 149, 152–3, 159, 170, 182, 187–8, 219, 237, 250, 252, 262
To Sir J. Simon, **iii** 512, 517
Conversation with Signor Bastianini, **iv** 325–7
Conversation with M. Blondel, **i** 20
Conversation with M. Christitch, **iv** 333
Conversation with M. Chvalkovsky, **iii** 126–7
Conversation with Count Ciano, **i** 27–9, 261–2, 342–3, 353; **ii** 600–3, 642–4; **iii** 319–21, 324–7, 329, 336–9, 344–6, 356–7, 458–9, 467–70, 478, 490–1; **iv** 298, 306–8, 316–7, 319–20, 340; **v** 120–2, 128–9, 149–51, 172
Conversation with M. François-Poncet, **iii** 470–3, 488–9, 510–1; **iv** 296–7, 308, 325, 332–3; **v** 124

Perth, Earl of (*cont.*)
  Conversation with Comte de Kerchove, **iv** 297, 322–3
  Conversation with Signor Mussolini, **v** 262–4
  Conversation with Mr. Wm. Phillips, **ii** 608; **iv** 321–2
  Conversation with M. Wysocky, **i** 274
  Letter to Sir A. Cadogan, **iii** 466; **iv** 305, 332
  Letter to Viscount Halifax, **iii** 458
Perth, Lady, **iii** 536
'Pertinax' (André Géraud) (Foreign Editor of the 'Echo de Paris'), **iii** 393; **vi** 63; **vii** 130
Pétain, Henri Philippe (Marshal of France, French Ambassador to Spain, March 1939–May 1940), **ii** 535; **iv** 462; **v** 144, 223, 508
Peters, Dr. Gustave (a leader of Sudeten German party), **ii** 674; **iii** 216
Petitbon, Lt.-Col. (General Gamelin's Staff Officer), **iii** 557, 570–1; **vii** 136–7
  Conversation with Colonel W. Fraser, **ii** 609–10
  Conversation with Sir E. Phipps, **iv** 53–4
Peto, Geoffrey (a member of Lord Runciman's Mission to Czechoslovakia), **ii** 50, 69, 74, 115, 313, 662–3, 667, 672
Petravich, Dr. J. de (Hungarian Consul at Bratislava), **iv** 158
Petrovski, General, **i** 422
Petschek family (a German-Jewish family in Czechoslovakia), **i** 595; **iv** 561
Pfrogner, Dr., **i** 113
Philip, Percy (Paris correspondent of the 'New York Times'), **v** 384–5
Phillips, Godfrey (Secretary of the Shanghai Municipal Council, 1938–9), **viii** 365, 432, 454, 473–4, 476; **ix** 136–7
Phillips, H. (1938 Sir Herbert) (H.M. Consul-General at Shanghai, Sept. 1937–July 1940), **viii** 112, 123, 281, 361, 375–6, 386, 432, 446, 447*n*, 491, 506, 533; **ix** 72, 74, 101, 152–4, 203, 444, 489
  To British Embassy, Shanghai, **viii** 365, 453, 464, 466, 471, 473, 476, 481, 489, 538; **ix** 4, 37, 60–2, 71, 203, 446, 459, 489
  To Sir A. Clark Kerr, **viii** 41*n*, 483; **ix** 9, 14, 53, 68, 135
  To Viscount Halifax, **ix** 9, 14, 53, 135, 336
Phillips, Rear-Admiral T. (1941 Sir Tom) S. V. (Deputy Chief of Naval Staff, 1939–41), **vii** 3*n*, 367*n*
Phillips, William (U.S. Ambassador at Rome, 1936–41), **iii** 335, 536; **iv** 297; **v** 756, 784; **vi** 284; **vii** 165, 244, 448
  Conversation with the Earl of Perth, **ii** 608; **iv** 321–2
Phipps, Sir Eric C. E. (H.M. Ambassador at Berlin, April 1933–April 1937; then at Paris until Oct. 1939), **i** 50, 91, 144, 146, 149, 151,

153, 158*n*, 241, 295, 299 361*n*, 388*n*, 418, 425*n*, 460, 463*n*, 491*n*, 498*n*, 503*n*, 507*n*, 522*n*, 524*n*, 545, 577*n*, 602, 647; **ii** 71, 142, 159, 198, 271*n*, 272, 282*n*, 289, 314*n*, 523*n*; **iii** 87*n*, 89, 244*n*, 286, 397*n*, 401*n*, 510*n*; **iv** 1*n*, 105, 341, 348, 351*n*, 410, 466, 467*n*, 472, 490, 639; **v** 96–7, 123*n*, 162, 183*n*, 255, 274, 316, 330, 405–6, 427, 444*n*, 456, 460*n*, 569, 609, 689*n*, 691*n*, 743*n*, 763, 776, 778; **vi** 33, 329, 351, 358*n*, 399, 514, 520, 753; **vii** 303*n*, 401, 404, 489, 512, 520, 530; **viii** 94*n*, 195*n*, 259, 371, 394, 497–8; **ix** 187, 226*n*, 313, 342, 447
  To Sir A. Cadogan, **ii** 543; **iv** 381
  To Viscount Halifax, **i** 14, 41, 50, 53, 94, 142*n*, 143, 157, 160, 197, 253, 324, 336, 340, 343, 357, 360, 363, 366, 384, 388*n*, 425, 452, 460, 476–8, 503, 522, 526, 536, 539, 577; **ii** 215–641 *passim*; **iii** 59, 67, 87, 156, 250, 257, 262, 284, 346, 352, 355–6, 376, 389–90, 396, 401, 420–1, 425, 438, 447, 465, 479, 489, 493, 512, 556, 568, 573, 575, 579, 606, 608, 630; **iv** 1–2, 9, 48–51, 53, 60, 71, 74, 108, 137, 145, 154, 156, 167, 169, 221, 223–4, 228, 236, 243, 261, 263, 265, 274, 298, 323*n*, 330, 333, 335, 337, 339, 341, 345, 354, 363, 371, 373, 375–6, 523, 535, 540, 549, 567, 596, 639–40, 642, 645; **v** 55, 70, 105, 108, 130, 148, 151, 160, 178, 183, 216–7, 222, 239, 251, 272, 276, 278–9, 294, 315, 342, 347, 356, 377, 381, 404, 406, 413, 432, 438, 467, 488, 494, 505, 508, 523, 526, 533, 535, 590–1, 700, 730, 737, 746, 775, 790; **vi** 2, 56, 87, 146, 180, 212, 215, 227, 236, 261, 298, 304; **vii** 202, 206, 227, 244–5, 269, 277–9, 294–5, 312–3, 320, 340–1, 371, 378, 398, 406, 420, 449, 463, 471, 476, 489, 493, 495, 499, 500, 502–4, 515, 536, 538; **viii** 181, 394, 534; **ix** 38, 111, 187, 192, 247, 251
  To Sir J. Simon, **iii** 583; **viii** 392
  Conversation with M. Blum, **ii** 278–9, 568–9; **vii** 244–5
  Conversation with M. Bonnet, **i** 157, 197, 336–7, 357, 366–7, 476, 526–7, 577–8; **ii** 215–6, 219–20, 245–6, 255–6, 282, 287, 303*n*, 309, 310–1, 322–3, 336–7, 420, 451, 493, 558–9, 571–2; **iii** 67, 244–5, 257–8, 262–3, 389–90, 425–6, 465, 489, 493–4; **iv** 263, 339, 345, 640, 645; **v** 130, 148, 151–2, 160, 178, 222–3, 347, 381, 432, 737; **vi** 64, 146, 150–1; **vii** 278, 340–1; **ix** 192–3
  Conversation with Mr. Bullitt, **ii** 218–9; **v** 251–2; **vii** 202–3
  Conversation with M. Caillaux, **ii** 513–4
  Conversation with M. Charvériat, **iv** 48–9
  Conversation with M. Chautemps, **vii** 279–80
  Conversation with M. Daladier, **ii** 269–70, 311–2, 329; **iii** 257–8; **iv** 50–1, 354–5;

v 148, 151–2, 239–40, 276–8; **vi** 2, 357–8; **vii** 449, 463–4

Conversation with M. François-Poncet, **i** 452; **iii** 619–21

Conversation with Viscount Halifax, **vii** 518

Conversation with M. Herriot, **ii** 337

Conversation with M. Jeanneney, **ii** 560

Conversation with M. Léger, **ii** 234–5, 291–3; **iii** 421

Conversation with M. Marin, **ii** 579–80; **vii** 313–4

Conversation with M. Paul-Boncour, **i** 50, 94–5

Conversation with Col. Petitbon, **iv** 53–4

Conversation with M. Reynaud, **ii** 337

Conversation with Cardinal Verdier, **vii** 341–2

Conversation with Lt.-Col. de Vitrolles, **iv** 74–5

Conversation with Count Welczeck, **iv** 9–10

Letter to Sir A. Cadogan, **v** 143, 356n

Letter to Mr. Chamberlain, **vi** 357

Letter to Viscount Halifax, **ii** 303n, 444n; **iii** 244, 269, 618–9, 621; **v** 795, 799; **vi** 62–4, 150, 185, 302

Letter to Sir O. Sargent, **iii** 568n; **v** 250, 260; **vi** 220

At Anglo-French conversations, Nov. 1938, **iii** 285; Jan. 10, 1939, **iii** 513–5; Mar. 22, 1939, **iv** 457

Views on attitude of France towards possible outbreak of war, Sept. 1938, **ii** 510, 588

Pichon, Commandant (a member of French Delegation at Anglo-Franco-Soviet Military conversations), **vii** 565

Picot, Guillaume Georges (1st Secretary, French Embassy in China: acted as Chargé d'Affaires), **viii** 300, 310, 322, 341, 389, 474, 491, 507, 512,

Piedmont, Umberto Nicholas, Prince of (Crown Prince of Italy), **v** 130; **vii** 258, 419

Piekenbrock, Colonel, **vi** 326n

Pierlot, Hubert (Belgian Prime Minister, Feb. 1939 and April 1939–Feb. 1945; Minister for Foreign Affairs, April 1939–Jan. 1940), **iv** 106n; **v** 256, 269; **vii** 270–1, 338–40

Piétri, François, **ii** 219

Piggott, Major-General F. S. G. (British Military Attaché at Tokyo, 1921–6 and May 1936–Sept. 1939), **viii** 162–3, 168, 172, 298, 532, 533n; **ix** 1–2, 119, 134, 173, 324, 357, 431

Pilch, M. (Polish Commercial Counsellor at Berlin), **vii** 207

Pilsudski, Marshal Jozef (Polish Chief of State, 1918–22; Premier, 1926–8, 1930; Minister of War, 1926–35), **ii** 318; **iii** 430, 578; **iv** 60, 215, 540; **v** 2, 12, 37, 304, 384, 390, 423, 547, 582; **vi** 246–7, 249, 289, 405, 517, 710, 717

Piñeyro, C. (Argentine Consul-General at Danzig, 1934–9), **vi** 178

Pinsent, G. H. S. (Financial Adviser at H.M. Embassy, Berlin, Nov. 1932–April 1939), **iv** 598

Report by, **iii** 647; **iv** 537, 608–10

Pipinelis, Panoyotis (Greek Minister at Budapest, 1936–9), **v** 614

Pirelli, Alberto (Italian Minister of State), **iv** 319

Pirow, Dr. Oswald (South African Minister of Defence, 1933–9), **iii** 563

Pittman, Senator K. (Chairman of U.S. Senate Standing Committee on Foreign Relations, 1933–40), **iv** 37; **ix** 43–4

Pittman Resolutions, Mar. 20, 1939, **v** 356n; **ix** 43; April 1939, **ix** 43–4, 99, 147, 371, 417, 482

Pius XI, His Holiness Pope (1922–39), **iii** 358, 536; **iv** 475; **vii** 183

Pius XII, His Holiness Pope (1939–58), **v** 411, 420, 432, 435–6, 451–2, 456, 458, 467, 476–7, 480, 482, 489–90, 498–9, 505, 524, 581, 610–1, 653, 685–6, 718–9; **vi** 46, 292, 303–4, 316, 332, 370–2, 633, 704; **vii** 63, 117–8, 183, 213, 301, 308, 401–2, 404

Broadcast appeal for peace, Aug. 24, 1939, **vii** 253–5; *referred to*, **vii** 216n, 223, 227, 253

Peace appeal to Germany and Poland, Aug. 31, 1939; **vii** 448, 455, 495

Planetta, Sgt. Major Otto, **i** 129

Plymouth, 2nd Earl of (Parliamentary Under-Secretary of State for Foreign Affairs, July 1936–May 1939), **iv** 462

Speech in House of Lords, Dec. 6, 1938; **viii** 303, 345

Pohl, Major-General A. (Austrian Military Attaché at Berlin, 1936–8), **ii** 65

Poniatowski, J. (Polish Minister of Agriculture, 1934–9), **vii** 54

Ponomarev, Military Engineer I. (Soviet interpreter at Anglo-Franco-Soviet Military conversations), **vii** 561

Porsche, Herr (District head of Sudeten German party, Liberec), **ii** 32

Posdniakoff, Nikolai (1st Secretary, Soviet Legation at Kovno: acted as Chargé d'Affaires), **iv** 286

Pospisil, Dr. Vilem (Governor of National Bank of Czechoslovakia), **iii** 560, 631, 637–8; **iv** 13–4, 26

Potemkin (Potyomkin), Vladimir P. (Deputy People's Commissar for Foreign Affairs in U.S.S.R., 1937–9), **ii** 266; **iv** 45, 503, 568–9, 629; **v** 224, 341, 413, 460, 544–5, 564, 567, 571, 589, 604, 634, 648, 657, 678, 698, 701, 710–1, 726; **vi** 79, 84, 89, 116–7, 119, 138–41, 230, 251, 522, 572, 612, 615, 641, 781; **vii** 46, 385

Conversation with Colonel Beck, **v** 500–1

Conversation with M. Massigli, **v** 380

Note to Viscount Chilston, **iv** 629

Visit to Angora, **v** 282, 287, 342, 380, 399, 400, 411, 433–5, 537, 542; **vi** 623

Visit to Sofia, **v** 341–2, 380, 530

Visit to Warsaw, **v** 476, 500, 542

Potocki, Count Joseph
  At Anglo-Polish conversations, April 1939, **v** 1, 9, 30
Potworowski, Gustave (Polish Minister at Stockholm, 1936–9), **v** 466
Pound, Admiral of the Fleet Sir Dudley (British Commander-in Chief, Mediterranean, 1936–9; 1st Sea Lord and Chief of Naval Staff, 1939–43), **v** 127, 145; **vii** 35
Pownall, Major-General H. R. (Director of Military Operations and Intelligence, War Office, 1938–40), **vii** 600, 604
Prasca, General Count S. Visconti (Italian Military Attaché at Paris), **ii** 147; **iv** 330; **vii** 489
Prati, Signor (Italian Vice-Consul at Danzig), **vi** 728–9
Preiss, Dr. Jaroslav (Head of Zivnostenska Bank, Czechoslovakia), **ii** 261, 267, 668, 670, 673
Presti, Signor (Prefect of Rome), **iii** 533, 536
Preston, T. H. (H.M. Chargé d'Affaires at Kovno, June 1930–Sept. 1940)
  To Viscount Halifax, **iv** 639, 642; **vii** 510
  To Mr. Orde, **iv** 390, 421, 454, 456, 517, 550; **v** 282
  Conversation with M. Mironas, **iv** 285–7
  Conversation with M. Urbsys, **iv** 454–5
  Conversation with M. J. Urbsys, **iv** 517–8, 639–40
Prételat, General, **vii** 463
Pretzell, Major (German Assistant Military Attaché, Rome), **ii** 356; **iii** 334–5; **iv** 311–2, 328
Price, G. Ward (Special Foreign Correspondent of the 'Daily Mail'), **i** 82, 149, 449; **ii** 653
Prideaux-Brune, H. I. (Acting Chinese Secretary, British Embassy, China, Oct. 1938–Nov. 1939), **ix** 240n, 390, 476n
  To British Embassy, Shanghai, **ix** 240, 260, 341, 478, 481
Priestwood, Victor (The Crown Advocate, Shanghai, 1934–9), **ix** 456, 520, 524
Protitch, Dr. Vasilije (Yugoslav Minister at Prague, 1935–9), **ii** 25, 415–6; **iii** 112
Prunas, R. (Counsellor of Italian Embassy at Paris: acted as Chargé d'Affaires), **iii** 482–3
  Conversation with Mr. R. I. Campbell, **iii** 487–8
Prussia, Prince Friedrich of, **vi** 12n
Pruzinsky, Dr. Mikulas (appointed Slovak Minister of Finance, Mar. 14, 1939), **iv** 219–20, 408
Prytz, Björn Gustaf (Swedish Minister at London, 1938–47), **iii** 445, 554
  Conversation with Mr. R. A. Butler, **vi** 107
Psaroudas, Constantin (Greek Minister at Berne, 1936–41), **v** 145
Puaux, Gabriel (French Minister at Vienna, 1933–8), **i** 13

Puhl, Dr. Emil (a Director of the Reichsbank), **iv** 597, 604
Pu Yi, Emperor of Manchukuo (1934–45), **viii** 334
Pyatakov, G. L. (Vice-Commissar for heavy industry in U.S.S.R., shot for alleged conspiracy in Feb. 1937), **iv** 415

Quo, Dr. P. W. *See* Kuo, Dr. P. W.
Quo Tai-chi, Dr. (Chinese Ambassador at London, 1935–41), **viii** 7n, 19, 21, 30–1, 38, 66–7, 93, 152–3, 198n, 257–8, 391, 401, 410, 455, 472, 483n, 540; **ix** 7–8, 25, 78, 132, 147, 334–5, 341, 368, 374, 386, 467–8, 490
  To Viscount Halifax, **viii** 198, 482; **ix** 375, 455
  Conversation with Mr. R. A. Butler, **viii** 93–4; 104–5
  Conversation with Viscount Halifax, **viii** 4–5, 58–9, 145–7, 173–4, 203–4, 244–5, 308–9, 336–7, 381–2; **ix** 5–7, 12–4, 46–7, 53, 144, 209–11, 236–8, 248–9, 292–3, 332–4, 389–92, 506–7
  Conversation with Mr. Howe, **ix** 47n, 58–9
  Letter to Sir A. Cadogan, **viii** 417

Raczynski, Count Edward (Polish Ambassador at London, 1934–45), **ii** 315, 460n; **iii** 15, 16n, 574, 580; **iv** 110, 423–5, 433, 463–4, 473, 496, 519, 524, 581; **v** 47, 96, 201, 203, 254–5, 299, 300, 324, 329, 416–7, 418n, 419, 604; **vi** 118, 206, 353, 379–80, 463, 502, 508, 570, 635, 644, 683, 717, 759n; **vii** 301, 311, 333–4, 359, 514, 529, 534
  To Viscount Halifax, **iii** 14
  Conversation with Sir A. Cadogan, **vi** 132, 679–80
  Conversation with Mr. Chamberlain, **v** 778–9
  Conversation with Viscount Halifax, **i** 247–8; **ii** 317–8; **iii** 3, 13, 189–90, 430–2; **iv** 11, 32, 434–6, 500–3, 510–1, 575; **v** 51–2, 97–9, 539–40, 747–9; **vi** 198–201, 244–6, 321–5, 365–6, 378, 418, 564–6, 649–50, 669–70; **vii** 168–70, 249–50, 290–2, 310–1, 380, 496, 532
  Conversation with Sir O. Sargent, **iii** 7; **vi** 410–1
  Conversation with Mr. Strang, **iii** 557–8; **iv** 112–3; **v** 383–5; **vi** 24–5
  Letter to Viscount Halifax, **vi** 654; **vii** 425
  At Anglo-Polish conversations, April 1939, **v** 1, 9, 30, 35; *at* discussion on Anglo-Polish Treaty, **vii** 63–6
Raczynski, Count Roger (Polish Ambassador at Bucharest, 1938–9), **iii** 197; **iv** 35, 370, 396, 428, 435, 510; **v** 94, 106, 657
Radford, C. A. Ralegh (Director of the British School at Rome, 1936–9), **iii** 536
Raeder, Admiral Erich (Commander-in-Chief

of the German navy, 1935–43), **ii** 66; **iii** 670; **iv** 482; **vi** 744, 747
Conversation with Admiral Cunningham, **iii** 671

Ramishvili, Captain (Deputy Chief of Staff of the Commander-in-Chief of the Soviet Baltic Fleet), **vii** 45

Ramsay, Sir Patrick W. M. (H.M. Minister at Copenhagen, Oct. 1935–Sept. 1939)
To Viscount Halifax, **v** 462

Randall, A. W. G. (Adviser on League of Nations affairs in the Foreign Office, 1939), **v** 561n; **viii** 391

Raphael, Raphael (Greek Minister at Angora, Jan. 1936–Oct. 1939, then Ambassador till 1946), **v** 447, 550; **vii** 238

Rasin, Dr. (a member of Czechoslovak Parliamentary Committee of Six), **ii** 70, 662–3

Rath, Herr vom (a Secretary at German Embassy, Paris), **iii** 261, 268–9, 272–3, 275–7, 286; **iv** 187

Rauschning, Dr. Hermann (President of Danzig Senate, 1933–4), **vi** 735

Rawlings, Captain H. B. (British Naval Attaché at Tokyo, Jan. 1936–Jan. 1939), **viii** 168, 174n, 285–6; **ix** 287n

Rawson, S. W., **vi** 745–7, 751, 756; **vii** 66, 176, 552

Rayski, General (Head of the Polish Air Force), **i** 482; **v** 39

Rechenberg, Herr (a member of Press Department, German Ministry of Economics), **iv** 597

Rediess, Herr (Head of the S.S. in East Prussia), **vi** 212

Redward, F. G. (British Press Attache at Budapest, July 1935–April 1941), **iii** 238

Reek, General (Chief of Estonian General Staff), **vi** 326

Refik Saydam, Dr. (Prime Minister of Turkey, 1939–42), **v** 516, 532, 537
Speech announcing Anglo-Turkish Declaration of May 1939, **v** 537

Rei, August (Estonian Minister at Moscow, 1938–40), **iv** 568; **v** 214, 698

Reich, Kier (German legal adviser to Sudeten German party), **ii** 273

Reichenau, General Walther von (Commander of the Army district at Leipzig; appointed Chief of German General Staff, Aug. 29, 1939), **i** 295, 581n; **ii** 66, 684–5, 687; **iv** 596; **vi** 238, 330, 710–1, 729; **vii** 415–6, 417n
Conversation with Mr. Kirkpatrick, **vi** 5

Reinhardt, Major-General W. (Head of the German Kyffhäuserbund), **iv** 19n

Rendel, G. W. (H.M. Minister at Sofia, June 1938–Mar. 1941), **v** 159n; **vi** 412
To Viscount Halifax, **iii** 142; **v** 341, 756; **vi** 344–5

Conversation with King Boris, **iii** 142–5
Conversation with M. Kiosseivanoff, **iii** 145–6; **v** 756–7; **vi** 344–5

Renondeau, General G. (French Military Attaché at Berlin until Nov. 1938), **i** 271; **ii** 68, 137, 309, 616; **iii** 162, 571, 619

Renwick, Sir Robert, **vi** 751n

Requette, Colonel, **iv** 450

Reuss, Prince of, **vi** 11–2

Revay, Julian (a member of Mgr. Volosin's Government of Province of Ruthenia, 1938–9), **iii** 377

Reynaud, Paul (French Deputy President of the Council of Ministers and Minister of Justice, April–Nov. 1938; Minister of Finance, Nov. 1938–Mar. 1940), **i** 325; **ii** 220, 535; **iii** 257, 392; **iv** 1n, 596; **v** 799; **vi** 150, 411; **viii** 495n
Conversation with Viscount Halifax, **i** 325–6
Conversation with Sir E. Phipps, **ii** 337

Reynaud, Madame Paul, **iii** 392

Reynolds, Major B. T. (a member of Corps of Observers in Czechoslovakia, Oct. 1938), **iii** 84

Rezac, M., **ii** 671

Rhoda, Colonel (Italian Military Attaché at Prague, 1935–7), **iii** 163

Ribbentrop, Joachim von (German Ambassador at London, 1936–8; Minister for Foreign Affairs, Feb. 1938–May 1945), **i–vii** *passim*; **viii** 89, 179, 182, 536n; **ix** 539
Conversation with Lord Allen of Hurtwood, **ii** 88
Conversation with Mr. Ashton-Gwatkin, **iv** 602–3
Conversation with M. Bonnet, **iii** 389, 396–7
Conversation with King Boris III of Bulgaria, **iii** 143–4
Conversation with M. Burckhardt, **iii** 658–9; **vi** 43, 721–3, 727–8
Conversation with Mr. Chamberlain, **i** 21–3
Conversation with Count Ciano, *see below,* Visit to Milan, Rome, *and* Ciano, Count G. (*Visit to* Germany)
Conversation with Viscount Halifax, **i** 4–6, 13, 21–3
Conversation with Sir N. Henderson, **i** 284–7, 290, 329–30, 334–5, 542–3; **ii** 205–6, 216–7, 283; **iv** 110–1; **v** 387–90; **vii** 429–30, 432–3, 493–4, 511
Conversation with M. Mastny, **i** 332–3
Conversation with M. Noël, **iv** 33
Conversation with Sir H. Wilson, **ii** 353–4
Conversation with Mr. Hugh Wilson, **iii** 278
Letter to M. Bonnet, **vi** 514; *referred to,* **vi** 399, 591; **vii** 18
Letter to Viscount Halifax, **ii** 127; *referred to,* **ii** 138
Letter to Sir N. Henderson, **ii** 430
Statement in Paris, Dec. 6, 1938, **iii** 395–6

Ribbentrop, J. von (*cont.*)
  Visit to Milan, May 1939, **v** 454, 461, 473,
    516, 523–4, 654, 733, 801–3; **ix** 57
  Visit to Moscow, Aug. 1939, **vii** 118, 122–
    212 *passim*, 384–5, 594, 604, 606–7, 620
  Visit to Paris, Dec. 1938, *projected*, **iii** 273,
    284, 286, 296, 299, 363, 365, 375–6;
    account of, **iii** 389–97; *referred to*, **iii** 366n,
    400, 420–1, 427, 465, 476, 511, 513, 515,
    530, 545, 638; **vii** 631
  Visit to Rome, Oct. 1938, **iii** 358–60; **viii**
    174, 179, 239
  Visit to Warsaw, Jan. 1939, *projected*, **iii**
    580, 582, 585–6, 603, 606; *account of*, **iv**
    15–6, 31, 68–9, 80–1; **vi** 530; *referred to*,
    iv 18, 33, 47, 51, 87, 102, 146, 154, 166,
    168, 202; **v** 374, 813
  Views on probable British reaction to a
    German attack, on Czechoslovakia, **ii**
    204, 234, 240, 684–5; on Danzig, **v** 232,
    424, 478, 525; **vi** 555; **vii** 416, 547
Ribbentrop, Frau von, **i** 21; **iii** 390–3
Ricciardi, Dr. A. (Italian Commercial Coun-
  sellor at Berlin), **iii** 130–1, 177, 642, 644–5
Richert, Arvid G. (Swedish Minister at Berlin,
  1937–45), **ii** 569
Richthoven, Herr von (German representative
  on Sub-Committee C of International Com-
  mission set up in Oct. 1938), **iii** 131–2
Ridsdale, William (a member of News Dept. of
  the Foreign Office)
  Memorandum by, **vi** 705
Riley, H. ('Professor' Riley) (Headmaster of
  Strathallan School, Perthshire), **vii** 17
Rintelen, Colonel E. von (German Military
  Attaché at Rome), **ii** 356; **iv** 170, 328
Rist, Professor Charles (a Director of the Banque
  de Paris et des Pays-Bas), **iii** 249
Ritter, Dr. Karl (German Ambassador at Rio
  de Janeiro, 1937–8; Acting Chairman of
  Ambassadors' Commission, Nov. 1938), **iii**
  130–1, 176–8, 234–5, 240–1, 644–5, 647–9,
  654–6; **iv** 564
  Conversation with Mr. Ashton-Gwatkin, **iii**
    151–2
  Conversation with Sir G. Ogilvie-Forbes, **iii**
    235, 242
Rizo-Rangabé, Alexander (Greek Minister at
  Berlin, 1933–41), **v** 777
Roberts, F. K. (a member of Central Dept. of
  the Foreign Office), **i** 138; **vi** 22, 151, 759n;
  vii 176n, 219n, 232n, 242n, 356
  Conversation with M. Cambon, **iii** 77–8
  Conversation with M. Dahlerus, **vii** 537n
  Conversation with Mr. Spencer, **vi** 216–7;
    vii 357, 368, 552
  Letter to Mr. Dew, **vi** 681
  Memorandum by, **iv** 238, 470
  Minute by, **iii** 77; **vi** 216, 411, 563, **vii** 88n,
    166–7, 190, 195, 281, 357, 368, 552, 554

Notes by, on Anglo-Franco-Soviet Military
  conversations, **vii** 558
At Anglo-French conversations, April 1938,
  i 198; Sept. 1938, **ii** 373, 520, 536
Robertshaw, Commander B. I. (Staff Officer to
  Admiral Drax during his mission to Moscow,
  Aug. 1939), **vii** 35, 562
Rochat, Charles (Head of European Depart-
  ment, French Ministry of Foreign Affairs)
  At Anglo-French conversations, April 1938,
  i 198; Sept. 1938, **ii** 373, 520, 536; Nov.
  1938, **iii** 285
Roche, Émile (Editor of the 'République'), **ii**
  305; **vi** 495
Rogers, Cyril (Acting Financial Adviser to the
  Chinese Government), **viii** 256, 308, 389,
  409, 486–7; **ix** 8, 12, 24, 58n, 246n, 248, 251,
  268, 275, 353, 419
  To Viscount Halifax, **ix** 490
  To Sir F. Leith-Ross, **viii** 377
  To the Treasury, **viii** 379; **ix** 105, 114, 117,
    163, 188
Roman, Antoni (Polish Minister of Industry and
  Commerce, 1936–9), **iii** 105; **vi** 359
Romanos, J. (Counsellor of Greek Legation at
  Rome: acted as Chargé d'Affaires), **v** 117n,
  170
Romer, Thaddée de (Polish Ambassador at
  Tokyo, 1937–9), **vi** 249; **viii** 138; **ix** 42
Romier, Lucien (Editor of the 'Figaro'), **iv** 60
Romrée de Vichenet, Comte de. *See* Vichenet,
  Comte C. de Romrée de
Ronald, N. B. (a member of Far Eastern Dept.
  of the Foreign Office)
  To Sir R. Craigie, **ix** 422
  To Mr. Randall, **viii** 391
  Conversation with Mr. Herschel Johnson,
    viii 456–8
  Letter to Sir R. Craigie, **viii** 548
  Letter to Mr. Mallet, **viii** 456
Roosevelt, Franklin Delano (President of the
  United States, Mar. 1933–April 1945), **ii**
  149, 174, 213, 218, 293, 301, 541n, 546, 612,
  617, 620, 625; **iii** 59, 103, 157, 279, 296, 322,
  343; **iv** 4, 6, 9, 27, 29, 40, 51, 83, 85, 103–4,
  125, 139, 159, 423–4, 463, 465, 495, 555, 602;
  v 56, 169, 251–2, 263, 287, 302, 436, 441, 458,
  775, 793; **vi** 678; **vii** 78, 164–5, 202–3, 245,
  295, 379, 630; **viii** 107–8, 116, 146, 379, 381–2,
  384–5, 416, 456n, 458, 509; **ix** 43–4, 109, 193,
  204n, 233, 371, 395, 415, 494, 518
  Conversation with Sir R. Lindsay, **vii** 261–2,
    627–9
  Conversation with Marquess of Lothian, **vii**
    428–9
  Message to Herr Hitler, Sept. 27, 1938, **ii**
    608, 617n
  Message to Congress, Jan. 4, 1939, **iv** 29n;
    viii 381n, 382, 402–3
  Message to Col. Beck, Aug. 1939, **vii** 63

Peace appeal, Sept. 26, 1938, **ii** 546*n*, 547; **iv** 295; **viii** 107

Peace appeal, April 14, 1939, *text of*, **v** 212; *referred to*, **v** 218, 239, 250, 253, 256, 271, 275, 280, 360, 372, 382, 462, 489, 505, 584, 803; **ix** 13, 107

Appeal to King of Italy, Aug. 24, 1939, **vii** 199, 223

Appeals to Herr Hitler and President Moscicki, Aug. 25, 1939, **vii** 223*n*; *referred to*, **vii** 226, 261, 263, 280, 321, 372

and Neutrality Laws, **iv** 366; **v** 356; **vii** 262, 628–9; **ix** 284*n*

Rootes, W. E., **iv** 598

Rosche, Dr. (Representative of Sudeten German party), **i** 501, 543*n*; **ii** 49, 265, 672, 674

Rose, Dr. Adam (Polish Vice-Minister of Commerce, 1936–9), **iii** 182; **vi** 244*n*

Rösel, Dr. R. G. (London correspondent of the 'Essener National Zeitung'), **iv** 272*n*; **v** 430*n*

Rosenberg, Alfred, **iii** 181

Rosengoltz, A. P. (Commissioner for Trade in U.S.S.R., shot for alleged conspiracy in Mar. 1938), **iv** 414

Ross, Lt.-Col. A. (British Military Attaché at Angora, Feb. 1936–Aug. 1939), **v** 593, 675

Rougetel, J. H. le. *See* Le Rougetel, J. H.

Rowe-Dutton, E. (Financial Adviser at H.M. Embassy, Paris, Oct. 1934–April 1939), **ii** 535, 558; **iii** 249, 631; **viii** 494; **ix** 112

Roy, Fernand (French Consul at Amoy, 1935–43), **ix** 267, 288, 339, 361*n*

Rublee, George (Director of Intergovernmental Committee on Refugees), **ii** 149; **iii** 262, 278–9, 296, 519, 677

Conversation with Dr. Schacht, **iii** 675–7

Rucinski, Dr. J. (Financial Counsellor at Polish Embassy, London), **vi** 570

Rucker, A. N. (Principal Private Secretary to Prime Minister), **vii** 520, 529

Letter to M. Wenner-Gren, **vi** 742

Rueff, Jacques (a member of French Ministry of Finance), **iv** 597–8; **vi** 269, 271, 605

Rumbold, Sir Horace G. M., Bart. (H.M. Ambassador at Berlin, 1928–33), **i** 294

Runciman, Leslie (elder son of 1st Viscount Runciman), **vii** 66, 547–8

Conversation with Field Marshal Göring, **vii** 548–50

Runciman, Walter, 1st Viscount (Head of Mission to Czechoslovakia, 1938), **i** 567, 583, 607, 620; **ii** 4–405 *passim*, 444*n*, 646–81 *passim*; **iii** 625; **iv** 563; **vii** 50, 548, 628; arrival in Prague, **ii** 49; departure from Prague, **ii** 677

To Mr. N. Chamberlain, **ii** 329*n*

To Viscount Halifax, **ii** 164, 188, 196, 198, 223, 253–4, 264, 274, 304, 312

Conversation with Dr. Benes, **ii** 50, 171, 221, 254*n*

Conversation with Herr Frank, **ii** 82

Conversation with Herr Henlein, **ii** 122, 333–4, 656–7

Conversation with Dr. Hodza, **ii** 304

Letter to Dr. Benes, **ii** 675

Letter to Viscount Halifax, **ii** 50, 56, 74, 81, 115, 142, 149, 192, 248

Proposals of, **ii** 223–4, 677–9

Runciman, Lady, **ii** 51, 69, 115, 209, 662–3, 665, 667, 670

Rundstedt, General Gerd von, **vii** 416

Rushcliffe, 1st Baron, **v** 675

Rüter, Herr, **iv** 610

Ryan, Sir Andrew (H.M. Minister at Durazzo, Sept. 1936–June 1939), **v** 123, 129, 132*n*, 138, 191–2, 194, 615

To Viscount Halifax, **iv** 357; **v** 116, 119, 127, 168, 195, 229, 382, 436, 750

Letter to Mr. Ingram, **v** 174

Ryan, Lady, **v** 175–7, 191, 194

Ryan, Mr. (son of Sir Andrew Ryan), **v** 190

Rydz, E. Smigly. *See* Smigly-Rydz, Marshal E.

Rykens, Paul (a director of Lever Bros. and Unilevers), **vi** 362–3

Rykov, A. I. (a former Soviet leader; shot in Mar. 1938 for alleged conspiracy), **iv** 414–5

Sadek, Dr. Vlastimil (Czechoslovak Minister of Commerce, 1938–9), **iii** 376; **iv** 62

Sahm, Dr. H. (German Minister at Oslo, 1936–9), **iii** 659

Saint, M. (a member of French delegation at Anglo-French conversations, Nov. 1938), **iii** 285

Saint-Cyr, Carra de Vaux. *See* Vaux Saint-Cyr, Carra de

Saint-Hardouin, J. Tarbé de (Counsellor of French Embassy, Berlin, July and Aug. 1939: acted as Chargé d'Affaires), **vi** 399, 519–20

Saint-Quentin, Comte R. Doynel de (French Ambassador at Washington, 1938–40), **iv** 530; **viii** 23, 495; **ix** 193, 261, 264, 331*n*, 418, 421, 447, 450, 518

Saionji, Prince Kimmochi (the last of the Japanese Elder Statesmen), **viii** 493

Saito, Hirosi (Japanese Ambassador at Washington, 1934–8), **ix** 102*n*

Saito, Mr. (a Japanese police officer), **ix** 10

Sakoh, Shyuichi (Japanese Ambassador at Warsaw, 1937–9), **vii** 217; **ix** 42

Sakurauchi, Yukio (Japanese Minister of Finance, Jan.–Aug. 1939), **ix** 45, 517

Salazar, Dr. Antonio de Oliveira (Portuguese Prime Minister since 1932), **vi** 203–4

Salland, Lt.-Col. R. (French Military Attaché at Vienna), **i** 67

Sander, Professor Fritz (Rector of the German University in Prague), **ii** 657, 665

Sandler, R. J. (Swedish Minister for Foreign Affairs, 1932–9; *rapporteur* of League of Nations Committee of Three on Danzig questions),

Sandler, R. J. (*cont.*)
  iii 445, 587–8, 596–7, 605–6; **iv** 68; **v** 394, 466, 654; **vi** 48, 107, 639; **vii** 422; **viii** 111, 145
    Conversation with Viscount Halifax, **iii** 594–5
    At meetings of Committee of Three, **iii** 591, 598–603, 612–4; **vi** 725
Sandner, Rudolf (a member of Sudeten German party), **i** 70, 249
Sanford, Mr. (Paris correspondent of the 'Daily Herald') **iii** 160
Sansom, Sir George B. (Commercial Counsellor, H.M. Embassy, Tokyo, Mar. 1925–Sept. 1940) **viii** 264–5, 313, 359; **ix** 36, 57
    Memorandum by, **ix** 528
Saracoglu (Sarajoglu), Sükrü (Turkish Minister for Foreign Affairs, 1938–42), **iv** 374–5, 386; **v** 57–8, 105, 115, 162–7, 181, 187, 189–90, 194, 199, 222, 228, 230–1, 241–3, 282, 287, 296, 334, 336–7, 366, 380, 387, 397, 399, 400, 442, 444–5, 447–8, 490, 494, 498–500, 509, 518–9, 522n, 532, 534–6, 548, 550, 552–4, 573–4, 592–3, 646, 681–2, 687, 693, 725, 739–40, 743, 760–1, 766, 786, 789–90; **vi** 18, 29n, 30, 52–4, 68, 70, 74, 78–9, 83, 93, 102–3, 111, 151–2, 169–70, 188–9, 228–9, 241, 260, 272, 304, 321, 341, 354, 403, 434, 463, 574–5, 596, 599, 620, 625, 661, 673, 686; **vii** 140, 155, 184, 200, 214, 238, 248, 264, 269, 272, 276–7, 287, 308, 321, 325, 356, 360, 364–6, 418–9, 423, 449, 454, 471, 487, 503, 528
    Conversation with King Carol of Roumania, **vi** 673–4
    Conversation with Sir H. Knatchbull-Hugessen, **v** 109–10, 162, 188, 194, 220, 259–60, 288, 340–1, 389, 433–5, 463–6, 519, 729–30; **vi** 229, 387, 449, 622–3; **vii** 198–9, 273
    Conversation with Herr von Papen, **v** 354–5, 442, 574; **vii** 214–5
    Letter to Sir H. Knatchbull-Hugessen, **v** 226, 693
Sargent, Sir Orme Garton (Assistant Under-Secretary of State for Foreign Affairs, Aug. 1933–Sept. 1939), **i** 387, 444, 592; **ii** 119, 125, 137, 172; **iii** 1, 447; **iv** 305, 321n, 337n; **v** 142; **vi** 286n, 359, 520n; **vii** 424n; **ix** 272n
    To Sir H. Knatchbull-Hugessen, **v** 682
    Conversation with M. de Barcza, **iii** 19–20
    Conversation with M. Roger Cambon, **ii** 167–8; **v** 778
    Conversation with M. Corbin, **iii** 634–5; **vi** 180–1, 242–3, 511–2
    Conversation with M. Florescu, **iv** 576
    Conversation with M. Jazdzewski, **ii** 82–3
    Conversation with Count Raczynski, **iii** 7; **vi** 410–1
    Conversation with M. Simopoulos, **v** 122–3
    Conversation with M. Tilea, **iv** 284–5; **v** 746–7
    Letter to Mr. Campbell, **ii** 72n

Letter to M. Corbin, **vi** 122–3, 352
Letter to Sir N. Henderson, **ii** 41n, 172n; **vi** 707
Letter to Mr. Holman, **vi** 488
Letter to General Ismay, **vi** 221n
Letter to Sir P. Loraine, **v** 762
Letter to Mr. Norton, **vi** 508
Letter to Sir E. Phipps, **iii** 366n, 437, 444, 636; **iv** 331
Minute by, **iv** 218n, 268, 576; **v** 122, 665n, 746, 778, 783; **vi** 180, 242, 410, 467, 511; **vii** 354n, 478, 529
At Anglo-French conversations, April 1938, **i** 198
Sarraut, Albert (French Minister of the Interior, 1938–40), **ii** 622; **iii** 392; **v** 799
Sarraut, Madame, **iii** 392
Sato, Colonel Kenryo (official spokesman of the Japanese Ministry of War)
    Article by, **viii** 289–90
Sato, Naotake (Adviser to Japanese Ministry of Foreign Affairs, 1938), **viii** 182
Satow, Sir Ernest (British diplomatist and historian), **vi** 115
Sauerwein, A. J. (a French journalist), **i** 142, 476
Saulys, Dr. Jurgis (Lithuanian Minister at Warsaw, 1939), **iv** 430–1
Sawada, Renzo (Japanese Vice-Minister for Foreign Affairs, Oct. 18, 1938–Sept. 1940), **viii** 171, 180, 194, 211–2, 219, 229, 283–4, 287–8, 294, 312, 324n, 339, 347, 349, 368, 390–1, 419, 479, 499, 551, 553; **ix** 3, 49, 53, 64, 71, 74, 78, 80–1, 85, 139, 146, 161, 167–8, 178, 185, 232
    To Sir R. Craigie, **viii** 220, 377
    Conversation with M. Arsène-Henry, **ix** 399–400
    Conversation with Sir R. Craigie, **viii** 279–80, 281–2, 344, 476, 502–4; **ix** 44–5, 91n, 214, 226, 526–7
    Letter to Sir R. Craigie, **viii** 377; *referred to*, **viii** 378, 390, 402, 420
Saxe-Coburg-Gotha, Duke Leopold of (President of the *Deutsche-Englische Gesellschaft*), **iv** 154; **vii** 631
    Speech by, **iv** 591–2, 594
Saydam, Dr. Refik. *See* Refik Saydam, Dr.
Schacht, Dr. Hjalmar (President of the Reichsbank, Mar. 1933–Jan. 1939), **i** 552; **ii** 23–4, 66; **iii** 434, 551, 675n; **iv** 605; **v** 673; **ix** 271–2, 273n, 329
    dismissal of, **iv** 5, 10, 23, 39, 599
    Conversation with Mr. Ashton-Gwatkin, **ix** 273n
    Conversation with Sir N. Henderson, **ii** 23–4
    Conversation with Lord Winterton, Mr. Rublee and Sir F. Leith-Ross, **iii** 675–7
Scheel, Dr. (German Students' Leader), **iv** 62
Scheel, Paul (Danish Consul-General at Shanghai, 1935–47), **ix** 62, 140, 446

Schell, Colonel von (Director of Mechanization, German General Staff), **vi** 296

Schicketanz, Dr. (Sudeten German representative in talks between Czechoslovak Government and Sudeten Germans), **i** 452, 466; **ii** 274, 671, 674

Schiessl, Dr. (a member of the staff of Dr. Benes), **i** 547-8

Schilhawsky, General (Inspector-General of Austrian Army), **i** 18, 137

Schilling, Herr (a German newspaper correspondent), **vii** 19

Schipa, Tito (Italian tenor), **iii** 536

Schlitter, Oskar (Secretary, German Embassy, London), **iii** 451*n*

Schmidt, August (Estonian Minister at London, 1934-40), **vi** 95-6, 325, 327; **vii** 426
   Conversation with Viscount Halifax, **vi** 281-2, 382

Schmidt, Dr. Guido (Austrian Minister for Foreign Affairs, Feb.–Mar. 1938), **i** 1, 2, 7, 128, 132

Schmidt, Dr. Paul Otto (Chief Interpreter to Herr Hitler, 1935-45), **ii** 339, 353, 362, 401, 428, 430-1, 505, 554-6, 631, 635*n*; **iii** 190; **iv** 606; **vii** 231, 351, 387-8, 393, 427, 536

Schmitz, Dr. Richard (Mayor of Vienna, 1934-8), **i** 134

Schneyder, Herr (Berlin representative of the 'Essener National-Zeitung'), **iv** 597

Schniewind, Rear-Admiral
   Speeches at Anglo-German Naval conversations, Dec. 30, 1938; **iii** 664-71

Schnurre, Julius (Head of Economic Policy Division IV (Eastern Europe) in German Foreign Ministry), **iv** 15, 34, 54, 67, 82, 115, 134; **v** 622, 634, 746; **vi** 447; **vii** 99

Schoenfeld, Rudolf E. (1st Secretary, U.S. Embassy, London), **viii** 411

Schönborn, Count (Host of members of Lord Runciman's Mission), **ii** 667

Schubert, M. (Counsellor of Czechoslovak Legation at Berlin: acted as Chargé d'Affaires), **iii** 645
   Conversation with Sir N. Henderson, **ii** 428-30, 578-9
   Conversation with Baron von Weizsäcker, **ii** 371-2

Schulenberg, Count Friedrich Werner von der (German Ambassador at Moscow, 1934-41), **ii** 140, 141*n*, 163-4, 168; **iv** 34, 115*n*, 385, 446; **v** 460, 746; **vi** 22; **vii** 41, 188
   Conversation with M. Litvinov, **ii** 140-1, 179

Schuschnigg, Dr. Kurt von (Austrian Federal Chancellor, July 1934–Mar. 1938), **i** 1-60 *passim*, 70, 81, 127-35, 149, 155, 173, 175, 177, 603, 621, 629; **ii** 40, 121, 238; **v** 424, 546, 803; **vi** 741; **vii** 428

Announcement of resignation, Mar. 11, **i** 137; *referred to*, **i** 16-18, 134
Speech at Innsbruck, Mar. 9, 1938, **i** 2; *referred to*, **i** 3, 98, 132, 179

Schwarzenberg, Prince Adolf (Host of Lord Runciman in Czechoslovakia), **ii** 663

Schwerin, Lt.-Col. Count von (Sub-Chief of the Attaché-Gruppe, German War Ministry), **v** 806; **vi** 295-8, 305-7, 413; **vii** 123

Schwerin von Krosigk, Count Ludwig (German Minister of Finance, 1932-45), **ii** 690-1

Scott, A. L. (a member of Far Eastern Dept. of the Foreign Office; Acting Chinese Secretary at Peking, 1933-7), **viii** 332*n*, 392

Sebekowski, Dr. Wilhelm (a member of Sudeten German party), **i** 249; **ii** 49, 166, 254, 265, 665, 674

Seeds, Sir William (H.M. Ambassador at Moscow, Jan. 1939–Jan. 1940), **iii** 280*n*; **iv** 448*n*, 453, 485; **v** 463, 566, 622*n*, 683-4, 698, 766-8, 786; **vi** 33-4, 84, 99, 106, 122, 138, 152, 243, 349, 383-4, 606, 611, 703, 780; **vii** 3*n*, 34, 40, 42, 164, 225, 247, 563, 594, 606-7; **ix** 58*n*
   Instructions for, June 1939, **vi** 33-41
   To Sir A. Cadogan, **v** 634
   To Viscount Halifax, **iv** 14, 24, 33, 45, 52, 54, 115, 123, 128, 188, 372, 385, 411, 429-30, 445, 448, 467, 485, 503, 509, 511-2, 523, 568, 574, 584; **v** 45, 104, 198, 215, 221, 223, 228, 282, 319, 400, 410, 412, 460, 469, 471, 483, 491, 520, 542, 558, 567, 589, 604, 647, 678, 701, 707, 710, 722, 725, 736, 743, 753, 784; **vi** 22, 54, 65, 77, 79, 84-5, 89, 91, 98, 109-10, 112, 115, 129, 134, 140, 142-3, 151, 160, 179, 208-9, 217, 229-30, 249, 251, 256, 272, 308, 310, 313-4, 332, 345, 375, 377, 379, 447, 450, 456, 460, 475, 491, 493, 509-10, 521, 531, 543, 559, 570, 575-6, 612, 615, 641, 674, 682-3; **vii** 1, 3, 21-2, 41, 45, 74, 98-9, 101, 114, 118-20, 141-2, 154, 156, 184, 187-8, 197, 225, 237-8, 305, 346, 383, 430
   Conversation with M. Baltrusaitis, **vi** 256-7
   Conversation with M. Kalinin, **iv** 45-6
   Conversation with M. Litvinov, **iv** 24-5, 123-4, 128, 372, 385, 429, 509, 574-5; **v** 215, 221-2, 400
   Conversation with M. Molotov, **v** 469-71, 483-7, 558-9, 567-8, 701-2, 710-2, 722, 726-7; **vi** 79, 89-91, 116-20, 140-3, 230-2, 249-51, 308-12, 375-9, 456-60, 509-10, 521-5, 570-4; **vii** 142-3, 237
   Letter to Sir L. Oliphant, **iv** 132; **v** 571

Seeds, Lady, **iv** 568-9

Seguin, J. de (French Counsellor at Warsaw: acted as Chargé d'Affaires), **iii** 242

Selter, Karl (Estonian Minister for Foreign

Selter, K. (*cont.*)
Affairs, 1938–9), **v** 698; **vi** 35, 55, 116, 118, 281
 Conversation with Mr. Gallienne, **v** 697–8; **vi** 325–7
 Visit to Berlin, **v** 775
Selzam, Dr. Edwart von (Counsellor of Legation in the German Embassy at London), **iii** 515–6; **vi** 200n
 Letter to Mr. Perowne, **iv** 635
Sereggi, General Zef (Albanian Minister at Rome, Mar.–April 1939), **iv** 358; **v** 116, 119, 128, 169, 176
Serrano Suñer, Ramon (Spanish Minister of the Interior, Dec. 1938–Oct. 1940), **vi** 284, 453
Seton-Watson, Professor R. W. (Masaryk Professor of Central European History in the University of London, 1922–45), **i** 520
Seyss-Inquart, Dr. Artur (Austrian Minister of Interior, Feb.–Mar. 1938; Federal Chancellor, Mar. 11–15, 1938), **i** 1, 7–40 *passim*, 45, 58–9, 99, 129–35; **iv** 247, 438; **vii** 96, 623
 appointed Statthalter, **i** 135
Shaposhnikov, Army Commander B. M. (Chief of General Staff of the Soviet Army), **i** 422; **vii** 46
 At meetings of Anglo-Franco-Soviet Military Delegations, **vii** 561, 563, 565, 573, 575, 591, 593, 611
Sharonov, Nikolaj (Soviet Ambassador at Warsaw, 1939), **vi** 441, 447; **vii** 217, 499
Shepherd, E. H. G. (H.M. Consul-General at Danzig, Nov. 1937–July 1939), **iii** 280n, 281n, 657; **iv** 507; **v** 100, 538, 732; **vi** 226n
 To Sir A. Cadogan, **v** 625
 To Viscount Halifax, **iii** 441, 552, 561, 572; **iv** 46, 80, 151, 156, 159, 186, 265, 280; **v** 24, 211, 510, 560, 576, 608, 764, 788; **vi** 1, 7, 9, 31, 65–6, 87, 108, 136, 148, 164, 177, 187, 223–4
 To Sir N. Henderson, **v** 752; **vi** 32
 To Mr. Livingston, **iv** 261
 To Sir J. Simon, **iii** 581
 Conversation with Dr. Böttcher, **vi** 1, 9–10
 Conversation with M. Burckhardt, **iii** 441–2; **vi** 187
 Conversation with Herr Greiser, **iii** 552–3
 Conversation with Mr. Troutbeck, **vi** 356–7
Shepherd, F. M. (H.M. Consul at Dresden, June 1938–July 1939; in charge of Consulate-General, Danzig, July 10–Sept. 1, 1939), **ii** 360; **iv** 233, 441; **vi** 226n, 355n, 421, 494; **vii** 296
 To Viscount Halifax, **vi** 364, 386, 388, 391, 394, 401, 432, 451, 454, 461, 477, 480, 487, 507, 513, 532, 547, 560–1, 568, 577, 586, 593–4, 610–1, 613–4, 620, 622–4, 636, 640, 652, 659, 661–2, 666, 685; **vii** 10, 24, 55, 89, 96, 100, 104, 123, 152–4, 156, 224, 269, 298, 363, 402, 450, 483, 541

To Mr. Norton, **vi** 462, 480
 Conversation with M. Burckhardt, **vi** 451–2, 454–5
 Letter to Mr. Kirkpatrick, **vi** 419, 490
 departure from Danzig, **vii** 541–2, 545–6
Shibayama, Colonel K. (Head of Japanese Special Mission, Tientsin), **viii** 445–6, 458–9, 500, 526
Shigemitsu, Mamoru (Japanese Ambassador at London, Oct. 1938–Dec. 1941), **iv** 161; **v** 482; **viii** 78n, 247, 260, 457; **ix** 28n, 62–4, 151–2, 165, 171, 210, 215, 218, 241–2, 481–2, 511, 519
 Conversation with Mr. Butler, **ix** 513–4
 Conversation with Mr. Chamberlain, **viii** 262–3
 Conversation with Viscount Halifax, **viii** 422–4; **ix** 27–9, 57–8, 86–8, 202–3, 205–6, 507–8
Shigeyasu, Lt.-Col. (Officer in charge of Foreign Affairs Department of the Japanese Headquarters in Peking), **viii** 351, 380–1, 557n, 558
Shima, S. (Japanese Consul at Tientsin), **viii** 230, 233, 314, 322–3, 427, 527–8
Shiono, Suyehiko (Japanese Minister of Justice, 1937–9), **viii** 369n
Shiratori, Toshio (Japanese Ambassador at Rome, 1938–9), **iii** 358; **iv** 107, 161; **viii** 237, 253, 437n, 482; **ix** 42, 64
Shone, T. A. (1st Secretary, H.M. Legation, Belgrade, Nov. 1936–Nov. 1939; acted as Chargé d'Affaires), **vi** 166–7
 To Viscount Halifax, **ii** 25, 135, 151, 260, 268
 Conversation with M. Antitch, **ii** 25
 Conversation with M. Brugère, **ii** 135–6
Shumenkovitch, Ilija (Yugoslav Minister at Angora, 1939), **v** 346, 447, 667
Sidor, Karel (Minister without Portfolio representing Slovakia in Czechoslovak Government, Dec. 1938–Mar. 1939; President of Council of Province of Slovakia, Mar. 12–14; Minister of the Interior of Republic of Slovakia, Mar.–April 1939), **i** 465, 551; **iii** 189, 199, 217, 222, 377–8; **iv** 95, 183, 219–21, 225–6, 229, 234, 238–9, 241, 246, 406–8, 438–40; **v** 85
Siemens, Captain Leopold (German Naval Attaché at London), **ii** 286, 290n, 295–6
 At Anglo-German Naval conversations, Dec. 1938, **iii** 664
Silex, Dr. Karl (Editor of the 'Deutsche Allgemeine Zeitung'), **iv** 582n
Simmons, Major-General F. K. (Commander, Shanghai Area, British Troops in China, 1939–40), **viii** 106, 234, 376, 428, 431, 538–9; **ix** 204, 336–7
Simon, Sir John (Chancellor of the Exchequer, May 1937–May 1940: in charge of Foreign Office, Jan. 1939), **i** 345n; **ii** 189; **iii** 512n,

629, 635–6; **iv** 109; **v** 539, 748–9; **vi** 199, 366, 380, 401, 410, 508, 567, 570, 753; **viii** 7*n*, 48; **ix** 59, 249, 293, 391, 513
  To Sir R. Craigie, **viii** 387, 397
  To Sir G. Ogilvie-Forbes, **iii** 515
  To Sir E. Phipps, **iii** 634
  To U.K. Delegation (Geneva), **viii** 391
  Speech at Lanark, Aug. 27, 1938, **ii** 172–5; *referred to*, **ii** 189, 196, 205, 210, 214, 247, 286, 295, 681
  Statements in House of Commons, Oct. 5, 1938, **iii** 128; Mar. 8, 1939, **viii** 505; Mar. 15, **iv** 278; April 13, **v** 470, 485; July 4, **ix** 248; July 25, **vi** 479
  At Anglo-French conversations, Sept. 1938, **ii** 373, 520, 526–9, 536
Simopoulos, Charalambos (Greek Minister at London, 1935–42), **iv** 521; **v** 138, 148, 158–9, 236, 412, 614–6, 750
  Conversation with Viscount Halifax, **iv** 497–9; **v** 157–8, 185
  Conversation with Mr. Ingram, **v** 163, 550–1
  Conversation with Sir O. Sargent, **v** 122–3
Simovitch, General D. T. (Yugoslav Chief of General Staff), **iv** 102
  Conversation with Lt.-Col. H. C. T. Stronge, **iv** 103–4
Sinclair, Sir Archibald (M.P. for Caithness & Sutherland), **i** 630; **vi** 577–8
  Conversation with Herr Henlein, **i** 633–5
Singloh Hsu (a Chinese banker), **viii** 42
Sinka, Major A. (Estonian Military Attaché at Moscow), **i** 165
Sirovy, General. *See* Syrovy, General
Sivak, Josef (President of the Council, Province of Slovakia, Mar. 10–12, 1939; Minister of Schools, Mar. 12–14; Minister of Public Instruction in 1st Government of Republic of Slovakia), **iv** 219, 221, 225, 229, 406, 408
Skeferis, Pericles (Greek Minister at Durazzo, 1935–9), **v** 116, 120, 122–3, 136, 138, 168, 174, 229–30, 348, 382–3, 436–7, 750–1
Skirpa, Kazys (Lithuanian Minister at Berlin, 1938–40), **iii** 548; **iv** 483–4, 640, 642
Skubl, Dr. (Austrian State Secretary for Security, 1937–8), **i** 130, 135
Slavik, Dr. Juraj (Czechoslovak Minister at Warsaw, 1936–9), **i** 315–6, 429–30, 464–5; **iii** 27, 35, 40, 46–7, 80, 82, 198, 212; **iv** 32
  Conversation with Sir H. Kennard, **i** 464–5; **iii** 188–9, 199
Slawoj-Skladkowski, General F. (Polish Prime Minister and Minister of the Interior, 1936–9), **iv** 87–8; **v** 605; **vi** 322; **vii** 319
Slessor, Group Captain J. C. (Director of Plans, Air Ministry, 1938–41), **iv** 237
Smetona, Antanas (President of Lithuania, 1926–40), **iv** 454, 483, 518
Smigly-Rydz, Marshal Edward (Inspector-General of the Polish Armed Forces, 1935–9

and First Citizen of the Republic after the President), **i** 431, 444*n*, 445, 480; **ii** 538–9; **iii** 22, 27–8, 33, 103–5, 181; **iv** 154, 543, 549–50, 572, 581; **v** 39, 203, 305, 570; **vi** 234, 247, 274, 317, 322–3, 359, 379, 381, 386, 400, 406, 415–9, 445–6, 476, 584, 724, 733; **vii** 85–6, 117, 211, 216, 236, 309, 338, 364, 371, 477, 498, 559–60
  Speech by, Aug. 6, 1939, *referred to*, **vi** 628, 635, 638, 643
  Statement to press, July 1939, **vi** 404, 448
Smith, A. C. (British Council assistant to H.M. Legation, Tallinn), **v** 698
Smith, Captain R. H. Tottenham (H.M. Consul at Turin, Nov. 1937–June 1940), **iii** 346
Smith, Lt.-Col. T. (U.S. Military Attaché at Berlin), **i** 414; **ii** 309
Smogorzewski, M. (Editor of the 'Gazeta Polska'), **vi** 365
Smorodinov, Corps Commander V. (Deputy Chief of General Staff of the Soviet Army), **vii** 45–6
  At meetings of Anglo-Franco-Soviet Military Delegations, **vii** 561, 563
Smutny, Dr. P. (Czechoslovak *Chef du Protocol*), **ii** 667, 673
Snow, Thomas Maitland (H.M. Minister at Helsingfors, Mar. 1937–Feb. 1940), **vii** 184
  To Viscount Halifax, **v** 223, 253, 495; **vi** 120
  Conversation with M. Erkko, **v** 495–6
  Conversation with Field-Marshal Baron Mannerheim, **vi** 120–2
Sokol, Dr. Martin (Chairman of the Slovak Diet, 1938–9; Minister of Schools in M. Sidor's Government of Province of Slovakia), **iv** 219, 221, 225, 229, 246
Sokolnicki, Michel (Polish Ambassador at Angora, 1936–9), **vii** 273
Solymossy, Lt.-Col. V. de (Hungarian Military Attaché at Prague), **iii** 210–1
Soong, T. V. (Secretary-General of Aeronautical Affairs Commission, National Government of China), **viii** 102, 104, 160, 161*n*, 284, 308, 377, 430; **ix** 14, 276
Sorensen, R. W. (M.P. for West Leyton), **iv** 240
Sorgo, Dr. N. M. (Yugoslav Minister at The Vatican, 1937–41), **vi** 675
Soubotitch (Subotitch), Ivan (Yugoslav delegate to League of Nations, 1935–9; Minister at London, June 1939–41), **v** 663; **vi** 166
Soudan, Eugène (Belgian Minister for Foreign Affairs, Feb.–Mar. 1939)
  Conversation with Sir R. Clive, **iv** 508–9
Souritz, Y. Z. *See* Suritz, Y. Z.
Soviche, Captain (a member of French Military Delegation to U.S.S.R., Aug. 1939), **vii** 562
Spaak, Paul Henri (Belgian Minister for Foreign Affairs, June 1936–Jan. 1939; Prime

Spaak, Paul Henri (*cont.*)
Minister, May 1938–Feb. 1939), **iii** 287*n*; **iv** 106*n*

Spann, Professor Othmar (Professor at Vienna: political theorist), **i** 250

Speaight, R. L. (a member of Central Dept. of the Foreign Office)
Memorandum by, **v** 415
Note by, **ii** 419

Spear, Lt.-Col. C. R. (British Military Attaché in China, Oct. 1938–Dec. 1939), **ix** 152, 197, 265, 287, 401, 415, 508

Spechel, A. (Italian Consul-General at Danzig, 1938–9), **v** 25–6; **vi** 187

Spencer, C. F. (a Director of John Brown Ltd.; intermediary between M. Dahlerus and British Foreign Office officials), **vi** 743*n*, 745–7, 751*n*, 759; **vii** 66, 176*n*, 194–5, 232*n*, 281–2, 286*n*, 320*n*, 537*n*, 551, 554–5
Conversation with M. Dahlerus, **vii** 219, 356–7, 368, 474–5, 485
Conversation with Mr. Roberts, **vi** 216–7; **vii** 357, 368, 552

Sperrle, General Hugo (a German General of Aviation), **iv** 258

Sportiello, Admiral (an Italian Naval Commander), **v** 191

Sramek, Mgr. Jan (Chairman of Czechoslovak People's Catholic party), **i** 311, 510, 517, 530, 570; **ii** 34, 415; **iii** 96

Ssu Ching-wu (Leader of anti-Japanese guerrilla force in Tientsin area), **viii** 156*n*, 368*n*, 378, 390, 402, 416–7, 420–1, 459–60, 468, 471, 479, 499, 551–60; **ix** 2, 19, 20, 325, 357, 364, 416, 424, 427, 431*n*, 432, 470, 493, 515, 524, 533

Stachiewicz, General (Chief of Polish General Staff), **iii** 33; **iv** 142; **vi** 234; **vii** 54, 61, 70, 107–8, 208
Conversation with Colonel Godfrey, **i** 480–4
Conversation with Lt.-Col. Sword, **vii** 84–5, 91–2, 195–6, 208–11

Stalin, Joseph V. (General Secretary of Central Committee of Communist Party of U.S.S.R. and member of the Politburo), **i** 165, 305, 423; **iii** 193; **iv** 64, 191–2, 422, 459, 511, 535, 557, 569; **v** 21, 104, 206, 217, 413, 429, 451, 484, 542–5; 620, 727, 744, 802, 808; **vi** 331, 461, 500, 702, 704–5; **vii** 41, 138, 155, 188, 244, 245*n*, 256, 258–9, 291, 354*n*, 431, 550, 593, 600; **ix** 506
Speech on Mar. 10, 1939, **iv** 411–9; **v** 202*n*, 209, 312, 332, 357, 359, 450, 462; **vi** 280, 780; **vii** 197, 431, 618–9, 621

Stamp, 1st Baron, **ii** 672

Stanhope, 7th Earl (President of the Board of Education, May 1937–Oct. 1938; 1st Lord of the Admiralty, Oct. 27, 1938–Sept. 1939)
Speech in House of Lords, Oct. 5, 1938, **iii** 328

Stanley, Oliver F. G. (President of the Board of

Trade, May 1937–Jan. 1940), **iv** 36, 107, 111, 138*n*; **v** 209; **vi** 244*n*
Speech in House of Commons, Nov. 1, 1938, **viii** 178–9
Visit to Germany, *proposed*, **iv** 131, 139, 250, 255; *postponed*, **iv** 260, 261*n*, 271, 273, 364, 595; **v** 586, 717; **vi** 497

Stano, Julius (Secretary-General of Slovak People's party), **iv** 229

Stapelmann, Herr, **vi** 66

Starace, A. (Secretary-General of the Fascist party in Italy, 1931–9), **iii** 533, 536; **v** 781; **vii** 93

Starzynski, Stefan (President of the City of Warsaw, 1934–9), **i** 429

Steed, Henry Wickham (author and journalist), **i** 520; 529

Steel, C. E. (Secretary, H.M. Embassy at Berlin, July 1936–June 1939), **ii** 71
To Mr. Mallet, **ii** 77

Stefenelli, F. (Italian Consul at Tientsin), **viii** 71–2, 232, 248, 323, 328–9, 452, 459, 511, 555

Stein, Boris E. (Soviet Ambassador at Rome, 1935–9), **iii** 359; **v** 376

Steinhardt, L. A. (U.S. Ambassador at Moscow, 1939–41), **vii** 42*n*, 156

Stepanic, Colonel (Czechoslovak representative on Military Sub-Committee of International Commission set up in Oct. 1938), **iii** 162

Stepanov, S. (Deputy People's Commissar for Foreign Trade in U.S.S.R.), **iv** 568–9

Stephens, David (a member of Lord Runciman's Mission to Czechoslovakia), **ii** 668

Stevenson, Ralph C. Skrine (League of Nations Adviser in the Foreign Office, 1937–8), **ii** 293, 683; **viii** 67–8, 83
Conversation with M. Burckhardt, **ii** 689–91
Letter to Mr. Strang, **ii** 689

Stilwell, Colonel J. W. (U.S. Military Attaché in China), **ix** 341

Stirum, Count John de Limburg. *See* Limburg-Stirum, Count John de

Stöhrer, Dr. Eberhard von (German Ambassador at Burgos, 1937–43), **ii** 651

Stoica, Basile (Roumanian Ambassador at Angora, 1939–41), **v** 57, 387, 447, 490–1, 681, 686–7, 720, 724–5, 762; **vi** 68

Stoller, Dr. W. (German Consul-General at Tientsin, 1936–41), **viii** 61, 63, 71–2, 233, 248, 328

Stopford, R. J. (British liaison officer in Prague), **ii** 50, 69, 74, 115, 155, 404, 663, 665, 668, 670–1; **iii** 117, 120, 632; **iv** 277*n*, 278
To Mr. Ashton-Gwatkin, **ii** 150, 448
Conversation with Herr Kundt, **ii** 674–5
Note by, **ii** 667

Stoyadinovitch, Dr. Milan (Yugoslav President of the Council and Minister for Foreign

Affairs, 1935–9), ii 25, 135–7, 144, 151, 157–8, 204, 241, 260; iii 19, 46; iv 388n, 618, 620; v 314, 346
resignation of, v 34n

Strang, William (Counsellor in the Foreign Office, 1933–9: Head of Central Department, 1937–9), i 365, 375, 427, 614n; ii 13–5, 112, 143, 409; iv 136, 149, 156, 180n; v 286n, 418n, 716, 777, 786, 790; vi 2, 4, 6–7, 20n, 22, 25, 29, 50, 79, 84, 89, 92, 103, 112–3, 116, 118–9, 431, 448, 573, 781; vii 16, 99, 190, 358n, 373, 514n, 552, 594
arrival in Moscow, vi 115; *return to* London, vi 592; vii 99n
To Mr. Ashton-Gwatkin, iii 119, 149
To Sir G. Ogilvie-Forbes, iii 264
Conversation with M. Cambon, iii 553–4; v 565–6; vii 106–8
Conversation with Mr. Kirkpatrick, iii 93n
Conversation with M. Maisky, v 506–7
Conversation with M. Masaryk, ii 536
Conversation with Count Michalowski, iii 15
Conversation with M. Raczynski, iii 557–8; iv 112–3; v 383–5; vi 24–5
Conversation with Mr. Troutbeck, ii 536, 544
Conversations with members of H.M. Legation at Prague, i 403–12; of H.M. Embassy at Berlin, i 412–6
Letter to Sir R. Clive, iv 576
Letter to Sir N. Henderson, July 21, 1938, i 610; *referred to,* ii 14–5; July 30, i 614n
Letter to Sir H. Kennard, iii 267, 557; iv 112
Letter to Mr. Kirkpatrick, vi 539
Letter to Mr. Mack, iv 82
Letter to Sir G. Ogilvie-Forbes, iv 115n
Letter to Sir O. Sargent, vi 138, 422
Minute by, ii 409, 411, 421, 536; iii 589; iv 41, 260; v 273, 286n, 383, 506, 565; vi 20, 24, 105–6, 760n; vii 2n, 106, 108n, 119n, 121, 132, 286–7, 401, 404, 529
At Anglo-French conversations, April 1938, i 198; Sept. 1938, ii 373, 520, 536; Nov. 1938, iii 285; Mar. 21, 1939, iv 422; Mar. 22, 1939, iv 457
At Anglo-Polish conversations, April 1939, v 1, 9, 30
At Anglo-Roumanian conversations, April 1939, v 296, 309, 321
At discussions for Anglo-Polish treaty, Aug. 1939, vii 64

Strong, Major K. W. D. (British Assistant Military Attaché at Berlin, Jan. 1938–Aug. 1939), i 16–17, 344, 352, 358, 363, 451; ii 169; iv 244, 397–8; v 806
To War Office, iv 264
Conversation with Major von Mellenthin, ii 126–7

Stronge, Lt.-Col. H. C. T. (British Military Attaché at Prague, Nov. 1936–Oct. 1938; at Belgrade, Nov. 1936–Mar. 1939), i 120,

126, 251, 267, 302n, 352, 368, 375, 389, 397–8, 406, 411–2, 428n, 441, 446, 449, 462–3, 471, 474, 492, 495n; ii 34–5, 81, 90, 99, 185, 258, 260, 268, 280–1, 308, 336, 357, 364, 368, 411–2, 457, 567, 581, 591, 612; iii 124, 368; iv 102
To Mr. Newton, i 104, 121, 432; ii 185, 258
Conversation with Colonel Count Valfre di Bonzo, ii 146–7
Conversation with Colonel Hajek, ii 90–1
Conversation with General Krejci, i 462–3; ii 370
Conversation with General Simovitch, iv 103–4
Conversation with Colonel Toussaint, ii 143–6; iii 254–5

Stuart, James (M.P. for Moray and Nairn), vi 295

Stuckart, Dr. Wilhelm (State Secretary of German Ministry of the Interior), iv 280

Stülpnagel, Lt.-Gen. von (a member of Military Sub-Committee of International Commission set up in Oct. 1938), iii 162; iv 279

Suat Davaz (Turkish Ambassador at Paris, 1932–40), iv 143, 465

Subotitch, Ivan. *See* Soubotitch, Ivan

Sugiyama, General (Commander-in-Chief, Japanese forces in North China), viii 338, 351, 532; ix 160, 168, 361, 454

Sükrü Saracoglu. *See* Saracoglu, Sükrü

Sun Fo (President of Chinese Legislative Yuan), viii 42, 219, 250

Suñer, Ramon Serrano. *See* Serrano Suñer, Ramon

Suritz, Yakov Zakharovich (Soviet Ambassador at Paris, 1937–40), ii 219–20; iv 422–3, 471; v 198, 215–7, 228, 406, 542, 572, 683–4, 693; vi 22, 398

Surzynski, M. (Vice-Marshal of the Polish Diet), iv 88; v 514

Sutton-Pratt, Major R. (Observer in Czechoslovakia, June–Oct. 1938), i 411n; ii 90, 94n, 99n, 176, 265n, 304–5, 319, 366–7, 671; iii 73n, 74, 82
Report by, ii 319n; iii 83

Suvorov, Colonel (Military Commandant of City of Moscow), vii 45

Swida, M., v 764

Swinton, 1st Viscount (Secretary of State for Air, June 1935–May 1938), iii 616

Swire, G. Warren (Chairman of the China Association), viii 191

Swirski, Admiral (Commander-in-Chief of the Polish Navy), vii 309

Sword, Lt.-Col. E. R. (British Military Attaché at Warsaw, June 1938–Sept. 1939), iv 362, 476, 497n, 507, 514; v 38, 58, 245, 579–80, 757; vi 80, 486–7, 617, 684–5; vii 61, 107, 126, 208, 321, 330, 404, 453, 559–60
To Sir H. Kennard, iv 477; v 39, 246–8, 583; vii 133, 208

Sword, Lt.-Col. (*cont.*)
  To War Office, **iii** 23; **v** 203
  Conversation with General Musse, **v** 757–8
  Conversation with Colonel Pelevaynski, **iii** 17
  Conversation with General Stachiewicz, **vii**
    84–5, 91–2, 195–6, 208–11
Syrovy, General Jan (Czechoslovak Prime
  Minister, Sept.–Oct. and Oct.–Nov. 1938;
  President of the Republic *ad interim*, Oct. 5–
  Nov. 30, 1938; Minister of Defence, Dec.
  1938–Mar. 1939), **ii** 147, 493*n*, 518, 561, 640;
  iii 21–2, 96*n*, 216, 377; **iv** 98, 126, 563; **v**
  594–5; **vi** 705
    Speech by, Oct. 5, 1938, **iii** 124*n*; Oct. 28,
    iii 214–5
Sziller, M., **v** 764
Sztojay, Döme (Hungarian Minister at Berlin,
  1935–44), **i** 34*n*; **vi** 215
Szymanski, Lt.-Col. A. (Polish Military Attaché
  at Berlin), **i** 93; **ii** 309; **iv** 23; **v** 67, 101, 210–1,
  433, 546
    Conversation with Colonel Mason-Mac-
    farlane, **iv** 184–6, 504

Tabouis, Madame Geneviève (Diplomatic cor-
  respondent of the 'Œuvre'), **iv** 293; **vi** 342
Tada, Lt.-Gen. Hayao (Vice-Chief of Japanese
  General Staff), **viii** 77
Talati, Mr., **ix** 538
Taliani de Marchio, Marchese F. M. (Italian
  Ambassador in China, 1938–43), **viii** 232, 341
Tanaka, Baron G. (Japanese Prime Minister &
  Foreign Secretary, 1927–9), **ix** 6*n*
Tanaka, H. (Japanese Vice-Consul at Tientsin),
  ix 2, 216, 324, 357–8, 364–5, 387, 409, 436,
  470, 481
Tani, Masayuki (Minister in Charge of Japa-
  nese Embassy at Shanghai, 1938), **viii** 12,
  18, 24, 55–6, 156, 159, 552
Tarbé de Saint-Hardouin. *See* Saint-Hardouin,
  J. Tarbé de
Tardini, Mgr. Domenico (Under-Secretary of
  State, The Vatican), **v** 411, 436, 458, 498;
  vii 63, 253, 350
    Conversation with Mr. Osborne, **vii** 183, 196
Tashiro, S. (Japanese Consul-General at Tientsin), **viii** 35, 61, 119–20, 125, 226, 230–1, 233,
  252–3, 328–9, 335, 350, 378, 383, 388–9, 391,
  421, 445, 459, 468, 471, 489–92, 507*n*, 509,
  511, 527, 551*n*, 552, 554–6; **ix** 2, 12., 132,
  145, 164, 168–9, 179, 182–3, 205*n*, 208, 221*n*,
  278, 322, 505
    Conversation with Mr. Jamieson and M.
    Lépissier, **viii** 338–9
Tatarescu, Georges (Roumanian Ambassador
  at Paris, 1938–9), **iv** 375, 410, 422, 459; **v**
  312, 329
Tatsumi, Colonel E. (Chief of European-Ameri-
  can Department of Japanese General Staff),
  viii 457*n*, 468

Taub, Siegfried (a leader of the German Social
  Democrat party in Czechoslovakia), **ii** 451
Taurines, M. (Vice-President of the French
  Parliamentary Group 'Alliance Démo-
  cratique'), **ii** 623
Tauschitz, Stefan (Austrian Minister at Berlin,
  1933–8), **i** 12
Taylor, Wayne C. (Fiscal Assistant Secretary of
  the U.S. Treasury), **viii** 311, 335–6, 462
Teleki, Count Paul (Hungarian Prime Minister,
  Feb. 1939–April 1941), **iv** 129, 265, 277, 289;
  v 60, 210*n*; **vi** 437, 585; **vii** 83, 92–3, 152, 377
Tellier, Pol le. *See* Le Tellier, Pol
Temperley, Major-General A. C. (Military
  Correspondent of the 'Daily Telegraph',
  1935–9), **i** 622
Temperley, Professor H. W. V. (Professor of
  Modern History in the University of Cam-
  bridge), **i** 520
Teplansky, Pavel (Slovak Minister of Finance,
  Dec. 1938–Mar. 1939), **iii** 377; **iv** 157, 183–4,
  219, 221, 225, 230, 406
Terentiev, Alexei (Soviet Ambassador at An-
  gora, 1938–40), **v** 766; **vi** 169, 449, 623, 661;
  vii 276
Tevfik Rüstü Aras. *See* Aras, Dr. Tevfik Rüstü
Thaon di Revel, Count Paolo (Italian Minister
  of Finance, 1935–43), **iii** 501
Thermann, Dr. E. Freiherr von (German Ambassador at Buenos Aires, 1936–41), **ii** 651;
  vi 490
Thierry, Adrien (French Minister at Bucharest,
  1936–9; Ambassador there, April 1939–40),
  iii 197; **iv** 42, 410, 423, 433, 515, 567
Thomsen, Hans (German Chargé d'Affaires *ad
  interim* at Washington, Nov. 1938–Dec. 1940),
  iv 481
Thouvenin, M., **iv** 266
Thwaites, J. A. (H.M. Vice-Consul at Katowice, 1938–9; Consul there, April–Oct. 1939),
  v 246; **vii** 203, 533
Tilea, Viorel V. (Roumanian Minister at
  London, 1939–40), **iv** 370–1, 379, 384–5,
  391, 395, 398–9, 401, 409–10, 422, 448–50,
  471, 494, 576, 619; **v** 68, 74–5, 83, 105, 111–2,
  343, 403, 501, 531, 801; **vi** 324
    Conversation with Sir A. Cadogan, **iv** 389,
    520; **v** 65–6, 207
    Conversation with Viscount Halifax, **iv** 283–4,
    360–1, 366–7, 375–6; **v** 395–6, 480–3;
    vi 263, 582–5
    Conversation with Sir O. Sargent, **iv** 284–5;
    v 746–7
    At Anglo-Roumanian conversations, April
    1939, **v** 296, 309, 321, 325, 329, 332–3, 342
Timoshenkó, Army Commander (Soviet Commander of military district of Kiev), **i** 422;
  vii 46
Tinkler, R. M., **ix** 152
Tippelskirch, General Kurt von (Chief of

Intelligence, German Ministry of War), **ii** 291, 309, 408
  Conversation with Colonel Mason-Mac-Farlane, **ii** 120–1, 616
Tippelskirch, Werner von (Counsellor of German Embassy, Moscow), **ii** 298
Tipper, A. E. (Chairman of the Municipal Council, British Concession, Tientsin, 1938–9), **viii** 9; **ix** 112, 145, 493
Tiso, Dr. Josef (a leader of Slovak People's party; President of Council of Province of Slovakia, Dec. 2, 1938–Mar. 10, 1939; Prime Minister of Republic of Slovakia, Mar. 14–Oct. 26, 1939), **ii** 279; **iii** 114, 140, 185, 377, 413; **iv** 92–3, 96, 98–9, 219–21, 239, 243–4, 246, 406, 442; **v** 86, 91, 291, 546, 616–7
  Conversation with Mr. Pares, **iv** 92–3
  Visit to Herr Hitler, Mar. 1939, **iv** 233, 235, 241–2, 407, 438–9, 443; **v** 616; April 1939, **v** 88–90
  Request to Herr Hitler to assume protectorate over Slovakia, **iv** 280, 288
Titulescu, Nicolas (Roumanian Minister for Foreign Affairs, 1932–6), **iii** 182; **v** 91, 310, 672, 747
Todd, F. H. (Commercial Secretary, H.M. Embassy, Moscow, Aug. 1938–May 1940)
  Memorandum by, **iv** 197
Todt, Dr. Fritz (German General Inspector of Road Communications), **iii** 240, 623
Tofer, Karl (Estonian Minister at Berlin, 1936–9), **v** 803
Togay, Hulusi Fuat. *See* Hulusi Fuat Togay
Togo, Shigenori (Japanese Ambassador at Moscow, 1938–40), **ix** 519
Tojo, Lt.-Gen. Hideki (Japanese Vice-Minister of War, May–Dec. 1938), **viii** 270, 289–90
  Speech by, **viii** 270, 290
Tokugawa, Marquis Raitei, **ix** 173–4
Tokugawa, Yoshitomo (son of Marquis Tokugawa), **ix** 173
Tönnisson, Jaan (a member of Estonian Chamber of Deputies), **vi** 281
Torr, C. J. W. (1st Secretary, H.M. Legation, The Vatican, April 1937–Sept. 1939)
  Conversation with Cardinal Pacelli, **ii** 136–7
Toussaint, Colonel (German Military Attaché at Prague), **i** 61–2, 329, 349, 359, 361, 392; **ii** 143; **iii** 253
  Conversation with Lt.-Col. H. C. T. Stronge, **ii** 143–6; **iii** 254–5
Toussaint, General J. (French Military Attaché at Rome), **iv** 304–5; **v** 117, 170, 240
  Conversation with Colonel Burrows, **v** 172–4
Trajanovitch, Lt.-Col. R. (Yugoslav Military Attaché at Rome), **iii** 335; **iv** 328; **v** 426
Trant, J. P. (H.M. Consul-General at Moscow, June 1939–Mar. 1943), **vi** 301
Trautmann, Dr. Oscar (German Ambassador in China, 1935–8), **viii** 21, 341

Trenchard, 1st Viscount (Marshal of the Royal Air Force), **iii** 616
Trentham, E. N. R. (Financial Adviser at H.M. Embassy, Berlin, April–Sept. 1939), **v** 425
Treue, Herr (of the Reichsbank), **iv** 598
Tripiccione, Colonel (Italian Director of Military Operations and Intelligence)
  Conversation with Col. Burrows, **v** 118–9
Tripura, Maharajur of, **ix** 370
Trotski, Lev Davidovich, **iv** 414–5
Troubridge, Captain T. H. (British Naval Attaché at Berlin, Aug. 1936–April 1939), **ii** 204*n*; **iv** 177, 455
  At Anglo-German Naval conversations, Dec. 1938, **iii** 664
Troup, Rear-Admiral J. A. G. (Director of Naval Intelligence, 1935–9), **ii** 286
Troutbeck, J. M. (1st Secretary, H.M. Legation at Prague, Oct. 1937–May 1939; acted as Chargé d'Affaires), **i** 138, 190*n*, 406, 568; **ii** 33, 50, 143, 450, 536, 596; **iii** 379; **v** 84; **vi** 705
  To Viscount Halifax, **ii** 170, 176–7; **iii** 223, 225–7, 234, 631*n*; **iv** 7–8, 13, 55–6, 61, 64, 85, 92–3, 108, 113, 116, 125–6, 136, 147, 149, 158, 162; **v** 93, 554
  Conversation with M. Chvalkovsky, **iv** 129–30
  Conversation with Dr. Masarik, **iv** 7–9, 13
  Conversation with Mr. Shepherd, **vi** 356–7
  Conversation with Mr. Strang, **ii** 536, 544
  Letter to Mr. Strang, **iv** 129
  Minute by, **vi** 356, 678
Tsehio, Mr. (Japanese Vice-President of Hua Hsing Commercial Bank), **ix** 30
Tuan Mao-lan (Senior Secretary, Ministry of Foreign Affairs, China), **viii** 197
Tuka, Dr. Vojtech (Deputy Prime Minister of Republic of Slovakia, Mar.–Oct. 1939), **iii** 217; **iv** 63, 221, 226, 246, 407–8, 455; **v** 85, 87–9
Tukhachevski, Marshal (Marshal of the Soviet Union: shot in June 1937), **i** 163–4, 420, 422; **iv** 414
Turauskas, E. (Lithuanian Minister at Prague, 1934–9), **iv** 430–1
Turin, Senior Lieutenant (Soviet interpreter), **vii** 561
Türkmen, Lt.-Col. B. (Turkish Military and Air Attaché at Moscow), **vii** 46
Twardowski, Dr. Fritz von (Deputy Director of Cultural Policy Department of German Ministry of Foreign Affairs), **iii** 653
Tweedsmuir, 1st Baron (Governor-General of Canada, 1935–40), **ii** 54
Tweedy, Mr. (a press representative of the Palestine Government), **iv** 12

Uborevitch, General I. P. (Soviet Assistant Commissar for Defence; shot in June 1937), **i** 422; **iv** 414

Uchida, Goro (Japanese Consul-General at Amoy), **ix** 70, 178*n*, 189, 256, 288

Udet, General (Head of technical office of the German Air Force), **iv** 302, 306

Ugaki, General K. (Japanese Minister for Foreign Affairs, May–Sept. 1938), **viii** 1, 5, 6*n*, 12–4, 17, 23–4, 26, 36–7, 41, 43, 46–50, 53–4, 56–7, 62, 70*n*, 71, 73–9, 84, 87–90, 96, 105–8, 120–2, 130, 139, 156, 158*n*, 171, 180–2, 206, 211, 281–2, 292, 378; **ix** 198, 200, 498
   resignation of, **viii** 110; *referred to*, **viii** 114–6, 118, 120–2, 215
   Conversation with Sir R. Craigie, **viii** 5*n*, 12*n*, 13*n*, 26–8, 34–5, 73, 86–7, 91, 96–101

Uhlenberg, M., **vi** 149-50

Ulanova, Galina (Soviet *prima ballerina*), **iv** 569

Umberto, Crown Prince of Italy. *See* Piedmont, Prince of

Unden, Osten (M. Sandler's representative on Committee of Three), **iii** 595

United Kingdom Delegation (Geneva)
   To Sir A. Cadogan, **v** 623, 626, 630, 632, 637–8, 648–9, 654; **ix** 100
   To Viscount Halifax, **ii** 293, 365–6, 497, 594; **iii** 5, 18, 591–2, 594, 598, 604–5; **viii** 93, 104, 110, 402, 408; **ix** 104, 113
   To Sir J. Simon, **iii** 585–7, 595, 597

United Kingdom Delegation (Munich)
   To Viscount Halifax, **ii** 627, 630
   To Mr. Newton, **ii** 629

Urbsys, Juozas (Secretary-General of Lithuanian Ministry of Foreign Affairs, 1936–8; Minister for Foreign Affairs, Dec. 1938–40), **iv** 285, 483–4, 642–3
   Conversation with Mr. Preston, **iv** 517–8, 639–40
   Visit to Berlin, **iv** 397–8, 421, 430, 454, 456, 475–6, 493, 643

Urbsys, M. (Secretary-General of Lithuanian Ministry of Foreign Affairs), **iv** 390, 517
   Conversation with Mr. Preston, **iv** 454–5

Urdarianu, E. (Minister of Court, Roumania), **iv** 433

Usborne, Vice-Admiral C. V., **iv** 265; **vii** 33

Vachell, Group Captain J. L. (British Air Attaché at Berlin and Warsaw, Oct. 1937–Sept. 1939), **iii** 617; **iv** 116, 177, 586; **v** 38, 42, 100; **vii** 522
   To Sir N. Henderson, **iv** 117
   To Sir H. Kennard, **v** 43
   To Sir G. Ogilvie-Forbes, **iv** 586
   Memorandum by, **v** 100

Valentino, Baron Pietro Arone di (Italian Ambassador at Warsaw, 1936–9), **v** 567, 718

Valera, Eamon de (Prime Minister of Eire, Dec. 1937–Feb. 1948), **ii** 133, 594; **vi** 753; **vii** 67

Valeri, Mgr. Valerio (Apostolic Nuncio in France, 1936–44), **v** 432, 467

Valin, General (a member of French Military Delegation to Moscow, Aug. 1939), **vii** 1, 2*n*, 3*n*, 5, 26, 558–9, 562, 569, 581–2, 598

Vanco, Dr. Milos (Slovak Minister of Justice, Dec. 1938–Mar. 1939), **iii** 377; **iv** 98, 219

Vandenberg, Arthur Hendrick (U.S. Senator from Michigan), **ix** 348
   Vandenberg Resolution, **ix** 348*n*, 371

Van den Bergen, Lt.-Gen. *See* Bergen, Lt.-Gen. E. M. Van den

Vansittart, Sir Robert (Chief Diplomatic Adviser to Secretary of State for Foreign Affairs, 1938–41), **i** 112*n*, 299, 300, 416*n*, 418*n*, 556; **ii** 673, 683; **iii** 1; **v** 565*n*, 578; **vi** 14, 745, 754, 759*n*; **vii** 80; **ix** 272*n*
   Conversation with Herr Henlein, **i** 298–9, 630–3
   Conversation with Herr von Kleist, **ii** 683–6
   Conversation with M. Maisky, **v** 564–5, 639*n*
   Minute by, **v** 564; **vii** 355*n*
   At Anglo-French conversations, April 1938, **i** 198; Sept. 1938, **ii** 373, 520, 536

Van Zeeland, Paul. *See* Zeeland, Paul van

Von Zuylen, Baron. *See* Zuylen, Baron van

Vauhnik, Colonel V. (Yugoslav Military Attaché at Berlin), **iv** 102
   Conversation with Colonel Mason-Mac-Farlane, **iii** 564–5

Vaux Saint-Cyr, Carra de (French Consul-General at Munich, 1934–8; Chargé d'Affaires at Berlin, April 1939), **i** 310; **v** 250

Vavrecka, Hugo (Head of Propaganda Department of Czechoslovak Ministry of Foreign Affairs, 1938–9), **iii** 377

Velics, Lázló de (Hungarian Minister at Berne and. Permanent Delegate to the League of Nations)
   Conversation with Mr. R. A. Butler, **iii** 5

Verdier, Cardinal (Archbishop of Paris), **ii** 535, 568*n*; **vii** 177
   Conversation with Sir E. Phipps, **vii** 341–2

Vereker, G. G. M. (Counsellor of H.M. Embassy, Moscow, Nov. 1937–Feb. 1940; acted as Chargé d'Affaires), **iv** 14, 24–5, 417; **vii** 45
   To Viscount Halifax, **i** 280, 303, 346, 391, 402, 419; **iii** 541, 575
   Conversation with M. Coulondre, **i** 303–7, 402
   Conversation with M. Payart, **ii** 229
   Views on 'Ukrainian' question, **iii** 575

Vichenet, Comte C. de Romrée de (Belgian Ambassador at Madrid, 1939–41), **vii** 287

Victor Emmanuel III, King of Italy (1900–46), **i** 627; **ii** 626; **iii** 348, 496, 500, 535–7, 539; **iv** 42; **v** 130, 134, 219*n*, 411; **vii** 93, 136, 185, 220, 258, 316
   Visit (projected) to Berlin, **v** 586; **vi** 706

Villani, Baron Frederic de (Hungarian Minister at Rome, 1934–41), **iii** 358; **iv** 492; **v** 551

Viola di Campalto, Count Guido (Italian Ambassador at Burgos, 1937–9), **iii** 314

Viscafé, Major, **iii** 336

Vissarion, Mgr. *See* Djuvanni, Mgr. Vissarion

Vitrolles, Baron Régis d'Arnauld de (French Minister at The Hague, 1931–40), **iv** 28; **vi** 227; **vii** 349

Vitrolles, Lt.-Col. de (Head of the Deuxième Bureau of the French Air Force)
Conversation with Wing Commander D. Colyer, **iii** 583–5; **v** 488–9
Conversation with Col. Fraser, **iv** 74–5
Conversation with Sir E. Phipps, **iv** 74–5

Vogüé, Marquis L. de (President of Suez Canal Company), **iii** 309, 504

Voigt, F. A. (Diplomatic correspondent of the 'Manchester Guardian'), **ii** 189

Volosin, Mgr. Augustin (Prime Minister of Province of Ruthenia, Oct. 1938–Mar. 1939), **iii** 377; **iv** 281

Voorst Evekink, Lt.-Col. D. van (Netherlands Military Attaché at Brussels and Paris), **iv** 52, 78, 450, 576
Conversation with Lt.-Col. Blake, **iv** 451–2

Voorst Tot Voorst, Lt.-Gen. Baron J. J. G. van (Commander-in-Chief of Netherlands Field Army), **iv** 78.

Vörnle, Jean (Secretary-General of Hungarian Ministry of Foreign Affairs, 1938–9), **iv** 248, 253, 511n; **v** 60, 62

Voroshilov, K. E., Marshal of the Soviet Union (People's Commissar for Defence in U.S.S.R.), **i** 164–5, 305–6, 422; **v** 463n; **vi** 615, 641, 674; **vii** 4–5, 23, 34–5, 46, 74, 86, 102, 114–5, 119, 141, 143, 161, 167, 188, 210, 225, 237, 305–6, 346–8, 385, 558–613 *passim*, 621
Conversation with General Doumenc, **vii** 609–13
Conversation with Colonel Firebrace, **v** 471

Vos van Steenwijk, Baron G. W. de (Netherlands Minister in China, 1935–40), **ix** 125

Voska, Captain Emanuel (Head of the Czechoslovak Maffia during the First World War), **iv** 561

Vuillemin, General (Head of French Air Mission to Berlin, Aug. 1938), **ii** 122–4, 140, 158, 218

Vukchevitch, Dr. Alexandre (Yugoslav Minister at Warsaw, 1938–9), **iii** 138

Wakefield-Harrey, C. O. (H.M. Consul at Florence, Sept. 1936–Mar. 1939), **iv** 301

Walewski, M. (*Rapporteur* of the budget in Polish Ministry of Foreign Affairs), **i** 429–30

Waley, S. D. (a Principal Assistant Secretary in H.M. Treasury), **vi** 635

Walker, E. A. (First Secretary, H.M. Embassy, Angora, May 1939–May 1941), **vii** 299n

Wallace, Captain D. Euan (Financial Secretary to the Treasury and member of U.K. Delegation to League of Nations), **ii** 293, 361n
To Viscount Halifax, **ii** 365–6, 594

Walters, Frank (a Deputy Secretary-General of League of Nations), **iii** 441–2, 587, 611; **v** 392–4; **vi** 639, 660
Conversation with M. Burckhardt, **v** 561–2
Conversation with Mr. Makins, **iv** 383n
Letter to Mr. Randall, **iv** 383

Wang, Dr. C. T. (Chinese Ambassador at Washington, 1937–8), **viii** 16, 19, 66n, 245, 257; **ix** 78, 147

Wang Ching-wei (President of the National People's Political Assembly, China), **viii** 197, 249–50, 356
flight to Hanoi, **viii** 362–4, 415; **ix** 92
proposed as head of new Central Government of Japanese-occupied China, **ix** 242, 252, 254, 259–60, 312, 343, 353, 368, 418, 450

Wang Chung-hui (Vice-President of the Executive Yuan and Chinese Minister for Foreign Affairs, 1937–41), **viii** 2–4, 7, 16, 18, 196, 249–50, 478; **ix** 19, 43–4, 53, 78, 316
Conversation with Mr. Greenway, **viii** 294–5

Wang Ke-min (Head of the Japanese-controlled Provisional Government at Peking), **viii** 535; **ix** 260

Wang Wen, **ix** 180, 362

Wang Wen's brother, **ix** 111, 118, 122–4, 126–7, 180

Wardlaw-Milne, Sir John (M.P. for Kidderminster), **viii** 163

Warlimont, Colonel von (Head of Operations Section of the High Command of the German Army), **iii** 176–7; **iv** 176–7

Warner, Sir George (H.M. Minister at Berne, Jan. 1935–Dec. 1939), **ii** 691
To Viscount Halifax, **ii** 242

Warr, Earl de la. *See* De la Warr, 9th Earl

Water, C. T. te (High Commissioner for South Africa in London, 1929–39), **vi** 588, 633; **vii** 49
Conversation with Viscount Halifax and Mr. Bruce, **vi** 588–90

Waterlow, Sir Sydney Philip (H.M. Minister at Athens, Dec. 1933–May 1939), **v** 163
To Viscount Halifax, **iv** 374, 387, 396; **v** 136, 145, 160, 182, 186, 280, 444
Conversation with M. Metaxas, **v** 145

Watkinson, A. E. (H.M. Consul at Tripoli, Oct. 1938–July 1940), **iv** 313

Weber, Dr. W. M. (First Secretary of German Embassy, London)
Conversation with Mr. Ashton-Gwatkin, **v** 791–2

Weininger, M., **ii** 669

Weizmann, Dr. C. (President of the World Zionist Organisation), **iii** 264

Weizsäcker, Baron Ernst von (State Secretary of German Ministry of Foreign Affairs, 1938–43), i 12, 66, 323, 328, 349–50, 355, 362, 371, 392–4, 417, 427–8, 448, 504, 544, 581, 592–3, 603, 613, 622; ii 9, 12–3, 24, 66, 108, 205, 240, 249, 284, 297, 300, 310, 324–5, 351, 372n, 400–2, 421, 423–4, 428, 430, 499, 512–3, 630, 650, 652–3, 655, 683; iii 56, 64, 74, 76, 93, 117, 123, 129–30, 134, 148, 151, 167–9, 175, 186–7, 191, 200, 208, 221, 241, 265, 268–9, 271, 273, 442, 446, 587, 610, 654–5, 657, 659; iv 122, 160, 167, 204, 232, 242, 245, 253, 260, 263, 371, 383, 443, 461; v 28, 94, 232, 244, 265, 398, 713–4, 720, 752, 782, 798, 804; vi 15, 123–4, 201, 211, 215, 235–9, 318, 331, 348, 355, 368–9, 412, 456, 519–20, 580, 634, 636, 644–5, 651, 663, 692, 697, 701, 703–4, 707, 711, 713, 726, 754; vii 36–8, 62, 68–9, 78, 89, 101, 123, 139, 159, 162, 181, 186, 190, 192, 199, 212–4, 216, 222, 269, 294, 301, 372, 400, 432n, 435n, 437, 440, 451, 457, 466, 631
  Conversation with M. Burckhardt, ii 690–1; vi 43–4, 727
  Conversation with M. Coulondre, iv 264–5; v 527–8
  Conversation with Sir N. Henderson, i 335, 344–6, 348, 393–4, 426–8, 485–6, 537–8, 568–9, 596–7; ii 6, 11, 24, 109–10, 123, 203–4, 216, 283, 325–6, 417–8, 584–5; iii 149–50; iv 122–3, 244, 250, 590–1; v 337–9, 562–3, 807; vi 28, 59–62, 75–6, 359, 362–4, 381–2, 609–12; vii 29–31
  Conversation with Sir G. Ogilvie-Forbes, iii , 203–4
  Conversation with M. Schubert, ii 371–2
  Conversation with Sir H. Wilson, ii 353
  Letter to Sir N. Henderson, i 609
Welczeck (Welczek), Count J. von (German Ambassador at Paris, 1936–9), i 265, 357, 384; ii 216, 219, 262, 542, 651; iii 262–3, 269, 286, 309–10, 389–93, 513, 620; iv 263, 269, 368; v 429; vi 236, 381, 399, 514, 517, 519
  Conversation with M. Bonnet, i 384; ii 216; vi 237
  Conversation with Sir E. Phipps, iv 9–10
Welczeck (Welczek), Countess von, iii 391
Welles, Sumner (U.S. Under Secretary of State, 1937–43), iii 279, 295, 344; iv 9, 159, 161, 481; vii 164, 261; viii 239n, 299, 428, 433, 435–6, 438–9, 456n, 457–8, 497; ix 189, 204n, 205, 283, 342, 404, 492, 514
  To Herr Hans Thomsen, iv 481
  Conversation with Sir R. Lindsay, iv 124–5; vii 41–2, 154; viii 278–9; ix 187–8, 235, 284, 443–4
  Conversation with Marquess of Lothian, ix 518

Conversation with Mr. Mallet, viii 384–5; ix 395–6
Statement by, March 17, 1939, iv 482
Wells, H. G. (British writer), iii 560, 566
Wen, Mr. (Superintendent of Customs, Tientsin; appointed Mayor of Tientsin, Mar. 1939) viii 243, 445–6, 460, 470
Wenda, Colonel Z. Z. (Vice-Marshal of the Polish Diet), vi 262
Wenner-Gren, Axel L., vi 745–8, 750; vii 67, 327, 551, 554
  Conversation with Mr. Chamberlain, vi 736–8
  Conversation with Field-Marshal Göring, vi 738–9
  Letter to Mr. Chamberlain, vi 740, 742
  Letter to Captain Margesson, vi 739
Wenninger, Lt.-Gen. R. F. A. (German Air Attaché at London), iv 123
Werdt, Colonel H. von (Swiss Military Attaché at Berlin), ii 309
Wernher, Sir Harold (President of Anglo-Swedish Society), vi 483–4; vii 286, 537n
  Conversation with M. Dahlerus, vii 320n
Werth, General (Chief of Hungarian General Staff), iii 239; vii 92
Westman, K. G. (a member of Swedish Delegation to League of Nations), iii 587; viii 111, 145
Wettstein de Westersheimb, Jean (Hungarian Minister at Prague, 1933–9), iii 43, 51, 76, 79, 81, 86
  Note to Dr. Krofta, iii 44, 51, 86
Weygand, General Maxime, ii 535; iii 37, 249; v 434, 452, 465, 646
Whitamore, C. E. (H.M. Acting Consul-General at Hankow, May 1938–Sept. 1939), viii 3, 361; ix 79, 96, 157, 225
  To British Embassy, Shanghai, ix 73, 81, 110
Whittall, L. H. (H.M. Acting Consul at Hankow, Mar. 1939–Feb. 1940), ix 73
Wiart, Major-General Carton de. *See* Carton de Wiart, Major-General A.
Wiedemann, Captain Fritz (a confidant of Herr Hitler), i 602, 613, 618–9; ii 2, 10, 19, 24, 44, 78–9, 92; iii 563; iv 6, 23, 39; vii 626
  Conversation with Viscount Halifax, i 584–9
Wiehl, Emil K. J. (Director of Economic Department in German Ministry of Foreign Affairs, June 1937–Sept. 1944), iii 390; iv 134, 597–8
  Conversation with Mr. Ashton-Gwatkin, iv 603–4
Wienke, Herr (of the Reichsbank), iv 598
Wiesner, M. (Polish Senator), iv 88
Wiley, J. W. (U.S. Consul-General at Vienna), i 359, 363
Wilhelmina, Queen of the Netherlands (1890–1948), vii 340, 349, 447
Willaume, Captain (a member of French Mili-

tary Delegation to Moscow, Aug. 1939), **vii** 562, 580

Willecot de Rincquese, Captain de (a member of French Military Delegation to Moscow, Aug. 1939), **vii** 562

William, Crown Prince of Germany, **ii** 65–6; **vi** 11

William II, Emperor of Germany (1888–1918; d. 1941), **i** 179, 226; **ii** 396; **iii** 143, 154; **iv** 19; **v** 593; **vi** 692, 711

Williams, Frank S. (U.S. Commercial Attaché at Tokyo), **viii** 317
  Memorandum by, **viii** 318

Williams, W. H. (H.M. Pro-Consul at Shanghai, May 1938–Sept. 1942), **viii** 243

Wilmowski, Herr von (of Krupps), **iv** 600

Wilson, Sir Horace J. (Chief Industrial Adviser to H.M. Government, 1930–9; seconded to the Treasury for service with the Prime Minister, 1935–9), **i** 619; **ii** 462, 537, 539–40, 541n, 543–5, 569, 571, 576, 588, 643, 653, 670; **vii** 475; **viii** 247, 260; **ix** 510
  To Mr. Chamberlain, **ii** 552, 563
  Conversation with M. Dahlerus, **vii** 441–2
  Conversation with Dr. von Dirksen, **ii** 351–3; **vi** 579–82
  Conversation with Dr. F. Hesse, **ix** 539
  Conversation with Herr Hitler, Sept. 1938, **ii** 552–7, 563–7
  Conversation with Herr von Ribbentrop, **ii** 353–4
  Conversation with Baron von Weizsäcker, **ii** 353
  Conversation with Herr Wohltat, **vi** 389–91
  Notes on conversations during Mr. Chamberlain's visit to Berchtesgaden, **ii** 351–4
  Note on the Munich Conference, **ii** 630–5
  Note on interview with Dr. F. Hesse, **ix** 539
  At Anglo-French conversations, Sept. 1938, **ii** 373, 520, 536
  At Meeting at Godesberg between Mr. Chamberlain and Herr Hitler, **ii** 472, 499

Wilson, Hugh R. (U.S. Ambassador at Berlin, 1938–40; recalled Nov. 1938, did not return to post), **i** 238, 290, 348, 359, 414–5, 614–5, 617; **ii** 12, 57, 149, 213, 217, 646–7; **iii** 272, 279, 296; **iv** 381; **vii** 630
  Conversation with Herr von Ribbentrop, **iii** 278
  recall to Washington, **iii** 272

Wilson, Woodrow (President of the United States, 1912–20), **i** 71, 182; **ii** 486

Winslow, Major J. S. (U.S. Military Attaché at Prague), **i** 381

Winterton, 6th Earl (Chancellor of Duchy of Lancaster, May 1937–Jan. 1939), **iii** 172, 432
  Conversation with Dr. Schacht, **iii** 675–7
  Speech by, Sept. 1938, **iii** 29n, 31; Oct. 1938, **iii** 153, 158, 194

Wirsen, K. E. T. (Swedish Minister at Rome, 1938–40), **iv** 293, 297; **vii** 422

Witos, Wincenty (leader of Peasant party in Poland; in exile 1933–9), **iv** 497

Witz, Herr, **vii** 204

Witzleben, Baron (leader of the Germans in Roumania), **iv** 42

Witzleben, General Erwin von, **vii** 517

Woermann, Dr. Ernst (Head of Political Department of German Ministry of Foreign Affairs, with title of Under State Secretary, April 1938–April 1943), **i** 21, 80, 259, 262, 265, 273, 277, 281, 303, 304n, 402; **ii** 38, 105–6; **iii** 230, 269, 271, 657, 668; **iv** 644; **vi** 679; **vii** 192
  Conversation with Sir A. Cadogan, **i** 80–2
  Conversation with Sir N. Henderson, **i** 260, 304n; **ii** 87–8, 91–3
  Conversation with Sir G. Ogilvie-Forbes, **iii** 271

Wohltat, Dr. Helmut (of the German Ministry for Economic Affairs: Commissioner of the Four-Year Plan), **iii** 677; **iv** 369, 433, 598, 600–1; **vi** 580; **vii** 549
  Conversation with Mr. Ashton-Gwatkin, **v** 791–2
  Conversation with Mr. R. S. Hudson, **vi** 407–10; *referred to*, **vi** 464–6, 480–3, 495, 555, 580, 607, 648; **vii** 548
  Conversation with Sir H. Wilson, **vi** 389–91

Wolf, Dr. (a representative of Polish minority in Czechoslovakia), **ii** 667

Wolf, V. L. R. (appointed German Consul at Brno, Jan. 1939), **iv** 63

Wolf, Dr. Wilhelm (Austrian Minister for Foreign Affairs, Mar. 12–15, 1938), **i** 129, 135

Wolff, Johanna, **v** 245

Wollner, Deputy (of Sudeten German party), **ii** 457

Wong, C. C. (a member of the Chinese Trading Commission), **viii** 472

Wong Chu-lin (Chairman of the Chinese Chamber of Commerce), **viii** 354

Woo Zung-yui (of the Reformed Government at Nanking), **ix** 11

Wood, Sir Kingsley (Secretary of State for Air, May 1938–April 1940), **iii** 158, 172, 250n, 291, 293; **iv** 115n, 123, 532; **vii** 368

Woodhead, H. G. W. (Chairman of the China Association, Shanghai), **ix** 137

Wszelaki, M. (Economic adviser to the Polish Ministry of Foreign Affairs), **vi** 427
  Conversation with Mr. Hankey, **vi** 405–7

Wühlisch, Johann von (Counsellor of German Embassy at Warsaw: acted as Chargé d'Affaires), **vi** 679

Wu Pei-fu, Marshal, **viii** 297, 356, 362

Wyndham, Mr. (Assistant clerk to British Military Attaché, Rome), **iv** 313

Wysocky, Alfredo (Polish Ambassador at Rome, 1933–8)
    Conversation with Herr Hitler, **i** 274
    Conversation with the Earl of Perth, **i** 274

Yada, Shichitaro (Japanese Minister at Berne, 1930–4), **ix** 173

Yakir, General I. E. (Soviet Commander-in-Chief at Kiev; shot in June 1937), **iv** 414

Yamamoto, Vice-Admiral Isoroku (Japanese Vice-Minister of Marine), **viii** 71

Yanguas y Messia, José Maria de (Spanish Ambassador at The Vatican, 1938–42), **vii** 448

Yarnell, Admiral Henry E. (Commander-in-Chief of U.S. Asiatic Fleet), **ix** 223n

Yehia, Abdul Fattah. *See* Abdul Fattah Yehia

Yencken, A. F. (First Secretary, H.M. Embassy at Rome, Jan. 1937–April 1939), **iii** 328–9; **iv** 293, 338; **v** 188
    Conversation with Signor Buti, **v** 250–1

Yevtitch, Pavle (Yugoslav Press Attaché at London), **v** 595

Yonai, Admiral Mitsumasa (Japanese Minister of Marine, 1937–9), **viii** 79, 369; **ix** 412, 517

Yoshida, Shigeru (Japanese Ambassador at London, 1936–8), **viii** 78n, 83, 91, 95, 164, 528–9
    Conversation with Viscount Halifax, **viii** 78–9

Young, Dr. (Financial adviser to Chinese Government), **viii** 433n, 435, 516; **ix** 8, 24, 112

Young, G. P. (Secretary, H.M. Embassy in China, Oct. 1935–Oct. 1938), **viii** 2n, 10n, 32n, 552
    To British Embassy, Shanghai, **viii** 10, 70
    To Viscount Halifax, **viii** 31

Yrjö-Koskinen, Baron A. (Finnish Minister at Moscow, 1930–9), **iv** 568; **vi** 265

Yuki, Toyotaro (Governor of Bank of Japan), **viii** 369, 493; **ix** 45

Yvonne, Signor (of police inspectorate at Kulangsu), **ix** 480

Zalitis, Lt.-Col. (Latvian Military Attaché at Moscow), **i** 165

Zamfirescu, A. D. (Roumanian Minister at Rome, 1938–9), **v** 396

Zanchi, Signor, **iii** 645

Zarine, Charles (Latvian Minister at London, 1933–40), **vi** 48, 158

Zarske, Herr (Editor of the 'Danziger Vorposten'), **vi** 395, 507; **vii** 542n

Zatko, Dr. Peter (Secretary-General of Slovak Industrial Union), **iv** 98, 229

Zay, Jean (French Minister of National Education, 1936–9), **iii** 392–3; **ix** 193

Zech-Burkersroda, Count Julius von (German Minister at The Hague, 1928–40), **vii** 349

Zechlin, Erich (German Minister at Kovno, 1933–40), **iv** 454

Zeeland, Paul van (Belgian Prime Minister, Mar. 1935–Nov. 1937), **v** 792

Zekai Apaydin (Turkish Ambassador at Moscow, 1935–9), **v** 282, 573, 590, 604, 672, 707–8; **vii** 276

Zenkl, Dr. Peter (Mayor of Prague), **ii** 51; **iii** 21; **iv** 561

Zernatto, Guido (Secretary-General of Austrian Patriotic Front), **i** 2, 132

Zhdanov, A. A. (a member of Presidium of the Supreme Council in the U.S.S.R.)
    article by, June 29, 1939, **vi** 217, 225n, 325n, 781

Zinoviev, G. E. (a former Soviet leader; shot for alleged conspiracy in Aug. 1936), **iv** 414

Zog I, King of the Albanians (Sept. 1928–April 1939), **iv** 357, 498; **v** 119–23, 127–9, 133–5, 137, 139–40, 149–50, 160, 163, 169, 175–7, 191–3, 195–7, 230
    arrival in Greece, **v** 136, 158, 170

Zuylen, Baron van (Political Director of Belgian Ministry of Foreign Affairs), **iv** 109

Zvrskovec, M. (of Slovak Ministry of Foreign Affairs), **v** 88, 90

Part IV: Subject Index

Aachen, **ii** 453; **iii** 98, 583; **vii** 416

Aaland Islands, **ii** 368n; **v** 496n; **vi** 265; **vii** 116, 155, 268, 577, 604

Abyssinia, i 127; **ii** 133, 562, 585; **iii** 366n, 472, 479–80, 484, 490, 496–7, 502n, 528; **vi** 753
recognition of Italian Empire, by France, **iii** 157, 296–7, 344, 486, 513; **v** 614; by Great Britain, **iii** 315, 322–3, 341, 352, 354–5

Addis Ababa, **iii** 475, 485

Adelsheim, **ii** 26

Aden, **vi** 127

Adler-Gebirge, **iii** 641

Adriatic Sea, **v** 589; **vi** 599

Aegean Sea
Bulgarian claim to outlet, **vi** 30, 68

Ainazi, **viii** 577

Air warfare, **ii** 637; **iii** 434–5; **vi** 766; **vii** 287, 293, 428, 485, 522, 628
in China, **viii** 3, 25–6, 37, 42–3, 45–6, 65–6, 73, 102, 146n
League of Nations Resolution of May 27, 1939, **viii** 104; **ix** 105, 113, 121, 141–2

Ajaccio, **iii** 475

Aland Islands. *See* Aaland Islands

Albania
Italy and, **iv** 161, 352, 357–8, 402n, 498; **v** 35, 50, 56, 70, 116–7, 119–23, 125, 127
Italian occupation, **v** 128–97 *passim*; *referred to*, **v** 97, 107, 113, 229–30, 319, 354, 376, 422; **vi** 72, 497, 659
effect of Italian action on:—Anglo-Italian relations, **v** 82, 120–1, 125, 128, 131–2, 135–7, 141–2, 147, 149–50, 154, 156, 164, 219, 705, 755, 765, 780; Balkan Entente, **v** 348, 530; Franco-Italian relations, **v** 130, 172, 256, 258, 278; Greece, **v** 127, 141–2, 146, 348, 437; Turkey, **v** 355, 464, 615; Yugoslavia, **v** 137, 139, 141–2, 146, 148, 150; *see also* Guarantee (to Greece)
Italian troop concentrations, **v** 382n, 383, 412, 426, 444, 615, 750–1
partition of, between Italy and Yugoslavia, **v** 122; **vi** 439

Aldershof, **i** 611

Aleutian Islands, **vii** 428

Alexandretta, Sandjak of, **iii** 587; **vi** 346–7

Algeria, **iii** 287; **iv** 325

Algiers, French garrison in, **iv** 316

Allenstein district, **vii** 204

Almeria, **vi** 208

Alsace-Lorraine, **i** 274, 296, 455; **ii** 338, 345, 375, 381; **iii** 151–2, 244–5, 479; **v** 302

Alto Adige, **vi** 255, 283n, 284, 323–4, 659n

Altsdorf, **iv** 57

Alzenau, **ii** 26

Amada Unida margarine factory in Danzig, **vi** 547, 568, 653, 685; **vii** 55

Ambassadors' Commission. *See* Commissions (International)

Ambassadors' Conference. *See* Conferences

Amoy (Kulangsu International Settlement), **ix** 83, 87, 94, 108, 139, 231
Japanese landing, **ix** 66, 80; protest by Great Britain, **ix** 67, 78–81
British and U.S. landings, **ix** 81n, 119, 340, 361, 371, 433, 461
Japanese demands, and negotiations, **ix** 70, 140, 155, 178, 189, 210, 256, 266–7, 288–9, 339, 361, 462, 480
blockade of, **ix** 203, 288

Amsterdam, **ii** 616; **iv** 37; **vii** 474

Anglo-Belgian Staff conversations, **iv** 78, 104–5; **vi** 221n

Anglo-Franco-Soviet military conversations
proposals for, **v** 470, 485, 529, 564, 565n, 726, 794; **vi** 2, 37, 50, 105, 111–2, 141, 312, 352, 377, 425–6, 429, 457–61
agreed to by Great Britain, **vi** 478, 484–5
preparations for, **vi** 492–3, 509–12, 521–4, 527–8, 533–5, 543, 546, 561–4, 570, 576–7, 595, 606, 611–2, 615, 641
British and French Military Missions, arrival and reception, **vii** 45–7, 558, 598; credentials and instructions, **vi** 674, 682–3, 762–89; **vii** 8–10, 21, 563, 589, 603; departure from Moscow, **vii** 184, 187–8, 190, 224, 237, 247, 613–4
conversations in Moscow, **vi** 674; **vii** 3–5, 22–3, 32–5, 102, 114–5, 121, 141, 225, 558–60, 616–7; record of, **vii** 560–614
passage of Soviet troops through Poland and Roumania, **vii** 1–4, 21, 25–8, 39–42, 53–4, 61, 70, 77, 85–9, 91–2, 101–2, 105–8, 112–3, 115–7, 119–21, 130, 133–6, 142, 149–50, 155, 158, 161, 164, 166–7, 170, 177, 209–11, 237, 305, 347, 559–60, 572–4, 592, 594, 599, 601–2, 604, 608–13

Anglo-Franco-Soviet negotiations, April–Aug. 1939, **v** 202–794 *passim*; **vi** *passim*; **vii** 74, 143, 430, 615–6, 622
main stages: — suggested unilateral declarations by U.S.S.R., April 14, **v** 202, 206, 209–10; French proposal, April 14, **v** 216, 261–2; Soviet counter-proposals, April 17, **v** 228–9; French proposal for Tripartite Agreement, April 24, **v** 295, 317; British revised draft, April 28, **v** 357, 359;

Anglo-Franco-Soviet negotiations (*cont.*)
modified French proposals handed to M.
Suritz, May 2, **v** 406, 641; British proposals
of May 6, **v** 450; Soviet proposals of May 15,
v 558; draft of proposed triple mutual guarantee pact, May 25, **v** 679; Soviet proposals
of June 2, **v** 753-4, 785; Anglo-French proposals dated June 6, handed to M. Molotov,
June 15, **vi** 34-41, 79; Soviet reply, June 16,
vi 85-7, 89-90; Anglo-French proposals,
June 21-2, **vi** 134-5, 140-2; Soviet reply,
June 22, **vi** 143; political articles of draft
Agreement, as at July 23, **vi** 539-42, 681-2
Baltic States and Finland, guarantee to,
v 558-9, 564, 565*n*, 568, 572-3, 578, 591,
604, 624, 649, 669, 689, 697, 736-7, 775;
vi 3-4, 35-6, 49, 50, 54-6, 86, 89-91, 95-6,
98, 103-4, 106, 116-8, 135, 144-5, 161-2,
168, 173-4, 179, 218, 225, 230-1, 250-1,
256, 264-7, 277, 280-2, 307-8, 313, 335,
350, 376, 414, 559, 571
'indirect aggression', definition of, **vi** 251,
277, 309-11, 313-4, 319, 324, 332-5, 339,
346, 349, 375, 382-4, 396-8, 424, 428-30,
450-1, 457-8, 460, 478, 485, 494, 511,
521-2, 525, 531, 544, 559, 571-3, 575-6,
578, 591, 594, 650, 682-3; **vii** 42-5, 74
simultaneous signature of political and
military agreements, **vi** 312, 319, 328, 332,
335-6, 339, 346, 349-50, 355, 360, 376-8,
383-4, 424-7, 429-30, 457, 459, 762
Belgium, **vi** 163, 168, 174, 230, 251, 280,
313
Bulgaria **v** 756-7
Denmark, **vi** 162, 168, 173, 225
Germany, **v** 272; **vi** 61, 74, 184, 197, 216, 287,
321, 331, 389, 467-8, 560-1, 580, 616, 620,
705, 708-12, 755-6
Greece, **vi** 174, 230, 251, 280, 313
Italy, **iv** 492; **v** 737; **vi** 126, 284, 444, 700;
vii 72
Japan, **v** 482; **iv** 23, 25, 27-8, 57, 64-5, 77,
91*n*, 99, 131, 516
Luxemburg, **vi** 167-8, 179, 181-2, 184, 194,
225, 230, 267-8, 276-7, 309, 311, 335, 346,
349-50, 360, 376, 428
Netherlands, **vi** 3-4, 36, 90, 103-4, 135, 144-5,
162-3, 167-8, 173-4, 179, 209, 219, 225-8,
230-1, 240, 243, 249-50, 254, 267-8, 276-80,
307, 309, 311, 314, 328, 335-6, 339, 346,
349-50, 360, 375-6, 428
Poland, **v** 236, 449, 657, 670; **vi** 24, 117-8,
163, 168, 174, 199, 200, 230-1, 250-1, 280,
311, 313, 339-40, 376, 440-1, 493-4, 545,
548, 565-6; **vii** 113
Roumania, **v** 597-8, 653, 658, 670; **vi** 117-8,
163, 168, 174, 230, 251, 280, 313, 583-4
Switzerland, **vi** 3-4, 36, 90, 103-4, 135, 144-5,
162-3, 167-8, 173-4, 179, 209, 219, 225,
230-1, 243, 249-50, 267-8, 276-80, 309, 311,

Anglo-Franco-Soviet negotiations (*cont.*)
314, 328, 335-6, 339, 346, 349-50, 360, 375-
6, 428
Turkey, **v** 573, 647, 672; **vi** 163, 168, 174,
230-1, 250-1, 280, 311, 313, 376, 387, 403,
623; **vii** 384
Anglo-Franco-Turkish negotiations. *See* Guara-
antee (to Turkey); Turkey (Great Britain)
Anglo-French conversations
Nov. 1937 (in London), *referred to,* **i** 85, 216
April 28-29, 1938 (in London), **i** 198-234;
referred to, **i** 235-7, 239-43, 246-7, 251*n*, 254,
256-8, 266, 293, 305, 326, 336, 546
Sept. 18 (in London), **ii** 373-40; *referred to,* **ii**
372, 404, 409, 452
Sept. 25 (in London), **ii** 520-35
Sept. 26 (in London), **ii** 536-41
Nov. 24 (in Paris), **iii** 285-311; *referred to,* **iii**
440, 444, 447, 461; **iv** 462; **viii** 244, 308-9
Jan. 10, 1939 (in Paris), **iii** 512-5; *referred to,*
iv 17, 82
Mar. 21 (in London), **iv** 422-7; *referred to,* **iv**
471-3, 495, 527
Mar. 22 (in London), **iv** 457-63; *referred to,* **iv**
495, 500, 514-5, 527, 532
May 20 (in Paris), **v** 608-14
Anglo-French Staff conversations
Air Staffs, **i** 84, 88, 90, 143, 145, 199-202, 208,
233-5, 245, 247, 256
Army Staffs, **i** 203-4, 206, 209, 211, 235; **iii**
289, 292, 427; **iv** 43-4, 79, 83, 101, 105, 108,
115, 133, 135-6, 145-6, 152, 154-6, 170-1,
223, 228, 236-7, 274, 577; **v** 49-50, 242; **vi**
85; representatives at: British, **iv** 237;
French, **iv** 223, 228
Naval Staffs, **i** 200, 203, 205, 207-10, 226-7;
iv 146, 155
at Singapore, **ix** 53*n*, 238, 372, 496*n*
Anglo-German conversations on Naval Agree-
ments, Dec. 1938, **iii** 455-6, 664-71; *see also*
Germany (Great Britain)
Anglo-German Declaration, Sept. 30, 1938, **ii**
640; *see also* Munich Conference (Hitler-
Chamberlain Declaration)
Anglo-German Fellowship, **iv** 18
Anglo-German Society (in Germany), **iv** 591*n*,
593
Anglo-Italian conversations. *See* Italy (Great
Britain)
Anglo-Japanese negotiations. *See* Tientsin
(British Concession: negotiations in Tokyo)
Anglo-Polish conversations, April 4-6, 1939
record of, **v** 1-19, 30-6; summary of con-
clusions, **v** 47-9; *see also* Poland (Great
Britain, visit to London of M. Beck)
Anglo-Polish Staff conversations, **v** 735, 749; **vi**
29*n*
preparations, **v** 53, 200, 234, 238, 379, 398
Anglo-Roumanian conversations, April 23-6,
1939, **v** 295-315, 321-34, 342-4, 374

Anglo-Soviet discussions, 1933, *referred to*, **iv** 207
  for Anglo-Soviet negotiations, 1939, *see* Anglo-Franco-Soviet negotiations
Anglo-Turkish negotiations. *See* Guarantee (to Turkey); Turkey (Great Britain)
Anhwei, **ix** 86
Annaberg, **i** 61
Anti-Comintern Pact, **iii** 590; **iv** 71, 516, 528, 548; **v** 520, 660; **vii** 138, 281
  attitude of:—General Franco, **iv** 124; **v** 144; Greece, **v** 331; Hungary, **iv** 55*n*, 618; Italy, **iii** 280; **iv** 5, 38, 70–1, 107, 185; **viii** 85*n*; **ix** 213; Japan, **iii** 280; **iv** 5, 38, 49, 70–1, 107, 125, 161; **vii** 275, 341, 428; **viii** 85, 90, 92, 115, 154, 176–7, 179, 189, 239, 267, 276–7, 290–1, 342, 407, 415, 437–8, 441–3, 451, 452*n*, 453, 456–8, 460–1, 468–9, 478, 482, 485, 493, 498, 536; **ix** 23, 26, 40, 42–3, 56, 64–5, 91, 98–9, 128–32, 233–4, 441–2, 516–7; Poland, **iii** 374, 589; **iv** 69, 185, 504, 513, 543, 581; **v** 24, 69, 276, 290, 416–7; Roumania, **v** 313, 331, 660; Turkey, **v** 331; Yugoslavia, **v** 331, 588, 660
  proposal to transform into military alliance, **iii** 280, 360; **iv** 27, 37, 49, 71; *see also* subhead (attitude of: Italy, Japan) *above*
Arcachon, **ix** 234*n*
Armaments, limitation of, **i** 110, 139, 175, 454; **ii** 637–9; **iii** 518–9, 527; **vi** 61
Armed Forces of the British Empire (a Russian reference book), **iv** 128
Arnau, **iii** 640
Arys, **ii** 408
Asch, **ii** 231, 313, 321, 334–6, 415, 455, 457, 572, 611, 619, 621, 659, 669, 672–3
Aschaffenburg, **ii** 26
Asia Development Council, **viii** 246*n*, 294, 371, 404
Asiatic Petroleum Company, property damaged in Tientsin, **ix** 322
Aspern, **i** 27, 135
Assab, **iii** 508
Associated British Committee (Tientsin), **viii** 123*n*, 421–2; **ix** 66, 112
Augustow, **vi** 246
Aussig, **i** 187, 594; **ii** 319; **iv** 249
Australia, **iii** 295; **vi** 747; **viii** 314, 347
Austria, **i** 1–60 *passim*, 126–37, 146–9, 155–7; **ii** 74, 281
  air force, **iv** 587–8
  army, incorporation into German army, **i** 43–4, 92–3; **vi** 297
  Czechoslovakia, **i** 366
  Germany. *See* Germany (Austria)
  Italy, **i** 127
  National Bank of Austria, **i** 136
  Press, **iv** 235
    'Reichspost', **i** 133; 'Wiener Journal', **ii** 65
Austrian 'Anschluss'. *See* Germany (Austria)
Austrian Legion, **i** 15, 24, 30, 45

Axis, Rome–Berlin, **i** 37, 127, 176, 208, 226; **ii** 20*n*, 172*n*; **iii** 160–1, 187, 218, 253, 287, 344, 349, 357–9, 389, 400, 427, 472, 474, 476, 478–9, 481, 498–9, 508, 511, 518; **iv** 30, 32, 124, 143, 178–9, 296, 309, 350, 403, 492*n*, 531, 616, 618, 620–1, 625; **v** 124, 162, 428, 481; **vi** 216, 253, 443; **viii** 17
Bad Reichenhall, **ii** 60
Baden, **ii** 26; **vii** 464
Bahnschutz (German Railway Protective Troops), **i** 611; **ii** 15
Baku, **iii** 658
Balearic Islands, **iii** 299, 315, 329, 479, 483, 506; **iv** 104; **v** 150
Balkan Entente (Greece, Roumania, Turkey, Yugoslavia), **iv** 104, 361, 367, 372, 374*n*, 386–7, 396, 409, 420, 424, 465, 470, 473, 497–8, 555, 576, 620; **v** 49, 58, 207, 221, 241, 296–7, 308, 314, 322, 334, 395, 403, 447, 463, 481, 530, 659, 796
  Anglo-Turkish Declaration of May 1939 and, **v** 473, 491, 493, 498, 531, 537, 552, 563, 589, 595–7, 660–3, 667, 671–2, 676, 681, 686–7, 701, 708, 720, 723, 725, 729, 739–40, 761–2; **vi** 17–8, 23–4, 51–2, 54, 66–71, 101–3, 130, 147, 164–5, 170, 228, 242, 260–1, 304–5, 463–4
  Bulgaria, admission to, **v** 109–10, 199, 207, 221, 296–7, 307–8, 326–8, 346, 348, 374, 380, 387, 464, 530, 550; **vi** 68, 84
  Germany, **v** 355, 464, 550
  See also Albania (effect of Italian action on Balkan Entente)
Balkan States. *See* South-east Europe
Baltic Sea, **iv** 479; **vi** 405; **vii** 134, 209, 460
Baltic States
  H.M. diplomatic representation, **iv** 390*n*
  U.S.S.R., **v** 214, 350, 404–5, 528, 564, 568, 604
  See also Anglo-Franco-Soviet negotiations (Baltic States and Finland, guarantee to); Estonia; Finland; Latvia; Lithuania
Baranowicze, **vii** 135
Barcelona, **iii** 329, 521
Barcelona Government. *See* Spain and Spanish Civil War
Bari, **v** 175; anti-British broadcasts, **iii** 312, 316, 318; Italian troop concentrations, **iv** 358; **v** 117
Baring Bank balances, **iv** 504; **v** 208
Bärnsdorf, **i** 124
Batang, **viii** 207
Batoum, **v** 259, 282
Bautsch, **iii** 641
Bavaria, **ii** 26–7, 42, 66
  military preparations, **i** 7, 9–12, 19, 20, 24, 40, 57, 61, 321, 559; **ii** 104–5, 127, 161, 237, 281, 453, 491; **iv** 24, 39; **vi** 617
Bayreuth, **ii** 24, 59, 60
Behnisch, **iii** 642

Behr and Mathews Ltd., **viii** 331
Belgium, i 22, 97, 191, 194, 209, 315; **ii** 269, 449, 594, 637; **iii** 159, 260, 263, 291, 556, 570, 583, 618; **v** 31, 213, 280, 302, 722, 727, 758; **vii** 514
attitude towards:—possible attack by Germany, **v** 256, 269–71; **vi** 222–3; possible German invasion of Netherlands, **iv** 44, 53, 58, 66–7, 69, 70, 75–8, 84, 451, 509
British and French commitments, **i** 96, 199; **iii** 287n; **v** 5, 270; **vii** 270–1, 293, 304, 312, 329, 338
German commitments, **i** 455, 649; **ii** 344, 375; **iii** 287n; **iv** 58, 76, 602; **v** 269–70; **vii** 270–1
Government changes, Feb. 1939, **iv** 106
invasion, 1914, **v** 617; **vii** 112
joint offer of 'good offices' by Belgium and Netherlands, Aug. 1939, **vii** 340, 349, 379, 447, 464
King Leopold's proposal for conference, April 1939, **v** 314
neutral position, **i** 648–50, 652; **ii** 395; **iii** 287n; as model for Czechoslovakia, **i** 55, 153, 497, 625; **ii** 393; **iv** 129–30
Press: 'L'Indépendance Belge', **iv** 451; 'Het Laatste Nieuws', **v** 270; 'La Libre Belgique', **v** 269; 'Le Matin', **v** 270; 'La Meuse', **v** 271; 'Le Peuple', **iv** 509; **v** 270; 'De Standaard', **v** 270; 'Le Vingtième Siècle', **v** 271
Staff conversations: with France, **iv** 58, 70, 76, 105, 509; Great Britain, **iv** 78, 104–5; **vi** 221n; Netherlands. **iv** 78, 450, 452
See also Anglo-Franco-Soviet negotiations (Belgium)
Bensheim, **ii** 26
Bérard Agreement, **iv** 461n; **v** 508
Berat-Scutari, **v** 127
Berchtesgaden, **i** 286, 348–9, 362, 552, 568n, 628; **ii** 49, 57, 60, 78, 184, 205, 217, 231, 362–4, 418, 423, 428, 649; **v** 46; **vi** 470
meeting between Herr Hitler and M. Beck, **iii** 566n, 573, 580–2, 585, 589–90; *referred to,* **iii** 525. 568, 581, 587; **iv** 4, 11, 32, 35, 68, 87, 102, 112, 146, 154, 168; **v** 52, 384, 390, 418–9, 441, 455, 601, 619, 699, 813; **vi** 13, 248, 518, 531
meeting between Herr Hitler and M. Burckhardt, **vi** 691–6; *referred to,* **vi** 640, 642–3, 657–9, 662–8, 677, 690–1, 760n; **vii** 6, 8, 11, 13, 16, 23, 31–2, 36, 73, 78, comments on, by Mr. Campbell, **vii** 16–9; by Sir N. Henderson, **vii** 37–8; by Sir H. Kennard, **vii** 49, 51
meeting between Herr Hitler and Mr. Chamberlain, **ii** 338–51, 374–8; *referred to,* **ii** 351–4, 356, 361–2, 404, 407–8, 413, 421–2, 427, 479, 673–4; **iii** 3, 67, 626
preparations for, **ii** 314, 322, 324–6, 331, 334, 647–8
reactions of French Government, **ii** 329, 336–7, 359, 373, 452

Berchtesgaden (Hitler-Chamberlain) (*cont.*)
Herr Schmidt's record of, **ii** 342, 400–1, 410, 428, 430–1
meeting between Herr Hitler and M. François-Poncet, **iii** 244, 618–9
meetings between Herr Hitler and Sir N. Henderson, **vii** 145, 150, 161–3, 201–2, 212–3, 227–31, 251–3, 256–7, 267, 427
meeting between Herr Hitler and Dr. Imredy and M. Kanya, **iii** 9
meeting between Herr Hitler and Mgr. Orsenigo, **v** 462–3
Berchtesgaden Agreement. *See* Treaties (Austria–Germany)
Beregszasz, **iii** 86
Bergen, **ii** 127
Berlin, **i** 18, 155–6, 179, 358, 404; **ii** 60, 68, 76, 87–8, 104–5, 109, 127, 134, 190, 192, 371, 552, 616; **iii** 251, 275, 417; **vi** 175
conference, suggested by Mr. Chamberlain, Sept. 1938, **ii** 587, 590
Herr Hitler's birthday celebrations, **v** 204, 290–3
Berlin-Bernau, **iii** 256
Besigheim, **ii** 26
Bessarabia, **iii** 577; **iv** 619; **v** 104; **vi** 584
Beuthen, **iv** 245
Bezinok, **v** 88
Bialowieza, **iv** 154, 177
Bialystok, **v** 407; **vii** 135
Bielitz, incident, **vii** 231, 235
Bielsko, **v** 246–7; **vi** 204, 552; **vii** 425
Bilbao, **iii** 521
'Bismarck', launching, *referred to,* **iv** 589
Bizerta, internment of Spanish Republican fleet, **iv** 461–2
Black Sea, **iii** 577–8, 668; **v** 589; **vi** 169, 599
Bled, **i** 614; **ii** 144, 261
meeting of permanent Council of Little Entente, **ii** 157–8, 241, 260
provisional agreements between Little Entente and Hungary, **v** 64n, 332; **vi** 642n
Böblingen, **ii** 26
Bodenbach, **i** 437
Bodenstadt, **iii** 136, 641
Bogumin (Oderberg), **iii** 46, 49n, 60, 82, 104–5, 136, 223, 228–9; **iv** 513, 617; **v** 246–7; **vi** 13, 710
Bohemia, **i** 105, 107, 183–4, 190, 193, 223, 251, 279, 300–3, 327, 404–5, 465, 479, 487, 491, 502, 515, 613; **ii** 80, 186, 364, 368, 522, 549, 552, 570, 592; **iii** 118, 134, 139, 165, 207, 216, 225, 626; **iv** 56, 244, 248–9, 260, 267, 270, 362, 379; *see also* next heading
Bohemia and Moravia
German occupation, **iv** 255–8, 260–1, 267, 275, 379, 404–5, 444, 560–1; *referred to,* **v** 304, 616–7, 684; **vi** 5, 13–4, 72, 133, 277, 280, 290–1, 297, 306, 373, 408, 497, 616, 659, 693, 712, 750, 754; **vii** 38, 48

Bohemia and Moravia (German occupation) (*cont.*)

reactions of: France, **iv** 273, 368, 371, 376–7, 394–5, 461; Great Britain, **iv** 263, 267, 271–3, 291, 350n, 364–5, 371–2, 376, 379, 381, 402–3, 526, 583–4, 595–6, 615; **v** 9, 245, 337, 600, 617, 619, 675, 713–4, 780, 791, 801, 804; **vi** 76, 114, 751; **vii** 60, 111, 550; Hungary, **iv** 618, 625; Italy, **iv** 273, 281–2, 294, 350–2, 379, 461; Japan, **viii** 536; Netherlands, **iv** 450; Poland, **iv** 616; **v** 9, 10, 424–5, 563, 570, 580, 601; **vi** 57–8, 258; Roumania, **iv** 284, 618–9, 625; **v** 301; Scandinavian and Baltic States, **iv** 622; Turkey, **v** 615; U.S.S.R., **iv** 385, 391, 445–8, 621–2; United States, **iv** 364, 366, 481–2; Yugoslavia, **iv** 620–1, 625; **v** 529

Bohemia and Moravia, Protectorate of
formation and administration, **iv** 272, 275–6, 279, 287–9, 470, 481, 561–6, 583; **v** 554–7; **vi** 581
importance to Germany, **iv** 393–4, 477, 536–9, 586–8, 624

Böhler Bros. Ltd., **i** 93
Böhmerwald, **iii** 83
Böhmisch Kamnitz, **ii** 662
Böhmisch-Krumau, **iii** 640
Böhmisch Leipa (Ceska Lipa), **i** 182, 432; **ii** 232, 552, 660; **iii** 640
Böhmisch Trübau (Ceska Trebová), **iii** 207; **iv** 57
Bohnsack, **vi** 32–3, 149, 393
Bohumin, **iii** 73, 225
Bolivia, **v** 701, 711
Bologna, **iv** 338
Bolzano, **iv** 338; **v** 171, 173; **vi** 659; *see also* South Tyrol
Bordeaux, **ii** 262
Boulogne, **ii** 532; **iii** 617
Boxer Indemnity, **viii** 14n, 138n, 516; **ix** 150, 246, 353
Brackenheim, **ii** 26
Brandenburg, **ii** 161
Bratislava (Pressburg), **i** 106–7, 171, 302, 342; **ii** 281, 667; **iii** 111, 152, 188, 198, 200, 203, 217, 230, 384, 412–3, 639; **iv** 95–6, 220, 231, 233–7, 241–2, 244, 255, 264, 287, 362, 408, 438, 440, 442, 595; **v** 89; **vi** 137
Braunau, **i** 579–80; **iii** 641
Brazil, **iii** 519; **iv** 25
Bremen, **iii** 85, 98; **vi** 171–2, 184
Brenner frontier, **ii** 309; **iv** 23; **vi** 488, 554–5 guaranteed by Herr Hitler, **ii** 147, 345; **vi** 324 proposed meeting between Herr Hitler and Signor Mussolini, **vi** 667; **vii** 24, 103
Breslau, **i** 61, 301, 358; **ii** 6, 95, 203n, 370; **iii** 91, 123, 235, 240, 417; **iv** 232, 234, 245, 443; **v** 204; **vii** 515
Breslau Festival (German National Gymnastic Festival), **ii** 39, 59, 81, 91, 102, 133

Breslau–Vienna motor road, **iii** 235, 240, 409, 415–7, 441, 449, 648
Brest-Litovsk, **vii** 496
Briand-Kellogg Pact, **i** 63–4; **ii** 546n; **v** 350
Brindisi, **iv** 358; **v** 117
Brioni, **iii** 174
British-American Tobacco Company, **ix** 86
British Broadcasting Company (B.B.C.), **v** 236–7, 253, 275, 384, 385n
British Chamber of Commerce (Shanghai), **ix** 292, 326
British Commonwealth of Nations (British Empire), **i** 84, 89, 96, 227, 602; **ii** 53, 59, 84–5, 95, 132, 159, 174, 262, 293, 303, 365, 394–5, 429, 568, 681, 688; **iii** 142–4, 245n, 246, 351, 500, 571, 590; **iv** 46, 251, 309, 527; **v** 371, 423, 617, 791–2; **vi** 61, 73, 416, 487, 722, 730, 756, 758–9; **vii** 355n; **viii** 345–7
commercial relations with Japan, **viii** 264–5, 305, 314, 347
Germany's offer relating to, **vi** 43; **vii** 229, 320
Jewish problem and, **iii** 295–6
British Guiana, **iii** 295, 343
British Legion of Ex-Service Men, **ii** 57n, 572, 622; **iii** 65–6, 75, 85–6, 98, 112, 117, 120, 130, 148, 169, 172–3, 551
British Somaliland, **iii** 528; **iv** 302; **v** 457
Brittany, **iii** 479
Brno (Brünn), **i** 107, 171, 349, 373; **ii** 449, 475, 549, 632; **iii** 86, 148–50, 196, 207, 228, 417, 627, 640; **iv** 56–7, 63, 231, 235, 251, 261, 264, 270, 442, 562; **v** 555–6, 803
Bromberg. *See* Bydgoszez
Bruck, **iv** 234–5
Brunswick, **ii** 127
Brüsau, **iv** 57
Brüx, **ii** 183, 446, 663; **iii** 640
Brzesc, **v** 407
Bucharest, **ii** 291
meetings of Balkan Entente, **v** 297n, 308, 491n, 686
suggested conference, Mar. 1939. *See* U.S.S.R.
Buchen, **ii** 26
Budapest, **ii** 218, 615
Büdingen, **ii** 26
Budweis, **i** 106; **ii** 596, 603; **iii** 84; **iv** 267
Bukovina, **iii** 565
Bulgaria, i 79; **ii** 651; **iv** 104; **v** 159, 169, 181, 227, 241, 531; **vi** 18, 102
France, **v** 395, 403
Germany, **v** 109–10, 213, 285, 464; **vi** 111–2, 216, 263, 324, 344–5, 412, 496–7, 746
Italy, **v** 285; **vi** 18
minorities, **vi** 583
Roumania, **iii** 46; **iv** 333, 433, 498, 620; **v** 109n, 207, 296, 308–9, 326–8, 380, 387, 464, 530; **vi** 18–9, 30, 53, 68, 84, 147, 583
Turkey, **vi** 195, 438
U.S.S.R., **v** 411, 433–4, 530–1

Bulgaria (*cont.*)
war in Europe, probable attitude, **vi** 344, 496, 618
Yugoslavia, **v** 285, 334, 672; **vi** 344, 438, 583
See also Anglo-Franco-Soviet negotiations (Bulgaria); Balkan Entente (admission of Bulgaria)
Burgenland, **i** 148; **ii** 281; **iii** 185
Burgos. *See* Spain and Spanish Civil War (Gen. Franco's administration)
Burma, and Sino-Japanese conflict, **viii** 160, 293, 306
Burma–Yunnan Air Service, **viii** 142
Burma–Yunnan railway project, **viii** 130, 142
Burma–Yunnan road, **viii** 4*n*, 142, 147, 173, 184, 245; **ix** 395
lorries for, **viii** 142, 147, 173, 245, 309, 312, 330, 335, 540
Butterfield and Swire, Messrs., **viii** 288, 350, 441*n*, 528; **ix** 61, 156, 178, 322
Bütow, **vii** 461
Bydgoszcz, **iv** 525, 545*n*; **v** 42, 247–8; **vi** 94, 551–2; **vii** 432, 460

Cadca, **iii** 82, 186, 188, 219
Cadiz, **iii** 320, 322, 325; **v** 56, 143–4
Calabria, **iv** 338
Calais, **ii** 532
Calatayud, **iii** 314
Calw, **ii** 26
Cameroons, The, **vi** 348
Campania, **iv** 338
Canada, **ii** 174, 451; **vii** 628; **viii** 147
Canton, **vii** 629; **viii** 25, 37, 43, 88, 125–6, 189–90, 195, 207, 215; capture by Japanese, **viii** 176, 177*n*, 216–7
Customs Administration, taken over by Japanese. *See* Chinese Maritime Customs Administration
Capital ships: limitation of tonnage, **iii** 670; **iv** 628–37
Capri, **iv** 338
Carbonia, **iii** 489
Carinthia, **i** 43
Carlsbad, **i** 217, 250, 436, 438, 595; **ii** 69, 304–5, 319, 664, 671–2
Carlsbad Programme (i.e. Herr Henlein's eight demands in speech at Carlsbad), **i** 185; *referred to*, **i** 186–7, 215, 238, 249–50, 252, 255, 285, 297, 299, 308–9, 372, 415, 449, 453, 458, 461, 496, 555, 596; **ii** 111, 177, 180–2, 192, 196, 199, 200, 207–8, 210, 221, 223, 227–8, 232–3, 238, 240, 245–6, 248, 250, 252–4, 257, 261, 266–7, 274, 280, 289, 309–10, 315, 327, 331–2, 647, 656–7, 666, 668, 670, 675–6
Carpathians, **ii** 474
Cawnpore, **vi** 127
Central China Telecommunications Company, **viii** 124

Cernova massacre (1907), **iv** 98
Cervenka, **iii** 641; **iv** 57
Ceska Budejovice. *See* Budweis
Ceska Lipa. *See* Böhmisch Leipa
Ceska Trebová. *See* Böhmisch Trübau
Cesky Tesin. *See* Teschen
Chabowka, **v** 246–7
Chahar Province, **viii** 32
Cham, **i** 61; **ii** 27
Chamuria, **v** 751
Changkufeng, **viii** 26*n*, 40*n*, 149; *see also* Japan (U.S.S.R.)
Changsha, **viii** 27, 169
Chang Yin Sha, **ix** 153
Chapei, **viii** 28*n*; **ix** 336
Chefoo, **viii** 52*n*, 279, 284–5, 287–8; **ix** 349–50, 355, 383
Chefoo Harbour Improvement Commission, **viii** 287
Chekiang, **viii** 203
Chemnitz, **i** 358
Chiesch, **iii** 640
China, viii and **ix** *passim*
Banks and currencies: Bank of China, **viii** 11, 100, 120*n*, 225–6, 230, 255, 397, 486; **ix** 23, 188, 390, 536–8; Bank of Communications, **viii** 10, 35, 100, 225, 230, 255, 486; **ix** 188, 246, 380, 426–7, 430, 447, 502, 536–8; Banque Franco-Chinoise, **viii** 10; Banque de l'Indo-Chine, **viii** 10; **ix** 113, 168, 467, 538; Bank of Japan, **ix** 57, 273*n*; Chartered Bank of India, Australia and China, **viii** 225, 297, 486–7, 505; **ix** 467; Chase Bank, **viii** 120*n*, 123*n*, 133; Federal Reserve Bank, and currency, **viii** 72, 100, 225–6, 240, 316–9, 331, 389, 398, 490, 494, 500, 513; **ix** 17*n*, 18, 31, 45–6, 224, 244, 247, 250, 325, 330, 350, 380, 393, 420, 427, 447, 449, 452, 483, 537; Hongkong and Shanghai Bank, **viii** 14*n*, 123, 257, 280, 297–8, 329, 374, 400, 486–7, 505; **ix** 55, 246; Hua Hsing Commercial Bank, and currency, **ix** 30, 35–6, 46, 54–6, 58*n*, 61, 63, 87, 93–5, 103, 107, 115, 125, 145–6, 347, 454, 507, 538; Yokohama Specie Bank, **viii** 14*n*, 63, 233, 409, 496; **ix** 154, 330, 350, 380, 427, 447
Customs administration. *See* Chinese Maritime Customs Administration
extraterritorial rights, **viii** 215, 332–3, 340, 342, 373, 405; **ix** 532
Germany, **viii** 21, 189
Government of Nationalist China (and the Kuomintang), **viii** 2*n*, 6*n*, 177*n*, 218–9, 249–50, 284; **ix** 92–3, 423; *see also* Chiang Kai-shek, Generalissimo, in Index of Persons
Great Britain
British diplomatic representation, **viii** 2*n*, 179*n*
British policy towards, **viii** 178–9, 198–9, 217–9, 381, 441, 474

China (Great Britain) *(cont.)*
  British troops in, **viii** 9*n*, 106, 114–5, 137–8, 233*n*, 234
  Chinese troops offered for defence of Hong Kong, **ix** 52, 53*n*, 238, 240, 372, 476
  financial aid to China, **viii** 1*n*, 59, 130, 196, 217–8, 257–8, 262, 281, 295, 308–9, 337, 341, 391, 455, 467; **ix** 59, 335, 341, 391
    export credits, **viii** 1*n*, 14,.58–60, 68, 93, 102–3, 130, 142–3, 147, 173, 245, 309, 312, 329–30, 335–6, 342, 344–5, 373, 430, 470, 472–3, 540–1; **ix** 8, 19, 24, 293–4, 334, 353*n*, 355, 367–8, 373, 389–91, 485
    refusal of loan, July 1938, **viii** 7*n*; effect on China, **viii** 6, 7, 10–1, 93; on Japan, **viii** 27, 29, 44, 48–50, 54
    support of Chinese currency. *See* Chinese Currency Stabilization Fund; Tientsin (negotiations in Tokyo)
  suggested visit to Great Britain of T. V. Soong, **viii** 377, 379
  International Settlements and Concessions. *See* Amoy (Kulangsu Settlement); Shanghai (International Settlement); Tientsin (British, French and Italian Concessions); Japan (International Settlements in China, statement relating to)
  Japan
    policy towards Kuomintang régime, **viii** 30, 31*n*; *see also* Japan (East Asia); Sino-Japanese conflict
    trading relations, **ix** 104, 115
  Japanese-occupied districts
    administration: Provisional Government (at Peking), **viii** 3*n*, 10*n*; **ix** 63–4, 132, 246, 252, 260*n*, 280*n*, 369, 393, 424–5, 463, 499; Reformed Government (at Nanking), **viii** 2*n*; **ix** 11, 30, 36, 93; suggested new Central Government, **viii** 74, 277, 297, 355–6; **ix** 242, 252, 254, 259, 392; *see also* Wang Ching-wei in Index of Persons
    anti-British activities, **ix** 308, 388, 397–8, 401, 438–40, 445, 452–3, 459, 491–2
    attitude of Great Britain, **viii** 297; **ix** 342 *n*, 343, 379
    trade and exchange control, **viii** 490–1, 494–8, 500, 513; **ix** 17–8, 40, 63–4, 114–5, 124, 164, 246, 252, 274–5, 330–1
    withdrawal of foreign troops and warships suggested, **ix** 526–7
  Kuomintang, The. *See above*, Government of Nationalist China
  League of Nations. *See* Sino-Japanese conflict (sanctions against Japan)
  Press, **ix** 21, 66*n*, 87; 'Chungking joint Daily News', **ix** 343; 'Peking and Tientsin Times', **viii** 126*n*, 335, 511, 512*n*; 'Sin Shun Pao', **ix** 336; 'Yung Pao', **viii** 446, 458
  proposal for joint action by China, France,

China *(cont.)*
  Great Britain and U.S., **ix** 5–8, 13 ,25, 31, 52
  silver reserves in North China, **viii** 10*n*; **ix** 467–8, 536–8; at Tientsin, **viii** 35, 100, 119–20, 123, 125, 133, 186, 225–6, 230–1, 256, 270, 308, 316–7, 327, 338, 388–9, 417–8, 440; **ix** 246, 268, 275, 331, 355–6, 380, 393, 430, 452, 460, 463, 484; *see also* Tientsin (negotiations in Tokyo)
    Peking–Tientsin Silver Custody Committee, **viii** 35, 226; **ix** 452, 538
    Reserve Fund Custody Committee (Currency Reserve Board), **viii** 35; **ix** 536–8
  U.S. and financial assistance, **iii** 308; **viii** 66, 69, 127*n*, 199, 212, 246, 249, 296*n*, 302, 311, 335–6, 340, 374, 379, 384–5, 428–9, 461–2; **ix** 23, 249
  U.S.S.R., **viii** 8, 11, 102, 198, 219, 249
  war in Europe, probable attitude, **ix** 5*n*, 17, 31
  See also Japan (East Asia, Japanese policy); Sino-Japanese conflict
China Association, **viii** 191; **ix** 66, 292, 326
China Egg Produce Company, **viii** 331
China Purchasing Commission, **viii** 540; **ix** 334
Chinese Bondholders Committee, **viii** 483*n*
Chinese Currency Stabilization Fund
  establishment of, **viii** 486–7, 505–6; exhaustion of, **viii** 104, 115–6, 188, 248, 292–3, 490
  France, **ix** 105, 112–3, 118, 150, 163, 167–8, 214, 248
  Great Britain, **iii** 309; **viii** 161*n*, 257, 280–1, 297–8, 301, 329, 369, 374, 416–7, 422, 431, 442, 477; **ix** 29, 110, 117–8, 128, 150, 163, 167–8, 214, 248–9, 293, 295; attitude towards further contribution, **ix** 513
  Japanese reaction to establishment of, **viii** 503–4, 518–9, 537*n*; **ix** 12, 31; *see also* Japan (Great Britain, effect on Anglo-Japanese relations of Great Britain's financial aid to China)
  United States, **viii** 311, 335, 384–5, 428–9
Chinese Maritime Customs Administration, **viii** 52, 153
  Anglo-Japanese Agreement of May 2, 1938, **viii** 14*n*
    implementation of, **viii** 14, 231, 261, 370, 387–8, 392–3, 399, 401, 416, 429–30, 433, 435–6, 442, 451, 516; **ix** 116, 150, 246, 276, 353
  Anglo-Japanese understanding of 1936, **viii** 213, 315
  demands for additional Japanese staff, **viii** 153, 160, 164–8, 181, 185, 213–4, 242–3, 315, 524–6, 533, 537, 539–40; **ix** 24, 37
  suspension by Chinese Government of payments on Customs loans, **viii** 396–7, 399, 401, 409–11, 416, 431, 436, 482–3
  take-over of Canton Customs by Japanese, **viii** 214, 224, 238, 240, 283, 334, 352
Chinese Trading Commission, **viii** 472–3

Chojnice, **iii** 251; **iv** 81; **vii** 327
Chorzele, **vii** 484
Chungking, **viii** 2*n*, 42, 158
Chusenji, **ix** 478
Chust, **iii** 384, 413
Cieszyn. *See* Teschen
Cologne, **i** 156; **ii** 350, 418; **vi** 657
Comintern, The, **i** 391, 511; **iii** 280; **iv** 603
Commissions
  Czech–Polish Boundary, **iii** 219, 223
  Danube, European Commission, **v** 300*n*
  Elbe, International Commission, **iv** 63
  Evian, **iii** 432
  International (Ambassadors' Commission)
    provided for in Munich Agreement, **ii** 628–
    30, 632–5; **iii** 56–7, 61, 64–7, 93*n*, 100, 122–3,
    148–51, 163, 165, 167–8, 172, 207–8, 234–5,
    239, 241–2, 375, 379, 408, 432, 639–56
    proposed formation, **ii** 391–2, 464, 475, 477,
    496, 505, 522, 525, 530–1, 550, 571–3
    members, **ii** 629
    meetings, **iii** 56, 91, 109, 128–35, 169–70,
    175–8, 235, 241, 654–6
    Sub-Committees, **iii** 56, 108, 116, 129–35,
    162–5, 170, 176–8, 196, 207–8, 639–49
Committees
  in Bohemia and Moravia, Protectorate of:
    Committee of the National Community, **iv**
    470, 565–6; **v** 557
  in Czechoslovakia: Committee of Six Deputies
    (Dr. Meissner's Committee), **i** 546–7, 570,
    579; **ii** 50, 70, 75, 93*n*, 662–3, 665, 668;
    National Committee formed Mar. 1939, **iv**
    280, 565; National Local Committee in
    Silesia, 1918, **iii** 12
  Hong Kong Committee, **viii** 537
  of League of Nations
    Committee of Three on Danzig. *See* Danzig
    (League of Nations)
    Far East Advisory Committee, **viii** 67–8,
    144; **ix** 105, 121, 142
  Non-Intervention Committee. *See* Spain and
    Spanish Civil War
Communism and Communists, **i** 274; **ii** 11, 14,
65, 118; **iii** 499
  Austria, **i** 17, 20, 24, 59, 129, 147
  China, **viii** 85, 198, 219, 381
  Czechoslovakia, **i** 126, 280, 350, 377, 390–1,
    398, 490; **ii** 9, 167, 177, 466; **iii** 75, 83, 111–2,
    165, 215, 217, 410, 412; **iv** 62, 562; **viii** 85
  Danzig Free State, **vi** 455
  France, **ii** 270, 544, 568*n*, 580, 588, 622–3;
    iii 88, 156–7, 160, 479, 483, 516; **vi** 150–1;
    vii 245, 313, 342
  Germany, **ii** 508
  Poland, **iii** 105; **vii** 87
  Slovakia, **iii** 217
  Spain, **ii** 636–7; **iii** 320, 325
Conferences
  Ambassadors', **iii** 33; **v** 125, 132, 141

Conferences (*cont.*)
  Brussels, of 1937, **viii** 199, 301*n*; **ix** 42, 237,
    348*n*
  Evian, **iii** 295
  Hague Reparations, **i** 366
  Inter-Parliamentary, Oslo, Aug. 1939, **vii** 67
  Montreux, **v** 530
  Munich. *See* Munich Conference
  Nyon, **v** 530
  Palestine, **iv** 208–9
  Paris Peace (1919), **i** 182–4, 188, 192, 301–3;
    ii 333, 358, 403; **iv** 294; **vi** 15
  San Remo, **vi** 346–7
  Stresa, **i** 47, 303; **iv** 297
  Versailles. *See above*, Paris Peace (1919)
  Vienna. *See* Vienna Award and Conference
  Whaling, **v** 793; **vi** 467, 482
Conferences, suggestions for. *See* Belgium,
  Italy, Sudeten German question, U.S.S.R.,
  United States, Vatican
Conversations between representatives of Great
  Britain and:—
  Belgium. *See* Anglo-Belgian Staff conversations
  France. *See* Anglo-French conversations;
    Anglo-French Staff conversations; Anglo-
    Franco-Soviet military conversations
  Germany. *See* Germany (Great Britain, Naval
    Agreements)
  Italy. *See* Italy (Great Britain)
  Poland. *See* Anglo-Polish Staff conversations;
    Poland (Great Britain, visit of M. Beck)
  Roumania. *See* Anglo-Roumanian conver-
    sations
  U.S.S.R. *See* Anglo-Franco-Soviet military
    conversations
Corfu, **v** 82, 116, 120, 141–3, 145–7, 154–5,
  157–9, 164, 167
Corsica, **iii** 390, 463–7, 474–5, 480, 487, 512,
  608; **iv** 317; **v** 614, 797
Cottbus, **i** 358
Cracow, **i** 445; **iii** 16–7; **iv** 177; **v** 246–7, 407;
  vii 415, 474, 476, 485, 496, 533
Croatia, **iv** 352, 379
Cruisers, German decision to increase arma-
  ment. *See* Germany (Great Britain, Naval
  Agreements)
Csap, **iii** 86
Cyprus, **vi** 127
Czaca, **vii** 160
Czarny-Dunajec, **v** 246–7
Czechoslovak Co-operative Society, **iii** 648
Czechoslovakia
  air force, **ii** 320; absorption into German air
    force, **iv** 587–8; **v** 102
  Anglo-French economic and financial assis-
    tance, **i** 232, 628; **ii** 661, 672; **iii** 81, 195–6,
    221, 380–1, 401, 418, 560, 629–38; **iv** 1–3,
    13–5, 85*n*, 109, 277–8; **viii** 218
    text of financial agreement, Jan. 1939, **iv**
    25–6

Czechoslovakia (*cont.*)

army, **i** 105-7, 218, 221, 271, 462-3, 566-7, 609; **ii** 258-9, 281, 539, 575*n*, 581-2, 609-10; **iii** 253, 255

attitude towards concessions to Sudeten Germans, **i** 116, 439; **ii** 35, 281, 336, 357, 641; statement by Officers' Association, **ii** 81, 89, 90, 100, 111, 145

disbandment, **iv** 393

General Staff, **i** 61-2, 67, 104-7, 181, 327-9, 349, 368, 380-1, 397, 400, 405, 411, 424, 433, 446, 449, 451, 462, 471, 473, 543, 566; **ii** 81, 89, 90, 99, 132, 146-7, 176, 186-7, 258-9, 280-1, 304*n*, 308, 364, 368, 411-2, 544, 563, 567, 591-2

three years' service, **i** 463, 471, 473-5, 478, 486, 492-4, 504, 569, 577, 590; **ii** 46, 116, 125, 192

reorganization, after Sept. 1938, **iii** 165, 306; **iv** 65, 126, 204

strength and readiness for war, **i** 105-7, 218, 221, 271, 462-3, 566-7, 609; **ii** 258-9, 281, 539, 575*n*, 581-2, 609-10; **iii** 253, 255

See also sub-head (military measures)

Finance Guards, **ii** 186

France, **i** 73, 86, 102, 126, 140, 143-6, 153, 158, 160-1, 195, 232, 242, 253, 277, 299*n*, 314, 325, 332, 336, 351-2, 357, 360, 366, 379, 383-4, 415, 419, 459, 462, 468, 477-8, 497, 499, 500, 503, 523-4, 527, 545-6, 548-9, 577, 600, 605-6, 618, 620, 647, 650; **ii** 1, 38-9, 96-7, 125, 147, 194, 216, 272, 353 395-6

French commitments, **i** 36, 50-4, 72, 83, 85, 94, 105, 108, 139, 152, 213, 218, 236, 340, 342, 379, 496-7, 545; **ii** 1, 73, 123-4, 160, 263, 314, 323, 380-1, 383-7, 396, 444*n*; **iii** 88; **iv** 241; *see also* Treaties

See also sub-head (Anglo-French economic and financial assistance) *above*; Sudeten German question (attitude of France and Great Britain)

Germany

agreement between, suggested, **i** 72-3

economic relations, **i** 50, 55-6, 87, 111, 140*n*, 153-4, 219, 237, 268, 301, 315,˙405, 578, 580-1; **ii** 268, 661; **iii** 92, 131, 167*n*, 176, 178, 192, 204, 410-1, 565, 634-5; **iv** 2, 7-8, 62, 64-5, 86, 173, 393, 477, 505, 535-9, 567; **v** 456

German assurances after Austrian 'Anschluss', **i** 24, 33-7, 40-1, 47, 51, 61-2, 65-6, 76, 87, 95, 104, 112

military preparations against, Mar. 1938, **i** 20, 61-2, 66-7, 95, 104; May, **i** 317-8, 321, 323, 327-9, 331-2, 335, 337, 339, 342, 344, 349, 352-5, 358-9, 361, 363, 368-9, 380-1, 411-4, 457, 585; **ii** 46, 113*n*, 145, 506; **iii** 546; *see also* Germany (Great Britain, *démarche* of May 21-2); June, **i** 448, 450-1; July-Sept., **i** 554, 561, 568*n*,

Czechoslovakia (Germany) (*cont*).

580, 610-3; **ii** 13-6, 85, 126, 161, 319-20, 369-72, 382-3, 387-8, 424, 427, 451, 453-4, 461, 473-4, 491, 544-5, 552, 567, 570, 574, 578, 592, 615-6, 623-8; **iii** 625

reported decision of Herr Hitler to attack, **i** 611; **ii** 125, 212, 242, 245, 275, 291, 369, 473, 570, 574, 578-9, 585

possible German attack, attitude of:—

France and Great Britain. *See* Sudeten German question; Germany (Great Britain)

Hungary, **i** 271; **ii** 516, 562, 575*n*; **iii** 36, 628

Italy, **i** 265; **ii** 233*n*, 234, 239-40, 294, 516, 562, 588, 600, 614, 626, 643, 691; **iii** 161, 334-6, 346-52

Poland, **i** 257, 258*n*, 265, 267, 271, 431*n*, 444-5, 512, 551; **ii** 288, 294, 318, 516, 538-9, 543, 562, 575*n*; **iii** 8, 33, 36, 101, 628

U.S.S.R., **i** 65, 108, 162, 172-3, 213, 265, 267, 280-1, 289, 305-7, 346; **iii** 141*n*, 164, 168, 220, 229, 255, 270, 272, 323, 354*n*, 355, 441, 480, 484, 489, 497-8, 509, 532, 550*n*, 575*n*; **iii** 67, 143, 153, 628; **iv** 426

United States, **ii** 149, 213, 219, 284-5, 293*n*, 296, 301, 317, 617, 687; **vii** 627-9

Yugoslavia, **i** 108, 615; **ii** 260, 562

relations after Munich Agreement, **iii** 114, 118, 121, 123-4, 151, 174, 187, 190-2, 201, 221-2, 241, 367-8, 380, 385, 407-17, 446, 548, 550, 584, 608; **iv** 2, 56, 121, 129-31, 215, 222, 227*n*, 232, 234-49, 255, 263, 441-5, 604; *see also* Bohemia and Moravia

Great Britain

Czech. gold in Great Britain, **iv** 366; **v** 713

Czech. request for intervention of Great Britain, with Germany, **i** 114, 158-60, 374; with Hungary, **iii** 115, 140, with Italy, **iii** 140; with Poland, **iii** 49, 50*n*, 61

guarantee by, **ii** 405, 445, 447, 469, 628; **iii** 116*n*, 118, 120, 127, 186, 222, 303, 398-9, 440, 515, 619; **iv** 17, 267, 273; *see also* Guarantee (to Czechoslovakia)

See also sub-heads (Anglo-French economic and financial assistance) *above* and (Hungary), (Poland) *below*; Munich Conference and Agreement; Sudeten German question; Teschen area

Hungary, **i** 257, 265, 271, 338; **ii** 157, 459-60, 475; **iii** 6, 11, 18, 29, 37, 43; **iv** 8, 204

attitude of Great Britain towards Hungarian claims, **ii** 459-60; **iii** 1-2, 4, 11, 18, 20, 29, 30, 37, 48-9, 75, 113-4, 116, 121, 125-6, 141-2, 153, 189, 191, 194, 200-3

negotiations: preparations for, **iii** 66, 74-6, 79-81, 86, 113-6, 140-2; course of, **iii**

Czechoslovakia (Hungary) (*cont.*)
152, 155, 170–1, 173–5, 184–9, 191, 197–8, 200–6, 209–11, 237; arbitration by Germany and Italy, **iii** 211–2, 218, 220–1; *see also* Vienna Conference and Award
See also sub-head (minorities) *below*; Ruthenia; Slovakia
Internal conditions, **i** 71, 124, 191, 268, 301, 489, 518, 522, 556, 594–5; **ii** 34, 166–7, 661–2, 664, 677, 679; **iii** 81, 192, 214–9, 385, 401–2, 410–3, 634–5; **iv** 61–2
Italy. *See* sub-head (Germany; possible German attack) *above*; Ruthenia
Legionaries, **i** 116; **iv** 61
Little Entente, **ii** 157–8
local defence corps (Straž Obrany Statu), **ii** 552*n*
local elections, **i** 77–8, 124, 126, 186–7, 215, 242, 269, 275–6, 278, 283, 319, 323–4, 329–30, 344, 350*n*, 353, 363, 371, 374, 378, 382, 385, 390, 395–6, 400, 430–1, 448–9, 462, 466, 478, 499, 544; **ii** 1, 29, 468, 470, 524
military measures, **i** 328–494 *passim*, 559, 566–7, 576, 579–81, 584, 599, 609, 654; **ii** 9, 320, 334, 349, 351, 368–73, 387–8, 551–2, 661, 664; **iv** 42; **vii** 625–6
mobilization, **ii** 369–70, 372–4, 388, 492–3, 501, 506, 511, 543–5, 548–9, 591–2, 675; *see also* Sudeten German question (attitude of France and Great Britain)
National Defence Law, **i** 347–8, 556; **ii** 661
national defence unions (Narodni Jednota organizations), **ii** 90*n*, 357
See also Sudetenland (martial law)
minorities. *See also below* (nationality policy of)
   decision of Munich Conference, **ii** 629, 632, 635; **iii** 53, 74–5, 80, 125, 139, 186, 209, 224
   Germans in Sudetenland, *see* Sudeten German question; other German minorities, **iii** 223, 225, 385, 409, 413, 415; **iv** 7, 54, 62–3, 86, 126–8, 144, 149–50, 204, 230–1, 240, 242–4, 251, 255–7, 261, 270, 282, 404, 443
   Hungarians (Magyars), **i** 77, 188–91, 237, 300, 471, 625; **ii** 147, 157, 279, 315, 340, 345, 376, 381–2, 392, 465, 467, 475, 629, 632, 635, 655, 662, 667; **iii** 2, 4–5, 10–1, 17, 19, 21, 26, 37, 42, 44, 49, 111–3, 115, 141, 171, 184, 220–1, 385
   Jews. *See* Jews (Czechoslovakia)
   Poles, **i** 189–91, 237, 300, 471, 512; **ii** 190, 279, 315, 392, 465, 467, 475, 655, 667; **iii** 80, 228
      Committee for defending rights of Poles in Czechoslovakia, **iii** 8
      demand for same treatment as Sudeten Germans, **i** 315, 465, 481, 560; **ii** 82–3, 340, 345, 376, 381–2, 441; **iii** 3, 6–8, 13–7, 19, 24, 101

Czechoslovakia (minorities) (*cont.*)
   promised any concessions granted to Sudeten Germans, **i** 315, 465; **ii** 190, 475; **iii** 1, 17, 39, 43
   Ruthenes (Ruthenians) and Ukrainians, **i** 189–90, 443; **ii** 315, 345, 403; **iii** 97, 112–3, 141, 184, 201, 222–3, 525, 576
   Slovaks, **i** 77, 166–8, 182, 429–30, 443, 465, 512, 540; **ii** 315, 340, 347, 381–2, 403, 465, 467; **iii** 80, 82, 91, 97, 111–2, 114, 122, 125, 137, 171, 184, 216–7, 223, 407–8, 412, 615; **iv** 94, 157, 183, 200, 219, 238
      agreement of October 6, 1938 (The Sillein Agreement), **iii** 114, 122, 125, 141, 187; **iv** 219
      autonomy law of Nov. 22, 1938, **iv** 238
      See also Slovakia (independence movement); (internal conditions)
   nationality policy of, **i** 73–4, 77–8, 95, 113–8, 125–6, 138, 142, 152, 158–60, 167–72, 179–82, 186, 188–636 *passim*; **ii** 10, 23, 28–9, 33–5, 75–6, 95, 97, 111, 114, 121–2, 220–1, 402–4, 433, 475; **iii** 385
      administrative reforms, **i** 77, 192–4, 311, 459, 470, 518–9, 521–2, 547; **ii** 165, 228–9, 656, 662, 675
      agreement with Activist parties, Feb. 1937, **i** 191–2, 228, 509; **ii** 33, 228
      Language Law, **i** 192, 279, 509, 521–2, 530–1, 540, 543*n*, 547, 557, 559–60, 576, 598–9, 609, 641–2; **ii** 49, 165, 675
      draft Statute of Nationality Laws of Czechoslovak Republic, **i** 126, 183–4, 192–4, 215, 243, 269, 278, 319, 338, 394–5, 443, 447–9, 453, 458, 462, 466–7, 486, 502, 504, 518, 521, 537–8, 540–3, 547, 556–7, 560, 567, 569, 577, 579, 582, 590, 598, 608, 613–4; **ii** 11, 49, 63–4, 110, 130, 165, 222, 675
         text of, **i** 170–2
         communicated to France and Great Britain, **i** 158, 160, 180–1, 215–6
         Mr. Newton's comments on, **i** 167–70, 181
      suggested 'State of Nationalities', **i** 114–5, 215–6, 242–3, 260, 262–4, 269–70, 273, 277, 291, 308, 312, 556, 596, 613, 624; **ii** 36, 40; **vii** 623–4
      See also Sudeten German question (negotiations between Czechoslovak Govt. and Sudeten German representatives)
   neutralization of, **i** 55, 73, 139–40, 152–4, 279–80, 379, 405, 410, 452, 458, 497, 498*n*, 535, 549–50, 552, 614, 625, 647–52; **ii** 20, 72, 150, 347, 393–6, 661; **iii** 527; **iv** 129–31, 136, 141–2; *see also* Guarantee (to Czechoslovakia)
   Poland, **i** 110, 213–4, 247, 315–6, 338, 351, 364, 421, 429–31, 445, 464–5, 474, 478–81, 512, 550–1; **ii** 218, 287–8, 318, 459–60, 604; **iii** 7–8, 12, 16, 24–5, 31–6, 38–43, 46, 48, 49*n*, 51–5, 58–64, 66, 68–73, 82, 97, 100–6, 110,

Czechoslovakia (Poland) (*cont.*)
146, 156, 179–82, 188, 199, 211–2, 228–9, 364, 366n, 378–9, 384, 419–20, 424, 430–1, 565; iv 204, 262
  Agreement of Nov. 1, 1938, iii 212, 218–20, 222, 239
  attitude of Great Britain towards Polish claims against Czechoslovakia, ii 459–60; iii 1, 13–4, 18, 23–4, 28–9, 31, 40–1, 50, 53–4, 59, 60, 189–90; *see also* Teschen area
  expected reaction to German attack on Czechoslovakia. *See* sub-head (Germany) *See also* sub-head (minorities: Poles) *above*; Slovakia (Poland); Teschen area
  political parties: Activist parties, the, i 64, 69, 74, 102, 124, 183, 191, 250, 311, 509n; ii 31, 33, 674; Aufbruch group, i 69n, 249–50; Communist party, *see* Communism (in Czechoslovakia); Czech. Agrarian Republican party, i 309, 313; ii 167; iii 217; iv 157; Czech. People's Catholic party, i 74, 311, 472; iii 96, 214; v 85; Czech. Small Traders party, iii 96, 214; Czech. Social Democratic party, i 377, 390; iii 214, 410; *Deutsch-Demokratische Freiheitspartei*, i 70; German Agrarian party (*Bund der Landwirte*), i 64, 69, 70n, 74, 117, 487; German Christian Socialist party, i 69, 70n, 250, 487; ii 31–2, 34; German party (in Province of Slovakia), iii 413; iv 95–6, 158, 226, 229, 406–8; v 86, 90–1; German Social Democratic party, i 64n, 69, 170, 172, 180, 283, 440n, 471–2; ii 32, 57, 69, 94n, 404, 450–1, 665; iii 195n; Henlein party, *see below* Sudeten German party; National Alliance party (Party of National Union), i 283, 510; iii 96; National Labour party, iv 61; National Party of the Working People, iii 214–5, 412; National Socialist party, iii 96, 214–5, 410; iv 55, 63; Party of Czech. National Unity (M. Béran's bloc), iii 214–5, 376–7, 412; Slovak National party, iii 377; iv 157–8; v 85; Slovak People's party (Hlinka party), i 166–7, 429–30, 465, 480, 530; ii 279; iii 21, 80, 91, 96; iv 241–2; v 85–6
  Sudeten German party (Henlein party), i 64–616 *passim*; ii 3–222 *passim*, 404, 662, 674, 676, 679
    attitude towards Nazi principles, i 185, 248–50, 275, 279, 309, 511, 555
    Freiwilliger Schutzdienst (F.S.), ii 32
    manifesto of Aug. 26, 1938, signed by Deputies Frank and Kollner, ii 167, 171, 176, 183, 210
    proposed Parteitag at Böhmisch-Leipa, Oct. 1938, ii 232, 244, 249, 660, 670
    dissolution of, ii 404n
    See also Sudeten German question
  Press, i 126, 272, 284, 288, 292, 311, 320, 328, 360, 377, 462n, 468n, 542, 548, 556, 567, 617;

Czechoslovakia (Press) (*cont.*)
ii 1, 7n, 8, 23, 28n, 91, 111, 200; iii 212, 215; iv 61–3; v 555–7
  Austrian 'Anschluss', i 68–71, 76
  Mr. Chamberlain's speech of March 24, 1938, i 141, 150
  proposed concessions to Sudeten Germans, i 506–9, 516–8, 521, 567, 595
  attitude towards Lord Runciman's Mission, ii 29, 37, 49, 69
  manifesto by Officers' Association, ii 81–2, 89–90
  'Gablonzer Tagblatt', ii 30; 'Hlas Mladych', iv 61; 'Hranicar', ii 28n; 'Národní Osvobozeny', iv 61; 'Prager Presse', i 567; ii 110, 139, 279, 404n, 580; iii 377, 409; 'Prager Tagblatt', i 461; iv 63; 'Pritomnost', i 517; 'Reichenberger Zeitung', i 68; 'Rote Fahne', i 280–1; 'Rundschau', i 594; ii 183; 'Slovak', i 166; iv 408, 438; v 85–8; 'Slovenska Pravda', iv 406; 'Venkov', iv 183; 'Volksdeutsche Zeitung', iv 126; 'Die Zeit', i 69, 70, 125n, 276, 382n, 518; ii 90, 110; iv 126, 227, 235, 562
  public opinion, ii 33, 333, 368n
  Roumania, ii 355; iii 45, 141, 182, 385; *see also* Roumania (armament contracts with Czechoslovakia)
  State Defence Guard, ii 186
  strategic position, i 56, 85, 87, 104–8, 120–2, 141, 144, 213, 218, 220–1, 236, 241–2, 267–8, 271–2, 282, 302, 411–2, 421, 492–3; ii 226; iii 306
  U.S.S.R., i 54, 62, 64–5, 85, 105, 108, 110, 115, 139, 153, 162, 164–5, 172–3, 181, 197, 213, 236, 255, 280–1, 289, 297, 305–7, 314–5, 321, 346, 385, 390–1, 415, 419–24, 482, 628, 647, 654; ii 1, 73, 85, 97, 107, 141, 147, 164, 166, 168, 220, 229, 255, 266, 272, 318, 340, 347, 376, 393, 498, 603; iii 40; iv 412; *see also* Treaties (Czechoslovakia and U.S.S.R.)
  United States, i 615; ii 357; iii 385; iv 366, 441; vii 627–8
  Yugoslavia, ii 241, 260
  See also Missions; Munich Conference and Agreement; Refugees; Ruthenia; Slovakia; Sudeten German question

Czestochowa, v 246; vii 186n, 515

Dachau, i 19
Dagö, viii 577
Dakar, i 203
Danube, R., navigation, iii 131
Danube Basin, i 79, 80, 195–6; ii 158; iii 44, 233; iv 178
Danube–Oder canal, iii 235, 240, 408–9
Danzig, Free City of
  M. Burckhardt's position. *See* sub-heads (League of Nations) and (Poland) *below*

Danzig, Free City of (*cont.*)
customs arrangements, **vi** 26, 624–5; *see also* sub-head (Poland) *below*
disturbances in, **iv** 145, 151–2, 157, 159, 163, 166, 168, 177, 181, 187, 203; **v** 547, 558, 622–3, 625–6, 635–7, 667, 692, 731, 733–4, 764, 768, 788, 816; **vi** 9, 30, 32–3, 42, 65, 81, 148–50, 177, 204, 402, 417, 432–3, 436, 452, 455, 461–2, 487, 505, 513–4, 527, 653, 662, 681, 689–90, 692, 726; **vii** 12, 22, 25, 51, 59, 152–3, 186n, 190, 219, 249, 296, 318, 355, 363, 403, 405–6, 450–1
economic conditions, **v** 27, 101, 511, 515, 813; **vi** 505–6; **vii** 402
establishment of Free City, **v** 810
France, **iii** 282–3, 406, 438, 552–6, 567, 587–8; **iv** 169–70, 382, 384, 385n; **v** 413–4, 438–9, 527n; **vi** 213, 236–7, 291, 372, 399, 516, 519, 697–8, 728; **vii** 19, 68
Freikorps, **vi** 87, 164, 176–7, 223, 505
German-Polish dispute. *See* Germany (Poland) and sub-heads (Great Britain), (Italy) *below*
Great Britain
attitude towards German-Polish dispute, **iv** 424, 436, 500, 502, 510; **v** 27, 199, 282, 285, 401, 410, 478, 490, 492–3, 501–2, 517–8, 525–7, 549, 581, 601–2, 609–10, 675, 684–5, 690, 731–2, 783n, 806; **vi** 58, 85, 130–3, 171, 212, 249n, 255–60, 274, 283, 291–3, 304, 306, 316, 322, 337, 342, 353, 356–7, 363, 372, 431–3, 456, 482, 488, 502, 530, 584, 595, 597, 643, 728; **vii** 6–7, 58–60, 62, 68, 73, 76, 82, 117, 124n, 146, 159, 186, 215, 241, 246, 250, 367n, 465, 470; *see also* Guarantee (to Poland by Great Britain)
economic mission (alleged) to Danzig, **vii** 17–8, 98–9
history of Danzig question, memorandum, **v** 809–16
Italy
attitude towards German-Polish dispute, **v** 523, 567, 589, 654, 705; **vi** 124, 253, 288–9, 658, 665, 675, 724; **vii** 71, 80; *see also* Germany (Italy)
League of Nations, **iii** 206, 281, 283–4, 401–6, 431, 438–9, 442–4, 542–4, 552–8, 561, 567, 572n, 573–4, 580–1, 586–9, 591–606, 610–4; **iv** 11, 46–7, 68, 81, 112, 145, 147, 151, 166–7, 169–70, 187, 224, 261, 383, 507, 617; **v** 3, 17–8, 51–2, 391–4, 430–1, 466, 476–7, 525, 527, 561–2 627–30, 654, 682, 709–10, 783n, 810–3; **vi** 45–6, 48, 107, 639, 660, 668, 691, 697, 700; **vii** 11, 17, 104, 222, 237, 261, 542n
Resolution of June 22, 1921, **v** 709n
military preparations, **v** 576–7, 606, 608; **vi** 177–8, 207, 211, 224, 236, 242, 247, 257, 291, 322, 338, 356, 369, 387–9, 391–4, 399, 400, 421, 454, 476–7, 487, 505, 532–3, 547, 549,

Danzig (military preparations) (*cont.*)
563, 586–7, 617, 654, 685, 689, 728; **vii** 29, 156–7, 160, 200
partition of territory, possibility of, **vi** 186; **vii** 50
Poland
importance of Danzig to Poland, **v** 579, 581–3; **vi** 291–2
in favour of *status quo*, **iii** 281, 284, 401, 405, 431, 439, 544, 555, 557, 592–4, 597, 600, 604–5, 612, 659; **iv** 68, 147; **v** 18, 476–7; *see also* sub-head (League of Nations)
Polish-German disputes relating to Danzig. *See* Germany (Poland) and sub-heads (Great Britain) and (Italy) *above*
relations between Danzig Senate and Polish representative at Danzig
customs disputes, 1935, **vi** 547n, 612; June–Aug., 1939, **v** 764, 768; **vi** 7–9, 26–7, 31, 148–50, 402, 547–9, 559, 562–4, 568–9, 577, 592–4, 597, 609–14, 620–2, 624, 627–8, 635–6, 638, 644–5, 647, 649, 651–3, 679–80, 684–5, 689–90, 696; **vii** 55, 87, 152, 190
herring industry and margarine factory disputes, **vi** 547, 569 593, 621, 653, 690; **vii** 55, 403
Polish note to Senate of Aug. 4, 1939, **vi** 594
direct intervention of Germany, Aug. 9–10, *see* Germany (Poland, disputes relating to Danzig and Polish Corridor)
position of M. Burckhardt as intermediary, **vi** 388–9, 402, 420, 433, 435, 448, 452, 455, 462, 477, 480, 490–1, 494–5, 577, 594, 614, 621–2, 624, 652–4, 662, 689–91, 696–7, 716, 718; **vii** 6, 9, 12, 49, 50, 224, 261, 296, 542
question of notification of Polish military trains, **vi** 364, 388, 402, 452, 494, 532, 546, 561, 689
suggested détente, **vi** 388, 401, 433, 448, 475, 482, 549–50, 557, 652–4, 662
Herr Greiser not informed, **vi** 594, 614, 653, 689; **vii** 11
meetings between Polish representative and Herr Greiser, July 17, **vi** 365, 386, 652; Aug. 16 and 18, **vi** 685, 697; **vii** 12, 24–5, 55
Press, **vi** 9, 148, 394; 'Danziger Neueste Nachrichten', **v** 514, 764; **vi** 179; 'Der Danziger Vorposten', **iv** 47, 143; **v** 25, 510–2, 514–5, 764; **vi** 9, 31, 66, 401, 480n, 547, 593; **vii** 96–7
S.A. and S.S. in, **iii** 599; **v** 560, 608, 665, 732; **vi** 32–3, 80–1, 87, 136–7, 177–8, 193, 223, 392, 402, 454, 685; **vii** 104, 544, 546
visits of German vessels to. *See* 'Königsberg'; 'Leipzig'; 'Schleswig Holstein'

Dardanelles, The, **v** 75, 77, 589, 796; **vi** 599
Darmstadt, **ii** 26
Datyne, **iii** 223
Dauba et Hühnerwasser, **iii** 640
Deblin, **iii** 23
Denmark, **ii** 530; **iv** 129; **v** 6; *see also* Anglo-Franco-Soviet negotiations (Denmark)
Deutsch-Eylau, **vii** 484
Deutsch Gabel, **i** 432; **iii** 640
Devin (Theben), **iv** 96
Dieburg, **ii** 26
Dire Dawa (Diré-Dauoa), **iii** 485; **iv** 303
Dirschau. *See* Tczew
Djibuti, **iv** 10; **v** 457; **vi** 202, 471, 488, 554-5, 724
Döberitz, **ii** 125, 236
Dobrudja, **iii** 46; **iv** 333, 433, 498, 620; **v** 109*n*, 380, 464; **vi** 30, 68, 202
Dodecanese, The, **v** 593
Dolni Sobesovice, **iii** 223
Domazlice area, **iii** 408
Dresden, **i** 317, 358; **ii** 126-7, 281, 491, 551-2; **iii** 417; **iv** 234, 245, 248
Durazzo, **v** 127-8, 140, 168-9, 175-7, 190-3, 437*n*, 750
Düsseldorf, **iv** 21, 138*n*
Dutch East Indies. *See* Netherlands East Indies
Dux, **i** 436
Dzialdowo, **vii** 323

East Prussia, **i** 451; **ii** 21, 27, 45, 62, 105, 269, 309, 408, 453; **iii** 548; **iv** 265, 362, 369, 398; **v** 67, 203, 248, 338, 371, 538, 576, 582, 692, 814; **vi** 393, 477, 549, 684; **vii** 3*n*, 4, 40, 90, 126, 135, 160, 204, 298, 327, 337-8, 375, 415, 496, 515, 545, 549
Eastern Galicia. *See* Galicia
Eastern Pact of 1934, **iii** 374
Eastern Pomerania, **ii** 127
Eger, **i** 251, 428*n*; **ii** 327, 348
  border incident, May 21, 1938, **i** 330, 333, 336-7, 340, 342, 358-61, 378, 414, 619
  disturbances, Sept. 13-4, 1938, **ii** 304-5, 319-20, 354, 457, 468, 472, 544, 611, 619, 621, 669, 672-3
Egerland, **ii** 333, 457, 546, 554, 572, 586, 591, 621, 655; **iii** 625, 627
  question of cession of, **ii** 358, 360, 364
Egypt, **i** 96; **iii** 287, 493, 498; **iv** 308, 329, 336, 342-3; **v** 54, 143, 150, 152, 264; **vi** 438; **vii** 418
  British forces, **iv** 329, 348*n*; **vii** 266*n*
  dispatch of Indian troops to, **vi** 579, 628
Elbasan, **v** 177, 750
Elbe, R., navigation, **iii** 131
Elbe canal, **iii** 240, 409
Elbing, **v** 27, 608; **vi** 393, 587
Elbogen, **ii** 672
Encirclement. *See* Germany; Italy; Poland
Engerau, **iv** 408

Erbach, **ii** 26
Erfurt, **i** 451
Estonia, **v** 104
  Anglo-Franco-Soviet guarantee, question of, **v** 350, 558, 572-3, 669, 689, 697, 737; **vi** 35, 55, 95-6, 174, 230, 251, 280, 282, 313, 325-7, 382-3; *see also* Anglo-Franco-Soviet negotiations (Baltic States and Finland)
  Anglo-Polish treaty negotiations, **vii** 65
  attitude towards Great Britain, **v** 350; **vi** 326; **vii** 426
  policy of neutrality, **v** 352; **vi** 35, 382-3; **vii** 426
  Press, **vi** 326-7; 'Baltic Times', **v** 698; **vi** 281, 327; 'Uus Eesti', **vi** 327
  Soviet declaration of Mar. 28, 1939 and Estonian reply, **v** 349-52; *referred to,* **v** 214, 404-5, 604, 775-6; **vi** 161
  See also Germany (Estonia)
Esztergom, **i** 321*n*
Ethiopia. *See* Abyssinia
Eupen, **i** 174
Ewo Cotton Mills, Shanghai, **ix** 14-6

Falkenau, **ii** 305, 457
Far East, **ii** 96; **iii** 280, 291, 308-9; **iv** 412; **v** 152, 160; **vii** 549
  inter-relationship of situations in Europe and Far East, **i** 305, 423; **vi** 126, 179, 186, 197, 208, 236, 706, 709-10, 720; **viii** 54, 134, 143, 188, 291, 320-1, 362; **ix** 458, 531
  See also China; Japan; Sino-Japanese War, Tientsin
Fascism, in Czechoslovakia, **iii** 192; **v** 556; in Italy, **i** 37; **iii** 466-7
Finale Ligure, **iv** 338
Finland
  Anglo-Franco-Soviet guarantee, question of, **v** 496, 522, 558-9, 568, 573, 590, 737; **vi** 35, 55, 120-1, 168, 174, 230, 251, 264-6, 280-1, 307-8, 313, 413-5; *see also* Anglo-Franco-Soviet negotiations (Baltic States and Finland)
  attitude towards: assistance from U.S.S.R., **v** 223, 253, 495-6; Germany, **v** 495, 759
  trade delegation to U.S.S.R., **iv** 621
First World War. *See* War (1914-1918)
Fiume, **iii** 475
Florina, **v** 136, 158
Florisdorf, **ii** 281
Foreign Bankers' Association, Shanghai, **ix** 125, 146
Four-Power Declaration proposed, Mar. 1939, **iv** 392, 424-5, 429, 431, 433, 453, 456, 467, 469, 492, 494, 498, 513, 522, 542, 544, 558, 574, 585; **v** 20, 22, 205, 642-3; **vi** 110
  text of, **iv** 400, 427, 486*n*
  reaction of France, **iv** 425-6, 434, 457, 467, 473, 486-7, 490-1, 495, 498, 528
  reaction of Poland, **iv** 425, 428, 432, 436, 453,

Four-Power Declaration (*cont.*)
458, 472–3, 494, 496, 498, 508–9, 519, 528;
v 20, 22; counter-suggestion for Anglo-
Polish bilateral understanding, iv 463, 466,
500–1, 510–1, 524
reaction of U.S.S.R., iv 429, 467, 472, 495,
498, 508–9, 528, 530, 585, 622
decision to modify, iv 457–61, 515–7, 527–30,
544, 567, 574–5; v 20–3, 45, 83, 104
See also Anglo-Franco-Soviet negotiations;
Germany (Roumania, threat of German
aggression); Guarantee (to Poland), (to
Roumania)
Fourteen Points of President Wilson, ii 486
France
armed forces
air force, i 200, 202, 205–7; ii 474, 528,
532–3; iii 142, 289–91; v 103; vi 63, 788;
vii 582
aircraft production, i 205–6, 611; iii 289–
91; iv 50, 118, 462, 488–9, 532; vii 582
army, i 205, 207; ii 218, 513; iii 291, 569–
70, 609; iv 426; vi 757, 769; vii 566;
General Staff, ii 191; iii 483, 557, 579; iv
53, 262; vi 88; vii 247–8, 420, 504
navy, v 152, 239; vii 576–80
See also Anglo-French Staff conversations
attitude towards possible outbreak of war in
Sept. 1938, ii 190–1, 220, 303*n*, 309–11, 314,
322–3, 509–10, 513–4, 532, 544, 558, 571;
see also France (military measures) and
(public opinion)
Austria, i 13, 25, 232
Belgium, iii 569–70; iv 58, 70
Bulgaria, iv 395, 403
Czechoslovakia. *See* Czechoslovakia (France);
Bohemia and Moravia (occupation by
Germany); Sudeten German question (atti-
tude of France and Great Britain)
Far East
attitude of France towards Japan's policy
in China, viii 392, 394–6, 419; ix 192–3
embargo on certain exports from Indo-
China to Japan, viii 148, 184; ix 238
See also Chinese Currency Stabilization
Fund; Hainan Island; Indo-China;
Shanghai (French Concession) and (Inter-
national Settlement); Sino-Japanese conflict (reprisals against Japan); Tientsin
(French Concession)
French North Africa. *See* North Africa
Germany, i 274, 614; ii 13, 86, 122–4, 216,
338, 345, 350, 374–5, 395, 562; iii 244–5,
437, 545, 562, 618–21; iv 167–8, 170, 461;
v 213, 354, 370; vi 515–9; vii 277–8
economic negotiations, iii 397, 618; iv 167,
601
Franco-German Agreement, suggested, iii
250, 257–62, 269, 273, 282, 286; attitude
of Great Britain, iii 252–3, 259–60, 267

France (Franco-German Agreement) *cont.*
summary of proposals, iii 262
text of, iii 286, 310–1, 391, 394
signature, Dec. 6, 1938, iii 284, 286, 376,
391, 421
referred to, iii 287, 363, 392–3, 395–6, 400–
25, 437, 530, 531*n*; iv 51, 168, 241, 264,
267, 269, 299, 602–3, 643–5; vi 237,
515–8, 591
French Air Mission to Germany, ii 122–4
German attack on France reported
imminent, v 54–6, 71
handing over of Czech. Legation in Paris to
German Embassy, iv 363–4, 379
visit of Herr von Ribbentrop to Paris, iii
389–97; *see also* Ribbentrop, J. von, in
Index of Persons
Great Britain
commitments between, i 84–5, 91, 96, 144,
199, 211, 233–4, 247, 347, 356; ii 303, 307,
310–1, 681; iii 260, 288–9, 366*n*, 425,
446–7, 472; iv 90*n*, 101, 114, 311
relations after Munich settlement, iii 251–3,
257, 259–60, 263, 267, 389, 511
French request for postponement of
announcement of date of General Election
in Great Britain, vi 62–3, 357, 489, 491
See also Anglo-French conversations; France
(Italy, attitude towards questions affecting Franco-Italian relations); Sudeten
German question
Greece, v 148
internal situation, ii 270, 278; iii 87–90,
157–8, 365*n*, 462; vi 62; vii 313–4
Italy, i 14, 20, 28, 37, 208, 325*n*; ii 191, 197,
222; iii 157, 257, 296–7, 428, 461, 471–2,
474–524 *passim*; iv 139–40, 273, 308, 314–5,
332, 339, 531, 533, 589–90, 593, 608; v 51,
119, 251, 551, 578, 737; vi 31, 146, 150
attitude towards questions affecting Franco-
Italian relations of:—Germany, iii 389–
90, 420, 489, 493, 512, 530–1, 545, 556,
572; iv 4, 10, 38, 42, 49, 61, 69, 89, 140,
165, 293–9, 304, 319, 336, 594–5
Great Britain, iii 509–10, 514, 516; iv 90,
139–40, 292–3, 309–11, 324, 329–55,
358–9; v 124, 126–7, 130, 237, 252, 255–6,
258–9, 272*n*, 276–9, 344–6, 386, 427, 432,
612–4, 651, 664–5, 691, 703, 730, 763,
774, 793, 799, 800, 808; vi 32, 64, 185,
301–2, 317, 330, 350–1, 353, 357–8, 471,
555, 587; *see also* Tunis
Poland, iv 143, 179
the Vatican, v 718–9; *see also* Vatican (suggestion for 5-Power Conference)
M. Baudouin's mission to Rome, iv 323,
335; v 263–4, 345, 347
demonstration in Italian Chamber against
France, iii 463–74, 478, 480, 482, 484,
486–7, 506, 524; iv 299, 347; v 614*n*, 797

France (Italy) *cont.*

Franco-Italian Agreement of 1935, denunciation by Italy, **iii** 491; *see also* Treaties

Italian claims against France, **iii** 390, 420, 437, 471, 477, 493; **iv** 123, 292–4, 296–7, 317, 320–3, 325, 353–5, 359, 402*n*, 440, 488; **v** 263–4, 347, 427–8, 611–4, 650–1; **vi** 358, 471–4, 724; **vii** 350

statement of claims, April–May, 1939, **v** 347, 611

question of direct Franco-Italian negotiations, **v** 122, 124, 130, 237, 252, 258, 263–4, 277–9, 344–5, 347, 428, 432, 477, 480, 651, 663–4, 774, 797, 799, 800; **vi** 220–1, 351, 357–8, 587

See also Abyssinia (recognition of Italian Empire); Albania (effect of Italian action on Franco-Italian relations); France (Turkey: Sandjak of Alexandretta); Spain (effect of Spanish issue on Franco-Italian relations)

Japan. *See* France (Far East)

military measures, Sept. 1938, **ii** 197, 234*n*, 249–50, 270, 310, 451, 456, 461, 509, 527–8; **iii** 335; March 1939, **iv** 423; April, **v** 239–40; Aug.–Sept., **vii** 96, 102, 120, 123, 137, 158, 249, 317, 340, 489, 500, 504

Poland, **i** 72, 172–3, 444–5; **ii** 538–9; **iii** 104, 107, 110, 182, 365–6, 397*n*, 526, 577; **iv** 32, 33*n*, 69, 182, 205 423, 616

expected French reaction to German attack on Poland, **iii** 366*n*, 494, 568*n*, 569–70; **v** 438; **vi** 237*n*, 399, 517–9; **vii** 166, 245, 278–9, 342, 420, 463, 495; *see also* Poland (Great Britain, implementation of undertakings)

financial aid, **v** 539–40, 734, 758; **vi** 411; **vii** 79

negotiations, May 1939, **v** 608–9, 611, 638–9, 700, 757–8, 772

See also Danzig (France); Treaties (France and Poland)

political parties, **ii** 508, 573, 605–6, 622–3; **iii** 157, 346, 355, 462, 479, 483; *see also* Communism (France)

Press, **i** 337, 340, 360, 384, 392, 549, 556, 581*n*; **ii** 117, 216, 337, 361, 414*n*, 420, 532, 544*n*; **iii** 245, 284, 346, 389, 393; **v** 505, 578, 599, 780, 795; **vii** 16–7, 166

Mr. Chamberlain's speech on Mar. 24, 1938, **i** 141, 150

Franco-Italian relations, **iii** 320, 322, 470, 472, 480–1, 494, 506, 524; **iv** 320, 346–7

German occupation of Bohemia and Moravia, **iv** 265–6

Anglo-Franco-Soviet negotiations, **v** 272, 785; **vi** 377–8

Danzig question, **v** 413–4; **vi** 247, 638, 691

Hudson–Wohltat conversations, **vi** 464*n*, 480–1, 495

France (Press) *cont.*

'L'Action Française', **v** 414; 'Agence Économique et Financière', **iii** 393; 'L'Époque', **v** 439, 785; **vi** 55, 495; 'Excelsior', **vi** 489; 'Le Figaro', **iii** 393; **iv** 60–1; **v** 264; **vi** 495; 'Gringoire', **iii** 481; 'L'Homme Libre', **iv** 266; **v** 439; 'L'Humanité', **ii** 623; **iii** 393, 481, 506; **iv** 266; **v** 439, 505; **vi** 199; **vii** 244; 'L'Intransigeant', **vi** 495; 'Le Jour-Écho de Paris', **ii** 606, 623; **iii** 156, 481; 'Le Journal des Débats', **iv** 266; **v** 413, 439; 'La Journée Industrielle', **vi** 495; 'La Liberté', **ii** 622; 'Le Matin', **ii** 322; **iii** 156, 481; 'L'Œuvre', **iii** 157, 481; **v** 414, 439; 'L'Ordre', **ii** 623; **iii** 393; 'Paris-Midi', **iii** 246; **vi** 677; **vii** 16–7; 'Paris-Soir', **vi** 495; 'Le Petit Journal', **v** 439; 'Le Petit Parisien', **i** 53; **iii** 322, 481; **v** 439, 505; **vi** 215, 481; 'Le Peuple', **iii** 393; **iv** 266; **v** 505; 'Le Populaire', **ii** 623; **iii** 392–3; **iv** 266; **v** 439, 505; **vi** 495; 'La République', **ii** 305, 622; **vi** 495; 'Le Soir', **v** 785; 'Le Temps', **ii** 337, 568, 606; **iii** 394, 481, 484; **iv** 266; **v** 414, 790; **vi** 481; 'La Victoire', **v** 785

public opinion, **ii** 305, 322, 413, 482, 509–10, 514, 544, 547, 558; **iii** 394, 420, 480; **v** 638; **vii** 116, 500, 512

Roumania. *See* Guarantee (to Roumania)

Spain. *See* Spain

Syria, **iii** 307; **vi** 347

Turkey

Hatay negotiations, **v** 465, 504, 507, 518, 522, 526, 532–4, 536, 549–50, 578, 746

Sandjak of Alexandretta, cession to Turkey, **v** 796; **vi** 346; protest by Italy, **vi** 346–7

Trade and Clearing Agreement, **vi** 362, 686

See also Guarantee (to Turkey); Turkey (Anglo-Franco-Turkish negotiations)

U.S.S.R. *See* Anglo-Franco-Soviet negotiations; Treaties (France–U.S.S.R.)

United States, aircraft for France, **iii** 290–1; **iv** 462–3

Frankenstein, i 358

Frankfort-on-the-Oder, i 156, 178, 358; **v** 782; **vii** 160

Franzensbad, i 594

Frankstadt, iii 641

Freiburg, vii 416

Freiheit, iii 640

Freistadt, iii 41, 46, 52–3, 58, 62, 82, 97, 179–82

Freiwaldau, i 580*n*; **ii** 99*n*; **iii** 83

Freiwilliger Schutzdienst, iv 407, 438*n*

French Somaliland, iv 303

Freudenstadt, ii 26

Freudenthal, ii 630

Friedland, i 432; **ii** 596, 603

Frydek, iii 82, 104, 146, 186–8; **iv** 162

Frystat, iii 225, 229; **v** 246

Fukien, viii 203

Gablonz, **i** 123–4; **ii** 552, 664; **iii** 640

Galatz, **v** 62

Galicia, **iv** 80; **vi** 44; **vii** 3*n*, 4, 70, 87

Garches, **ii** 270

Garing, **vii** 474

Garmisch, **i** 317, 318*n*

Gastein, **i** 535, 613

Gdynia, **i** 429; **ii** 288; **iii** 274; **iv** 514; **v** 27, 101, 249, 304, 324–5, 538, 560, 577, 579, 583, 610, 628, 706, 813; **vi** 32, 338, 357, 404; **vii** 134, 200, 432, 460–1, 479

Gelnhausen, **ii** 26

Geneva, League of Nations meetings. *See* League of Nations

Genoa, **i** 325; **iii** 293, 532–3; **iv** 338

Gera, **i** 451

'German Day', March 27, 1938, **i** 2, 132

Germany

air force, **i** 26, 67, 611; **ii** 140, 162, 218–9, 284, 310, 347, 371, 454, 474, 533; **iii** 294, 546, 550, 563, 570–1, 608–9, 616–7; **iv** 30, 116–120, 185, 258, 264, 479, 586–8, 627; **v** 433; **vi** 772, 788; **vii** 416, 522, 526

  compared with British and French air forces, **iv** 118–9; **v** 102–3; **vi** 757

army, **i** 43–4, 381, 462–3, 480, 576, 609; **ii** 2, 14–6, 66–7, 76, 121, 132, 258, 539, 610, 655; **iii** 140, 166, 191, 255, 546–7, 570–1, 609, 624; **iv** 5, 23–4, 30, 160, 162, 625–7; **v** 38, 72, 338, 595, 792; **vi** 44, 374, 757; **vii** 56, 125, 416, 419, 422; *see also* Brauchitsch, Colonel-General W. von, in Index of Persons

  attitude towards possible outbreak of war, **i** 614; **ii** 16, 40, 162, 171, 356, 379, 684, 687, 691; **iii** 624; **iv** 596; **v** 107; **vi** 708, 710, 715

  General Staff, **i** 129, 327–8, 413–4, 420, 422–3, 450; **ii** 15, 60, 104, 126–7, 162, 184, 237, 242; **iii** 125, 159, 571, 583, 619; **v** 646; **vi** 296, 306; **vii** 140, 415–6, 514, 517; *see also* Beck, Colonel-General Ludwig; Halder, General F.; Reichenau, General W. von, in Index of Persons

    Attaché Gruppe, **i** 9, 16; **ii** 42–5, 47, 65, 126–7, 169; *see also* Albedyl, Hauptmann von; Mellenthin, Major von; Schwerin, Lt.-Col. Count von, in Index of Persons

    Herr von Kleist's mission to Great Britain, **ii** 683–8

  High Command, **i** 225, 451; **ii** 16, 27, 42–4, 46, 62–3, 238; **iii** 372, 427, 547, 549, 624; **iv** 258; **v** 478, 595; *see also* Keitel, General W., in Index of Persons

  in control in Protectorate of Bohemia and Moravia, **iv** 564–5

  Pioneer battalions, **iii** 623

  strength and readiness for war, **i** 92–4, 102, 111–2, 122, 271–2, 318, 413–4, 484, 494, 614; **ii** 16, 66–8, 98, 172, 184, 191, 233, 266, 281, 284, 454; **iii** 368–73, 427, 550,

Germany (army) (*cont.*)

617, 624, 626; **v** 768; **vi** 185, 368–9, 434, 512, 698–9, 770–1; **vii** 15

  See also Germany (military measures)

Austria, **i** 1–60 *passim*, 80–2, 95, 127–36, 176, 178, 295, 318

  annexation (Austrian 'Anschluss'), **i** 42–3; *referred to*, **i** 48, 63, 68, 97–100, 111, 119, 135–7, 139, 173, 178, 181, 197, 217, 223, 226, 260, 294, 301–2, 323*n*, 326, 368, 381, 457, 533, 603, 610, 621, 625; **ii** 33, 40, 84, 99, 121, 229, 263, 345, 347, 375; **iii** 104, 160, 179, 397, 496, 622; **iv** 236, 279, 564; **vi** 72, 290, 506, 555, 753

  attitude of: France and Great Britain, **i** 46–7, 58, 217; Italy, **i** 28–9, 37–8, 47, 100, 173; **ii** 345; **iii** 160, 496

  effect of German action on: Anglo-German relations, **i** 57, 80–1, 109, 176, 653; Czechoslovak economic and strategic position, **i** 85, 87, 104–8, 119, 124, 157, 218, 221, 236, 267–8; **iii** 101; Germany's economic and military ✓ position, **i** 119; **iii** 369; Herr Hitler's personal position, **i** 119, 157, 179; Sudeten Germans, **i** 68, 121, 123–4, 140, 212, 266, 321, 405, 487, 509; **ii** 9, 31, 33, 429

  conditions in Austria after the 'Anschluss', **i** 60, 67, 120, 124, 136–7, 146–7, 155, 250; **ii** 66, 70; military preparations, **i** 317; **ii** 27, 42, 48, 62–3, 105, 120, 126–7, 161, 237, 453, 554, 561, 615, **iv** 23–4

  Greater Germany, **i** 119, 156–7, 179, 266, 268, 294; **ii** 63; **iii** 387

colonial question, **i** 5, 81–2, 109–10, 175, 177, 232, 287, 294, 622–4, 655; **ii** 85, 129, 345, 688; **iii** 159, 244–6, 250, 254, 256–7, 262, 310, 397, 437, 590, 618; **iv** 5, 38, 59, 65, 80, 165, 176, 213, 215–6, 591–4, 601; **v** 10, 302, 304, 360, 371, 618; **vi** 202–3, 408, 412, 737; **vii** 319, 354*n*, 362–3, 387

  Colonial-Political School at Ladeburg, **iii** 256

  Reich Colonial League, **iii** 256

Council for Defence of the Reich, **vii** 464*n*

Czechoslovakia. *See* Bohemia and Moravia; Czechoslovakia (Germany); Munich Agreement; Sudeten German question; Sudetenland

Danzig. *See* Germany (Poland)

Denmark, **v** 213, 775; **vi** 73; *see also* Germany (Scandinavian countries)

Egypt, **v** 213

Enabling Act, **ii** 343

encirclement, fear of, **v** 216, 244–5, 272, 299, 301, 313, 315, 318–9, 355, 361, 377, 381, 423, 430, 473*n*, 584, 592–3, 600, 644, 646, 671, 675, 713, 724, 771*n*, 804; **vi** 47, 72–3, 75, 78, 88, 94, 113–4, 133, 154, 172, 197, 202, 298, 467, 469–70, 490, 529, 580, 708, 710, 712, 734; **vii** 30, 53

Germany (*cont.*)

Estonia, **v** 213, 280, 803; **vi** 326–7
Non-aggression pact between, **v** 437, 461, 560, 697–8, 775; **vi** 281; attitude of Great Britain, **v** 560, 590
Finland, **v** 213, 253; **vi** 282, 413; *see also* Germany (Scandinavian countries)
Great Britain, **i**–**vii** *passim*
co-operation in Far East suggested, **viii** 11, 12n, 21–2, 267–8; Dr. Schacht's proposals ✔ on currency problems, **ix** 271–2, 273n, 329, 351, 399
German assurances to Gréat Britain after Austrian 'Anschluss', **i** 24-5, 32, 43-4, 59, 228-30, 236
British approaches on questions affecting Czechoslovakia:—
démarche of May 7–11, 1938, **i** 260, 284–8; *referred to*, **i** 231, 241, 243–7, 252–7, 261, 264, 270, 281–2, 289–90, 303–4, 308
démarche of May 21–2, 1938, **i** 331–2, 334–5, 341, 348; *referred to*, **i** 336, 346, 353, 376, 382, 409–10, 412–4, 426, 440, 456, 535, 551, 575, 590, 615; **ii** 30, 58, 64, 76, 97–8, 107, 118, 145, 206, 225, 233, 283, 324, 429, 666; **iii** 254, 619, 622–3; **iv** 33, 590; **vi** 330, 730; **vii** 162
memorandum of Aug. 11, 1938, **ii** 78–80
notes of protest, Mar. 15 and 17, 1939, **iv** 250, 259, 291, 444, 455
visits by Mr. Chamberlain. *See* Berchtesgaden, Godesberg, Munich Conference
Naval Agreements
Anglo-German conversations, Dec. 1938, **iii** 455–6, 664–71; preparations for, **iii** 422–3, 429, 432–3, 435–6, 439–40, 445, 450–5, 672–4
denunciation by Germany, **iv** 455–6; **v** 360–2, 371; *referred to*, **v** 374, 388, 520, 584, 619, 792; **vi** 61, 73
British reply, **vi** 153–8; *referred to*, **vi** 184, 212, 469
See also Treaties *bilateral* (Germany—Great Britain); *multilateral* (Naval Armaments)
propaganda in Great Britain against Germany, **vi** 374, 385, 442, 529, 714–6, 719–20
R.A.F. visit suggested, **iv** 111, 115n, 123
trade negotiations, **iv** 131–2, 138n, 165, 173–7, 260–1, 271, 591n, 604–10; **v** 586, 602, 791–2
visit to Herr Hitler of German-speaking British representative suggested, **v** 287; **vi** 390, 661, 695–6; **vii** 6, 11, 17, 32, 36–7, 56, 66, 68, 73, 75, 81, 83, 89–90, 97, 109, 113, 123, 125n, 138, 232, 284, 476, 552n
warning of Sept. 1, 1939, **vii** 488–9, 493, 509, 512; *see also* Poland (Great Britain, implementation of undertakings)
Greece, **v** 213, 280; **vi** 101

Germany (*cont.*)

Hungary, **i** 611; **ii** 140, 345, 469; **iv** 373, 477–8, 618, 625; **v** 77, 211, 213, 300, 332, 606, 620, 657; **vi** 263, 285, 324, 452, 630n, 642; **vii** 71, 83–4, 92, 141, 152n, 377
attitude of Germany towards:—Hungarian demands on Czechoslovakia, *see* Ruthenia; Slovakia; Vienna Conference and Award
Hungarian demands on Roumania, *see* Hungary (Roumania)
See also Horthy, Admiral and Csaky, Count in Index of Persons
internal conditions, **i** 155, 584; **ii** 66–7, 161, 184–5, 238, 243, 268; **iii** 388, 545, 550, 562, 565, 584, 592; **iv** 5, 39, 74–5, 164–5, 168, 175–6, 186, 598–601, 604–10; **v** 456, 673, 717; **vi** 133, 408–9; **vii** 274, 372–3, 419, 464
Catholic church, **iii** 388; **iv** 60; **vi** 294, 706
debts, foreign, **iv** 600, 606, 609–10; **vi** 407
Four-year Plan, **i** 318, 494; **iii** 545, 562; **iv** 599, 600, 602–3; **v** 673; **vii** 258
Dr. Funk's financial plan, **iv** 604–5, 610
law regarding military service, **i** 584; **ii** 21, 52; **iii** 623
passport regulations, **ii** 26
'Wehrsport' training decree, **iv** 19–23
Italy, **i** 109, 173, 552; **ii** 89, 191, 247, 279, 332, 626; **iii** 160–1, 389–90, 466n, 496, 498, 562, 584, 616; **iv** 22–3, 27, 55, 59–61, 160, 461, 531; **v** 354, 426, 488, 567, 589, 593, 650, 733; **vi** 253, 284, 323–4, 443–5, 705–6, 731–2; **vii** 7, 258, 327
German guarantee of Brenner frontier, **ii** 147, 345; **iv** 215; **v** 302, 685; **vi** 324
German declaration of support, Feb. 1939, **iv** 59, 301–4
Italy as restraining influence on Germany, **ii** 590, 624, 626, 642–4; **v** 257–8; *see also* Munich Conference (part played by Signor Mussolini)
Italy not prepared to join Germany in war against Poland, Aug. 1939, **vii** 71, 80, 119, 136, 139, 147, 322, 397, 459
Political and Military Pact, signed May 22, 1939, **v** 461; consultative clause, **vi** 596, 708; **vii** 71, 492, 733; secret clause, **vii** 335–6
comments by Sir P. Loraine, **v** 473–5, 654–5; *referred to*, **v** 481–2, 520, 585, 598–9, 620, 650–1, 656, 671, 692, 716, 733, 742, 745, 802–3; **vi** 123; **ix** 131
See also Anti-Comintern Pact; Brenner frontier; Czechoslovakia (Germany, possible German attack: attitude of Italy); France (Italy, attitude towards questions affecting Franco-Italian relations); Germany (Austria, annexation: attitude of Italy); Rome-Berlin Axis; and in Index of

Germany (Italy) (*cont.*)
  Persons, Ciano, Count (visit to Germany);
    Ribbentrop, Herr von (visit to Italy)
  Japan, **iii** 280; **iv** 185; **v** 285; **vi** 61, 757, 759;
    vii 125, 258–9, 629; **viii** 87–90, 107, 122,
    174, 451, 475; **ix** 193, 415; *see also* Anti-
    Comintern Pact; Germany (U.S.S.R., Ger-
    man–Soviet Non-Aggression Pact: reaction
    of Japan)
  Kyffhäuser Bund (National ex-Servicemen's
    Organization), **iii** 85; **iv** 19, 20
  Latvia, **v** 213, 280, 461–2, 803; **vi** 301
    Non-aggression pact, **v** 437, 461, 648–9,
      697–8, 700; **vi** 45n, 159
  Lithuania, **iv** 286–7, 518, 523; **v** 213, 280,
    282, 455; *see also* Memel
  Little Entente, **ii** 158, 196; *see also* Germany
    (Roumania), (Yugoslavia)
  Luxemburg, **v** 213, 280
  military measures
    strengthening of W. frontier, **i** 552, 561,
      563; **ii** 13, 38, 48, 86, 104, 112n, 169, 237,
      290, 453, 552, 567, 651; **iii** 545, 619, **623**
    closing of W. frontier, Aug. 1938, **ii** 26–7,
      48
    See also Siegfried Line
    test mobilization, autumn 1938, **ii** 21–2,
      27–8, 39, 40, 42–9, 51–3, 60–4, 67–8, 71,
      77, 89, 92, 98, 101, 104–6, 109, 112n, 115,
      117–8, 120–1, 124, 127–8, 134, 137–8, 161,
      163, 184, 190–1, 195, 204, 210, 225, **232**,
      236–8, 243, 281–2, 289–91, 454; **iii** 624
    possible military action by Germany during
      1939, reports and views, **iii** 544–51, 556–**7**,
      565, 569–71, 583–5, 590, 592, 608–9; **iv**
      4–5, 16, 18, 22–4, 30, 38–9, 41–2, 49–54,
      65, 72–5, 84, 90, 117, 120, 125, 159–65;
      186, 214, 218, 590, 593, 596; **v** 67, 70–2,
      79, 80, 93, 100, 173–4, 423, 433, **758**,
      769–71, 782, 804–5; **vi** 14, 87–8, 359, 412,
      615–6, 632–3, 635, 657, 666, 668, **684**,
      698–9, 708; *see also* Germany (Poland)
    general mobilization, **vii** 270, 302
    military moves against Poland, Aug. 1939,
      vii 96–7, 100, 102, 126, 129, 151, 159–**60**,
      189, 196, 206–7, 266, 270, 302, 309, **316**,
      327, 337–8, 341, 375, 415–6, 434–5, **453**
    German announcement of state of **war**,
      Sept. 1, 1939, **vii** 473
    military action, Sept. 1–3, **vii** 474, 476, 479,
      482, 484, 491, 496–7, 499, 503, 514–5, 522,
      529, 532, 534
    See also Germany (army); Czechoslovakia
      (Germany)
  minorities
    Czechs and Slovaks, **iii** 196, 226; **iv** 86, 252
    Jews. *See* Jews (Germany)
    Poles, **iv** 88–9, 153; **v** 408, 582, 808; **vi** 200,
      205, 287, 553, 719; **vii** 12, 29, 204
    minority groups of Germans outside Germany,

Germany (minority groups) (*cont.*)
    i 103, 139, 174, 178, 294–6, 318, 624; **ii** 384;
    iii 241, 387, 498, 655, 658; **iv** 262, 271, 286;
    v 302, 309, 698; *see also* Sudeten German
    question; Poland (minorities: German)
  navy and naval policy, **vi** 73, 746, 767; *see
    also* (Great Britain, Naval Agreements);
    Treaties (*multilateral*: Naval armaments)
  Netherlands, **ii** 344, 375; **iii** 547; **v** 213, 302
    possible German invasion, **iii** 159, 556, 583,
      590, 592, 608; **iv** 4, 6, 16–7, 27–30, 36–40,
      43–4, 48–54, 72–3, 83–5, 100, 167, 214,
      450–2, 509, 531; **v** 5; **vii** 514
  Norway, **v** 213, 280; *see also* Germany (Scan-
    dinavian countries)
  Poland, **i** 431; **ii** 287–8; **iii** 25, 104, 182, 253,
    267, 365, 375, 436, 494, 550, 572, 580–1, 584;
    iv 22, 24, 31–2, 55, 60, 143, 154, 168, 504;
    v–**vii** *passim*; **viii** 100–1, 216, 230, 232–3,
    290–2
    commercial relations, **iii** 182; **iv** 82, 115
    Danzig and Polish Corridor, disputes, **i**
      108–9, 174, 624–5; **ii** 688; **iii** 104, 182,
      198, 206, 243, 264–6, 274–5, 281, 283, 365,
      375, 404, 431, 439, 442–3, 554–5, 557–9,
      567, 573–4, 580–1, 585–9, 594, 611, 657–9;
      iv 11, 32, 68, 80–1, 112, 146–7, 265, 271,
      280–1, 362–3, 383, 464, 504, 507, 513–4,
      519, 524–5, 528, 533, 543, 548, 551, 572,
      575, 581–2, 617; **v** 3, 17, 23, 25–9, 51–2,
      56, 70, 94, 100–1, 199, 200, 203–4, 212,
      216, 224, 231–4, 243, 255, 257, 275–6,
      281, 286, 290, 304–5, 311, 318–9, 324, 339,
      371, 378–9, 383–4, 390–1, 403–4, 415–20,
      423, 425, 440–1, 455, 492, 501, 523–4, 538,
      560–1, 563, 570, 577, 579–86, 593–4, 602,
      608, 610, 628, 630, 675, 709, 715, 739, 759;
      803, 805, 809–10, 812–7; **vi** 1, 10, 13,
      28–9, 45–7, 57–8, 60, 81, 108, 124, 132,
      164–5, 177, 186, 192–755 *passim*; **vii** 12,
      17, 50, 53, 71, 103, 129, 154, 178, 184,
      189–90, 222–3, 237, 240, 296, 301, 352,
      361, 373, 375, 389, 403, 432, 441, 450,
      460–1, 542–6, 548–8, 555
    German proposals, Mar. 1939, **iv** 543;
      v 23–4, 276, 281, 286–7, 290, 304, 318,
      371, 378, 388–90, 410, 467, 593, 770,
      807, 814; **vi** 516, 693, 727, 755; **vii** 230,
      286n, 352, 373, 398, 395, 402, 409
    Polish reply and counter-proposals, **v** 276,
      290, 390, 417–9, 440–1; **vi** 252, 290
    alleged influence on Polish reply of:
      Great Britain's guarantee to Poland, **v**
        28–9, 232, 255, 257, 265, 281, 290, 304,
        381–91, 397, 403, 455, 467, 585, 587,
        590, 705, 771; **vi** 13, 205, 248, 255–6,
        290, 468; **vii** 31, 178, 549
    Germany's protectorate over Slovakia, **v**
      424–5, 570, 771, 782, 816; **vi** 239, 607, 704
    expected occupation of Danzig by

Germany (Poland) (*cont.*)

Danzig and Polish Corridor (*cont.*)

Germany, **iv** 265, 363; **v** 26–7, 100–1, 391, 538, 561, 5;'5, 608, 654, 665, 732; **vi** 164–5, 177, 192–3, 198, 208, 211–4, 223, 234–6, 256, 258, 291, 306–8

suggestion for counter-moves by France, Great Britain and Poland, **vi** 211, 233–4, 292–3, 387, 476, 550

suggestion that Italy be asked to intervene, **vi** 588–90, 633; **vii** 49

direct German intervention in dispute between Danzig Senate and Poland, Aug. 9–10, 1939, **vi** 644–5, 651, 662–3, 667, 679, 690, 700; **vii** 13, 29, 63, 77

question of re-opening direct German-Polish negotiations, **vii** 118, 124, 144, 146, 184–6, 190, 198–9, 216, 222, 230, 256, 294–5, 303*n*, 311, 318*n*, 319, 322, 324, 327–8, 331, 353, 354*n*, 361, 368, 374, 376, 390, 394, 410–1, 433, 436–8, 440, 445–7, 451–2, 454, 457–8, 465, 468–70, 475, 482, 490, 553

German terms to Poland, Aug, 1939, *text of* the 16 points, **vii** 459–62; *referred to*, **vii** 361, 375, 389, 397, 400, 432, 437, 440–2, 446, 454–5, 469, 475, 509–10, 544

German announcement of state of war, **vii** 473–4

Danzig proclaimed part of Germany, **vii** 542

frontier incidents, Aug. 1939, **vii** 51, 214, 228, 249, 289, 294, 323, 376, 396, 434, 453

need for avoidance of, **vii** 223, 236, 294, 403, 405-6, 434

suggested corps of neutral observers, **vii** 241–2, 269, 294, 297, 301

suggested Polish-German frontier commission, **vii** 398

German-Polish Pact of 1934, denunciation by Germany, **v** 364; *see also* Treaties

outbreak of war between. *See* Germany (military measures)

See also Berchtesgaden (meeting between Herr Hitler and M. Beck); Danzig, Free City of (Italy), (Great Britain); Poland (minorities: Germans); Ribbentrop, Herr von (visit to Warsaw) in Index of Persons; Vatican (Pope as mediator between Germany and Poland)

police: Grenzschutz, **i** 62; 'green' Schutzpolizei, **ii** 66; **iii** 166; secret police, **i** 18, 44, 67, 136, **iii** 545; *see also below*, S.A., S.S.

Press, **i** 3, 57, 65, 76, 119, 345, 369; **ii** 18, 24, 102, 334; **iii** 161, 297, 529, 545; **v** 58, 69, 771; **vi** 701

Anglo-German relations, **i** 49, 370, 388, 392–3, 399, 411, 426, 455, 457; **iii** 158, 171–2, 247–8, 263, 268, 278, 282, 388, 434*n*, 449*n*, 450–1, 474, 549; **iv** 12–3,

Germany (Press) (*cont.*)

Anglo-German relations (*cont.*)

131–2, 272*n*; **v** 388, 603; **vi** 80, 113–4, 197, 261–2, 465, 470, 481, 484, 634, 759*n*; **vii** 48, 372

'bombs to Berlin' incident, **ii** 24

Czecho-German relations, **i** 295, 320, 325, 333, 343, 356, 413, 447, 474–5, 477, 486, 493–4, 511–2, 516, 520, 526–7, 533, 537–8, 542, 568, 574, 596, 599, 617; **ii** 38–9, 79, 103, 225, 234, 408, 479, 655; **iv** 222–3, 230–2, 240, 242, 251, 442–3, 456; **vii** 625

Neth.-German relations, **iii** 549; **iv** 4, 38

Polish-German relations, **iv** 168, 540–1; **v** 24, 46, 338, 390, 403, 585, 692; **vi** 9; **vii** 108, 163, 223, 291, 372, 425, 430, 555

Soviet-German relations, **v** 463, 594, 724

'Der Angriff', **iii** 247, 259, 261, 268; **iv** 54, 582; **v** 403*n*, 723; 'Basler Nachrichten', **iii** 256; 'Berliner Tageblatt', **iii** 259; 'Börsen Zeitung', **i** 3, 49; **ii** 77, 189; **iii** 261, 268, 384; **vi** 465, 481; 'Deutsche Allgemeine Zeitung', **i** 49; **ii** 22, 138; **iii** 158; **iv** 319*n*, 562, 582*n*; **v** 58*n*; **vi** 465; 'Deutsche Dienst', **vi** 261; 'Deutsche Wehr', **ii** 52, 77; 'Deutsche Zeitung in Grossbritannien', **iv** 272*n*; 'Frankfurter Zeitung', **ii** 138; **iii** 359; 'Hamburger Fremdenblatt', **iii** 256*n*; **iv** 222; **v** 425; 'Leipziger Zeitung', **i** 333; 'National Zeitung' ('Essener National Zeitung'), **i** 49, 238*n*; **iii** 247–8; **iv** 1–2, 7, 61, 63, 131–2, 180, 272*n*, 525–6; 'Neue Zürcher Zeitung', **vi** 255*n*; 'Reichsgesetzblatt', **ii** 26–7; **iii** 381; 'Das Schwarze Korps', **i** 295; 'Völkischer Beobachter', **i** 49, 320*n*, 344; **ii** 52, 71, 138; **iii** 171, 247*n*, 248, 256*n*, 263, 363, 367, 437; **iv** 50, 222, 231, 237, 251, 493; **v** 671; **vi** 113, 465, 481, 527; 'Vossische Zeitung', **ii** 65

public opinion, **ii** 289, 334, 360, 571, 620; **iv** 456; **vi** 197, 615, 708

Roumania, **ii** 135, 137, 144, 151, 168, 171, 179, 189, 204, 279, 355, 381, 384; **iii** 550, 562, 565, 584; **iv** 43, 214, 360, 363, 366–7, 369–70, 375, 385, 387, 389, 391, 396–8, 401, 409–10, 419–20, 422, 433, 465–6, 468, 478, 493, 497*n*, 519–20, 542, 618–9; **v** 81, 92, 213, 239 329, 483; **vi** 79, 101, 127–8, 263

German economic interests. *See* South-east Europe (German interests); Treaties (German-Roumanian Trade Agreement)

threat of German aggression, Mar. 1939, **iv** 284, 360–1, 366–7, 372, 374–5, 380, 382, 384, 386–8, 396, 400, 421, 465, 470, 472, 498

reaction of: France, **iv** 375, 395–7, 410–1, 423, 466, 468, 471–2, 486–7; Great Britain, **iv** 361, 372, 380, 386, 399, 409–10, 435; *see also* Four-Power Declaration; Guarantee (to Roumania); Poland, **iv**

Germany (Roumania) (*cont.*)
361, 371, 401, 423, 435, 458, 465, 469, 471, 510; **v** 23, 34; U.S.S.R., **iv** 361, 372, 449; *see also* U.S.S.R. (Conference at Bucharest [suggested])
threat of German attack, Aug. 1939, **vi** 665*n*, 666, 673
See also Gafencu, G. (visit to Berlin) in Index of Persons
S.A. (Sturm Abteilung), **i** 13, 19, 20, 136, 147, 358, 412; **ii** 90, 457, 652–4; **iv** 19–23, 247, 456; Chief of Staff, *see* Lutze, V., in Index of Persons; S.A. Leib-Standarte Adolf Hitler, **iii** 625
S.S. (Schutz Staffel), **i** 18–9, 26, 44, 67, 136, 147–8, 358, 412, 612; **ii** 90, 371, 457, 652–4; **iii** 166, 372, 564; **iv** 19, 22, 247; **v** 665; **vi** 12, 88
S.S. Death's Head formations, **iii** 625; **vii** 258*n*; S.S. Grenzpolizei, **ii** 15; S.S. Leibstandarte Adolf Hitler, **iv** 258, 264, 267; **vi** 178; S.S. Verfügungstruppen, **iii** 166, 625; **v** 88; **vii** 258*n*; Waffen S.S., **vii** 258*n*
Scandinavian countries, **v** 462, 505–6
Slovakia, **v** 88–90, 276, 289; *see also* Slovakia
Stahlhelm, **ii** 66
'Strength through Joy' organization, **vi** 192
Suez Canal Company, **iii** 309–10; **iv** 10
Sweden, **v** 213; *see also* Germany (Scandinavian countries)
Switzerland, **i** 494; **v** 213, 270, 302
possible German invasion, **iv** 18, 30, 43, 49, 73, 83–4, 101, 114, 167, 214, 508, 531–2
Turkey, **v** 213, 322, 355, 442; **vi** 497; **vii** 225, 264, 273, 299
commercial relations, **v** 574, 592–3, 777, 789–90; **vi** 97, 112, 362, 434, 686; German terms, Aug. 22, 1939, **vii** 140, 155–6, 214
See also Guarantee (to Turkey, reaction of Germany)
U.S.S.R., **i** 95, 404, 422; **ii** 141*n*, 179; **iii** 253–4, 526; **iv** 71; **v** 213, 310
commercial negotiations, **iv** 115, 613, 621–2; **v** 622, 634, 746; **vi** 22, 447; **vii** 383
visit of Herr Schnurre to Moscow, **iv** 14–5, 25, 33–5; cancelled, **iv** 54, 67, 71, 82, 106, 115, 134
Commercial Credit Agreement, Aug. 1939, **vii** 98–100; *see also* Treaties (Germany–U.S.S.R.)
rapprochement, **iv** 71; **v** 463, 594–5, 620, 625, 646, 724, 736; **vi** 17, 44, 47, 449, 705; **vii** 41–2, 154
German-Soviet Non-Aggression Pact, terms of, **vii** 156, 188–9; ratification, Aug. 31, **vii** 430; *referred to,* **vii** 118, 122–3, 127, 132, 136, 142, 153, 207, 248, 268, 274–5, 278, 281, 291, 302, 303*n*, 340, 384, 397, 431, 543, 594, 608, 617–8, 620–2; **ix** 490, 505

Germany (U.S.S.R.: Non-Aggression Pact) (*cont.*)
effect on Anglo-Franco-Soviet military conversations, **vii** 122, 128–9, 131, 142–3, 154–5, 164, 167, 184, 187–8, 190, 205–6, 217, 225, 237, 384–5, 621
reaction of: Estonia, **vii** 426; France, **vii** 121, 129, 131, 244–5, 313, 342; Great Britain **vii** 122, 124*n*, 127, 180–1, 201, 218, 274–5; **ix** 504; Hungary, **vii** 377; Italy, **vii** 181–2, 255, 287, 316, 482*n*, 491; Japan, **vii** 275, 287, 316, 341, 428, 609; **ix** 490, 492, 495, 500, 503, 506–7, 511, 517–8; Poland, **vii** 115–6, 169, 204–5, 291; Spain, **vii** 275, 287; Turkey, **vii** 155, 218, 248, 273*n*, 384; United States, **vii** 275; The Vatican, **vii** 196
proposed military alliance, **vii** 309, 454, 487, 491, 514; inclusion of Japan, **vii** 309
United States, **ii** 639; **iii** 279, 562; **iv** 55, 60, 139; **v** 107
Yugoslavia, **i** 174, 552, 615; **ii** 135–7, 144, 151, 158, 168, 171, 189, 204, 279, 345; **iv** 282, 352, 620; **v** 54, 213, 275, 329, 620; **vi** 11–2, 101, 166, 285
See also Anglo-Franco-Soviet negotiations; Balkan Entente; Belgium; Bulgaria; China; France; Memel; South-east Europe; Spain
Gibraltar, **iv** 104, 411; **v** 56, 71, 118, 143–4, 152, 160, 171, 239
Glatz, **i** 107, 358; **ii** 632
Gleiwitz, **iv** 526; **vii** 485
Gmünd, **ii** 281; **iii** 627
Gniezno, **ix** 408
Godesberg, meetings between Mr. Chamberlain and Herr Hitler, **ii** 462, 477–9, 497, 520–2, 647*n*; **iii** 33, 67, 142–3, 149, 168, 371, 626; **v** 617, 665, 803
preparations for, **ii** 398, 405–6, 410–1, 414, 417–9, 421–3, 426, 437–8, 442–3, 654
conversations at, **ii** 463–73, 499–508
exchange of letters, **ii** 481–91, 493, 521, 542
Herr Hitler's proposals and memorandum of Sept. 23, **ii** 468–73, 495–6; *referred to,* **ii** 477–8, 482, 484, 491, 515–6, 521–5, 547, 549, 554–6, 607, 616, 618, 627; *communicated to Czechoslovak Government,* **ii** 497, 512, 548, 580; *reply of Czechoslovak Government,* **ii** 511, 514, 517, 519, 534, 536, 541–2, 550, 560, 569, 576–7, 580–1, 618
Goerlitz, **i** 358
Gölcük, **vii** 140
Goslar, **iv** 21
Gotkowice, **v** 246
Grafenwöhr, **ii** 237
Grajewo, **vii** 484
Graslitz, **ii** 672
Gratzen, **iii** 640
Graudenz. *See* Grudziadz
Graz, **i** 28, 131, 133, 156

Great Britain
armed forces
army, **i** 200–4, 206–11; **vi** 754, 769; **vii** 568
Royal Air Force, **i** 200, 202–4, 207; **iii** 616–7; **iv** 91, 118–9, 463, 500, 532; **v** 102–3; **vi** 754, 771, 788; **vii** 581–2, 598
Royal Navy, **i** 200; **ii** 40; **iii** 335, 351; **iv** 216, 582; **v** 152, 160, 251; **vi** 414; **vii** 316, 576–80
   Far East, **v** 152, 160; **viii** 320–2, 455–6, 543–50; **ix** 496*n*, 504–5; H.M. ships, 'Birmingham', **ix** 433*n*; 'Gnat', **viii** 3; 'Grimsby', **viii** 329*n*; 'Lowestoft', **viii** 460; **ix** 182; 'Sandwich', **ix** 493; *see also* Japan (Great Britain, incidents involving British shipping)
   naval measures taken, Sept. 1938, **ii** 276, 284, 286, 290*n*, 295–6, 576, 602, 620
   See also Germany (Great Britain, Naval Agreements)
conscription, **iv** 50, 133; **v** 278–9, 284, 337–9, 342, 356, 613, 619, 799, 804–5; **vi** 744
   attitude of France, **iv** 73, 91, 489; **v** 240, 250, 262; of United States, **v** 251–2
Emergency Powers (Defence) Bill, Aug. 24, 1939, **vii** 124*n*, 181, 352*n*
Export Guarantees Act, Feb. 28, 1939, **vi** 191; **viii** 430, 470, 540; **ix** 353*n*, 485
General Election. *See* France (Great Britain)
military measures, Aug. 1939, **vii** 124*n*, 249, 265–6, 568; *see also* Rearmament
Overseas Trade Guarantees Act, July 28, 1939, **vi** 190–1; **ix** 293–4
Press, **i** 212, 233, 584*n*, 590, 618; **ii** 24, 58, 157*n*, 196, 200, 258, 282*n*, 298, 311, 350, 420, 499; **iii** 56, 74, 170, 258, 268, 322, 357, 475, 590, 618; **iv** 7, 9*n*, 137, 153, 250, 412, 607; **v** 80, 337, 499, 599; **vi** 465–7, 607; **vii** 8, 627; **viii** 36, 188
   Austrian 'Anschluss', **i** 2–3, 80–1
   Anglo-German relations, **ii** 128–9, 257; **iii** 389; **iv** 12, 593, 595; **v** 361, 388, 603, 799, 802; **vi** 483, 720, 745, 751, 753; **vii** 91, 387, 550
   Anglo-Italian relations, **iii** 460–1; **v** 140, 142, 155; **vi** 253; **vii** 161, 339–40
   Anglo-Japanese relations, **viii** 27, 122, 135, 346; **ix** 88, 243, 471, 473*n*
   Anglo-Polish relations, **v** 51, 403; **vi** 245, 247, 283, 342; **vii** 54, 366, 399
   Anglo-Soviet relations, **v** 224, 236–7, 648, 717, 785; **vi** 377–8, 386, 592; **vii** 122, 154
   Danzig question, **v** 285; **vi** 401, 420, 432–3, 442, 626, 628, 638; **vii** 13–4, 50, 97
   Sudeten German question, **i** 252, 260, 292, 300, 333, 345, 369–70, 377, 392, 444, 457, 519, 556, 590, 631; **ii** 271
   Beaverbrook Group, **ii** 257; **v** 51; **vi** 245; 'Daily Express', **i** 588; 'Daily Herald', **iii** 475; **v** 224; **vi** 80; **vii** 305, 306*n*, 347;

Great Britain (Press) (*cont.*)
   'Daily Mail', **i** 449; **ii** 293, 417, 653; 'Daily Telegraph', **i** 187; **ii** 142, 164, 200, 257, 279; **iii** 245, 560, 590; **iv** 317, 369; **v** 142, 513; **vi** 465, 467, 'Daily Worker', **vii** 17*n*, 98–9, 384; 'Evening News', **vii** 339; 'Evening Standard', **vii** 339, 'Financial News', **vi** 536; 'Manchester Guardian', **iii** 158–9, 245*n*, 475, 590; **v** 223; **viii** 45, 64; 'News Chronicle', **i** 581, 590; **ii** 6; **iii** 261, 367, 560, 566, 590; **iv** 303, 304*n*, 594, 603, 607; **vi** 536; **viii** 437, 457–8; 'Observer', **iv** 310; **v** 785; 'Star', **v** 164; **vii** 339; 'Sunday Express', **iv** 309; 'Sunday Times', **ii** 89; **iii** 271, 590; **iv** 350*n*, 351; **v** 785; **vi** 218–9; 'The Tablet', **iv** 293; 'The Times', **i** 316, 370, 444, 472, 498, 613; **ii** 24, 257, 267, 271, 293, 354*n*; **iii** 29, 227, 248, 259*n*, 266, 268, 482*n*, 551; **iv** 237, 369, 372, 561–2; **v** 51, 112, 454, 524, 588, 593, 675, 747, 803; **vi** 17, 80, 202, 327, 390, 536, 578, 716; **vii** 13–4, 20–1, 109, 290*n*; **viii** 36, 77, 188, 212, 244, 267; **ix** 193, 348*n*, 477; article of Sept. 7, 1938 (*re* Sudeten German question), **ii** 271*n*; *referred to*, **iii** 2; **v** 65
proposals for international collaboration against further German aggression. *See* Anglo-Franco-Soviet negotiations; Four-Power Declaration; Guarantee
public opinion, **i** 174, 221, 268, 516, 538, 546, 566; **ii** 17, 225, 302, 326, 328, 467, 470, 482, 490, 500, 541, 554; **iii** 37, 63, 142–3, 189–90, 247–8, 282, 313, 315–6, 326, 329, 340, 345, 456, 474, 507, 520, 664–6, 671; **iv** 30, 111, 120, 124, 140, 207; **v** 30, 150, 164, 290, 321, 337, 391, 402, 588, 638, 680, 711, 727, 736, 801; **vi** 74, 134, 215, 219, 277, 306, 353, 408, 580, 648, 659, 684, 701, 737, 740; **vii** 116, 212, 428, 512; **ix** 152, 218, 226, 266, 437–8, 443, 453, 475, 512
White Paper (Cmd. 5847 of Sept. 1938), correspondence relating to, **ii** 576, 607, 623, 675*n*; **iii** 92; **v** 666, 684
Greater Germany. *See* Germany (Austria)
Greece
   air force, **v** 382
   Bulgarian and Yugoslav claims, **v** 285
   Italy, **v** 56, 82, 120, 136, 160, 163, 170, 285, 780; Italian assurances, **v** 161; *referred to*, **v** 151, 155, 182; troop concentrations towards Greek frontier, **v** 382–3, 412, 436–7, 444, 615, 750–1
   Turkey's commitments, **v** 575, 591, 694
   See also Albania (effect of Italian action on Greece); Anglo-Franco-Soviet negotiations; Anti-Comintern Pact; Corfu; Guarantee (to Greece)
Grenzmark, vii 338, 375, 415
Grodno, vii 135, 496
Gross Born, ii 236

Gross Boschpol, **v** 577
Gross Gerau, **ii** 26
Grudziadz, **v** 42, 247–8; **vii** 327, 432, 460, 474
Grulich, **i** 580n; **ii** 630; **iii** 641
Grusbach, **iii** 640
Guadalajara, **iv** 295
Guam, **viii** 475
Guarantees to
  Belgium. *See* Belgium (commitments towards)
  Czechoslovakia, question of international
    guarantee to, **ii** 390, 392–7, 405–6, 409,
    412–3, 416, 425, 432, 445, 447–9, 465, 469,
    475, 518, 573, 624, 628, 679; **iii** 13, 116n,
    127–8, 190, 193, 222, 231–2, 239, 243, 300–6,
    364, 373–5, 378, 398–9, 414–6, 418–9, 421,
    423–4, 427–8, 440–1, 444, 446–9, 513, 515,
    527–8, 530, 575, 606–8; **iv** 17, 82–3, 87, 91–2,
    130, 141, 169, 171–3, 180, 204, 222, 226–7,
    238, 240, 267, 269, 377; **vi** 517; *see also*
    Czechoslovakia (Great Britain)
  Greece: by Great Britain and France, **v** 96–7,
    105, 114, 141, 146, 148, 162, 166–7, 169, 179,
    182–6, 236
    declaration of April 13, 1939, **v** 197
    referred to, **v** 198, 264, 267, 365, 412, 447,
      575, 591, 616, 619, 687, 694, 738, 741,
      743, 762, 766, 780; **vi** 602
    by Turkey, **v** 167–8, 179, 187–9, 230; **vi**
      82, 102–3
  Poland: by France, **vi** 237n
    by Great Britain, **iv** 544–50, 552
    announcement, Mar. 31, 1939, **iv** 553
    implementation of. *See* Poland (Great
      Britain, political relations)
    referred to, **iv** 554–5, 557, 571–2, 575–6; **v**
      passim; **vi** 57, 118, 124, 185, 213, 218,
      237–8, 416, 582, 608, 757, 762; **vii** 162,
      331, 359
    See also Germany (Poland: Danzig and
      Polish Corridor); Poland (Great Britain)
  Roumania: by Great Britain and France, **iv**
    360–1, 375, 397, 409–11, 465–6, 515–7,
    527–30, 540–1, 544, 553–6, 567, 576–8, 615,
    619; **v** 21–2, 46, 57, 66, 74–7, 81, 92, 95–7,
    105–9, 111–5, 178, 184, 186n, 190
    declaration, April 13, 1939, **v** 197
    referred to, **v** 198, 200, 202, 210–1, 264, 267,
      298, 301, 309, 313, 365, 447, 521, 529,
      531, 575, 591, 604, 613, 619, 624, 687,
      695, 738, 741–2, 762, 766; **vi** 77, 79, 127,
      215, 582, 602, 629, 631, 642, 762
    by Germany, **iv** 360–1, 367, 420; **v** 81, 92
    by Poland, **iv** 516, 555, 578; **v** 16, 48, 57,
      73, 76, 81, 94, 112, 200–1, 211, 218, 233,
      298–300, 324, 404, 657; **vii** 65
    by Turkey, **v** 105, 115, 190, 227, 230, 575,
      591, 741; **vi** 52, 54, 69–71, 78, 82–3, 93,
      100, 102–3, 109, 145, 673
  Turkey: by Great Britain and France, **iv**
    437; **v** 95–8, 179–81, 183, 188, 194, 206,

Guarantees (to Turkey) (*cont.*)
    219–20, 226–8, 230–1, 238, 240–3, 259–60,
    278–80, 288, 306–7, 320, 323–4, 335, 340–1,
    362–7, 375, 385, 444–7, 452, 459, 468, 471–3,
    482, 493–6, 499, 500, 502, 552–4, 589, 606–7;
    see also Turkey (Great Britain, Anglo-Franco-
    Turkish negotiations)
    bipartite or tripartite Declaration, **v** 385,
      397, 448, 459, 468, 475, 494, 496, 502–4,
      507–10, 516, 518–9, 522–3, 526, 532–5
    Anglo-Turkish Declaration, May 12, 1939,
      v 497, 531, 537
    reaction of: Balkan Powers, *see* Balkan
      Entente; Germany, **v** 464, 574, 592, 619,
      652, 671–2, 777, 789–90; **vi** 74–5; Italy,
      v 567, 588, 667, 704, 737, 752, 755, 780;
      vi 16, 127, 253, 444
    Franco-Turkish negotiations, May–June,
      1939, **v** 536, 549–50, 578, 746; **vi** 52, 101,
      130, 170–1, 175
    Franco-Turkish Declaration, June 23,
      1939, **v** 746n; **vi** 164; reaction of Italy,
      vi 242
Gyöngyös, **iii** 12, 27
Györ, **iii** 12

'Hai' ships, **viii** 98; **ix** 531
Hainan Island, **viii** 149n, 173, 184; occupation
  by Japanese, **iv** 124n; **viii** 451; **ix** 6, 40, 46, 48,
  238
Hamburg, **i** 155; **v** 515; **vi** 46, 439, 747, 749, 751
Hanau, **ii** 26
Hangö, **vii** 577
Hankow
  H.Q. of Generalissimo Chiang Kai-shek,
    viii 2n, 179n
  Sino-Japanese conflict, **i** 305; **viii** 2–4,
    10n, 14, 27, 42, 69, 74–5, 81–2, 88, 102,
    130–1, 146, 153, 159, 171, 176, 181, 189–
    90, 194, 201, 205, 207, 215–6, 227–8; fall
    of, **viii** 171n, 177n
  Japanese policy, **viii** 206, 361, 367–8, 376;
    ix 73–4, 79, 81, 86–7, 96, 110, 143, 147,
    225
Hanoi-Kunming railway, **viii** 252
Hanover, **ii** 127, 616
Hanyang, **viii** 177n
Hapsburg Monarchy, **ii** 469; **iv** 266; **vi** 297
Hasalau (Habstal), **viii** 577
Hatay, The, **v** 465, 504, 507, 518, 522, 526,
  532–4, 536, 549–50, 578; **vi** 605–6
Havre, Le, **iii** 478
Hawaii, **vii** 428
Haydarpasa, **v** 593
Hechingen, **ii** 26
Heilbronn, **ii** 26
Hel, **v** 249, 583; **vi** 317; **vii** 134, 441
Helsingfors, **iv** 569; **vi** 282; **vii** 187–8, 237
Hengyang, **viii** 102
Henkel and Co., **v** 408

Henlein movement. *See* Czechoslovakia (Political parties, Sudeten German party); Carlsbad Programme; Sudeten German question

Heppenheim, ii 26

Herby, v 583

Hermanice, iii 223

Hermann Göring Fund, i 147

Hermann Göring Werke, vi 133

Hesse, ii 26, 161

Himara, v 127

Hirschberg, i 358

Hirtenberger Patronen-, Zündhütchen- und Metallwaren-Fabrik, i 93

Hlinka Guard, iii 217, 412; iv 157–8, 220–1, 225–6, 233–4, 238, 264, 287, 406–8

Hochal, ii 94

Hof, i 358; ii 27, 370

Hof-Eger Gap, ii 237

Hohenstadt, iii 641

Hohkaido, viii 470

Hollabrunn, ii 281

Holland. *See* Netherlands

Holy Roman Empire, i 55*n*, 302; ii 368; iv 280; v 628

Honan, ix 86, 440*n*

Hongkew, viii 41, 96–7, 100, 118; ix 137

Hong Kong, vii 629; viii 2*n*, 4, 8, 9*n*, 10*n*, 27*n*, 146, 148, 150, 157, 217, 288, 293; ix 52, 53*n*

Hong Kong–Canton railway, viii 146–7

Honolulu, viii 321

Honositz, iii 640

Hopei Province, viii 32–3

Hopei-Chahar Political Council, ix 356, 380, 468, 537

Horb, ii 26

Horne Bludovice, iii 223

Hrusov, iii 199, 219, 223

Hsupukou, ix 153

Hunan Province, viii 27*n*, 203, 207

Hungary, i 79, 100, 110, 154, 196, 222–3, 257, 265, 315, 353, 405, 480, 514, 611, 615, 651–2; iv 617–8; vi 202, 498

    Anti-Comintern Pact, member of, iv 55*n*, 618

    army, iii 44, 224–5, 239; iv 248, 253, 277; v 63, 78; vi 771; vii 140

    Czechoslovakia. *See* Czechoslovakia (Hungary); Ruthenia; Slovakia

    Great Britain. *See* Czechoslovakia (Hungary) and sub-head Hungarian-Roumanian relations *below*

    Italy, iii 185; iv 618; v 332–3; vi 452; vii 71, 83

    Little Entente, ii 151, 157; iv 617; v 64*n*, 332; vi 642*n*

    military measures, i 321*n*; iii 6, 11–2, 18, 20, 25, 27, 44, 188–9, 237; iv 227, 248, 395, 433, 485, 496, 618; v 61–3

    minorities, i 190–1; ii 157; iii 238–9

        Czechs, iii 226; Germans, i 174; iii 226,

Hungary (minorities) (*cont*.)

    238; vii 377; Jews, iii 225–6, 238–9; iv 74; Poles, iii 238; Ruthenians, iii 184, 226, 238; Slovaks, ii 157; iii 184, 225–6, 238; iv 92, 408; v 86–7

    national socialism, i 196; vi 585; vii 377

    Poland, i 315; iii 6, 16, 22, 97, 104, 111; iv 460, 503; v 15, 32–3; vi 405, 666; *see also* Ruthenia (attitude towards Hungary's claims)

    Press, iii 5, 22, 116; v 64, 112; 'Pester Lloyd', iii 5*n*

    Roumania, iii 46, 565; iv 333, 395, 401, 428–9, 433, 460, 478, 510–1, 521, 618–9; v 61–4, 106, 110, 113, 326–7, 333; vi 53, 77, 147, 437, 583, 629–32, 641–2, 660, 687; vii 57–8, 92

    Hungarian-Roumanian relations and:

        Germany, ii 455; iv 370, 401, 433, 457, 478, 480, 496, 625; v 92, 302, 309, 319

        Great Britain, iv 484, 496; vi 77, 629–32, 660, 687; vii 57–8, 92–3, 152

        Poland, iii 431; iv 183, 370, 401, 435, 503; v 2, 8, 15, 63, 94, 106

        See also Roumania (minorities: Hungarians); Ruthenia (attitude to Hungary's claims); Transylvania

    war in Europe, probable attitude, vi 452; vii 141, 151, 377

    Yugoslavia, iv 617–8; v 334, 529, 551, 660, 662; vi 51, 66, 437

    See also Treaties (Hungary–Little Entente)

Hupeh Province, viii 207

Hura, v 577

Huszt, v 62

Iglau (Jihlava), ii 549; iii 627; iv 231, 242, 261, 267, 270

Iglo, v 78

Ilava, v 85

Import Export Bank, viii 311

India, i 344; iv 600; v 612; vi 127, 659; viii 293

Indian Ocean, vi 747

Indo-China, v 152; vii 629; viii 148, 184, 244, 293; ix 193, 238

Industrial Facilities Corporation, viii 104

Inner Mongolia, viii 343–4, 372, 404, 521

Innsbruck, i 1–3, 28, 129, 132, 156; v 93

International Brigade, iii 343

International Institute of Agriculture, iv 356

International Organization for Relief of Refugees from Germany and Austria, ii 149

International Volunteers, Shanghai, viii 137

Ipolysag, iii 86

Iraq, i 96; v 213, 264, 600; vi 127, 195

Ireland (Northern and Southern), i 22, 505, 579, 587, 593, 604, 624–5; ii 70, 247, 307, 368, 532; iv 753; vii 549

Isola, ii 222

Israel, Messrs. (Berlin), **iii** 276
Italian East Africa, **iv** 302, 306–7
Italy
 aeroplane factories, **iv** 338
 air force, **ii** 222; **iii** 501; **vi** 788; *see also* Italy (Spain)
 army, **i** 422; **ii** 221, 356; **iii** 501; **iv** 160–1; **v** 172–3, 420–2; **vi** 706; *see also* Italy (military measures), (Spain)
 conference proposed by, to meet Sept. 5, 1939, **vii** 442–5, 449, 471, 477–9, 481, 498, 504–8, 511–3, 516, 519–21, 524, 530–1, 537n, 540
 encirclement, fear of, **v** 319, 567, 704–6, 759, 784
 France. *See* Albania (effect of Italian action on Franco-Italian relations); France (Italy)
 Germany. *See* Germany (Italy); Rome–Berlin Axis
 Great Britain, **ii** 172n; **iii** 257; **v** 251, 255–6, 536, 551, 599, 655; **vi** 253, 273–4, 450, 453, 555–6; **vii** 75–6, 94–5, 97, 113, 144, 147, 224, 263, 265–6, 295–6, 299, 303–4, 359–60, 369, 386, 439, 444, 459, 478
  Anglo-Italian conversations, and Agreement signed April 16, 1938, **i** 2, 128, 176, 180, 198, 208, 211, 222, 239; **ii** 20n, 240, 644; **iii** 253, 312–62 *passim*, 426, 459, 462–4, 467, 469, 473–4, 478–80, 482, 487, 494, 499, 500, 514, 518, 520, 530–1, 537–9; **iv** 293–4, 302, 315–6, 320, 323–4, 326, 343, 345, 348n, 559; **v** 120–1, 125, 128, 131, 133–5, 137, 141–2, 147, 154, 156, 169, 171, 173, 219, 258, 422, 503; **vi** 241, 252, 444, 579; **vii** 624; **viii** 92, 179, 443
   Agreement brought into effect, Nov. 16, 1938, **iii** 355, 362
   question of denunciation of, **v** 704, 706–7, 718, 752, 755–6, 763, 765–6, 779–80, 784; **vi** 15–6, 252
  H.M. Ambassador and audiences with Signor Mussolini, **vi** 21, 115
  loan to Italy, **iii** 280; **vi** 488, 554–7
  reaction of events in Far East on Anglo-Italian relations, **vi** 126, 127n; **ix** 213
  visit of Mr. Chamberlain and Lord Halifax, Jan. 1939, **iii** 321, 356–8, 362, 458–540 *passim*; **iv** 87, 292–4, 306, 346–7, 402; **vi** 257; **viii** 437n
 suggested Anglo-Italian collaboration to preserve peace, Aug. 1939, **vii** 7–8, 28, 36, 49, 60, 62, 67, 72, 157, 186, 241, 302–3, 307, 310, 323, 326, 329, 358, 367, 373, 393, 459, 477, 520
 See also Albania (effect of Italian action on Anglo-Italian relations); Anglo-Franco-Soviet negotiations (Italy); France (Italy—attitude towards questions affecting Franco-Italian relations)

Italy (*cont.*)
 internal conditions, **iii** 496–7, 500–1, 572; **iv** 337–9; **v** 171, 489
 Japan, **viii** 180
 Libya, Italian troops in. *See* Libya
 military measures, **ii** 221–2; **iii** 335–6, 347; **iv** 41–2, 125, 160–1, 298–308 *passim*, 311, 315, 321, 328, 355–8; **v** 54, 117–9, 123, 134, 160, 170, 172–3, 421–2; **vi** 31, 284, 664; **vii** 15, 71, 220, 240
 neutrality, decision, **vii** 459
 Poland, **iii** 62n; **iv** 177–9, 182; **vi** 19; *see also* Count Ciano (visit to Warsaw) in Index of Persons
 Press, **iii** 336, 347, 352–3, 358, 511, 530; **iv** 301–2, 309–11, 350; **v** 173, 781, 784, 800; **vi** 466, 528–9, 555; **vii** 71, 220, 335
  Anglo-Italian relations, **iv** 320, 327, 340; **vi** 126–7, 240–1, 253, 273, 443–4, 470, 556, 588
  Franco-Italian relations, **ii** 197; **iii** 297, 322, 394, 464, 474–8, 480, 485–7, 499; **iv** 42, 139–40, 317, 319–20, 326–7, 339; 346–7; **vi** 472
  comments on British and French attitude towards Gen. Franco, **iv** 318, 327
  See also Gayda, Dr. V. in Index of Persons
  'Giornale d'Italia', **i** 37; **iii** 248, 476; **iv** 324, 355; **v** 182, 186, 443, 655; **vi** 127, 664; 'Informazione Diplomatica', **ii** 315n, 331; **iii** 336, 400; **iv** 311; 'Lavoro Fascista', **iii** 476; **vi** 529; 'Mattino', **iii** 352; 'Messaggero', **iv** 309, 350n; 'Popolo d'Italia', **iii** 473; **iv** 310, 318, 324, 327; 'Relazioni Internazionali', **iv** 310, 317, 319, 326, 340; 'Resto del Carlino', **iv** 318; 'Stampa', **iii** 476; **iv** 318; **vi** 466; 'Tribuna', **iii** 475; **vi** 466, 529; 'Voce d'Italia', **iii** 476
 public opinion, **iii** 320, 345–52, 466n, 468, 472, 475; **iv** 347, 350; **v** 377, 473; **vi** 488; **vii** 481, 498
 sanctions against, 1935, **ii** 184; **iii** 472, 484–5; **iv** 616
 Spain, Italian forces in, **ii** 197, 636; **iii** 297, 299, 312–27, 329, 334, 339–40, 342–5, 356–7, 465, 479, 496–7, 506, 509, 514, 516, 518, 520–3, 530; **iv** 104, 292, 295–6, 300, 319n; **v** 56, 71, 118, 143, 150, 153, 155, 171, 173, 219, 258; *see also* Spain and Spanish Civil War (attitude of Germany and Italy)
 Suez Canal Co., request for appointment of Italian to Board of, **iii** 309–10; *see also* France (Italian claims)
 Turkey, **v** 354–5, 442, 780; *see also* Albania (effect of Italian action); Guarantee (to Turkey, reaction of Italy)
 Yugoslavia, **iv** 352, 620; **v** 54, 56, 116n, 117, 120–1, 137, 154, 285, 314, 346, 376, 588–9; **vi** 12, 66; **vii** 93, 421–2; *see also* Albania (effect of Italian action); Cinkar-Markovitch, A. (visit to Italy) in Index of Persons

Italy (*cont.*)

war in Europe, probable attitude, **vii** 84, 93–4, 114, 119, 136, 139, 144, 147–8, 157, 159, 161, 165, 202, 220–1, 226, 244, 248, 255, 263, 279, 299, 315–6, 322, 335, 349–50, 361, 378–9, 397, 419, 421–2, 452, 482–3, 495

official decision, **vii** 459, 481, 486

See also Anti-Comintern Pact; Austria; Bulgaria; Czechoslovakia; Greece; Hungary; Munich Conference

Jablonkow (Jablunkov), **iii** 82, 199, 212, 225

Jagerndorf, **ii** 630

Japan, ii 220, 562, 638, 691; **iii** 143, 519; **iv** 4, 38, 216, 621; **v** 152, 377, 503; **vi** 443, 747

armed forces: army, **viii** 1, 5–6, 32, 77, 87, 121, 156, 172, 180, 270; **ix** 130, 397–8, 442, 506–7, 516–7

navy, **iii** 670; **viii** 544

East Asia, Japanese policy

proposed China Council, **viii** 2*n*, 33, 81, 108, 110, 120–1, 155, 182

proposed 'new order' (economic co-operation between Japan, Manchukuo and China), **viii** 177*n*, 214–5, 234–7, 241–2, 246, 251, 255, 265, 271, 273–5, 293, 305, 314, 343–4, 346, 349, 355–8, 403–4; **ix** 94

Asia Development Council, **viii** 246*n*, 294, 371, 404

Great Britain, **viii** and **ix** *passim*

anti-British demonstrations in Tokyo, July–Aug. 1939, **ix** 378, 384

British interests in China, and Japanese policy

Great Britain's five points as bases for negotiations, **viii** 6*n*, 14, 27, 56, 62, 70*n*, 81–2, 87, 103, 111–3, 171, 222

talks between Sir R. Craigie and General Ugaki, July–Sept. 1938, **viii** 5*n*, 27–9, 34–6, 41, 43–4, 46–50, 53, 56–7, 62, 70*n*, 71, 74–6, 81–2, 86–7, 89–92, 96–101, 103, 105, 109, 111–3, 117–8, 120, 171

question of reprisals against Japan. *See* Sino-Japanese conflict

See also Amoy; China (Japanese-occupied districts); Shanghai; Tientsin; Yangtse

Eden-Yoshida project of 1937, **ix** 510, 522

effect on Anglo-Japanese relations of Great Britain's financial aid to China, **iii** 309; **viii** 257*n*, 261, 295–6, 298, 303, 345, 397–8, 488, 502–4, 518–9, 537*n*, 539; **ix** 12, 22, 31, 354–5, 390–1

incidents involving British shipping: H.M.S. 'Cicala' and H.M.S. 'Robin', **viii** 168*n*, 174*n*; **ix** 531; S.S. 'Lalita' and 'Sagres', **ix** 21, 87; H.M.S. 'Ladybird', **viii** 170*n*; H.M.S. 'Sandpiper', **viii** 169, 170*n*, 278,

Japan (Great Britain) (*cont.*)

324, 330; *see also* Chefoo; Tsingtao; Yangtse

internal affairs, **viii** 79–81, 289–90, 359–60, 528–9

change of Government, Jan. 1939, **viii** 369; Aug. 1939, **ix** 489, 492, 497–8, 500, 506–8, 515–9, 524

Five Ministers' Conference, **viii** 1, 5*n*, 29, 79, 154, 182–3, 246*n*; **ix** 130–1, 442, 516

political parties (the Seiyukai and Taishuto), **ix** 516

politics (moderates *v.* extremists), **ix** 264–5, 276, 286, 458, 528

relations between Japanese Govt. and Japanese military and naval authorities in China, **viii** 5*n*, 73, 77, 90, 172, 188; **ix** 171, 199, 209, 221, 237, 397, 454

International Settlements in China, Japanese statement relating to, **ix** 108–9, 138, 149, 176, 187, 194; *see also* Amoy (Kulangsu Settlement); Shanghai; Tientsin

League of Nations. *See* Sino-Japanese conflict (sanctions against Japan)

Manchukuo. *See* sub-head (East Asia) *above*

Press, **viii** 49, 86, 118, 121–2, 130, 135, 139, 211, 229, 253, 480, 519; **ix** 108, 130, 195, 274, 302, 517, 519, 525

'Asahi', **viii** 121; **ix** 109, 131, 524; 'Chugai', **viii** 518; **ix** 131, 186; 'Chuo Koron', **viii** 182; 'Hochi', **viii** 464; **ix** 131, 378; 'Japan Advertiser', **viii** 355–6; 'Japan Times', **viii** 86; 'Kakushin, **viii** 289; 'Kokumin', **ix** 131; 'Nichi Nichi', **viii** 121, 139, 519; **ix** 131, 186, 461; 'Tairiku Shimpo','**ix** 336; 'Yomiuri', **viii** 211; **ix** 131

public opinion, **viii** 22, 27, 34, 44, 54, 77–8, 89, 107, 275, 503; **ix** 57, 276, 282, 367, 397–8, 474, 530

U.S.S.R., **iv** 621; **vii** 615; **viii** 85, 302, 362, 518; **ix** 26, 28, 516

Manchukuo border incident (Changkufeng affair), **viii** 26*n*, 31, 38–40, 49, 54, 149

United States, **iii** 308–9; **vii** 428; **ix** 518, 520

U.S. interests in China, and Japanese policy, **viii** 62, 82, 116, 124, 127, 151, 181, 185, 190, 192–4, 199, 204–5, 212, 216, 240–2, 246, 254–5, 275–6, 302, 316–9, 348, 353, 356, 374, 389, 448–9, 505, 513–4; **ix** 69, 94, 120, 202*n*, 205, 223, 284, 342, 396

proposed U.S.-Japanese co-operation in cause of peace in Europe, **ix** 102, 107–9, 134–5, 148, 172, 188, 197, 235, 284

U.S. denunciation of American-Japanese Commercial Treaty of 1911, **ix** 348, 352, 354, 360, 366–7, 371, 381–2, 391, 411, 415, 417, 482, 516, 524

Japan (*cont.*)
  war in Europe, probable attitude, **viii** 85, 87;
    ix 11, 38, 40, 52, 91, 429, 506, 521
    statement on 'non-interference', Sept. 4,
    1939, **ix** 525–7
    See also under Anglo-Franco-Soviet negotia-
    tions (Japan); Anti-Comintern Pact; France
    (Far East); Germany (Japan); Sino-Japa-
    nese conflict; Sudeten German question
    (Japan); Tientsin (British Concession)
Jardine Matheson & Company, viii 76, 98n,
  331; **ix** 16, 61, 82, 96, 156, 322; *see also*
  Matheson & Company
Jasina, iv 262
Jaworina, iii 219–20; **iv** 408
Jaworzyna, iii 199, 212, 219; **v** 246–7
Jechnitz, iii 640
Jenkau, vi 87
Jews, i 98, 617; **ii** 11, 14
  international Jewish propaganda, and murder
    of Herr vom Rath, **iii** 261, 268, 270, 277–8
  Jewish refugee problem, **iii** 294–6, 432, 519;
    iv 8; **v** 343
  Austria, **i** 24, 30, 42, 44, 67, 133, 136, 147, 155
  Bohemia and Moravia, Protectorate of, **iv**
    562, 566
  Czechoslovakia, **ii** 315; **iii** 195, 201, 225,
    375–6, 386, 401, 412, 418, 421, 559, 631–2;
    iv 2–3, 8–9, 13, 61–2, 108–9
  Danzig Free City of, **iii** 404, 543, 552, 559,
    591, 595, 598–602, 610, 613; **iv** 81, 187; **v**
    101, 813
  Germany, **i** 136; **ii** 66; **iii** 195, 262, 264, 266–
    7, 270–1, 273, 275–7, 294–6, 375, 381–4,
    388, 394, 397, 434, 520, 545, 562, 564; **iv**
    9–10, 59–60, 589; **v** 673
      expulsion of Polish Jews, **iii** 250–1, 274,
        365, 375, 432, 566, 568, 582; **iv** 206; **vi**
        206
  Hungary, **iii** 225–6, 238–9; **iv** 74
  Italy, **iii** 497
  Lithuania, **v** 282
  Poland, **ii** 287; **iii** 432; **iv** 203; **v** 35–6, 40,
    284; **vi** 269–70; **vii** 281; *see also* sub-head
    (Germany: expulsion of Polish Jews) *above*
  Roumania, **iv** 183, 203; **v** 36, 342–3
  Slovakia, **iii** 217, 226, 412; **iv** 97–8, 158, 229,
    238; **v** 90
  Sudetenland, **i** 124, 186–7, 263, 415, 594–5;
    ii 9; **iii** 381; expulsion from, **iii** 195, 205,
    208, 221, 230; right of option, **iv** 108, 113–4,
    150–1
Jibuti, iii 420, 437, 464, 466–7, 475, 477, 482n,
  483–4, 487–90, 493, 495, 508, 510, 512; **iv**
  296, 317, 319n, 322–3, 325–6, 336, 344, 353n,
  359, 590; **v** 124, 223, 347, 427, 611–3, 651,
  663; **vi** 44, 303, 358; **vii** 350
Jicin, i 579
Jihlava. *See* Iglau
Jilemnice, iii 236

Jüterbog, ii 105, 127, 236, 282

Kailan Mining Administration, ix 322
Kaiser Steinbruch, iv 235
Kalisz, v 247
Kalthof, v 622–3, 625–6, 635–6, 653, 667,
  733–4, 764, 768, 788; **vi** 8, 42, 45, 148–9,
  417, 452, 455, 726
Kamiensk, v 246
Karinhall, i 173n, 513, 591; **ii** 358n, 362, 543;
  iii 615; **v** 713, 715, 717; **vi** 11–2, 736, 744–5,
  754; **vii** 194–5, 547–8
Karlsbad. *See* Carlsbad
Kartuzy, v 27
Karwin (Karwina), iii 229; **vi** 81
Kaschau, vii 259
Käsemark, iv 222; **vi** 393, 454, 587n
Kassel, ii 190; **v** 771, 782
Katowice (Kattowitz), iii 8, 229, 251; **iv** 162;
  v 246, 511; **vi** 60; **vii** 203, 338, 375, 474, 485,
  496, 533
Kavaja, v 177, 383, 437n
Kiangsi, Province of, viii 33, 203, 207
Kiel, ii 123
Kielce, v 246–7, 407
Kiev, i 420–4; **v** 384
King-Hall news-letters, The, vi 374, 442, 734;
  vii 47, 213
Kipsdorf, ii 552
Kiukiang, viii 406
Kladrau, iii 640
Klagenfurt, i 156; **vii** 83
Klentsch, ii 596, 603
Kobe, viii 80
Kocurkovice, iii 223
Komarom, iii 86, 124, 140, 142, 152, 155, 184
Komotau, i 436–7; **ii** 666; **iii** 640
Königsberg, i 155; **iii** 641; **vi** 617; **vii** 134, 230,
  483, 546
**'Königsberg' (German cruiser), visit to Danzig,
  v** 788; **vi** 193, 207, 223, 233–4, 236, 557; **vii**
  55, 129, 152, 543–4; cancelled, **vii** 222n
Königsbruck, i 323n
Königgrätz, i 580n
Konstantynow, vi 552
Kosel, i 358
Kosice, iii 152, 188, 222
Kossovo, v 120
Kovno, vi 249
Kowel, vii 491
Krakow. *See* Cracow
Krappitz, i 358
Kronstadt, v 249; **vii** 134
Krumau, iii 74, 83, 85
Kufra, iv 302, 306
Kulangsu International Settlement. *See* Amoy
Kulm, vii 460
Kunming, ix 294
Kuomintang, The. *See* China (Government of
  Nationalist China)

Küstrin, **vii** 415
Kutno, **v** 247
Kuty, **iv** 57
Kwangsi Province, **viii** 27, 44, 207
Kwangtung Province, **viii** 127, 131, 137, 148–9, 364
Kwanto and Kwansai districts, **viii** 80
Kyšperk, **iv** 57

Ladeburg, **iii** 256
Lanark, Sir J. Simon's speech at, **ii** 172
Landsberg, **vii** 160, 416
Langfuhr, **vi** 454, 586; **vii** 105, 157
Lashio, **viii** 142
Latvia, i 172; **ii** 594; **v** 104, 648; **vi** 159
  Anglo-Franco-Soviet guarantee of, question of, **v** 558, 573, 604, 648–9, 669, 689, 700, 730, 737, 767; **vi** 35, 48–9, 55, 158–9, 168, 174, 230, 251, 280, 301, 313; *see also* Anglo-Franco-Soviet negotiations (Baltic States and Finland)
  Anglo-Polish treaty negotiations, **vii** 65
  German minority, **v** 698, 700; **vi** 159
  H.M. diplomatic representation, **iv** 390n
  neutrality, **v** 649; **vi** 49
  Soviet *démarche*, Mar. 1939, and Latvian reply, **v** 214–5, 404–5, 604
  See also Germany (Latvia)
League of Nations, i 54, 84–5, 91, 94, 96–7, 100, 143, 247, 294, 299n, 477, 497, 650–3; **ii** 173, 469, 489; **iii** 430, 479, 481; **iv** 60, 145n, 365; **v** 529n; **vi** 45n
  Abyssinian question, **iii** 480, 486; **vi** 753; **vii** 146
  Albania, **v** 120
  Anglo-Franco-Soviet negotiations, **v** 680, 688, 701–2, 711–2, 719, 726, 767; **vi** 35, 39
  Anglo-Franco-Turkish negotiations, **vi** 599, 602
  'Anschluss' of Austria, **i** 32, 41–2, 46, 49, 100, 127, 136
  Belgium, **i** 649; **iii** 287n
  China
    China's appeals to League, **ii** 595; **viii** 7n, 58–9, 66–9, 78, 83, 91, 93–6, 103–5, 111, 140, 143–6, 199, 245, 391–2, 398–9, 402–3, 408, 509; **ix** 100–1, 104–5, 113
    Resolutions relating to China (Oct. 1937, Feb. 1938, May 1938), **viii** 7n, 59, 96; of Jan. 1939, **viii** 418; **ix** 48; of May 1939, **ix** 121, 104–5, 113, 141–2
  Czechoslovakia: Sudeten German question, **i** 183, 229, 239, 255, 266, 298, 433, 534, 605, 635; **ii** 294, 323, 365–6, 498, 547, 594–5
  Danzig, guarantee of Constitution of Free City, **iii** 402, 404–5, 542–4, 552, 555, 591, 596, 604; **iv** 46; **v** 18; *see also* Danzig
  Japan. *See* Sino-Japanese conflict (sanctions against Japan)

League of Nations (*cont.*)
  Poland, **iii** 283–4; **iv** 616
  reform of, **ii** 157, 266, 293–4, 594n
  Switzerland, **i** 234n, 650–1
  U.S.S.R., **i** 62–4; **vii** 268
  Yugoslavia, **v** 588, 660; **vi** 166–7
  See also Air warfare; Committees (of League of Nations)
Leamington, **i** 84, 91
Lebanon, The, **vi** 347
Leipzig, **i** 18, 155, 301, 358, 561; **iii** 91, 417; **iv** 218, 245
'Leipzig' (German cruiser), visit to Danzig, 1936, **vi** 207
Leitmeritz, **i** 316; **ii** 660, 670; **v** 555
Lemberg. *See* Lwow
Leningrad, **v** 727; **vi** 535, 563–4; **vii** 45, 188, 237
Leonberg, **ii** 26
Leonding, **i** 43
Leszno, **vii** 484
Levice, **iii** 152
Libau, **viii** 577
Liberec. *See* Reichenberg
Libya, **iii** 485; **v** 304
  German military experts, **iv** 125, 161
  Italian troops, **iii** 312, 316, 318, 479; **iv** 161. 300, 302, 306–8, 312–3, 315–6, 324, 326, 328–34, 337, 339, 341–3, 345, 348; **v** 54, 422, 612–3, 703, 774; **vi** 31, 579
Lichtenau, **iv** 57
Lida, **vii** 135
Liebwerda, **ii** 663
Liechtenstein, **v** 213; **vi** 46
Liegnitz, **i** 358; **v** 204
Liessau, **v** 692
Lima, **iv** 602
Linz, **i** 43, 45, 82, 131–2, 135, 156; **ii** 281, 544, 596, 603; **iii** 417, 627
Lisbon, **v** 239
Lithuania, i 172, 421–2; **iii** 265–6, 274, 442; **iv** 617, 622; **v** 455; **vi** 218–9, 256n; **vii** 65, 112, 546
  Anglo-Franco-Soviet negotiations, **v** 568; **vi** 162, 256–7
  Great Britain, **iv** 287, 475
  Poland, **i** 63, 421–2; **iii** 104, 106; **iv** 286, 464, 518; **v** 3, 16, 34; **vi** 256, 607n
  Press, 'Lietuvos Aidas', **v** 282
  U.S.S.R., **iv** 286, 518–9, 622; **vi** 256
  See also Germany (Lithuania); Memel
Little Entente, **i** 252n, 257, 265, 615, 650–2; **ii** 1, 151, 157–8, 294, 575n; **iii** 51, 201; **iv** 69, 618; **v** 8, 123; **vi** 498
  Bled Agreement of Aug. 1938, **ii** 157; **v** 64n, 332; **vi** 642n
Lobositz, **iii** 640
Locarno settlement, 1925. *See* Treaties, *multilateral*
Lodz, **v** 69, 247, 407, 605; **vi** 94; **vii** 204, 425, 496

Löw Beer & Co., Messrs., **iii** 644
Low Countries, The, **iii** 160; **iv** 18; **vii** 293; *see also* Belgium; Netherlands
Lublin, **v** 43, 407; **vii** 259
Lubliniec, **v** 246; **vii** 485
Ludwigsburg, **ii** 26
Lukouchiao incident, July 7, 1937, **viii** 466; **ix** 100, 159
Lundenburg, **iii** 196, 207, 639; **iv** 57
Lunghai railway, **viii** 32, 535
Lungkow, **viii** 288
Lupkow, **v** 248
Luxemburg
  neutrality, **i** 648n, 649–50; **v** 628
  See also Anglo-Franco-Soviet negotiations
Lwow (Lvov), **i** 423; **v** 407; **vii** 306, 347, 453
Lyck, **vii** 135

Macao, **viii** 42n
Macedonia, **v** 530, 751
Maginot Line, **i** 94; **ii** 57, 86, 140, 269, 509, 513, 527–8, 569, 576, 585; **iii** 569, 579, 609; **iv** 18, 30; **v** 71, 758; **vi** 722, 773, 775; **vii** 514, 566–7
Mährisch-Altstadt, **i** 487
Mährisch-Neustadt, **iii** 641
Mährisch-Ostrau (Moravska Ostrava), **i** 121, 430, 479, 550–1; **ii** 264–5, 272, 274, 304n, 333, 671, 676; **iii** 104, 148, 196, 207, 228, 420, 642; **iv** 57, 162, 258, 261–2, 264, 404–5, 440, 444, 560; **v** 93, 204, 247, 556, 699; **vii** 547
Mährisch-Schönberg, **i** 487
Mährisch-Trübau, **iii** 641
Majorca, **iii** 355, 514
Malacky, **iv** 287
Malta, **iii** 466, 498
Manchukuo, **viii** 333, 448; *see also* Japan (U.S.S.R.)
Marbach, **ii** 26
Marburg, **iii** 564
Marienbad, **i** 276; **ii** 50, 177, 657, 664, 668; **v** 27, 625; **vi** 164, 178, 702, 706
Marienburg, **vi** 393
Marienwerder, **v** 721; **vii** 432n, 460
Marktheidenfeld, **ii** 26
Matheson & Company, **viii** 164
Matzkau, **vi** 586
Maulbronn, **ii** 26
'May 21–2, 1938'. *See* Germany (Great Britain, *démarche*)
Mediterranean, The, **i** 154, 176, 203; **iii** 252–3, 280, 344, 427, 472; **v** 239–40, 340, 589; **vi** 599, 747
  '*status quo*' and Italian action in Albania, **v** 128, 131, 133–5, 137, 149, 156
Mein Kampf, **i** 55–6, 154, 175, 226, 294, 303, 405, 603; **ii** 396; **iii** 191, 386–7; **iv** 214; **vi** 440, 500, 752; **vii** 256; **ix** 6
Melnik, **ii** 69; **iv** 264

Memel, **i** 108, 174, 515, 625; **ii** 339, 375; **iii** 436, 442, 548, 565, 585, 658; **iv** 121, 213, 215, 271, 362, 625; **v** 423, 560, 583, 721; **vi** 137; **vii** 134
  Convention and Statute of May 1924, **ii** 339, 375; **iv** 378, 474, 476, 638, 641, 645–6
  elections, Dec. 1938, **iv** 638–42
  Germany, **iv** 52, 285–6, 363, 369, 383, 390, 397, 421, 430–1, 454, 475–6, 493, 505, 517–8, 534, 547, 617, 622, 638–42, 646; **v** 618–9; **vi** 290–1, 498, 693
  occupation of Memel, **iv** 455–6
  cession to Germany, **iv** 474–6, 483; *see also* Treaties (Germany–Lithuania)
  reaction of: France, **iv** 363, 378, 382, 468, 639–46; Great Britain, **iii** 436n; **iv** 378, 436, 474, 534, 639, 641–7; Poland, **iv** 431, 452–3, 464, 466, 478–9, 497, 518; **v** 3, 16, 26, 709; **vi** 239
  visit of Herr Hitler, **iv** 482, 495; **v** 26
Merano, **iv** 338; **v** 171, 173
Messkirch, **ii** 26
Metropolitan-Vickers Electrical Co. Ltd., **iv** 34
Michalkovice, **iii** 223
Middle East, **iii** 318, 343
Milan, **iii** 476; **iv** 327, 338
  meeting between Count Ciano and Herr von Ribbentrop, **v** 473, 523, 585; *see also* Ciano, Count (visit to Milan) in Index of Persons
Milovice, **iv** 562
Miltenberg, **ii** 26
Minorities. *See* Czechoslovakia; Germany; Hungary; Poland; Roumania.
Minorities Declaration, Nov. 1938. *See* Munich Agreement (carrying out of)
Miskolc, **iii** 12
Missions
  British
    Lord Runciman's to Czechoslovakia, **ii** 3–405 *passim*, 446, 656–75, 680; **iii** 4, 101; **iv** 606; **vii** 99; attitude of: Czechoslovakia, **ii** 25, 29, 34, 38–9, 79; France, **ii** 20, 69, 72–3, 197, 246; Germany, **ii** 6, 13, 18–9, 24, 38, 64, 79, 88, 96–8, 102, 109–10, 112n, 126–8, 158–9, 168, 195, 646, 662, 667; Italian Ambassador at Berlin, **ii** 119–20; Poland, **ii** 190; *see also* Sudeten German question (attitude of France & Great Britain) and Runciman, Viscount, in Index of Persons
    Air, to Germany, **iv** 115n, 123
    Military, to Poland, **vii** 236n, 491n, 499, 515
    Trade, to Roumania, **iv** 419
    Trade, to U.S.S.R. (Mr. R. S. Hudson's), **iv** 132n, 568–71; press communiqué, **iv** 512, 523–4; **v** 235
  British and French Military, to U.S.S.R., **vi** 674n; *see also* Anglo-Franco-Soviet military conversations
  French Military, to Czechoslovakia, **i** 302n, 495n, 496, 503, 543

Missions (*cont.*)
  French (*cont.*)
    Air, to Germany, **ii** 122–4, 140
    aircraft production experts, to Great Britain,
      iv 462
    Air, to Poland, **iv** 142
    Military, to Poland, **vii** 236, 526
    Military, to Turkey, **vi** 434*n*
  German
    Air, to Great Britain, 1937, **iv** 123
  Polish
    Financial and economic, to Great Britain,
      vi 199, 215, 226
  Soviet
    Military, to Germany, **vii** 454
  Turkish
    Commercial, to France, **vi** 362
    Commercial, to Great Britain, **vii** 321*n*
    Military, to Great Britain, **vi** 191
Mistek, **iv** 162
Moldau Valley, **iii** 74
Montpellier, **iii** 478
Moravia, **i** 55*n*, 105, 107, 121, 183, 190, 193, 279,
  404–5, 487–8, 502, 570, 613; **ii** 524, 529*n*, 530,
  592, 630; **iii** 118*n*, 133, 139, 165, 207, 216,
  225, 626; **iv** 240, 247–9; *see also* Bohemia and
  Moravia
Moravičany L., **iv** 57
Moravka, **iii** 419
Moravska Ostrava. *See* Mährisch Ostrau
Morocco, **ii** 96, 636; **iii** 464; **iv** 307, 325; **v** 144
Moszczenica, **v** 246
Mukacevo, **iii** 152
Mukden incident, Sept. 18, 1931, **viii** 70, 73
Munich, **i** 19–20, 156; **ii** 281, 351, 353; **iii** 275,
  566, 581; **iv** 229
Munich, Conference at
  preparations, **ii** 542, 551, 553, 556, 561, 587,
    592, 594, 597, 599, 601, 604, 606–7, 614–5,
    623–4, 626, 644; **vi** 746, 752
  conversations, **ii** 630–40
  Hitler–Chamberlain Declaration, **ii** 640; *re-
    ferred to*, **iii** 60*n*, 159, 172, 252, 268, 273, 282,
    286, 293, 389, 525; **iv** 241, 267, 602, 641; **v**
    361; **vii** 621
  part played by Signor Mussolini, **ii** 587, 590,
    624, 626, 642–4; **iii** 322–3, 324*n*, 326, 328,
    336, 461–2, 480, 499, 500, 538, 620; **iv** 402;
    v 277; **vi** 330
  representation of Czechoslovakia, **ii** 601, 604,
    606–7, 614, 623–4, 631–2
  referred to, **ii** 616, 625–7; **iii** 67, 144, 149, 151,
    187, 248, 285, 298–9, 303–5, 314, 319–20,
    323, 326, 328, 330, 362, 392, 396, 415, 421,
    458, 460, 461*n*, 488, 498, 590, 626; **iv** 207,
    584; **v** 277, 458, 616; **vi** 63
Munich Agreement
  text of, **ii** 627–9, 634–5
  accepted by Czechoslovak Govt., **ii** 640–1; **iii**
    177

Munich Agreement (*cont.*)
  reaction of: Bulgaria, **iii** 144–6; China and
    Japan, **viii** 134, 138, 149, 158; leading
    Frenchmen, **iii** 88–90; Herr Hitler, **iv** 4;
    Italy, **iii** 346–52; Poland, **iii** 50, 102–3, 180;
    U.S.S.R., **iii** 144, 154, 193
  referred to, **ii** 630, 641; **iii** 50, 56, 58–9, 61, 86,
    93, 100, 105, 109, 118–9, 128–36, 147–8,
    162–3, 170, 175–8, 198, 200, 204–5, 227,
    231–2, 282, 292, 294, 323, 326, 343, 385*n*,
    408–9, 414–5, 423, 449, 461, 607, 626; **iv**
    41, 91–2, 113, 141–4, 220, 222, 227, 250, 252,
    264, 266, 268–9, 271, 291, 364, 368, 376–7,
    441, 443, 595; **v** 305–6, 337, 370–1, 456, 542,
    617; **vi** 21, 752, 754; **vii** 354*n*
  carrying-out of
    International Commission set up. *See* Com-
      missions
    Protocol of Oct. 5, 1938, **iii** 135–6, 169,
      176
    Executive Protocol of Oct. 28, **iii** 646
    German-Czech. conversations on fron-
      tier delimitation, **iii** 176, 196, 207, 213,
      226–7, 230, 234–5, 240–1, 654–5; Protocol
      of Nov. 20, **iii** 654
    questions of nationality and option, **ii** 628;
      iii 170, 176, 196, 208, 213, 235, 240,
      379*n*, 409–10; **iv** 85, 108–9, 113–4, 116,
      135, 143–4, 149–50, 158, 183
      Optants Agreement, Nov. 20, **iii** 649–52;
      Supplementary Agreement, **iv** 200
      Declaration on Minorities, Nov. 20, **iii**
        653; *referred to*, **iii** 235, 240, 410, 415
      Mixed Minority Commission, **iv** 7
    See also Guarantee (to Czechoslovakia);
      Plebiscite (in Czechoslovakia, suggested)
Munkacs, **iii** 239; **iv** 248, 253
Murmansk, **vii** 70, 134
Münsterlager, **ii** 127
Münster-Osnabrück, **vii** 514
Muszyna, **v** 248
Myslenice, **v** 246
Myszyniec, **vii** 484

Nachod, **i** 579, 580*n*
Nagold, **ii** 26
Naklo (Nakel), **vii** 453, 474, 479
Nanking, **i** 305; **viii** 2*n*, 6*n*, 28, 171, 200, 205,
  406
Naples, **iii** 293, 320, 322–3, 325, 475–6; **iv** 273
Naval construction, correspondence relating to
  exchange of information, **iv** 628–37; *see also*
  Germany (Great Britain)
Naval Staffs, British and French. *See* Anglo-
  French Staff conversations
Near East, **iii** 252, 307–8, 318, 343
Neckarsulm, **ii** 26
Neisse, **i** 358
Netherlands, **i** 315, 552, 648–9; **ii** 637; **iii** 278–
  9, 296, 309, 618

Netherlands (*cont.*)
as potential supplier of aeroplanes, **i** 206; **iii** 291
General Staff conversations, **iv** 78, 450–2, 577
joint offer of 'good offices' by Netherlands and Belgium, Aug. 1939; **vii** 340, 349, 379, 447, 464
possible German invasion. *See* Germany (Netherlands)
protest against mention of Netherlands in proposed Anglo-Franco-Soviet agreement, **vi** 226–7, 240, 254; *see also* Anglo-Franco-Soviet negotiations (Netherlands)
Netherlands East Indies (Dutch East Indies), **iv** 4, 38, 52, 577
Neu-Bistritz, **iii** 640
Neubrandenburg, **i** 325
Neuern, **ii** 596, 603, **iii** 640
Neuhammer, **v** 204
Neuhaus, **iii** 207, 640
Neuhausen, **ii** 415, 426
Neu Mittelwalde, **vii** 485
Neusiedlersee, **iv** 234
Neustadt, **i** 358
Neutralization, forms of, **i** 647–50; *see also* Czechoslovakia (question of neutralization of)
Neutrality Act (U.S.), **ii** 219; **iv** 29, 51, 366, 423–4; **v** 356; **vii** 428; **viii** 486; **ix** 43, 235, 284, 509
Pittman resolution concerning amendment, **v** 356*n*; **ix** 43*n*
Nice, **iii** 463–4, 466, 474–5, 480; **iv** 317; **v** 614, 797
Niegoreloye, **iv** 568
Nikolsburg, **ii** 86; **iii** 639
Nish, **v** 129
Nitra, **iii** 152, 188, 200
North Africa, **i** 203; **ii** 197; **iii** 287, 329; **iv** 348, 358
French military preparations, **iv** 316, 325–6, 330–6, 341
Moslem population, and Italian claims, **v** 278, 344, 612, 800; **vi** 358, 472
See also Libya, Tunis
North China Telephone and Telegraph Company, **viii** 124
North Sea, German naval manœuvres, **ii** 204*n*
Northern Rhodesia, **iv** 600
Notec, R., **v** 42
Norway, **i** 534; **iv** 622; **v** 506, 568
Nove Mesto, **iii** 141, 184
Nove Zamky, **iv** 92
Novogrodek, **v** 407; **vii** 306, 347
Nuremberg, **i** 9; **ii** 95; **iii** 98, 417; **iv** 245
Nazi party congress, Sept. 5–12, 1938, **i** 568*n*, 569, 611; **ii** 25, 39, 60, 64, 69, 98, 102, 112–257 *passim*, 272–4, 283–4, 289, 295–300, 306, 309–10, 330, 332–3, 348, 363, 413, 651–4, 671, 681, 685–7, 691; **iii** 624–5; **iv** 590; **viii** 48

Nuremberg (*cont.*)
Herr Hitler's speech, Sept. 12, 1938, **ii** 299, 304, 306, 308, 311, 314–5, 319, 322, 331, 333, 485, 647–8, 673, 676, 682; **iii** 101; **viii** 85–6
Nazi party congress, Sept. 1939, forward references to, **v** 620, 770; **vi** 42–3, 50, 60, 132, 187, 286, 413, 483, 560, 580–1, 616–7, 626, 633, 635, 637, 667, 700, 705, 711, 713, 733–4, 741, 750; **vii** 38, 51, 68, 80, 90, 97, 547; question of representation of Great Britain, France and Poland, **vi** 678; **vii** 243–4; cancelled, **vii** 297
Nuremberg Laws, **iii** 281, 401, 404; **iv** 566
introduced into Danzig Free City, **iii** 543

Oberhof, **iii** 223
Oberläutensdorf, **ii** 183
Obernberg, **ii** 26
Oberndorf, **ii** 26
Oberplan, **iii** 74, 84
Ober Polaun, **iii** 640
Obersalzberg, **ii** 351; **vi** 42, 721, 730
Observers (British) attached to H.M. Legation, Prague. *See* Sudeten German question (attitude of France & Great Britain)
Oder, R., **iii** 223; **v** 246
Oder–Danube Canal, **iii** 235, 240, 408–9, 648
Oderberg. *See* Bogumin
Offenbach, **ii** 26
Oliva, **vi** 186
Olmütz (Olomouc), **i** 107; **iii** 87, 148, 150, 627; **iv** 264, 562; **v** 93, 204
'Open Door' policy in: China, **viii** 8*n*, 116, 124, 190, 199, 202, 204–5, 212, 215, 229, 235, 244, 254, 271–6, 319, 348; **ix** 421, 482, 518
Congo Basin, **viii** 255, 272
Oppeln, **i** 358; **v** 408
Optants Agreement. *See* Munich Agreement (carrying-out of)
Oran, **v** 239
Oranienburg, **vii** 283, 322, 327, 337
Orava, **iii** 82, 138, 146, 186, 188
Orlawa, **v** 246
Orsovo, **v** 686
Ösel, **vii** 577
Oslo, **v** 506; **vii** 67
Ostrau (Ostrava). *See* Mährisch-Ostrau
Ostroleka, **vii** 484
Outer Mongolia, **ix** 28

Palestine, **i** 344, 505; **iii** 313, 316, 450, 551, 595, 601; **iv** 12, 172, 208–9; **v** 343; **vi** 126, 197; **vii** 541
Palma, **iii** 523
Paracel Islands, **viii** 149*n*, 470
Parkanynana, **iii** 86
Pärnu, **viii** 577
Passau, **i** 10

'Peace Plan', July 1939, **vi** 465–6, 481, 582, 749; *see also* Hudson, R. S. (*Conversation with Herr Wohltat*) in Index of Persons
Peihai (Pakhoi), **viii** 134
Peitaiho, **ix** 494*n*, 498
Peking, **viii** 2*n*, 3*n*; anti-British activities in, **ix** 86, 352, 384
Peking–Hankow railway, **viii** 32
Persia, trade delegation to Moscow, **iv** 621
Pfullendorff, **ii** 26
Piestany, **v** 88
Pillau, **v** 560
Pilnikau, **iii** 640
Pilsen, **ii** 50; **iii** 207, 417, 627, 635; **iv** 261, 264
Piotrkow, **v** 246
Pittman resolutions. *See* Pittman, Senator K. in Index of Persons
'Pittsburg Agreement', **i** 429, 465; **iii** 416; **iv** 219, 238–9
Plan, **i** 437
Plebiscite in:
   Austria, suggested, **i** 1–16 *passim*, 29, 31, 38, 40, 44–5, 54, 56, 58, 66, 82, 112, 130–4; *see also* Schuschnigg, Dr. Kurt von and Seyss-Inquart, Dr. Artur, in Index of Persons
   Austria and Germany, of April 10, 1938, **i** 42–3, 67, 82, 100, 119, 135, 146–9, 155–7, 176–9
   Czechoslovakia, suggested
      for Hungarians and Ruthenes, **iii** 2, 4, 111–2, 138, 152, 185, 191, 194, 198, 200, 202–3
      for Poles, **iii** 3, 7, 41, 46, 51–2, 146, 156, 186–9, 219
      for Sudeten Germans, **i** 249, 300, 403–6, 415, 434, 439, 444*n*, 447, 449, 462, 504–5, 534, 582, 596–7, 615, 617, 625; **ii** 12, 35, 85–6, 114, 133, 206, 225, 260, 279, 300, 350, 382, 385, 387, 651, 678
      attitude of: Czech. Govt., **i** 572–3, 578; **ii** 332, 368*n*, 390, 403, 619; France, **ii** 69, 305, 322–3, 381, 384, 388, 405; Great Britain, **i** 564, 566, 572, 654; **ii** 241, 405, 463–4; Herr Henlein, **i** 187, 297, 428, 498, 563, 634; **ii** 231, 252, 255, 334, 647, 659, 673
      proposals at Godesberg meetings, **ii** 468, 470–2, 478, 482, 486, 495–6, 505, 507, 521, 523–5, 577; at Munich Conference, **ii** 628, 634–5
      question of international force to supervise, **iii** 64–6, 75–6, 119, 130; *see also* British Legion of Ex-Servicemen
      decision not to have plebiscite, **iii** 135, 148, 169–70, 175–6
   Danzig, suggested, **v** 515, 561
   Polish Corridor, suggested, **vii** 397, 399, 432, 440–1, 460–1, 467, 469
   the Saar, **iv** 448; **vi** 691
   as precedent for plebiscite in Sudetenland, **i** 564, 587; **ii** 86, 350, 468–71, 478, 508,

Plebiscite in (the Saar) (*cont.*)
   628, 634–5, 661; **iii** 26, 79, 90, 95, 117, 129, 149
   Upper Silesia, **iv** 448; **vii** 352
Plunder and Pollak Co. (Leitmeritz), **iii** 644
Podmokly, **i** 121
Podolia, **vi** 44
Pohl, **iv** 57
Poland
   Air Defence loan, **v** 40, 44, 69, 283, 540
   armament production, **v** 34, 37–42, 398
   armed forces
      air force, **i** 482; **v** 38, 43–5, 102, 398, 488; **vi** 773, 788; **vii** 474, 477
      army, **i** 480; **ii** 144, 539; **iii** 570; **iv** 384, 479; **v** 38–41, 73, 538; **vi** 582, 769–70; **vii** 151, 160
      General Staff, **iv** 362, 478, 480; **v** 8, 570, 580, 749; **vi** 80, 262, 274, 416, 552, 617, 684; **vii** 1, 2*n*, 3*n*, 5, 21, 27–8, 40–1, 85, 87, 91–2, 112, 126, 136, 159–60, 210–1, 453, 502, 558–60; Chief of. *See* Stachiewicz, Gen., in Index of Persons
      Inspector-General. *See* Smigly-Rydz, Marshal, in Index of Persons
      navy, **v** 39, 205, 248–9, 560; **vii** 70, 134, 309, 502
   Association of Polish Citizens owning property in Germany, **iv** 206
   Camp of National Unity (O.Z.O.N.), **i** 429; **iii** 8, 22, 33; **iv** 179, 543; **v** 605
   colonial question, **iv** 179, 203, 205, 217; **vi** 19
   Czechoslovakia. *See* Czechoslovakia (minorities, Poles); Czechoslovakia (Poland); Teschen
   Danzig question. *See* Danzig, Free City of; Germany (Poland)
   decree relating to agrarian reform in frontier zone, Aug. 1939, **vii** 54
   encirclement, fear of, **iv** 480; **v** 306; **vi** 132, 138, 239, 704; **vii** 291
   Great Britain, **ii** 318; **iii** 9, 107, 110, 120–1, 182–3, 190; **iv** 142–3, 401–2 599, 600; **vi** 29, 249*n*, 385, 669, 680, 684; **vii** 146, 216, 503
      economic and financial relations, **iv** 142
         coal negotiations, **vi** 244*n*, 246, 365, 378, 536–8
         export credit guarantees, **vi** 226, 244, 509, 569–70
         question of financial aid, **v** 283–5, 289, 379, 398, 539–40, 588, 604–5, 734–5, 747–9, 778–9; **vi** 192, 198–9, 215, 244–6, 342, 365–8, 378–81, 400–1, 404–7, 410–1, 418, 427, 431, 436, 451, 463, 476, 479, 486, 503, 508–9, 526, 528–9, 536–8, 545, 557, 569–70, 635
         Polish desiderata, **v** 540–1
         conditions attached to loan, **vi** 269–71, 323, 366; not accepted by Poland, **vi** 358–9, 367, 378, 380, 386, 410, 479, 508

Poland (Great Britain) (*cont.*)

political relations

guarantee to Poland, Mar. 1939, **iv** 552-9; *see also* Guarantee

reciprocal Anglo-Polish assurances of assistance, **v** 98, 200, 234, 238; *see also* Anglo-Polish Staff-conversations and *below* visit to London of M. Beck

formal Anglo-Polish agreement, negotiations, **v** 35, 47-8, 98, 609, 611, 639, 700, 749, 772, 793; **vi** 323, 564-5, 649, 699; **vii** 63-6, 89, 168, 242, 282; Polish draft, Aug. 10, **vi** 654-6; signature of treaty, Aug. 25, **vii** 249

implementation, by France and Great Britain, of undertakings to Poland, Aug.-Sept. 1939, **vii** 225, 277, 478, 488, 495, 500-2, 504, 513-5, 518, 520-6, 531-9

visit to London of M. Beck, April 1939

preparations for, **iii** 591, 593, 596-7; **iv** 11, 32, 68, 110, 112, 142, 144-6, 151, 154, 181, 204, 373, 434-5, 454, 464, 513, 539, 581, 616; suggested subjects for discussion, **iv** 151, 167, 181, 205, 217, 290, 401, 522, 576

Anglo-Polish conversations, **v** 1-19, 30-6, 47-9

referred to, **v** 50, 53, 56-8, 65, 83-4, 94, 98, 180, 283, 286*n*, 401, 416, 423, 437, 609

visit to Poland of General Sir W. E. Ironside, July 1939, **vi** 274, 323, 353, 379, 400, 415-9, 426, 485-7

internal conditions, **iii** 179, 228-9; **v** 283-4, 398, 588

League of Silesian Insurgents, **iii** 22; **vii** 235

League of War Veterans, **iii** 8

military preparations, **iv** 497, 506, 514, 543; **v** 3, 26-7, 38-45, 246-9, 539, 581; **vi** 379

in Aug. 1939, **vi** 684-5; **vii** 126, 189, 195-6, 233, 300, 311, 321, 326, 330, 337, 339, 356

general mobilization, **vii** 364, 366, 370-1, 374, 376, 399, 404, 453; reaction of Great Britain, **vii** 378, 408, 424

See also (armed forces) *above,* and Germany (Poland: Danzig and Polish Corridor)

minorities, **iv** 479; **vi** 289

Czechs and Slovaks, **iii** 16, 225-6, 228; denunciation by Poland of Polish-Czech Minorities Agreement of 1925, **iii** 16, 228

Germans, **i** 139; **iii** 182, 225; **iv** 87-9, 111-2, 152-4, 205, 525-6, 540-1, 616; **v** 99, 203, 205, 246, 248, 338, 397, 406-9, 524, 582, 584, 587, 605, 782, 803; **vi** 10, 94, 105-6, 124-5, 200, 204-6, 247, 287, 343, 551-4, 694, 697, 719, 739-40; **vii** 12, 22, 29, 30, 38, 49, 51, 54, 58-9, 67, 73, 86,

Poland (minorities: Germans) (*cont.*)

104, 108-9, 163, 178, 184-5, 203-4, 230-1, 233, 235, 241, 298, 375, 389, 399, 405, 425, 430, 461

exchange of populations, **vii** 239, 267, 271, 286-7, 289, 294, 297, 301, 353, 409, 440, 450, 461

Jungdeutsche Partei, **vii** 51, 203-4

Polish Govt. communiqué, Aug. 30, **vii** 425, 531

See also Treaties (German-Polish Minority Declaration of Nov. 1937)

Ukrainians, **iii** 181, 227-8, 576; **iv** 616-7; **v** 40; **vii** 281

See also Jews (Poland)

Peasant party, **iii** 179; **iv** 497; **vi** 106

Press **iii** 22, 50, 179-80, 219, 364, 425; **iv** 153-4, 497; **v** 198, 379, 390; **vi** 400, 440, 482, 486, 527, 553; **vii** 12, 22, 54, 204-5

Anglo-Polish relations, **iv** 572; **v** 69; **vi** 536; **vii** 281

anti-Czech press campaign, **i** 315-6, 430, 465, 478, 481; **ii** 287; **iii** 7-8, 22, 25, 33-4, 41, 97, 101-3, 110-1, 138

Danzig question, **v** 391, 512-3, 547, 627, 635, 752; **vi** 248, 433, 448, 593, 621, 626, 628, 638, 657, 691; **vii** 12, 60, 151

general mobilization, **vii** 366, 376, 399

'A.B.C.', **vii** 204; 'Czas', **v** 69; **vi** 486, 536, 626, 634, 638, 643; **vii** 60; 'Dziennik Narodowy', **vi** 536; 'Express Poranny', **v** 512; **vi** 483, 536; **vii** 74; 'Gazeta Polska', **i** 430; **iii** 8, 111, 227, 364, 374; **iv** 177*n*, 497; **v** 69, 340*n*, 512; **vi** 486, 536, 587; **vii** 204; 'Kurjer Polski', **vi** 487, 536; 'Kurjer Poranny', **iii** 107; **v** 512; **vi** 486; 'Kurjer Warszawski', **i** 431; **iii** 425; **vi** 483, 486, 536; **vii** 74; 'Polska Zbrojna', **v** 69; **vii** 74; 'Robotnik', **i** 431; **v** 69, 512; 'Słowo', **iv** 88

public opinion, **ii** 287-8; **iii** 28*n*, 33-4, 49, 103, 179, 190; **iv** 143, 203, 206, 476, 497, 507, 514, 543, 582; **v** 31, 204, 605, 627, 635, 709, 731-2; **vi** 214, 245, 247, 269, 283, 318-9, 322, 400, 551; **vii** 146

Roumania, **i** 482; **ii** 355; **iii** 45, 104, 182; **iv** 183, 432, 435, 450, 559, 616; **v** 2, 8, 14-6, 36, 38, 48, 77; **vi** 405, 585, 674; *see also* Germany (Roumania, reaction of Poland to threat of German aggression); Guarantee (to Roumania); Hungary (Roumania); Treaties

strategic position, **iv** 477-80, 616-7; **v** 41-2, 246-8, 583

U.S.S.R., **i** 173, 257, 431*n*, 482; **ii** 107, 144, 498; **iii** 24, 104, 182, 577; **iv** 185, 500, 616; **v** 2, 6-8, 244; **vii** 217, 397

attitude towards help from U.S.S.R. in time of war, **iv** 428, 478; **v** 11-3, 73, 83, 104, 204-5, 249, 268, 295, 316-7, 398, 488; **vi** 24, 405, 440-1, 545 764, 772, 787; **vii**

Poland (U.S.S.R.) (*cont.*)
268, 499; *see also* Anglo-Franco-Soviet military conversations (passage of Soviet troops through Poland)
attitude towards U.S.S.R. joining guarantee of Czechoslovakia, **iii** 374, 418
conversations and communiqué of Nov. 27, 1938, **iii** 364–5, 374, 419, 430, 580, 582
trade negotiations, **iv** 15, 82, 613, 621; **v** 6; **vi** 441
Russo-Polish War of 1919–20, **i** 479; **ii** 287, 465; **iii** 8, 32–3
See also Anglo-Franco-Soviet conversations; Teschen; Treaties (Polish-Soviet Non-Aggression Pact of 1932)
Western Association (League), **iv** 525; **v** 407, 409; **vi** 552
Yugoslavia, **v** 34
See also Anti-Comintern Pact; France; Germany; Hungary; Italy; Lithuania; Ruthenia; Slovakia
Poldèves, The, **v** 414
Polish Corridor
anti-German demonstrations, **iii** 34; **iv** 111–2, 143, 153; **v** 524n; **vi** 9–10
extent of, **v** 815; **vii** 460
question of a corridor across, **iii** 198, 265, 439, 442–3, 581–2, 589; **iv** 32, 81, 147, 507, 525, 543, 548, 581; **v** 17, 28, 216, 232, 243, 276, 304–5, 318, 339, 415–20, 440–1, 570, 579–80, 594, 610, 630, 721, 809–10, 814–6; **vi** 530, 694, 755; **vii** 460–1, 549
See also Germany (Poland: Danzig and Polish Corridor)
Pomerania (Pommern, Pomorze), **ii** 44, 161; **iii** 251; **v** 204, 407, 409, 511; **vi** 239, 551; **vii** 97, 160, 338, 375, 415
Poprad, **iv** 99
Portugal, **i** 96, 581n, 649; **iii** 618; **v** 213, 239, 264; **vi** 162, 173, 225
Posen. *See* Poznan
Postelau, **vi** 455, 513
Postelberg, **iii** 640
Potsdam, **vi** 176
Povazska Bystrica, **v** 89
Poznan (Posen), **iii** 23, 251, 658; **iv** 152–3; **v** 42, 247–8, 372, 391, 407, 409, 423, 456; **vi** 44, 94, 385, 551
Prague, **i** 76, 107, 171, 181, 373, 404, 432, 436, 488, 611; **ii** 143, 147, 185, 259, 281, 522, 552; **iii** 86, 228, 417, 627; **iv** 62–3, 126, 240, 242, 249, 251, 260–1, 267, 282, 404; **v** 555
Lord Runciman in, **ii** 7n, 18, 49, 50, 57, 81–2, 87–8, 128, 175, 671
German entry, **iv** 264, 275, 279, 444, 560
Praszka-Krzepice, **vii** 485
Praust, **vi** 176, 178
Prerov (Prerau), **i** 107; **iv** 56–7
Presov, **iii** 368

Press, The, **v** 236; **vi** 691; **vii** 38; *see also* each country (Press)
Pressburg. *See* Bratislava
Prussia, **i** 649; **ii** 26, 66
Przemysl, **iii** 23
Przyszowice, **vi** 551

Rabka, **v** 247
Radom, **v** 246–7
Radvanice, **iii** 223
Rambouillet, **ii** 362; **vii** 79n
Rambouillet Loan. *See* Treaties (France-Poland)
Rangoon, **viii** 161
Rapallo, **iv** 338
Rashin, **viii** 40n
Ratibor, **i** 107; **v** 58; **vi** 205; **vii** 485
Ratisbon, **i** 302
Rearmament, **i** 120, 326; **iii** 144
France, **iii** 89, 158, 249–50, 252, 258; **iv** 73; *see also* France (armed forces)
Germany, **i** 93, 208, 586, 611; **iii** 294, 387, 525–6, 562, 616–7; **iv** 121, 185, 626–7; **vi** 616; *see also* Germany (air force, army)
Great Britain, **i** 87, 203–4, 326, 543, 611; **iii** 144, 158, 171–2, 247–9, 252, 257, 278, 282, 289–94, 387–8, 428, 520, 562; **iv** 6, 43, 50, 73, 120, 124, 137, 170, 585, 625, 627; **vi** 549, 754; **vii** 631–2; *see also* Great Britain (armed forces; conscription)
Italy, **iii** 501
Roumania, **iv** 284–5
U.S.S.R., **iv** 412
Rechlin, **i** 611
Reconstruction Finance Corporation, **viii** 311, 340
Refugees in
China, **viii** 245
Czechoslovakia, **iii** 195, 379, 418, 631–2, 635–8; **iv** 15, 26, 162
German refugees from Poland, **v** 203, 524, 782, 803; **iv** 10
International Organization for relief of refugees, **ii** 149
Spanish refugees in France, **iv** 345, 461–2
See under Jews (Jewish refugee problem)
Regensburg, **iii** 417
Reichenau, **ii** 669
Reichenberg (Liberec), **i** 69, 70, 121, 124–5, 251, 432–3, 438; **ii** 32, 304, 335, 658, 663–4, 669; **iii** 640; **iv** 126, 231
Reichenstein, **iii** 640
Reichsbank, The, **iii** 131, 178
Reparations
demanded by Sudeten Germans, **i** 125, 159, 169, 185, 249, 298, 309, 632, 638; **ii** 222
owed by Germany. *See* Germany (internal conditions; foreign debts)
Reval, **vii** 259
Revue des Deux Mondes, **iv** 307, 316, 331, 339

Rhineland, The **i** 75, 94, 451; **iii** 556
areas prohibited to foreign military personnel,
Aug. 1938, **ii** 26–7
re-occupation and re-fortification by Germany, **i** 128, 177, 199, 213, 217, 223, 225–6,
234, 267, 294, 379; **ii** 68, 140, 289, 453; **iii**
387, 479; **vi** 72, 753; attitude of Poland, **i**
72; **iii** 180
Riga, **ii** 218; **iv** 390n; **vi** 562–4; **vii** 483, 546
Rimavska Sobota, **iii** 152
Riyadh, **vi** 127n
Rochlitz, **iii** 640
Rome, **i** 29; **iii** 293, 475, 533; *see also* Chamberlain, Mr. N. (visit to Italy) and Hitler, Herr
(visit to Italy) in Index of Persons
Rome–Berlin Axis. *See* Axis, Rome–Berlin
Römerstadt, **iii** 641
Rominten, **i** 295; **ii** 423, 652; **iii** 9n
Rotterdam, **iv** 28, 37; **vi** 755
Rottweil, **ii** 26
Roumania, i 106, 217–8, 263, 307, 333 405,
423, 482, 514, 650; **ii** 429, 498, 532; **iv** 263
armed forces: army, **iv** 496; **v** 398; **vi** 770;
air force, **vi** 788
armament contracts with Czechoslovakia,
suspension, **iv** 284, 366, 375–6, 422, 477,
521, 619
foreign policy statement, Mar. 20, 1939, **iv**
521
Great Britain, **ii** 355; **iii** 45n, 232–3; **iv** 484;
vi 294, 320
British trade mission, **iii** 233; **iv** 283, 419,
619; **v** 483
question of financial loan and armaments,
iv 284–5, 366, 376, 520–1, 619; **v** 66, 112,
315, 343–4, 483; **vi** 585
question of raising Legation in Roumania
to an Embassy, **iv** 283–4; **v** 483
See also Anglo-Roumanian conversations;
Guarantee (to Roumania)
internal situation, **iii** 46
military measures, **iv** 281, 284, 395, 433, 496,
521; **v** 62–3; **vi** 294
minorities, **vi** 642
Bulgarians, **vi** 583
Germans, **iv** 262; **v** 271–2, 302, 309
Hungarians (Magyars), **iv** 262, 618; **v** 63,
332–3; **vi** 77, 215, 263, 629–31, 641–2
Ukrainians, **iii** 576
Nationalities Statute, **iii** 45n
National Front, **iv** 580; **v** 332
Poland. *See* Guarantee (to Roumania);
Poland (Roumania)
Press, reported press campaign against Hun-
gary, **vi** 294, 320, 583; 'Universul', **vi** 295
Turkey, **v** 57, 77, 115, 296–8, 322–3, 327–8,
694–5
Turco-Roumanian conversations, **v** 296–8,
328, 575
See also Guarantee (to Roumania)

Roumania (*cont.*)
U.S.S.R., **i** 197; **iii** 46; **iv** 422, 449, 621; **v**
310, 313, 331–2, 396, 482, 657; **vi** 170, 674
attitude towards transit through Rou-
mania of war supplies from U.S.S.R. to
Czechoslovakia, **i** 257; **ii** 144, 179, 229,
235, 255, 270, 355, 365, 489, 575n
attitude towards acceptance of aid from
U.S.S.R., **iv** 520, 579; **v** 76, 83, 91, 104,
222, 310, 330, 658; **vi** 764, 787
U.S.S.R. prepared to give assistance to
Roumania, **v** 202, 209, 221–2, 266, 368
Yugoslavia, **ii** 355; **iii** 565; **iv** 388, 621; **v** 106,
334, 395, 659–62; **vi** 66
See also Anglo-Franco-Soviet negotiations;
Anti-Comintern Pact; Balkan Entente;
Bulgaria; Germany; Hungary; Ruthenia
Roumanian Iron Guard, **i** 217; **v** 300, 343
Roznava, **iii** 152
Rudniki, **v** 246
Ruhr, The, **iii** 293; **vii** 293, 464
Rumburg, **i** 432; **ii** 596, 603
Rummelsburg, **v** 524, 803
Russia. *See* U.S.S.R.
Russo-Polish War of 1919–20. *See* Poland
(U.S.S.R.)
Ruthenia, i 105, 190, 279, 443, 480, 613; **iii**
112, 123, 126, 194, 199, 222, 239, 415, 418–20,
548; **iv** 56, 129, 178, 379
Hungary's claims, **iii** 33, 36, 38, 45, 111, 139,
141, 152, 181, 194, 236, 239, 242–3, 300;
invasion, Mar. 1939, **iv** 248–9, 253–4, 262,
277, 282, 289, 445, 448, 617; **v** 59–61
attitude towards Hungary's claims of:
France, **iv** 268
Germany, **iii** 118, 125, 159, 185–7, 190–
1, 200–4, 206, 212, 227, 236, 239, 242–3,
264n, 265, 275, 413, 419–20, 618; **iv**
80, 201, 261–2, 265, 282, 289–90, 362,
364, 370, 379, 434, 445, 624; **v** 60
Great Britain. *See* Czechoslovakia (Hungary: attitude of Great Britain towards
Hungarian claims)
Italy, **iii** 45, 121, 140, 170n, 174–5, 200)
202, 204, 206, 236, 525; **iv** 206, 262–3,
282, 445
Poland, **iii** 36, 45, 47, 82, 105, 110–1,
199, 232, 243, 374, 430; **iv** 225, 252,
262, 282, 364, 556; Poland's desire
for common frontier with Hungary, **i**
431n, 512; **iii** 111, 121–2, 138–9, 159,
181, 201, 205–6, 227–8, 242–3, 264n,
273, 364, 413, 418, 498, 525; **iv** 80, 178,
183, 261–2, 282, 617; **v** 59, 60
Roumania, **iii** 45, 114, 126, 138, 141,
153, 181, 197, 201, 206, 232, 242; **iv**
183, 202, 227, 262, 281, 291, 363, 389,
395, 401, 428–9, 433, 484, 496, 618–9;
v 61–4, 77, 327, 333, 396
Yugoslavia, **iii** 153, 232

Ruthenia (*cont.*)
internal condiuions, **iii** 217-8, 226, 377; **v** 60-1, 63; establishment of 'Sič', **iii** 413
Roumania's claims, **iii** 262, 281, 291; **iv** 618; **v** 61-3
See also Czechoslovakia (minorities, Ruthenes); Vienna Conference and Award
Ruzomberok, **i** 166
Rybnik, **iii** 105; **vii** 204, 453, 474
Rychtal, **vii** 485
Rzeszow, **iii** 23

Saadabad Pact, **v** 463, 796
Saar, The, **ii** 44, 139, 338, 345, 350, 374; **v** 370; **vi** 133, 691; *see also* Plebiscite (in the Saar)
Saarbrücken, **iii** 157, 244; **vii** 416, 464
Saghalien (Sakhalin), **ix** 516
Sahy, **iii** 184
Salonika, **v** 120, 296n
Salzburg, **i** 6-7, 43, 156; **vi** 643, 657-8, 666, 691, 712, 720; **vii** 16, 37, 162, 201
San Giovanni di Medua, **v** 127, 140
San Remo, **iv** 120, 443, 455; **v** 400, 546, 714, 801; **vii** 632
Santi Quaranta, **v** 127, 140, 437, 750
Sardinia, **iii** 523
Satoraljaujhely, **iii** 86
Saudi Arabia, **vi** 127
Saxony, **i** 61, 186, 321, 323, 327-8, 349, 451; **ii** 66, 161, 281, 309, 360, 396, 453; **vi** 617
Scandinavian countries, **i** 315; **v** 507, 653, 667, 786; **vi** 20, 29, 46
attitude towards proposed non-aggression pacts with Germany, **v** 462, 505-6
Scheles, **iii** 640
Schichts of Aussig, **i** 594
Schiewenhorst, **v** 788; **vi** 148, 393
Schildberg, **iii** 641
'Schleswig-Holstein' (German battleship), visit to Danzig, **vii** 222n, 224, 240, 249, 403, 542-4
Schlochau, **vii** 416
Schluckenau, **ii** 32
Schniedemühl, **vii** 416
Schönau, **iii** 639
Schönberg, **i** 488-9
Schönbrunn, **iv** 57
Schönlanke, **vii** 432, 460
Schotten, **ii** 26
Schutt Island, **iii** 152
Schneider-Creusot, **iii** 634
Second World War, outbreak. *See* War
Self-determination, principle of, **iii** 145; **iv** 448; **v** 685, 815
as basis of settlement of Sudeten German question, **i** 108, 111, 115, 182, 285, 345, 447, 534, 564, 597, 654; **ii** 85, 97, 143-4, 163, 195, 211, 234, 307, 327, 349, 352, 360, 363, 367, 371, 376-86, 389-91, 413, 426, 429, 463, 467, 486, 500-1, 506, 675, 678; **v** 713; *see also* Plebiscite (for Sudeten Germans);

Self-determination (*cont.*)
Sudeten German question (autonomy) and other minorities in Czechoslovakia, **iii** 3, 49, 80, 113, 155, 186-7, 198, 201, 203, 265
Senov, **iii** 223
Sesto Calendi, **iv** 338
Shanghai (French Concession), **viii** 475; **ix** 12, 60, 101, 111
Shanghai (International Settlement)
as base of operations for terrorists, **viii** 75, 99, 129, 139, 141, 463-7, 469, 471, 478, 506-7; **ix** 4, 21, 52, 62, 97, 336-7
emergency proclamation of Municipal Council, July 19, 1938, **viii** 465n, 472, 514, 524
See also Chen Lu, Hai Shih-tai, Marquis Li, in Index of Persons
British Embassy, **viii** 2n
Courts of Law
Chinese Courts, **viii** 96-8, 100, 105, 112-3, 118, 281-2; **ix** 44, 51, 54, 71, 75, 489
Supreme Court for China (British), **ix** 456, 525
French reaction to Japanese threat, **viii** 475; **ix** 111, 114, 187, 207
Land Regulations, **ix** 50, 54, 60, 68, 74, 76, 89
'lone battalion', **viii** 28n, 560
Municipal Council, suggested changes in constitution, **ix** 44-5, 50-2, 54, 71, 74-7, 85, 87-90, 135-8
police matters
negotiations between Shanghai Municipal Council and Japanese authorities, **viii** 464-5, 471-2, 474, 476-7, 480-1, 484, 489, 510-1, 514-5, 523-4, 538; **ix** 15, 49, 62
questions of: increased Japanese representation in Shanghai Municipal Police, **viii** 75, 82, 99, 111-2, 386n, 465, 481, 485; **ix** 9, 49
return of N. district to control of Shanghai Municipal Police, **viii** 100, 365, 385-6; **ix** 14-6, 21, 37, 68
maintenance of order in Western Extra Settlement area, **viii** 375-6, 428, 431, 440, 453-4, 467; **ix** 21, 44, 50, 203-4
rice deliveries interrupted, **ix** 444, 446, 454, 461, 478, 480, 487
suspected Japanese designs, **viii** 470, 476, 480, 488; **ix** 9-12, 60, 94, 101, 231
troops, British, **viii** 9n, 137n; Italian, **viii** 180, 234, 268
United States reaction to Japanese threat, **viii** 475, 501-2; **ix** 69, 102, 138-9
Shanghai (Japanese-controlled area), **viii** 467n; **ix** 4, 51, 489
Shanghai Inland Navigation Steamship Company, **viii** 124
Shanghai Volunteer Corps, **viii** 472; **ix** 51.

Shansi, **viii** 32

Shantung, **viii** 32, 279; **ix** 86

Shensi, **viii** 33

Shoreham, speech by Lord Winterton at, **iii** 158

Sicily, **iv** 338–9

Siegfried Line, **i** 568*n*, 613–4; **ii** 13, 56, 64, 68, 86, 112*n*, 113*n*, 269, 528, 531, 562; **iii** 526, 569, 579, 599; **vi** 88, 773; **vii** 233, 274, 566–7

Sighet, **iv** 281

Silesia
  Czechoslovak-, **i** 190, 487, 550; **ii** 186, 530, 630; **iii** 219, 235; **v** 93
  German-, **i** 55*n*, 61, 107–8, 317, 328, 404; **ii** 21, 49, 126, 237, 282, 453, 575*n*; **iii** 627; **vi** 552–3; **vii** 97, 160
  Haller-Korfanti *coup* in Upper-, May 1921, **vii** 352
  Polish Upper-, **i** 479; **ii** 288; **iii** 50, 105, 219, 229; **iv** 575; **v** 42, 73, 204, 423, 456, 561; **vi** 193, 338, 551; **vii** 204, 361, 375, 479, 485, 496
    treatment of German minority, **iv** 526; **v** 99, 407; **vi** 204, 551–3; **vii** 73, 86
  Trans-Olzan area, **iii** 22*n*, 228; **v** 247
  See also Teschen

Silesian Ostrava, **iii** 146, 156, 199, 219

Sillein (Zilina), **iii** 27*n*, 73; **iv** 408; **vii** 126, 160; *see also* Slovakia (administration)

Sinaia, meeting of Foreign Ministers of 'Little Entente', **i** 252*n*, 257, 266

Singapore, **vi** 754; **viii** 320–1, 422, 450, 456, 544–8, 550
  Anglo-French Staff conversations, **ix** 53*n*, 238, 372, 496*n*

Sinkiang, **ix** 28

Sino-Japanese conflict, **i** 305; **viii** and **ix** *passim*
  alleged Japanese conditions for peace, **viii** 158–9, 163–4, 277, 283–4, 535; **ix** 14, 17, 31, 96, 100, 159, 173–5, 365, 385
  attack on Chinese commercial aeroplane, **viii** 42, 45–6, 51, 55, 57, 64–6
  China's proposal to declare war on Japan, **viii** 218, 474, 485–6, 508–9
  interests of third Powers in China, **viii** 45–6, 69, 70, 131, 133–4, 137, 146–52, 159, 174–5, 207–8; *see also* Japan (G.B.); Japan (U.S.)
  Japanese blockade of Chinese coast, **viii** 98*n*
  reprisals against Japan, attitude of: France, **viii** 148, 184; **ix** 38–42, 57, 82, 90, 192, 207, 238
  Great Britain, **viii** 50–1, 109, 161, 183, 190–3, 245, 279, 291, 299, 301, 310, 325, 337, 359–60, 362, 412–4, 425–7, 446, 521–3; **ix** 47*n*, 57, 147, 215, 217, 226, 235, 239, 241, 257, 277, 292, 302, 327–8, 338–9, 485–6, 530
  United States, **viii** 146, 148, 153, 183, 193, 208–9, 245, 264, 279, 291, 313, 318, 436, 446, 449; **ix** 44, 84, 86, 90, 147, 328; *see also* Japan (U.S. interests in China)

Sino-Japanese conflict (*cont.*)
  sanctions against Japan, question of application by League of Nations, **viii** 58, 67–8, 94–5, 104–5, 108–11, 116–7, 138, 140, 144–8, 152, 509; **ix** 44, 46–9, 57, 100–1
  suggested offer of 'good offices' by foreign countries, **viii** 2–5, 11–25, 30, 38, 162–4, 175–6, 204*n*, 237, 253, 263, 304, 461, 479; **ix** 494, 501, 518, 520
  See also Air warfare; Canton; Hankow

Skalite, **iii** 219

Skoczow, **iii** 23

Skoda Works, **iii** 634–5; **iv** 65, 284, 376

Slovakia, i 105, 107, 188–90, 193, 223, 279, 405, 443, 465, 479, 502, 512, 613; **ii** 524, 549; **iii** 123, 139, 194, 222; **iv** 56, 379
  administration: Sillein agreement, Oct. 6, 1938, **iii** 114; **iv** 219; Slovak autonomy law, Nov. 22, 1938, **iv** 200, 238; Dr. Tiso's Govt., Dec. 1938, **iii** 377; **iv** 98; M. Sivak's Govt., Mar. 10, 1939, **iv** 219, 221, 225; M. Sidor's Govt., Mar. 12, **iv** 229–30, 233–4; Dr. Tiso's Govt., Mar. 14, **iv** 246, 408
  as possible compensation to Poland for loss of Danzig, **v** 306, 425, 570; **vi** 46, 137–8, 704; *see also* sub-head (Germany) *below*
  France, **iv** 243, 267–9
  Germany, **iii** 118, 185–7, 200, 203–4, 412–3, 548; **iv** 63, 95, 157–8, 184, 201, 218, 220, 223, 225, 227–32, 235, 238, 240–2, 244, 249, 261, 263, 267, 272, 287, 406–7, 438–44, 455; **v** 88–90, 204, 665; **vi** 80, 113, 132, 695, 754; **vii** 97, 327, 337–8, 375
    economic importance to Germany, **iv** 537–9
    F.S. (Freiwilliger Schutzdienst), **iv** 407, 438*n*
    German-Hungarian-Polish régime suggested, **v** 276, 289, 304, 306, 371, 378, 384, 390, 418–9, 441; **vi** 755
    German Protectorate over Slovakia, **iv** 246, 280, 282, 288, 444, 497*n*, 624; reaction of Poland, **iv** 362; **v** 425, 570; **vi** 239, 607, 704; **vii** 291
    military occupation, **vii** 424
  Hungary, **i** 443, 551; **iii** 38, 45, 111; **iv** 95, 201, 220, 247–8
    advance into E. Slovakia, Mar. 23, 1939, **iv** 619; **v** 77–8, 85–8
    agreement on frontiers, Apr. 4, **v** 78, 86–7
    attitude of Germany, **v** 78–9
    See also Vienna Conference and Award
  independence movement, **iii** 91, 111, 415–6; **iv** 201, 219–46 *passim*, 438–40; declaration of independence, Mar. 14, 1939, **iv** 245–6, 406–7
  internal conditions, **iii** 216–7, 225–6, 375*n*, 412; **iv** 63, 94–9, 157–8, 183–4, 200, 238–9, 407–8; **v** 84–91; *see also above* (administration)

Slovakia (*cont.*)
minorities: Germans, **iii** 226, 412–3; **iv** 93, 95–6, 227, 230, 234–5, 240, 438*n*
Magyars, **i** 188; **iii** 226, 412; **iv** 93, 235
Poles, **iv** 235
Ruthenians, **iii** 226, 412; **iv** 98, 235
see also Jews (Slovakia)
Poland, **i** 429–30, 465, 479–81, 512, 550–1; **ii** 287; **iii** 66, 80, 82, 97, 1,05, 110–1, 118, 120, 122, 138, 146, 181, 188–9, 199, 205, 211–2, 219, 378, 419*n*, 430; **iv** 95, 201, 220, 224, 231, 239, 245, 252; recognition of independence of Slovakia, **iv** 262
Press: 'Grenzbote', **v** 90; 'Narodni Noviny', **v** 85
Ruthenia, **iv** 98–9, 247
Slovaks: in Czechoslovakia, Germany, Hungary. *See* country heading (minorities)
in United States, **v** 86; delegation from, **i** 429–30, 465, 551; *see also* Pittsburgh Agreement
Smilow, **vii** 484
Smyrna, **vi** 97
Sokol Congress, **i** 441, 448, 463, 465, 488, 520, 524–5, 542, 548; **ii** 34, 258; **iii** 213
Soltau, **ii** 127
Soochow Creek, **viii** 99, 137
Sophienthal, **iii** 640
Sopron, **vi** 660*n*
South Africa, Union of, **i** 579, 602; **iv** 584
South America, **ii** 96; **iii** 296; **iv** 60, 602
South-east Europe
Anglo-French economic assistance, **i** 232, 326; **v** 311; *see also* Roumania (Great Britain)
German interests, **i** 75, 79, 80, 100, 108–9, 119, 154, 184, 217, 222, 225–6, 325, 379, 611, 627–8, 633; **ii** 96, 213, 375, 384, 474, 639; **iii** 45*n*, 161, 232–3, 246, 387–8, 541, 550, 571, 592; **iv** 22–3, 30, 60, 102–3, 165, 176–7, 213–4, 363, 468, 478, 509, 600–1, 604, 607, 618; **v** 14, 791–2; **vi** 407, 497, 731, 755–6, 760*n*; **vii** 274, 291, 556
See also Treaties (Germany–Roumania)
South Tyrol, **i** 7; **ii** 279; **iv** 215; **v** 302, 685, 783; **vi** 694; **vii** 239
negotiations regarding transfer of German-speaking population of the Alto Adige, **vi** 255, 283*n*, 284, 323–4, 659*n*
See also Germany (Italy, German guarantee of Brenner frontier)
Spain and Spanish Civil War, **i** 199*n*, 203, 205, 325*n*, 342, 385, 513, 580, 581*n*, 591, 611, 619; **ii** 66, 122, 197, 335, 509*n*, 528, 533, 636–7; **iii** 157; **iv** 124, 608; **viii** 98˙
attitude of: France and Great Britain, **i** 50*n*, 53; **ii** 220, 235; **iii** 297–300, 316–8, 330–3, 337, 340, 462, 512, 521, 530; **iv** 124, 318, 327, 461–2, 590, 593–4; **v** 51, 223, 508; **vi** 150; **vii** 631; Germany and Italy, **ii** 124*n*, 636; **iii** 298–9, 390, 427, 516, 520, 619; **iv** 10, 124; **v** 144, 377; **vi** 284, 443; **vii** 624

Spain and Spanish Civil War (*cont.*)
Barcelona (Republican) Government, **iii** 298, 317, 319–20, 324, 487
Bérard Agreement, Mar. 1939, **iv** 461*n*; **v** 508
effect of Spanish issue on Franco-Italian relations, **iii** 461–2, 465, 468, 479, 483, 485–7, 506, 509–10, 514, 516, 518, 520–4, 527; **iv** 10, 299, 330, 335, 353*n*, 590; **v** 259
Four-Power conference suggested, **iii** 157, 320, 332, 337–8
Gen. Franco's administration (at Burgos), **ii** 124; **iii** 297, 332, 337; **v** 223
recognition by: Czechoslovakia, **iv** 63; France and Great Britain, **iv** 318*n*
Non-Intervention Committee and Agreements, **i** 53; **iii** 297–8, 313–4, 316–7, 321, 325, 331, 333, 337–8, 346, 479, 481, 486, 506, 521; **iv** 295–6, 462
See also Anti-Comintern Pact (attitude of Gen. Franco); Italy (Spain, Italian forces in)
Spandau, **i** 380; **vii** 270
Spezia, **iv** 338; **v** 173
Spisz, **iii** 82, 138, 146, 186, 188
Sporvorice, **iii** 223
Spratley Archipelago, **viii** 475; **ix** 40, 46, 48
Staab, **iii** 640
Stablack, **ii** 408
Stanislawow, **v** 407; **vii** 306, 347
Starachowice Armament Factory, **v** 40–1
Starberg, **i** 20
Starkstadt, **iii** 640
Steglitz, **ii** 45
Steinbach, **iii** 136
Sternberg, **iii** 641
Stettin, **i** 485*n*, 494
Steyr-Daimler-Puch A. G., **i** 93
Stockholm, **i** 316, 351, 431; **vi** 749, 751; **vii** 551
meeting of four Scandinavian Ministers, May 9, 1939, **v** 462, 505–6, 568
Stolp, **v** 25, 27, 577
Stramberg, **iii** 641
'Strength through Joy' organization, **vi** 192, 208
Stuttgart, **i** 156, 610; **ii** 26, 140, 178; **iii** 409; **vii** 464
Styria, **i** 1, 43, 131–2
Submarines, **i** 239; **ii** 688; **iii** 279, 571; **iv** 50; **vi** 156; *see also* Germany (Great Britain Naval Agreements)
Germany's decision to increase total tonnage, **iii** 422, 429, 435, 440, 452–6, 664–6, 670–4
Sucha, **v** 246
Suchow, **viii** 207
Sudan, The, **iii** 528
Sudeten German question, i 33–7, 40–1, 47, 50–6, 61–655 *passim*; **ii** *passim*
attitude of France and Great Britain, **i** 35–6, 50–6, 83–554 *passim*, 563, 571–5, 581–3, 600, 605–9, 612–5, 618, 620; **ii** 1, 20, 101, 124, 126, 141–328 *passim*
Anglo-French approach to Czech. Govt.,

Sudeten German question (*cont.*)
attitude of France and Great Britain (*cont.*)
May 7, 1938, **i** 240–2, 251–2, 261, 263, 265–70
British 'observers' in Czechoslovakia, **i** 352, 362, 374–5, 397*n*, 406–7, 410*n*, 417, 463, 472, 485, 505, 555–7, 559, 576, 579, 580*n*, 606, 620; **ii** 9, 10, 12, 40, 99*n*, 110; **iii** 57–8, 65, 84, 120, 130, 163, 165
independent British mediator, suggested, **i** 401*n*, 501, 504–7, 515, 516*n*, 528, 531, 536–7, 541–2, 563, 565, 567, 575, 582–3, 600–2, 604–5, 607, 612–4; **ii** 4–8; accepted by Czech. Govt., July 1938, **i** 620; **ii** 10; *see also* Mission (Lord Runciman's)
conversations in London, Sept. 18, 1938, **ii** 373–99
proposals of Sept. 19, **ii** 404–5; *referred to*, **ii** 406–7, 409–11, 413–7, 420, 422–3, 425, 431, 436, 438, 440, 442–3, 447, 449–50, 460, 463–5, 477, 492, 521, 525–6, 544*n*, 548, 551, 580–1, 593, 604, 609, 628; **iii** 19, 21, 100, 102, 109, 128, 134, 232, 300, 304, 398, 634; **iv** 141, 240; **vii** 627
advice to Czechoslovakia on mobilization, **ii** 372–3, 457–62, 474, 480–1, 483, 485, 488, 491–2, 511, 517–8, 530, 548
suggestions on procedure for transfer of territory to Germany, **ii** 542, 551, 553, 561, 570–3, 584–6, 589–90, 592–3, 595–8, 601, 603–5, 610–624 *passim*
See also Berchtesgaden; Godesberg; Munich Conference and Agreement
attitude of Germany, **i** 110–2, 116–7, 174–5, 197, 221, 223, 238–40, 252–629 *passim*; **ii** *passim*; **iii** 622–6
attitude of Italy, **i** 261, 291, 297, 342–3, 353, 367–8; **ii** 130–1, 136–7, 172, 315–6, 356; *see also* Munich Conference (part played by Signor Mussolini)
attitude of Japan, **viii** 85–7, 90–2, 95, 107–8, 536*n*
autonomy, for Sudeten Germans, **i** 64, 76–7, 121, 125, 169, 185, 193–4, 240, 255–6, 282, 318–9, 344–5, 350, 363–4, 372, 378, 387, 395, 405, 410, 415, 442–4, 449, 466–7, 501, 511, 514–5, 530, 534, 557, 562, 596–7, 606–7, 634, 636–43; **ii** 30, 35, 69, 93, 97, 139, 144, 156, 166, 170, 172, 195, 209, 222, 231, 252, 254, 266, 306–7, 322, 657, 659, 678; military aspects of territorial autonomy, **i** 194; **ii** 185–8
conference, international, possible consideration of problems by, **ii** 88, 143, 147, 172, 661
demands and grievances of Sudeten Germans, **i** 34–5, 71, 116–7, 125, 139, 159, 169, 182–7, 249, 298, 309, 371, 555, 632, 638; **ii** 30–1, 36, 122, 222, 676–7; *see also* Carlsbad (Herr Henlein's eight demands)

Sudeten German question (*cont.*)
desire of Sudeten Germans for incorporation in Germany, **i** 68, 71, 121, 123–4, 219, 405, 555, 593, 634; **ii** 32, 40, 144, 335, 429
economic aspects. *See* Czechoslovakia (Germany); Sudetenland (economic conditions)
Herr Henlein's 'Freikorps' (Sudeten legion), **ii** 369, 414–5, 446, 448, 453–4, 455*n*, 457, 552, 677; **iii** 73*n*, 625
negotiations between Czech. Govt. and Sudeten German representatives, **i** 112–8, 122, 125*n*, 126, 138, 142*n*, 158–9, 195–6, 215, 264, 269, 275–6, 278, 283, 308–9, 312–3, 324, 331, 338, 349, 362*n*, 363, 365, 371–3, 377–8, 382–3, 385, 394–5, 401, 416*n*, 418, 452, 461, 464, 466–7, 469–71, 476, 478, 490, 493, 499, 501–2, 504, 506–11, 514–26, 530–3, 540–2, 543*n*, 547–8, 556–8, 562, 569–74, 598–9, 643–6; **ii** 4–5, 18, 25, 37–8, 49, 50, 57, 75, 80, 93, 100, 110–1, 116, 128, 142, 148, 150, 152–4, 165, 171, 178, 182, 198–9, 207, 209–10, 215, 222–3, 227–8, 231, 244–5, 248, 251, 253, 264–5, 272, 304, 309, 320–1, 327, 332–6, 662–3, 671–2, 675–6
proposals of Sudeten German representatives, **i** 365, 372, 383, 416*n*, 418, 442–3, 446, 453, 459*n*, 461, 466, 469–71, 490, 496, 504, 510–1, 515, 517, 531, 547, 556–8, 562; **ii** 231, 252–3
'sketch' of June 7, 1938, *text of*, **i** 636–43; *referred to*, **i** 490, 504, 510, 517, 531, 547, 562; **ii** 30–1, 49, 50, 75, 110, 165
memorandum of Sept. 2 (counter-proposals to Dr. Beneš' seven points), **ii** 215, 227–8
the Hitler–Henlein terms, **ii** 242, 245
Herr Frank's four points, **ii** 313, 321–2, 327, 335, 672–3, 676
proposals of Czechoslovak Govt., **i** 546–8, 557, 562, 570, 572–3, 606–9; **ii** 1, 5, 25, 49, 50, 74–5, 93, 100, 110–1, 165
Dr. Beneš' seven points, *text of*, **ii** 166, 657; *referred to*, **ii** 150, 153–4, 165, 171, 180–2, 188–9, 192–4, 196, 198–201, 207–10, 222, 226–7, 252, 664–5, 668
proposals of Sept. 5, **ii** 241, 253–4, 256, 261, 265–8, 272–4, 277–9, 281, 283, 332–3, 358, 403, 425, 669–72, 675–7
proposals of Sept. 13, **ii** 313, 672, 676
views and suggestions of
Sir N. Henderson, **i** 56*n*, 110–2, 115, 175, 238–9, 257–8, 262, 273–4, 297, 362–4, 376, 391–2, 447–8, 450, 458, 461, 475, 494–5, 521, 533–5, 564, 580, 590, 593, 597–8, 603–4, 613–4, 617–8, 621, 623–5, 629; **ii** 11–4, 35–6, 58–60, 63–5, 83–7, 102–3, 108*n*, 112*n*, 118, 120, 129–35, 138–40, 156, 170, 233–4, 239, 243, 250–1, 257, 299, 300, 306–7, 310, 330, 359–61, 363, 367, 371, 413, 423, 425–6, 436–7,

Sudeten German question (*cont.*)
439–40, 513, 515–6, 545, 574, 585–6, 599, 646–55
Mr. Newton, **i** 55–6, 139, 152–4, 167–70, 181, 300–3, 387, 439, 504–6, 520*n*, 573–5
See also Missions (Lord Runciman's); Munich Agreement; Plebiscite (for Sudeten Germans); Self-determination
Sudetenland
economic conditions, **i** 71, 124, 191, 489, 518, 522, 556, 594–5; **ii** 166–7, 661–2, 664, 677, 679
Employers' Committee oí the Industrialists' Association, **i** 250
disturbances, **i** 123, 126, 251, 258–9, 261, 276–7, 316, 342, 398–9, 428, 434–8, 487–8, 619; **ii** 167, 176, 183, 224, 304–5, 308, 313, 316, 319, 330, 333–5, 340, 348, 353–4, 356–7, 366–7, 374, 376, 495, 676–7; **iii** 74
frontier incidents, **i** 330, 333, 336–7, 340, 342, 358–61, 414, 442; **ii** 354, 419, 454–5, 457, 467, 472–3, 521, 544
international investigating commission suggested, **i** 386, 393–4, 402, 409, 410*n*, 417, 426
See also Eger, Egerland, Mährisch-Ostrau
Gymnastic Associations, **i** 250, 436, 489
maintenance of law and order, question of, **i** 71, 74, 122, 324; **ii** 316, 458, 476, 478, 482–3, 492–3, 507, 521, 523
Czech. police force, withdrawal suggested, **ii** 23, 28, 166, 186, 222, 224, 313, 321, 341, 349, 353, 377, 446, 476, 483, 495, 572–4
international police force suggested, **ii** 352, 446, 476, 492–3, 661, 679
martial law, **ii** 308, 313, 316, 319, 321, 336, 672, 677
occupation by German military forces, **iii** 162–7, 625, 628
Suez Canal Company, **iii** 88–9, 309; **iv** 10, 296, 322
Italian claims to representation on Board of, **iii** 309, 477, 483–4, 487–9, 493, 504–5, 510, 512; **iv** 299, 319*n*, 322–3, 325, 344, 353*n*, 359, 590; **v** 223, 347, 427, 611, 651, 663, 800; **vi** 44, 202, 303, 358, 471, 488, 554–5, 724; **vii** 350
Sui-fu, **ix** 294
Suiyuan Province, **viii** 32, 333–4
Sulz, **ii** 26
Suvalkai (Suwalki) district, Lithuania, **iv** 286
Swatow, **viii** 134; **ix** 223
Sweden, i 386, 649; **ii** 594; **iv** 622; **v** 508, 568
'Aftonbladet', **vii** 17*n*, 99
Swinemünde, **iv** 482
Switzerland, i 55, 153, 191, 234*n*, 237, 280, 378, 386, 434, 612–3, 625, 649, 652; **ii** 15, 58, 84–5, 97, 129, 144, 156, 282, 393, 678; **iii** 291, 590; **vii** 66; *see also* Germany (Switzerland)

Sylt, **vi** 746, 749
Syria, **iii** 307–8; **v** 213, 278; **vi** 347
Szechuan, **ix** 93
Szepetowka, **iii** 419

Taiyuanfu, **ix** 86
Taku Tug and Lighter Co. Ltd., The, **ix** 183
Tali, **viii** 207
Tallinn, **i** 431; **v** 249; **vi** 282
'Tanaka memorandum', **ix** 6
Tanganyika, **iii** 295, 564, 608
Tangier, **v** 239
Tangku, **viii** 338*n*; **ix** 322
Tannenberg celebrations, planned for Aug. 27, 1939, **vi** 557, 560, 633, 649, 666–7; **vii** 31, 57, 69, 89–90, 101, 543; cancelled, **vii** 265
Herr Hitler's proposed speech, **vi** 649, 667, 700–1, 713, 734; **vii** 31, 57, 69, 247
Tarnopol, **v** 407; **vii** 306, 347
Tarnowskie-Gory, **v** 246; **vi** 94; **vii** 485
Tarragona, **iii** 521
Tasaul, Lake, **iii** 233*n*
Tatra Mountains, **iii** 219; **v** 247
Tatra Works A. G., **iii** 644
Tauberbischofsheim, **ii** 26
Taus, **ii** 596, 603; **iii** 136, 236
Tavs Document, The, **i** 128
Tczew (Dirschau), **iv** 81; **v** 27, 538, 583; **vi** 149, 491; **vii** 461, 474, 477, 479, 484
Tempelburg, **vii** 416
Tepelini, **v** 750
Teplitz (Teplice), **i** 78, 438, 462; **ii** 446, 552, 658, 666
Teplitz-Schönau, **iii** 640
Teschen area (Cesky Tesin, Cieszyn), **i** 223, 351, 445, 465, 478–81, 512, 550–1; **ii** 287, 318, 441, 457, 465, 498, 538–40, 545; **iii** 6, 8, 17, 22–3, 25, 27, 32–5, 38*n*, 39–41, 43, 46, 49, 50, 52–4, 58–62, 82, 97, 101–7, 120, 180–2, 212, 219, 225, 228, 379; **iv** 95; **v** 246–7; **vi** 13, 551; **vii** 324
seizure by Czechoslovakia, 1919–20, **i** 479; **ii** 287, 465; **iii** 8, 32–3; **iv** 95
economic and military importance, **i** 479; **iii** 82, 103, 105; **iv** 617; **vi** 137
Polish demands for immediate cession, Sept. 1938, **iii** 41, 51–5, 59, 62, 70–2; Czechoslovak replies, **iii** 54, 64, 69, 70, 72–3, 82
attitude to Czech.–Polish dispute of: France and Great Britain, **ii** 538–40, 545; **iii** 38–40, 48, 50*n*, 53–4, 59, 60, 63–4, 97, 106–7; U.S.S.R., **ii** 498; **iii** 24, 104
frontier as fixed Nov. 1938, **iii** 212, 219, 223
Polish treatment of Czech. and German inhabitants, **iii** 228–9, 379; **iv** 162; **v** 246; **vi** 204, 551; **vii** 324
Tetschen, **i** 437
Therapia, **vi** 71
Theresienstadt, **ii** 552

Thorn, **iii** 658; **v** 247–8

Thornycroft & Co. Ltd., J. I., **viii** 312, 540

Thrace, **v** 464; **vi** 30, 68

Tientsin (British Concession)

anti-Japanese activities

treatment of offenders, **viii** 9, 15, 100, 156, 210–1, 368, 378, 380, 383–4, 390, 420–1, 445–7, 459–60, 462, 468, 471, 526, 551*n*; **ix** *passim*

legal issues, **ix** 109, 132, 158–60, 172–3, 179–80, 410–1, 455–6, 466, 469, 481, 493–4, 497, 519–20, 524–5, 533–5

question of mediation by U.S., **ix** 161–2 165, 167–9, 183, 185, 197

See also Cheng Lien-shi; Ssu Ching-wu; Li Han-yuan in Index of Persons

British forces, **viii** 9*n*, 115, 338*n*

customs administration, **viii** 232*n*, 243

evacuation of Japanese nationals, **viii** 55–6, 60–1, 63, 66, 71–3, 232–3, 243, 252, 300, 390*n*, 420, 494, 500

floods, **ix** 479, 493, 498, 504–5

Japanese aggressive acts, **viii** 494, 500

barriers at entrances to British and French Concessions, Dec. 1938, **viii** 314–5, 322–3, 328–9, 333, 335, 338–9, 341, 350–1, 354, 368, 377–8, 380, 391, 421, 427, 439, 445–7, 452, 459, 494, 500

live wire fences, **viii** 459, 471*n*, 489, 491, 494, 500, 509

reported Japanese terrorist organization, **viii** 70, 504, 507, 520

searching of foreigners, **viii** 527, 531–2, 534

trade restrictions. *See* China (Japanese-occupied districts)

blockade of British Concession, June 1939, **vi** 99, 127*n*, 176, 197, 208, 709; **ix** 169, 181–3, 186, 191–6, 198, 205–6, 210; text of Japanese statement of June 13, 1939, **ix** 211–2; situation reports, **ix** 236, 277, 419

searching of British subjects, June–July 1939, **ix** 182–3, 205, 221, 226–7, 229, 241–2, 245

interference with food supplies, **ix** 256, 262, 278, 322, 351, 397

anti-British demonstrations, **ix** 322, 494*n*

Japanese gendarmerie and Municipal Council police, **viii** 100, 492, 511–2, 517, 520; **ix** 2–3, 5, 18, 207; *see also* next heading, 'negotiations in Tokyo'

negotiations in Tokyo, **vi** 208, 503; **vii** 137

preparations for, **ix** 197–202, 214–5, 217, 219–32, 241, 255–7, 261–3, 267, 274, 278–83; preliminary formula, **ix** 278–9, 281, 283, 285, 290–1, 296–308; text of, **ix** 304–5, 313; *referred to*, **ix** 309–11, 316–20, 326–7, 334, 348, 388, 398, 453, 460, 472, 512, 527; reactions to formula of: Chinese,

Tientsin (negotiations in Tokyo) (*cont.*)

ix 332–3, 340, 343, 374–5, 386; Japanese military in N. China, **ix** 341

meetings, July 24–7, 1939, **ix** 321, 323–6, 337–8, 342–3, 344–7, 349–51, 355–8

currency and silver questions, **ix** 224, 243–5, 249–51, 314–5, 346, 350, 355, 359, 375, 378, 380, 392–3, 395, 420–2, 425–7, 440, 452, 457, 460, 463–5, 473–4, 477, 484, 488, 491, 501–2, 511–4, 521–2; Mr. Edwardes' formula, **ix** 509, 511, 514, 521; Mr. Myers' plan, **ix** 314, 315*n*; Dr. Schacht's proposal, **ix** 271–2, 273*n*, 329, 351, 399

legal points raised, **ix** 358–9, 369, 410, 414, 425–6, 452–3

consultation with French and U.S. Govts., **ix** 247, 289, 330–1, 342, 347, 359–60, 420–1, 465, 467; attitude of French Govt., **ix** 247, 251–4, 261, 312–3, 359, 379, 392, 399, 446*n*, 447–50; of U.S. Govt., **ix** 258, 283, 360, 372, 381, 394–5, 443–4

police matters, **ix** 376–7, 387, 416

draft agreement, **ix** 401–9, 419, 424, 434–6, 484

suspension of conversations, **ix** 389, 400, 415, 431, 439–41, 444–5, 451, 461, 469–70, 474–5, 478, 484, 495, 502, 512–3

proposed statement to press, **ix** 471–2, 474, 476–8

suggested reopening of negotiations, **ix** 495, 500, 504, 509, 514, 521–3

United States, and Anglo-Japanese relations in Tientsin, **viii** 83–4, 94; **ix** 184, 189, 204–5, 216*n*, 223, 227–8, 233–5, 283–4, 394, 520–1

visit of Major-General Piggott, **viii** 532, 533*n*; **ix** 1

Tientsin (French Concession), **viii** 10*n*, 294, 354; *see also* Tientsin (British Concession, Japanese aggressive acts)

Tientsin (Italian Concession), **viii** 232, 269, 459, 469

Tientsin–Pukow railway, **viii** 32

Tilsit, **vii** 546

Timisoara (Temesvar), **iv** 433

Tirana, **iv** 357; **v** 116, 127–8, 133, 149, 168, 176–7, 193, 195, 750

Togoland, **vi** 348

Tokyo: Anglo-Japanese conversations. *See* Tientsin (British Concession: negotiations in Tokyo)

Tomaszow, anti-German incidents, **v** 605; **vi** 552; **vii** 204

Torun. *See* Thorn

Toulouse, **iii** 478

Transolzan Volunteer Corps, **iii** 22, 103

Transylvania, **ii** 279, 381, 384, 575*n*; **iii** 181; **iv** 283

Hungary's claims, **ii** 455; **iv** 401, 478, 480, 618, 625; **vi** 77

See also Hungary (Roumania)

Trautenau, **i** 576, 579; **iii** 640
Treaties, Agreements, Declarations *bilateral*
Albania–Italy
  Treaty of Defensive Alliance, Nov. 1927,
  iv 357; **v** 120–1
Austria–Germany
  Agreement of July 11, 1936, **i** 7, 9*n*, 37–8,
  44, 47, 127–8, 130, 133
  Agreement of Feb. 12, 1938 (the Berchtes-
  gaden Agreement), **i** 1, 2, 5, 7, 8, 9*n*, 11,
  15, 21–2, 24, 28, 31, 39, 44, 59, 82, 98,
  129–31; **ii** 33*n*
Belgium–Germany
  German Declaration of Oct. 13, 1937, **i**
  649; **iii** 287*n*; **vii** 270
Belgium–Holland
  Treaty of April 19, 1839, **i** 648
China–Great Britain.
  Treaty of Tientsin, 1858, **ix** 455, 478*n*
  Chen–O'Malley Agreement, Feb. 1927,
  viii 206–7, 367–8
China–Japan
  Treaty of Shimonoseki, April 1895, **viii**
  13*n*
  Sino-Japanese Treaties of May 25, 1915,
  viii 7*n*
China–U.S.S.R.
  Sino-Soviet commercial treaty, June 16,
  1939, **ix** 249
Czechoslovakia–France
  Treaty of Alliance and Friendship, Paris,
  Jan. 25, 1924, **i** 72
  Treaty of Mutual Guarantee, Locarno,
  Oct. 16, 1925, **i** 83, 97, 218–9, 223, 260,
  456, 497, 647, 650; **ii** 107, 255, 386, 399,
  594; **iii** 88, 301, 607; **iv** 41, 267; **v** 200*n*
Czechoslovakia–Germany
  Arbitration Convention, Locarno, Oct.
  1925, **i** 37, 41, 47, 72, 349, 477; **ii** 386,
  422, 425, 433*n*, 435
  Frontier Agreement, Nov. 20, 1938, **iii**
  235, 240, 654
  Minorities Declaration, Nov. 20, 1938, **iii**
  235, 240, 410, 415; text of, **iii** 653
  Optants Agreement, Nov. 20, 1938, **iii** 235,
  240; text of, **iii** 649–52; Supplementary
  Agreement, Mar. 1939, **iv** 200
  Agreements of Oct. 27 and Nov. 23, 1938,
  relating to resumption of railway traffic,
  iv 57; Supplementary Agreement, Jan.
  1939, **iv** 56–8, 63, 65
  Agreement signed Mar. 15, 1939, **iv** 255–6,
  260, 265
Czechoslovakia–Poland
  Frontier Agreement, Nov. 5, 1918, **iii** 12
  Legal and Financial Convention, April
  1925: denunciation by Poland of Ch. III
  (Minorities), **ii** 459*n*; **iii** 16, 228
Czechoslovak Govt.–Slovaks
  Sillein Agreement of Oct. 1938, **iii** 114; **iv**

Treaties *bilateral* (*cont.*)
  Czechoslovak Govt.–Slovaks (*cont.*)
  219; *see also* Czechoslovakia (minorities)
Czechoslovakia–U.S.S.R.
  Treaty of Mutual Assistance, May 16,
  1935, **i** 54, 62, 64, 85, 172, 297, 346, 452,
  497, 634, 647, 650; **ii** 107, 255, 594; **iii**
  301, 374; **iv** 41
Danzig (Free City of)–Poland
  Treaty signed at Paris, Nov. 1920, **v** 810;
  vi 624
  Agreement signed at Warsaw, Oct. 1921,
  v 811; **vi** 7, 26, 547, 548*n*, 625; Protocol
  of Mar. 1922, **vi** 26
  Customs Agreement, Aug. 6, 1934, **vi** 7,
  26, 547, 569
Denmark–Germany
  Non-Aggression Pact, May 31, 1939, **v** 775
Estonia–Germany
  Non-Aggression Pact, June 7, 1939, **v** 775;
  see also Germany (Estonia)
Estonia–Latvia
  Defensive Alliance, 1923, **v** 697
Estonia–U.S.S.R.
  Treaty of Feb. 2, 1920, **v** 350
  Treaty of Non-Aggression, May 1932, **v**
  350–1, 697
France–Germany
  Agreement of Dec. 6, 1938, **iii** 286, 310–1,
  391, 394; *see also* France (Germany)
France–Great Britain
  Hoare–Laval Agreement, Dec. 1935, **iii**
  484, 506–7
  Notes exchanged April 1, 1936, **i** 144, 199,
  211, 234
France–Italy
  Agreement of 1896 relating to Tunis, **iii**
  475; **iv** 294, 323*n*; **v** 347, 386, 611, 800;
  vi 472–3
  Agreement of Jan. 1935 (Mussolini–Laval
  Agreement), **iii** 470–2, 475, 477, 479,
  483, 488–95, 499, 502–3, 507, 509, 516,
  518, 520, 524; **iv** 89, 293, 344; **v** 251, 611,
  613; **vi** 221
France–Poland
  Rambouillet Agreement, Sept. 1936, **ii**
  538; **iii** 104, 107, 366; **vii** 79*n*
  Political Alliance, Feb. 1921 and Treaty of
  Mutual Guarantee, Locarno, Oct. 16,
  1925, **i** 444*n*; **iii** 107; **iv** 182*n*, 426, 463,
  471, 473, 480, 496, 502, 516, 529, 616; **v** 4,
  6, 7, 371; **vi** 238, 399, 504, 517–8; **vii** 281
France–Roumania
  Treaty of Friendship, 1926, **iv** 480; **v**
  200*n*
France–Russia
  Treaty of Tilsit, 1807, **v** 809
France–Spain
  Bérard Agreement, Mar. 1939, **iv** 461*n*; **v**
  508

Treaties *bilateral* (*cont.*)
France–Syria
  Treaty of Friendship, Sept. 1936, **iii** 307;
  v 796
France–Turkey
  Franco-Turkish Joint Declaration, June
  23, 1939, **v** 746*n*; *see also* Guarantee (to
  Turkey)
France–U.S.S.R.
  Treaty of Mutual Assistance, signed at
  Paris, May 2, 1935 (Franco-Soviet Pact),
  i 62, 64, 111, 165, 172, 289, 314; **iii** 67,
  156, 193, 252–3, 307, 427, 526, 541, 619,
  621; **iv** 33, 124; **v** 7, 8, 216, 229, 261, 273,
  435, 470, 486, 624, 631, 641, 644, 737,
  767; **vi** 339, 517, 618; **vii** 205, 268; **ix** 28
France–Yugoslavia
  Treaty of Friendly Understanding, Nov,
  1927, **v** 200*n*
Germany–Great Britain
  Naval Agreements, June 18, 1935 and July
  17, 1937, and Protocol of June 30, 1938,
  i 110, 175–6, 455, 585; **ii** 339, 344, 346,
  375, 640; **iii** 244*n*, 248, 279, 526, 662–3;
  iv 628; **v** 302; **viii** 548; *see also* Germany
  (Great Britain, Naval Agreements)
  Payments Agreement, July 1, 1938, **iv** 603;
  vi 154
  Chamberlain–Hitler Declaration, Sept. 30,
  1938, **ii** 640; *see also* Munich Conference
  Agreement of June 1939 regarding exten-
  sion to Sudetenland of Anglo-German
  Transfer Agreement of July 1, 1938, and
  supplementary Agreement of Aug. 13,
  1938, **vi** 88*n*
  Coal Agreement, Jan. 1939, **iv** 138, 591*n*;
  vi 244*n*
Germany–Italy
  Political and Military Pact, May 22, 1939,
  v 461; *see also* Germany (Italy)
Germany–Latvia
  Non-Aggression Pact, June 7, 1939, **v**
  437, 461, 648–9, 697–8, 700; **vi** 45*n*, 159
Germany–Lithuania
  Treaty relating to Memel Territory, Mar.
  22, 1939, **iv** 483–4, 497, 518, 523, 534–5,
  550; **vi** 256*n*
Germany–Poland
  Declaration of Non-Aggression and Understanding, Jan. 26, 1934, **i** 72–3, 109, 274;
  ii 338, 344, 374; **iii** 182, 274, 425, 431,
  582, 585; **iv** 15–6, 60, 68, 215, 435, 540–1,
  575, 616; **v** 6, 52, 212, 423, 455, 582, 808,
  811; **vi** 503–4, 517; **vii** 621
    denunciation by Germany, **v** 360, 364,
    371–2, 378, 393, 404, 409, 520, 584,
    744; **vi** 73, 551
  Minority Declaration, Nov. 5, 1937, **iv** 88,
  152, 409
    denunciation by Poland, **v** 379, 409

Treaties *bilateral* (*cont.*)
Germany–Roumania
  Trade Agreement, Mar. 23, 1939, **iv** 497,
  519–20, 542, 619; **v** 63, 78, 300–1, 310–1;
  vi 72
Germany–Slovakia
  Treaty of Protection, Mar. 23, 1939, **iv**
  497; **v** 78, 89
Germany–U.S.S.R.
  Treaty of Rapallo, 1922, **vi** 756
  Neutrality Agreement, April 1926, **vii** 188,
  197, 620
  Commercial Credit Agreement, Aug. 19,
  1939, **vii** 98–100, 118, 122, 197, 207, 383,
  618
  Non-Aggression Pact, Aug. 23, 1939, **vii**
  132, 188–9; *see also* Germany (U.S.S.R.)
Great Britain–Greece
  Declaration announcing guarantee to
  Greece, April 13, 1939, **v** 197; *see also*
  Guarantee (to Greece)
Great Britain–Iraq
  Treaty of Alliance, June 1930, **vi** 195*n*
Great Britain–Italy
  Gentlemen's Agreement of 1937, **iii** 472
  Agreement, signed April 16, 1938, brought
  into effect, Nov. 16, 1938, **iii** 312–62
  passim; *see also* Italy (Great Britain)
Great Britain–Japan
  Commercial Treaty, April 3, 1911, **viii** 51,
  183, 192–3, 196, 413; **ix** 485, 530
  Customs Agreement, May 2, 1938, **viii**
  14*n*; *see also* Chinese Maritime Customs
  Administration
  'Arrangement' relating to local issues at
  Tientsin, June 19, 1940, **ix** 523*n*
Great Britain–Poland
  Declaration announcing guarantee to
  Poland, Mar. 31, 1939, **iv** 553; *see also*
  Guarantee (to Poland)
  Treaty of Mutual Assistance, Aug. 25, 1939,
  vii 242, 249, 279, 281, 314, 316, 322, 324
Great Britain–Portugal
  Treaty of Alliance, 1373, **vi** 162*n*
Great Britain–Roumania
  Declaration announcing guarantee to Rou-
  mania, April 13, 1939, **v** 197; *see also*
  Guarantee (to Roumania)
  Trade Agreement, May 11, 1939, **v** 483*n*
Great Britain–Turkey
  Guarantee Agreement of May 27, 1938,
  relating to export to Turkey of goods
  manufactured in U.K., **vi** 191
  Trade Agreement of May 27, 1938, **vii** 27*n*
  Anglo-Turkish Joint Declaration, May 12,
  1939, **v** 497, 531, 537; *see also* Guarantee
  (to Turkey)
Great Britain–U.S.S.R.
  Commercial Treaty of 1936, **iv** 35–6, 46,
  106, 132, 207

Treaties *bilateral* (*cont.*)
Great Britain–U.S.S.R. (*cont.*)
  Naval Agreement, July 17, 1937, and Protocol, **iii** 668; **iv** 628*n*, 629–33
Great Britain–United States
  Trade Agreement, Nov. 17, 1938, **iii** 279
Great Britain–Yugoslavia
  Payments Agreement, Nov. 1936, **vi** 437
Greece–Turkey
  Treaty of April 1938, **v** 189, 575
Greece–Yugoslavia
  Convention for regulating transit traffic *via* Salonika, May 1923, **v** 296*n*
Italy–U.S.S.R.
  Non-Aggression and Neutrality Pact, 1933, **vii** 619
  Commercial Agreement, Feb. 1939, **iv** 621
Italy–Yugoslavia
  Political and Economic Agreement, Mar. 1937, **v** 137, 596
Japan–U.S.S.R.
  Peace Treaty, 1905 (Portsmouth Treaty), **viii** 298
  Fishery Agreement, 1937, **viii** 356
Japan–United States
  Commercial Treaty of 1911, denunciation by U.S. *See* Japan (United States)
Latvia–U.S.S.R.
  Non-Aggression Pact of 1932, **v** 648; **vi** 159
Lithuania–U.S.S.R.
  Non-Aggression Pact of 1926, **vi** 256*n*
Poland–Roumania
  Treaty of Alliance, 1931, **iv** 363*n*, 371, 423, 435, 471, 478, 510; **v** 2, 74, 111–2, 217, 229, 233, 274, 298–9, 324, 434; **vi** 91; **vii** 64
Poland–U.S.S.R.
  Treaty of Non-Aggression, July 25, 1932, **ii** 498; **iii** 24, 364, 577; **v** 6; **vi** 405; **vii** 116, 217
  Trade Agreement, Jan. 1939, **iv** 621
Roumania–Yugoslavia
  Treaty of 1921, **iv** 388, 621; **v** 106, 660
Turkey–U.S.S.R.
  Treaty of Friendship and Neutrality, Dec. 17, 1925, **iv** 559; **v** 82; **vi** 83
Treaties, Agreements, etc., *multilateral*
Aggression, Convention for the Definition of, July 3, 1933, **vi** 158, 584*n*
Anti-Comintern Pact. *See* Anti-Comintern Pact
Austria: Anglo-Franco-Italian Agreements of Feb. 17 and Sept. 27, 1934, relating to independence of Austria, **i** 47
Balkan Pact, signed Feb. 9, 1934, **iv** 374*n*; *see also* main entry, Balkan Entente
Belgium: Anglo-French joint Declaration of April 24, 1937, **iii** 287*n*; **vi** 424; **vii** 270*n*, 304, 338
Belgium and Holland: Treaties signed at London, April 19, 1839, between Great

Treaties *multilateral* (*cont.*)
Britain, Austria-Hungary, France, Prussia, Russia and (a) Belgium, (b) Holland, **i** 649
Briand–Kellogg Pact. *See below* Pact of Paris
China: Peking Protocol, Sept. 7, 1901, **viii** 351*n*, 352
China: Treaty relating to principles and policies to be followed in matters concerning China, signed at Washington, Feb. 6, 1922 (the Nine-Power Treaty), **iii** 308*n*; **viii** 8, 161, 199, 212, 236, 250, 258, 269, 273, 303, 340, 356, 362, 371–2, 395–6, 404, 408, 418, 423, 448, 450, 522; **ix** 43, 63, 236, 263, 295, 375, 388, 422–3, 429, 460, 465, 473–4, 476–7, 491, 495, 502, 510, 513, 522, 530
China: Agreement of Feb. 17, 1930, relating to the Chinese Courts in International Settlement at Shanghai (Court Rendition Agreement), **viii** 97, 112; **ix** 489, 534
Czechoslovakia: Anglo-Franco-Czechoslovak Agreements regarding financial assistance to Czecho-Slovakia, signed in London, Jan. 27, 1939, **iv** 14, 25–6
Four-Power Pact (Great Britain, France, Germany, Italy), signed at Rome, July 15, 1933, **iii** 102, 518
Hague Convention of 1907, **vii** 379
Italy: Treaty of London, April 26, 1915, **iii** 477, 492, 500, 502*n*; **iv** 293–4; **v** 251
League of Nations: Geneva (Red Cross) Agreement, July 1929, **iii** 638–9
Little Entente (Czechoslovakia, Roumania, Yugoslavia) Treaty signed at Geneva, Feb. 16, 1933, **i** 615
Little Entente–Hungary
  Bled Agreements of Aug. 1938, **ii** 157; **v** 64*n*, 332; **vi** 642*n*
Locarno: Treaty of Mutual Guarantee, initialled at Locarno, Oct. 16, 1925, signed in London, Dec. 1, **i** 84–5, 96, 120, 199, 208, 211, 234, 649; **ii** 365–6; **iii** 260, 287*n*, 303–4; **v** 5*n*; **vii** 270*n*
Draft proposals reaffirming obligations under Treaty of Locarno adopted by Great Britain, Belgium, France and Italy, Mar. 19, 1936 (l'accord de Londres), **i** 84, 96, 199, 233–4, 247; **iii** 287*n*, 484
Luxemburg: Treaty of London, 1867, relating to Grand Duchy of Luxemburg, **i** 649
Memel Convention, signed at Paris, May 8, 1924: Annex I, Statute of the Memel Territory, **ii** 339, 375; **iv** 378, 474, 476, 638, 641, 645–6
Montreux Convention of 1936 (the Straits Convention), **v** 575, 615; **vi** 71, 109; **vii** 528
Munich Agreement. *See* this main heading
Naval Armaments
  Treaty for Limitation of, signed at Washington, Feb. 6, 1922 (the Five-Power Treaty), **ii** 637; **viii** 547

Treaties *multilateral (cont.)*
  Naval Armaments *(cont.)*
    Treaty for Limitation and Reduction of Naval Armaments, signed at London, April 22, 1930 (The London Naval Treaty of 1930), **ii** 637–8; **iii** 665
    Treaty for Limitation of Naval Armaments, signed at London, Mar. 25, 1936, and Protocol of June 30, 1938, **iii** 451*n*, 670*n*; **iv** 628*n*, 630–7; **vi** 156; **viii** 22*n*
  Pact of Paris (Briand–Kellogg Pact) for renunciation of war, signed by fifteen Powers, Aug. 27, 1928, **i** 63–4; **ii** 546*n*; **v** 350
  Peace Treaties, 1919–20, **i** 47, 49, 103, 131, 139, 177; **ii** 466; **iii** 10, 387, 499, 506, 593; **v** 318
    Treaty of St. Germain, **i** 127, 129, 135–6, 148, 182–4, 293; **viii** 85
    Treaty of Trianon, **vi** 77, 202*n*
    Treaty of Versailles, **i** 120, 148, 447, 621, 623, 649; **ii** 144, 169, 239, 315, 343, 349, 386, 613, 648; **iii** 248, 400, 406, 555, 662; **iv** 214, 266, 280, 475, 483, 492*n*; **v** 302, 455, 584, 705, 810; **vi** 72, 179, 286*n*, 624; **vii** 375, 389, 486, 530, 539–41
  Peking Protocol. *See above* China
  Roumania: Treaty of Bucharest, May 7, 1918, **vi** 72
  Russia: Treaty of Brest-Litovsk, Mar. 3, 1918, **vi** 72
  Saadabad Pact (Middle East Non-Aggression Pact), July 8, 1937, **v** 463, 796
  Spain: Non-Intervention Agreements of Aug. 1936 and Feb. 1937, **iii** 479, 481, 506; **iv** 295–6, 462
  Turkey: Anglo-Franco-Turkish Treaty of Mutual Assistance, Oct. 19, 1939, **vii** 537*n*
  Washington Five-Power Treaty. *See above* Naval Armaments
  Washington Nine-Power Treaty. *See above* China
Trebnitz, **i** 316
Trencin, **iv** 287
Trentino, **iv** 350
Trento, **iv** 338
Triebitz, **iv** 57
Trier, **ii** 104
Trieste, **i** 108; **ii** 414*n*; **iii** 498; **iv** 42, 49, 350; **v** 733
Tripoli, **iii** 475; **iv** 49
Trolle-Ljungby, **vi** 748
Troppau, **i** 576; **ii** 86; **iii** 641; **v** 204
Trzyniec, **iii** 82, 105, 229
Tsaribrod, **vi** 30, 68
Tsinanfu, **viii** 333–4
Tsingtao, **viii** 52*n*, 240, 279, 284–9, 330–1, 353, 490*n*; **ix** 349, 355
Tuh-er-wai Kong, **ix** 153
Tunis (Tunisia), **ii** 96; **iii** 608; **iv** 49, 51; **v** 54
  French military preparations, **iv** 307, 316, 325–6, 330–4, 336, 339, 341–3, 345, 348

Tunis *(cont.)*
  Great Britain's offer of 'good offices' with French and Italian Govts., **iv** 329–30, 334–6, 341–9, 353
  Italy's claims, **iii** 360, 390, 437, 463–7, 470–2, 474–5, 477, 479–80, 483, 487–92, 498, 510, 512; **iv** 107, 161, 293–4, 296–7, 299, 315, 317, 319*n*, 322–5, 344, 353*n*, 359, 590, 608; **v** 107, 117, 143, 251, 347, 386, 427, 611, 651, 663, 703, 797; **vi** 202, 303, 358, 471, 555
Turin, **iii** 532; **iv** 338
Turkey, **i** 515; **ii** 532; **iii** 154
  Great Britain
    Anglo-Turkish assurances, 1935, **vii** 366
    Anglo-Turkish Joint Declaration, May 12, 1939, **v** 497; *see also* Balkan Entente (Anglo-Turkish Declaration); Guarantee (to Turkey)
    Anglo-Franco-Turkish negotiations, May–Sept. 1939, **v** 366–7, 547–8, 574–6, 591, 682, 693–6, 738, 740–3, 760, 766, 785–8; **vi** 82–3, 93, 97, 100–3, 111, 145, 151–2, 159, 60, 165, 187, 194–6, 228–9, 241, 260–1, 279, 299, 300, 303, 313, 315, 336, 341, 355–6, 403, 434–5, 560, 567, 574–5, 596, 598–603, 617–9, 623, 625, 636, 646, 670–3, 676, 687–8; **vii** 183, 198–9, 226, 242, 264, 268, 271–3, 276–7, 299, 300, 305–6, 313, 320–1, 325, 327, 360, 364–6, 369, 372, 407–8, 412–3, 418–9, 423–4, 444, 446–7, 449, 454, 470, 487–8, 490, 493–4, 500–1, 527–8, 536–7
      Italy to be informed of Agreement before signature, **vii** 462–3, 494
      signature of Treaty of Mutual Assistance, **vii** 537*n*
    Anglo-Turkish Staff conversations, preparations for, **v** 242, 259, 280, 341, 576; **vi** 112, 188
    economic and financial aid to Turkey, **v** 335, 366; **vi** 97, 111, 189–92, 229, 353–5, 361–2, 435, 567, 574, 604–6, 618, 647; **vii** 226, 238, 264, 268, 271*n*, 272, 300, 320–1, 471–3, 484, 490, 536–7
    military supplies for Turkey, **v** 259–60, 548; **vi** 111, 188–90, 435, 567, 605, 625; **vii** 183, 238
    suggested special British mission to Turkey, Aug. 1939, **vii** 243, 272, 359
    suggested transfer of Anglo-Turkish trade to a compensation basis, **vi** 686; **vii** 26–7, 183
    Turkish Economic Delegation in Great Britain, **vii** 473
    Turkish Military Mission in Great Britain, **vi** 111, 567
  Political parties: National party, **vii** 360; Popular party, **v** 287–8, 445, 447; Republican People's party, **v** 445*n*

Turkey (*cont.*)

U.S.S.R., **v** 82, 259, 268, 282, 433–5, 449, 537, 796; **vi** 787

    proposed Turco-Soviet pact, **v** 336, 340–1, 380, 399, 400, 411, 434–5; **vi** 54, 250, 280, 311, 623, 661; **vii** 10, 200, 276, 508–9

war in Europe, probable attitude, **vii** 264–5, 277, 299*n*

Yugoslavia. *See* Balkan Entente (Anglo-Turkish negotiations)

See also Albania (effect of Italian action, on Turkey); Anglo-Franco-Soviet negotiations (Turkey's attitude towards); Anti-Comintern Pact; Bulgaria; France; Germany; Guarantee

Tuschkau, **iii** 640

Twenty-one Demands (Japan's), **viii** 7

Tyrol. *See* South Tyrol

Udine, **iii** 350

Ueberlingen, **ii** 26

Ukraine, **i** 108, 443; **iii** 201, 232, 274, 306–7, 368, 387, 415, 417, 436, 494, 513, 525, 541, 548, 550, 557, 562, 565, 570–80, 582–4, 589, 658–9; **iv** 4, 22–5, 35, 38, 55–6, 69, 71, 80, 102–3, 184–5, 214, 336, 412, 449, 607, 621; **v** 107, 384, 441, 455

Ulzen, **ii** 127

Ungvar, **iii** 239; **v** 78

Union of Soviet Socialist Republics (U.S.S.R.)

armed forces

    air force, **i** 95, 218, 305, 421–2; **ii** 312, 454, 533, 575*n*; **iii** 254; **iv** 196–7; **v** 73, 488; **vi** 775, 787–8; **vii** 134, 585, 599; Chief of, *see* Loktionov, Comm., in Index of Persons

    army, **i** 95, 161–5, 172–3, 213, 218, 305–7, 346, 420–4, 482–3; **ii** 270; **iii** 254, 577–8; **iv** 194–5, 412, 478; **v** 8, 73, 452, 797; **vi** 770, 785–6; **vii** 135, 575–6; **viii** 40; Chief of, *see* Shaposhnikoff, General, in Index of Persons

    navy, **iii** 456, 667–9, 673–4; **iv** 412, 630; **v** 249; **vi** 767–8, 783–5

Conference (six-Power) at Bucharest suggested, Mar. 1939, **iv** 385, 392, 423–4, 429–30, 466, 471–2, 574, 585; **v** 20, 45, 205; *see also* Four-Power Declaration

18th Congress of the All-Union Communist party, **iv** 411

Far East, **iv** 46, 107, 412, 621; **vii** 205, 615; *see also* Japan (U.S.S.R.)

Great Britain, **iii** 154; **iv** 45–6, 207–9, 485; **v** 205–6

    claims and debts question, **iv** 503–4, 569; **v** 208

    trade relations, **iv** 35–6, 46, 106, 132, 134, 207, 503–4, 511–2, 621; **v** 208–9; **vi** 533, 543; Mr. Hudson's Mission, **iv** 132*n*, 568–71; press communiqué, **iv** 512, 523–4; **v** 235

U.S.S.R. (Great Britain) (*cont.*)

    war trade agreement, **iv** 611–4

    see also Anglo-Franco-Soviet negotiations; Anglo-Franco-Soviet military conversations; Treaties (Great Britain–U.S.S.R.)

internal conditions, **i** 161–2, 218–9, 482–4; **iii** 232; **iv** 188–99, 207, 413–8, 613–4

resignation of M. Litvinov. *See* Litvinov, M. M. in Index of Persons

Press, **i** 305; **iii** 192–3; **iv** 128, 574; **v** 460

    Anglo-Franco-Soviet negotiations, **v** 413, 460, 520–1, 648, 785; **vi** 84, 119–20, 217, 781; **vii** 74, 102, 305–6, 346–8, 384–5, 588, 591–3

    German invasion of Czechoslovakia, **i** 280–1, 346; **iv** 446

    German-Soviet negotiations, **vi** 447; **vii** 98, 188, 197, 383

    Ukrainian question, **iii** 541, 575, 579

    visit of Mr. Hudson to Moscow, **iv** 509–10, 524, 570

    'Far Eastern Times', **iv** 523; 'Izvestiya', **iii** 193; **iv** 446; **v** 520, 545, 572, 590, 648; **vi** 559; **vii** 74, 98–100, 197, 305, 346; 'Journal de Moscou', **iii** 193, 280, 541, 575, 579; **iv** 25, 570; **v** 46; cessation of publication of, **v** 545; 'Krasnaya Zvezda', **iv** 128; 'Moscow News', **iv** 411, 413*n*; **vii** 385; 'Pravda', **iv** 446; **v** 785; **vi** 54, 161; article in, by M. Zhdanov on Anglo-Franco-Soviet negotiations, **vi** 209, 217–9, 781; **vii** 98–9, 197, 383–4, 615

See also Baltic States; Bulgaria; Czechoslovakia (Germany, possible German attack: attitude of U.S.S.R.); Estonia; Finland; Four-Power Declaration; Germany; Japan; Latvia; Lithuania; Munich Agreement; Poland; Roumania; Turkey

United States, **i** 79, 168, 518; **ii** 272, 439, 576, 688; **iii** 142–4, 278; **iv** 174, 216; **vi** 648

as source of munitions supply, **i** 203, 206–7, 422; **iii** 290–1; **iv** 462–3

Far East, question of Anglo-U.S. co-operation in, **viii** 11, 135–6, 173, 185, 190, 225, 249, 262, 264, 268–9, 278–9, 291, 295–9, 301, 341, 374, 400, 407, 409, 415, 425, 449–50, 497; **ix** 120, 135, 404–5, 423, 486, 510, 520–2; *see also* Amoy (Kulangsu International Settlement); China; Chinese Currency Stabilization Fund; Japan; Shanghai (International Settlement); Sino-Japanese conflict; Tientsin (British Concession: negotiations in Tokyo)

Fleet movements, **ii** 296; **v** 169, 251; **ix** 13

Great Britain, **ii** 132, 211, 213, 296, 682; **iii** 252, 278; **iv** 6, 27, 29, 364; **v** 169; *see also* sub-head Far East *above*

Jewish problem, **iii** 432, 519

Press, **ii** 200, 625; **iii** 278, 295; **iv** 412, 607; **viii** 183, 193, 346; **ix** 233–4; 'Baltimore

United States (Press) (*cont.*)
Sun', **vi** 63; 'New York Times', **vi** 63; **vii** 544; **viii** 456*n*
public opinion, **ii** 285, 301; **iv** 29, 37, 364, 380; **vi** 247, 678; **vii** 49, 63, 428; **viii** 449; **ix** 228
Slovaks in, **v** 86; delegation to Europe, **i** 429–30, 465, 551
suggestion relating to international conference, Sept. 1938, **ii** 617*n*; **vii** 628
war in Europe, probable attitude, **ii** 219, 285, 301; **iv** 103*n*; **vii** 203, 262, 287, 428–9, 628–9; **viii** 450; **ix** 234
See also Bohemia and Moravia (reaction of U.S. to German occupation); Czechoslovakia (Germany, possible German attack: attitude of U.S.); Czechoslovakia (United States); France; Germany; President Roosevelt in Index of Persons
Usti nad Orlici, **iii** 207; **iv** 57
Ustron, **iii** 23
Uzhorod, **iii** 152, 188, 217, 222; **v** 87
Uzok, **v** 87

Vaihingen, **ii** 26
Valona, **v** 119, 127, 140, 437, 750
van Zeeland Plan, **ii** 70; **v** 792
Vatican, The, iii 497; **v** 563
suggestion for Five-Power Conference, May 1939, **v** 411, 420, 432, 435–6, 439–40, 451, 458, 466–8, 476–7, 480, 482, 489–90, 499, 505, 524, 581, 685, 803; proposal dropped, **v** 498
the Pope as mediator between Germany and Poland, July/Aug. 1939, **v** 685, 718–9; **vi** 284, 293–4, 303–4, 316, 370–2, 550, 633, 675; **vii** 14, 20, 23, 63, 67, 117–8, 183, 301, 351, 401–4, 452–3, 495
peace appeal, Aug. 24, 1939, **vii** 216*n*, 223, 227, 253–5; appeal to Germany and Poland, Aug. 31, 1939, **vii** 448, 455, 495
Veldenstein, **ii** 652
Veliki Luki, **i** 421
Venice, **i** 37; **ii** 174, 339; **v** 287, 294, 314, 334, 550–1
Verona, **ii** 641
Vienna, **i** 24, 28, 38, 43, 45, 67–8, 76, 107, 116*n*, 133, 135–7, 148, 156, 301, 321, 404, 544, 612; **ii** 281, 370, 615; **iii** 91, 123, 228, 235, 240, 275, 367–8, 417, 627; **vi** 232–5, 443, 445; **v** 67*n*
Herr Hitler's entry, Mar. 14, 1938, **i** 48, 135
Vienna Arsenal, The, **i** 93
Vienna Conference and Award, Nov. 1938, **iii** 212, 218; text of Award, **iii** 220–1; *referred to*, **iii** 222–8, 236–7, 239, 300, 302, 385*n*, 413; **iv** 129, 172, 178, 206, 220, 222–3, 238–9, 241, 251, 439, 617–8; **v** 370
Vienna Congress, 1815, **i** 649; **iii** 218
Vilkaviskis, **iv** 286

Vilna (Wilno), **iii** 50; **v** 407; **vi** 441; **vii** 87, 116, 306, 347, 496
question of passage of Soviet troops through Vilna Gap, **vii** 3*n*, 4, 40, 70, 112
Vistula, R., **v** 42, 538; **vii** 484
Vitebsk, **i** 421; **iv** 189
Vitkovice. *See* Witkowitz
Volhynia, **v** 407
Vollmau, **iii** 640
Volpi financial and industrial group, Italy, **vii** 335–6
Vorarlberg, **i** 7, 148; **iv** 49
Vysi Lhota, **iii** 223

Waag, R., **iv** 262; **v** 78; **vii** 126
Walentynowo, **vii** 453
Wannsee, **v** 671
War (1914–1918), **i** 222, 225; **ii** 216, 348; **iii** 384; **v** 302, 309; **vii** 127, 202, 228, 620
War (1939), outbreak of, **vii** 473–4, 534–9; *see also* Germany (Poland); Poland (Great Britain, political relations)
Warnsdorf, **i** 432; **ii** 664
Warsaw, **i** 423, 429; **iv** 145, 152, 479; **v** 247, 407; German plan of attack, **vii** 327, 337–8, 415–6; bombing of, 496–7, 529, 532
Warta, R., **v** 42
Weiden, **i** 61
Weihaiwei, **ix** 383
Weimar, **i** 451; **iv** 245
Weimar Republic, **i** 155*n*
Weipert, **ii** 596, 603
Wejherowo, **vi** 66
Westerplatte, **vi** 164, 388, 393, 417, 421; **vii** 474, 476, 479, 542, 544, 546
Whangpoo Conservancy Board, **viii** 6*n*, 76, 82, 99; **ix** 21
White Paper (Cmd. 5847 of 1938). *See* Great Britain
White Russia, **iii** 274, 548, 577
Wiener Neustadt, **i** 24, 59*n*
Wiesbaden, **v** 515
Witkowitz (Vitkovice), **i** 479; **iii** 167*n*, 170, 189; **iv** 129*n*; occupation by German troops, **iv** 258, 264; **v** 699, 714; **vi** 750
Worthing, speech by Lord Winterton at, **iii** 158
Wscherau, **iii** 640
Wuchang, **viii** 82, 177*n*
Wuhu, **viii** 6*n*, 170*n*, 228, 266, 394, 406
Wunstorf, **i** 358
Württemberg, **ii** 26

Yalova, **vi** 52
Yangtze-kiang, navigation, **iii** 308; **viii** 6*n*, 75–6, 82, 99, 101, 170*n*, 171, 194, 199–201, 204–6, 213, 226–9, 244, 246, 254, 260, 262, 266–7, 280, 348, 394, 405–7, 432–4, 441, 445, 452, 525; **ix** 3–4, 36, 40, 61, 87, 139, 152–4
Kiangyin barrier, **viii** 99, 200, 227

Yangtze-kiang (*cont.*)
    reopening of Customs in Yangtze ports, *see*
    Chinese Maritime Customs Administration
    (demands for additional Japanese staff)
Yangtzepoo, **viii** $41n$, 75, 81, 96, 100
Yellow River, **viii** 32
Yemen, **vi** 127
Yochow, **viii** 228, 266
Yugoslavia, i 79, 106, 218, 222, 232, 257, 514,
  650; **ii** 144; **iii** 153, 232, 238; **iv** 579, 620;
  v 71
    armed forces, **iv** 102, 104, 388; **v** 334
    Croatian Peasant party, **iv** $352n$
    foreign policy, **iv** 522, 620–1; **v** 334, 551
    Great Britain, **v** 314, 322, 663; **vi** 102–3, 437
    Press, **v** 563, 589; 'Politika', **v** 563
    war in Europe, probable attitude, **iv** 104,
    388; **vi** 67
    See also Albania (effect on Yugoslavia of
    Italian occupation); Anti-Comintern Pact;
    Balkan Entente (Anglo-Turkish Declaration
    of May 1939); Bulgaria (Yugoslavia);
    Czechoslovakia (Germany, possible German
    attack: attitude of Yugoslavia); Germany
    (Yugoslavia); Hungary; Italy; Roumania

Yunnan Province, **ix** 93
Yunnanfu, **viii** 142

Zakopane, **v** 246–7
Zbaszyn, **iii** 251
Zdar (Zdiar), **ii** $70n$; **iii** 220; **v** 247
Zeitz, **i** 451
Zermanice, **iii** 223
Zilina. *See* Sillein
Zinnwald, **i** 61; **ii** 552
Zlabings, **iii** 640
Zlin, **ii** 662; **iii** 377
Znaim, **ii** 549; **iii** 237, 627, 640
Znojmo, **i** 106
Zoong Sing mill, **viii** 76, 99
Zoppot, **vi** 136, 186, 393, 586; **vii** 157, 546
  Congress of lawyers, **vii** 96, 101, 153, 543
Zory, **v** 246
Zossen, **i** 380
Zürich, **iii** 397
Zwardon, **iii** 199, 212, 219
Zwickau, **i** 432
Zwittau, **i** 487; **ii** 544; **iii** 86–7, 123, 151, 196,
  207, 641
Zywiec, **v** 247